D0787848

D

"Inventing the Nonprofit Sector"
and Other Essays on Philanthropy, Voluntarism,
and Nonprofit Organizations

Inventing the Nonprofit Sector

AND OTHER ESSAYS ON PHILANTHROPY, VOLUNTARISM, AND NONPROFIT ORGANIZATIONS

BY

PETER

DOBKIN

HALL

THE JOHNS HOPKINS
UNIVERSITY PRESS
BALTIMORE AND LONDON

© 1992 The Johns Hopkins University Press
All rights reserved
Printed in the United States of America

The Johns Hopkins University Press
701 West 40th Street
Baltimore, Maryland 21211-2190
The Johns Hopkins Press Ltd., London

The paper used in this book meets the minimum requirements of American National Standard for Information Sciences—Permanence of Paper for Printed Library Materials, ANSI Z39.48-1984.

Library of Congress Cataloging-in-Publication Data

Hall, Peter Dobkin, 1946–
Inventing the nonprofit sector and other essays on philanthropy, voluntarism, and nonprofit organizations / Peter Dobkin Hall.
p.   cm.
Includes bibliographical references and index.
ISBN 0-8018-4272-7 (alk. paper)
1. Charities—United States. 2. Corporations, Nonprofit—United States. 3. Voluntarism—United States. I. Title.
HV91.H263 1992
361.7'0973—dc20   91-26100

For Robert Wood Lynn

FRIEND AND MENTOR

Contents

Preface

In a very real sense, my work on the line of enquiry which produced this book was initiated in winter 1967, when I, an undergraduate at Reed College, approached Columbia University's eminent historian Richard Hofstadter to discuss my ideas about his interpretation of Progressivism, on which I planned to write my senior thesis. Hofstadter kindly and gently fielded my eager questions about *The Age of Reform*, readily acknowledging its many shortcomings and deficiencies.

"But why write about me?" Hofstadter asked at the conclusion of the interview. "Why write about me, when we know next to nothing about what really happened?" He held up copies of Evan Thomas' book on the Spanish Civil War and Graham Adams' monograph on the Walsh Commission. "This is the kind of work that really needs to be done. Don't waste your time writing about why *I* didn't discuss the role of industrial violence in the growth of Progressivism. Go out and study how the Progressives perceived industrial violence."

Hofstadter's wise belief in American historiography as an unfinished task, not a body of received wisdom, was soon confirmed by events. Within months of our talk, Hofstadter's own campus and the political traditions of which he had written so insightfully had been swept by revolution. Violence at Columbia and in Chicago—and in a hundred other campuses and cities—would transfigure everyone's expectations. The political forces that Hofstadter had seen as representing the best possibilities in American life had revealed their moral bankruptcy, while those he saw as representing the worst and darkest side of the American character were rapidly gaining strength. Within little more than a decade, they had taken control of the nation, promising to dismantle the liberal state that it had taken a century to create.

While the New Right (as Hofstadter called it) was no more than partially successful in dismantling the hated liberal state, challenges to it sparked a wide-ranging debate over the mission and goals of the nation and the values of American leadership. This debate necessarily involved a broad reexamination and reconceptualization of American institutions—the nature of family and community, the responsibilities of government and business corporations, the ethical obligations of individuals.

Scholars inevitably took part in this process, not only because of their expertise in these areas or because events had compelled them to broaden their interests to include public issues, but also because of fundamental changes in their relation to the public. Because opportunities for academic employment began shrinking in the early 1970s, at the very time that the first wave of baby-boom Ph.D.'s hit the job market, large numbers of would-be scholars, finding university jobs were unavailable, ended up working for corporations, foundations, and government agencies—as well as for museums and historical societies, and on the staffs of newspapers—while maintaining their scholarly interests. After decades of isolation in the rarefied and Olympian strata of national and international preoccupations, American scholars became passionately involved in the "world's work" as passionate participants rather than as detached observers.

In 1987, social critic Russell Jacoby, in *The Lost Intellectuals*, lamented the disappearance of "public intellectuals"—the writers and thinkers who in previous generations sought to "address a general and educated audience" (5). They had "been supplanted by high-tech intellectuals, consultants, and professors—anonymous souls, who may be competent, and more than competent, but who do not enrich public life" (x). He declared that the younger intellectuals were people "whose lives have unfolded almost entirely on campuses" and who directed themselves "to professional colleagues but are inaccessible and unknown to others."

The assertions of Jacoby were, more than anything else, a tribute to his own isolation from the main currents of intellectual life in the postliberal era of Nixon, Carter, Reagan, and Bush. To be sure, the professoriate—those lucky enough to find regular academic employment in an era of diminishing opportunities—was more insular and self-involved than ever. But, perhaps on a scale greater than in any other period of our history, the displaced men and women with advanced academic training were becoming an important force for reflecting on, and changing the direction of, American institutions. At the end of the twentieth century, Jacoby's "missing generation" of public intellectuals was not prophesying in the pages of the *Atlantic*, the *New Republic*, or the *New York Review of Books*. It was working in the infinitely more intimate and arduous settings of corporate, nonprofit, and public boards, trying to reshape conceptions of public and private responsibility. Whatever his shortcomings, management guru Peter Drucker, in *The New Realities* (1989), intuited correctly when he identified the nonprofit sector as the opening frontier of public life in the 1980s and 1990s—and as the particular arena for the "knowledge workers," his name for the new class of nonacademic intellectuals

(180-90). The nonprofit sector would be the common meeting ground where the real decisions about the future of American society and institutions would being made. This would be the arena in which the real calling of intellectuals—the capacity to provoke reflection and candid self-evaluation necessary for institutional renewal—would be exercised.

This book is an incomplete and fragmentary effort to sketch out an emerging institutional order—one in which familiar institutions of government, business, religion, culture, and voluntary action may play significantly different roles than they have in the past. Because I am so keenly aware of the defects and shortcomings of this book, I ask only that critical readers respond in the spirit of Richard Hofstadter's challenge to me so many years ago—by looking at the real issues and problems about which we know so little and about which we need to know so much.

Acknowledgments

Of the many colleagues who commented on various versions of this book, I particularly thank Clayton Alderfer, Paul J. DiMaggio, Bradford Gray, Barry Karl, Stanley N. Katz, Robert Wood Lynn, Richard Magat, George A. Marcus, Carl Milofsky, Waldemar A. Neilsen, Teresa Odendahl, William N. Parker, Robert L. Payton, Charles Perrow, Walter W. Powell, James A. Smith, Melissa Middleton Stone, Henry Suhrke, Jon Van Til, and Miriam Wood for their good counsel. I am also grateful to the members of the National Seminar on Trusteeship and the participants in the biweekly seminar of the Program on Non-Profit Organizations at Yale University for their comments and criticisms.

For their help in locating important sources, I especially thank Tom Rosenbaum of the Rockefeller Archive Center and Patty Bodak Stark of the Yale University Archives, as well as Pablo Eisenberg, Waldemar A. Neilsen, Gabriel Rudney, Leonard Silverstein, David Horton Smith, Hayden W. Smith, and Jon Van Til, who made available their personal recollections and papers.

This book would not have been possible without the generous support of the following funders: the American Council of Learned Societies, the AT&T Foundation, the Ellis Phillips Foundation, the Equitable Life Assurance Society of the United States, the Exxon Education Foundation, the General Electric Foundation, the Lilly Endowment, and the Walter Teagle Foundation. Portions of this book were also supported by the Connecticut Department of Labor, the National Seminar on Trusteeship, the Program on Non-Profit Organizations at Yale University, and the Rockefeller Archive Center.

Numerous essays in this book have appeared elsewhere in various guises. However, all have been extensively revised—some of them, such as chapter 1, almost beyond recognition. Chapter 2 is the only chapter that has been left pretty much as written, primarily because, as an artifact, it suggests so much about the difficulties involved in trying to conceptualize nonprofits—in particular, the difficulties of trying to bridge the gap between existing scholarship and the needs of the emerging institutional sector.

Jossey-Bass Publishers has graciously permitted me to use portions of "The History of Religious Philanthropy," which appeared in

Robert Wuthnow, ed., *Faith and Philanthropy in America* (1990); "Dilemmas of Research on Philanthropy, Voluntarism, and Nonprofit Organizations," which appeared in John Van Til, ed., *Critical Issues in American Philanthropy* (1990); and "Conflicting Managerial Cultures," which appeared in *Nonprofit Management and Leadership* 1, no. 2 (Winter 1990). Transaction Books has been kind enough to permit me to use portions of "Abandoning the Rhetoric of Independence: The Nonprofit Sector in the Postliberal Era," which appeared in Susan A. Ostrander, Stuart Langton, and John Van Til, eds., *Shifting the Debate: Public-Private Sector Relations in the Modern Warfare State* (1987). The Yale University Press has allowed me to use portions of "A Historical Overview of the Nonprofit Sector," which appeared in W. W. Powell, ed., *The Nonprofit Sector: A Research Handbook* (1987).

Jacqueline Wehmueller of the Johns Hopkins University Press deserves special thanks for her enthusiasm about the prospect of making the book available to readers and for her patience in seeing it through the editorial process.

My debt to Kathryn F. Bonese, who kept this work going through thick and thin, is incalculable.

"Inventing the Nonprofit Sector"
and Other Essays on Philanthropy, Voluntarism,
and Nonprofit Organizations

Introduction

This book has three major aims. First, it chronicles the intense and protracted political drama over private nonprofit institutions and their role in American democracy. Second and almost unavoidably, it explores the processes through which the public in a democracy defines itself and its collective purposes. Third, it examines scholarship and its crucial roles in these dramas of self-definition.

The terms now used to describe private charitable, philanthropic, and voluntary enterprise—such neologisms as *third sector, nonprofit sector,* and *independent sector*—obscure the controversies that have, for the past two centuries, raged around the claims of private groups to be able to act for and in the name of the public. These controversies came to a climax between 1961 and 1973, when tempering the growing numbers and power of these organizations stood near the top of the public agenda. Only in the past decade—perhaps for the first time since the end of the eighteenth century—have the oratorical guns fallen silent: all sides have come to accept these claims as legitimate, and the power centers all along the political spectrum are busying themselves with establishing and building up the privatized instrumentalities of public influence.

If history is any guide, the current consensus is only temporary. The sanitized language that renders the terms *nonprofit* and *nonprofit sector* so suitable as a basis for political accommodation also, in its essential ambiguity, assures future conflict. For what, after all, is really meant when people speak of *nonprofits?* For some, the term implies altruistic or charitable activity, but many nonprofits do neither.[1] For others, the term implies voluntarism; but many nonprofits are not voluntary organizations, nor do private agencies have a monopoly on voluntary action.[2] Although it makes sense to group institutions according to the products they provide, the services they deliver, or their forms of organization, the terms *nonprofit* and *nonprofit sector* have little to do with either, because any of the goods and services produced by nonprofits can be and are also supplied by businesses and government agencies.[3] Nor can nonprofits claim a distinctive way of raising revenue. Although much is said about their dependence on donations, sales of services, government grants and contracts, bonding, and investment income account for nearly 80 percent of nonprofit revenues.[4] Even tax exemption is not distinctive to nonprofits: governmental activities have always been tax exempt; at various times, the exemption has been extended to for-profit enterprises as well; finally, in some times and places nonprofits have been denied the exemption.

What, then, is so special about nonprofits? What has led commentators over the years—from Alexis de Tocqueville to John Gardner and Peter Drucker—make such extraordinary claims on their behalf? This book argues that their distinctiveness does not involve any set of abstract features such as tax-exempt status, constraints on the distribution of profits, or devotion to the production of public goods—features that are shared with nongovernmental organizations in other countries. What gives American nongovernmental organizations their special character and their crucially important function in the American polity is their concrete historical association with a particular institutional culture, a configuration of values, resources, organizational technologies, legal infrastructure, and styles of leadership. This institutional culture originated at the end of the eighteenth century, became dominant (though not unchallenged) in the twentieth, and entered a period of crisis—quite possibly a crisis of success rather than of failure—in our own time.

From this perspective, the climactic debate of two decades ago over the power and privileges of private institutions claiming to act in the public interest was more than a struggle over government's power to tax and regulate these entities. Although coinciding with the unraveling of American liberalism, beneath the challenge to the liberal political coalition that had dominated American government since the 1930s was a deeper struggle over the power of the institutions that set the public's moral and perceptual agendas and on which every national political regime had depended for its legitimacy and authority since the beginning of the century. It was nothing less than a struggle over the nature of democracy itself.

When struggles for political, economic, or social dominance are accompanied by major efforts to reinterpret the meaning of past events, it is a good sign that a fundamental reconfiguration of a culture and its institutions is in progress. Thus, the thoroughgoing reexamination of the American past which occurred over the past thirty years is emblematic of the depth and intensity of the political and institutional crisis of our generation. This reinterpretation has involved shifts not only in focus (from political events to broad social, economic, and political trends), in methods (from common-sense rationalistic models to deploying the full theoretical and technical capacity of the social sciences), and in evidence (from papers of political and cultural elites to the whole range of surviving artifacts, documentary and material). In addition, the reinterpretation has involved significant changes in the composition of the academic disciplines themselves, which had been almost exclusively made up of white male Protestants of Northern European origin. Thus, not surprisingly, the reinterpretation of the past has also been accompanied by a fundamental reappraisal of the role of scholars and scholarship, which has come to be seen as tied to the development of cultural institutions, which were themselves integral to emerging constellations of economic, political, and social interests. The reinterpretation of American history, the reappraisal of the role of scholarship, and the effort to come to grips with philanthropic, voluntary, and nonprofit organizations—which constituted the infrastructure of the enterprise of learning—were all of a piece.

The effort to reinterpret American culture, especially its development since the Civil War, has been at the center of historiographical concern since the 1950s, when Richard Hofstadter's *Age of Reform* began plumbing the motives and interests underlying the Progressive movement. Since then, looking beneath the ebb and flow of political tides, historians have discerned the deeper continuities and interrelationships in the development of the nation's social, economic, and cultural institutions.[5] Gradually, historians have agreed that a fundamental restructuring of public life began to take place in the 1870s and 1880s, which emerged as a national force with the Progressive movement at the turn of the century, and which, despite changes in regimes and electoral moods, framed public life for the rest of the century.

In its essentials, this restructuring involved an accommodation between government and private voluntary associations, which had coexisted uneasily—and often turbulently—through the first century of the republic's existence. In part because there were so few of them, in part because legal doctrines of the late eighteenth century treated voluntary associations as subservient to the state, the Founding Fathers had left unresolved their relation to government. Their growing number and power in early decades of the nineteenth century led to a series of sharp electoral and judicial clashes, whose overall effect was both to differentiate public and private sectors of activity and to leave the latter free to develop without significant governmental interference (though not, in certain places, without significant governmental encouragement).

By the last third of the nineteenth century, the disjunction between public and private sectors could no longer be ignored. On the one hand, the growing concentration of economic power by a few hundred entrepreneurs, and the growing restiveness of Americans in response to it, threatened the survival of the republic. On the other hand, those entrepreneurs, at least the most thoughtful among them, recognized that their enterprises' continued prosperity depended on governmental assistance and public approbation. Moreover, because the entrepreneurs shared the broader public's Christian and democratic convictions while possessing the power and the resources to enact their concerns, they became among the most active and influential agents in the effort to accommodate the new forces of industrialism to the traditional values.

The catastrophic depression that began in 1873, the violent labor disputes of 1877 and 1886, and the rising and ever more broadly based political insurgences presented the "wealthy, learned, and respectable" with a dilemma. To "crush the ignorant and vicious," as some advocated, would transform the United States into the kind of nightmarish industrial feudalism envisioned at the conclusion of Mark Twain's *Connecticut Yankee in King Arthur's Court*—an embattled cadre of technocrats surrounded by rings of Gatling guns, electrified barbed wire, and the rotting corpses of the protesting populace. A coercive solution was not only ethically unpalatable but also, men such as Andrew Carnegie argued, impractical, because institutionalized inequality would destroy the economic system's capacity for continuing growth and change.

The solution, gradually elaborated over the next quarter-century, involved a reinterpretation of social and economic life loosely based on Darwinian theories about the natural world.[6] From this perspective, inequality was seen being as inescapable a consequence of industrial production as the hierarchical diversity of life forms was the outcome of the struggle for existence in nature—and, indeed, was a product of the same competitive processes. While for some the social and economic hierarchies resulting from the division of labor presupposed coercive and exploitative relations, for thoughtful industrial leaders such as Andrew Carnegie and Marcus Alonzo Hanna inequality pointed more positively to interdependent and cooperative social imperatives. Simply put, the "man of affairs" could no more accomplish his great undertakings without the active and enthusiastic engagement of his foremen, clerks, and laborers than the generals in the late Civil War could have won battles without their staffs of officers and regiments of fighting men, all united by a desire to serve in a common cause.[7]

If the entrepreneurs could accept inequality as an inevitable consequence of social and economic life, their own experience as self-made men made it clear that the location of individuals in the hierarchy was not a birthright, but the reward of individual ability tested and tried in the competitive struggle. If so, it might be possible to substitute equality of opportunity for traditional goals of equality of condition, suggesting that the greatest beneficiaries of the industrial system had a positive obligation to use their wealth to establish institutions that could maximize opportunities for the masses, not only ensuring the continued recruitment of the talented and ambitious into leadership positions but also, in so doing, affirming—in a dramatically new way—the democratic and Christian values held by most Americans.

The lack of suitable organizational vehicles was the chief obstacle to enacting these ideas. By itself, government was inadequate because it was inherently corrupt and undependable. Business corporations were, in and of themselves, too limited and uncertain in their purposes for responsibilities of such magnitude. So Carnegie, Hanna, Rockefeller, and other industrialists with the necessary resources and influence began investing in the creation of new kinds of organizations—charitable foundations—and in the reconstruction of older ones—private universities. These entities, privately governed and supported, would become centers not only for the gathering of the scientific, social, and political, and economic intelligence needed to understand and control the accelerating processes of growth and change, but also for recruiting and training the leaders and experts capable, as Harvard's President Charles William Eliot said, of "fighting the wilderness, physical and moral" and of "working out the awful problem of self-government."

The ultimate outcome of these efforts would be a government whose growing scale and scope of concerns would by the 1920s touch on every aspect of American life, but whose policies, methods, and personnel, at least at the higher levels, were very much the products of privately governed and funded eleemosynary institutions—universities, foundations, professional societies, research institutes, and a host of other "voluntary cooperative" entities—which operated primarily on the national level.[8]

Scholars played key roles in the emergence of the new order. Not only did business investment in higher education make possible the establishment of the academic disciplines as powerful new elements in the process of political and industrial self-government, their reinterpretation of the world, from a familiar one governed by common-sense rules and untrained observation to a bewilderingly complex one, amenable only to the disciplined understanding of experts, was, depending on one's viewpoint, a powerful new instrument of social control, or of social betterment. Historians played an especially important role in this process because they recast the everyday historical experience of Americans into broad evolutionary patterns, which showed average citizens their place in the scheme of things—and revealed for the young the possibilities open to them. Historians were both propagandists and apologists for the new order and, at times, its most troubled doubters and dissenters.[9]

Needless to say, the emergence of the new order, which both vastly expanded the prerogatives of government while extensively privatizing important arenas of decisionmaking, was not unopposed. But the opposition, however numerous and eloquent, could never hope to match the determination, the massed resources, or the organizational genius of the champions of the new corporate state.[10] Looking back in 1918, Henry Adams would evoke the Rubicon the nation crossed in the turbulent 1890s:

> For a hundred years, between 1793 and 1893, the American people had hesitated, vacillated, swayed forward and back between two forces, one simply industrial, the other capitalistic, centralizing, and mechanical. In 1893, the issue came on a single gold standard, and the majority at last declared itself, once and for all, in favor of the capitalistic system with all its necessary machinery. All one's friends, all one's best citizens, reformers, churches, colleges, educated classes, had joined the banks to force submission to capitalism; a submission long foreseen by the mere law of mass. . . . A capitalistic system had been adopted, and if it were to be run at all, it must be run by capital and capitalistic methods; for nothing could surpass the nonensity of trying to run so complex and so concentrated a machine by Southern and Western farmers in grotesque alliance with city day-laborers, as had been tried in 1800 and 1828, and had failed even under simple conditions.[11]

Still, the dominance of the new order hardly meant the cessation of opposition. The new order was exiled from the center of political life just as thoroughly as the Federalists had been by the Jeffersonians and Jacksonians, and its anti-institutionalist traditions smoldered in various intellectual and political pockets, flaring up now and then—in the Walsh Investigation of Industrial Relations in the 1910s, in the Scopes Trial of the 1920s, in the Pecora and Temporary National Economic Committee (TNEC) hearings in the 1930s, in the House Un-American Activities Committee (HUAC) and McCarthy investigations of the 1940s and early 1950s—ultimately blazing forth in the 1960s and 1970s, with a broad and powerful challenge to the power of "government by people outside of government." The political extremes, Left and Right, had no monopoly on criticism. Partyless intellectuals such as Henry Adams, Randolph Bourne, and Thorstein Veblen questioned the new order's legitimacy even as it emerged. And their tradition was carried forward by a motley crew of literary doubters and dissenters, including Edmund Wilson (whose 1962 collection of essays on the Civil War, *Patriotic Gore,* drew devastating parallels among Lincoln, Bismark, and Stalin) and Kurt Vonnegut (whose satirical novels *Player*

Piano and *God Bless You, Mr. Rosewater* lampooned the pretensions of the alliance between plutocracy and technocracy).

The opposition eventually triumphed with the election of Ronald Reagan, but the New Right found, much as Jefferson had 180 years earlier under far simpler conditions, that national government "had to be run by capitalistic methods or not at all." Once in power, the New Right discovered that the welfare state against which it had railed for so long was less a vast national bureaucracy built along European lines than a subtly interwoven system of public and private enterprise. The voluntary sector, rather than constituting an alternative to the welfare state, was largely its creation: between 30 percent and 60 percent of its revenues came from direct or indirect government subsidies. Although this finding also came as a shock to proponents of voluntary, philanthropic, and nonprofit organizations, they took it in stride, using as the basis for building alliances with the Right in defense of the sector.

One reason for the attractiveness of the idea of strengthening the nonprofit sector over the past decade has been the assumption, shared by liberals and conservatives alike, that privatizing public initiative through the use of voluntary agencies was more flexible, responsive, economical, and "democratic" than statist alternatives. The government looked to the voluntary sector to monitor and serve human needs, voluntary organizations were busily preening their new identity as an independent sector, securing their privileges in law and tax policy, and perfecting their management and marketing acumen. Few seemed particularly concerned about the growing numbers of jobless, homeless, and apparently hopeless members of what was coming to be viewed as a "permanent underclass."[12] Moreover, neither the government nor the nonprofits could come to terms with the increasing pluralism of American society. The government steadfastly undermined affirmative action, while the key nonprofits—the big foundations and the elite universities—despite their advocacy of "principles and practices" that favored diversity and openness—remained largely white, male, Protestant preserves.[13]

The public, at least as it had come to define itself by the late 1980s, consisted of those individuals with resources to form organizations with sufficient visibility and influence to prompt public subvention of their particular causes, projects, and programs. In this setting, those without political or financial resources found themselves increasingly voiceless and powerless. Whereas voluntary action retained its potential as a vehicle for empowerment, increasing government regulation—imposed during the 1960s under the banner of making nonprofits more democratic—actually served to make voluntary organizations instruments of privilege and official policy, rather than advocates for social and economic justice.[14] Even when the powerless did succeed in acquiring nonprofit status, they still faced competing for funding in a setting in which unglamorous causes such as homelessness, poverty, and AIDs were unlikely to attract significant support.[15] The organizational technology of voluntary action—once relatively well-diffused—had, by the 1980s, become a monopoly of the articulate and propertied.

For private charity to stand accused of being an instrument of class domination is hardly new. However, in the past its critics believed that they could look to the state, if not as an alternative, then at least as a disinterested umpire capable of assuring fairness in the private sector's activities. Events since the 1960s have largely destroyed this faith, leaving a bleak vision of institutional life, public and private, as a mechanism for the reproduction of dominant interests—an iron cage, indeed![16]

A number of circumstances suggest that scholarship—not as apologist and propagandist, but as critical questioner—may play a role of unsuspected significance in finding a way out of this impasse. Had scholarship remained the captive of the corporate institutions of culture, there would be little to sustain this hope. But since the early 1970s, thousands of men and women with advanced academic training, rather than immuring themselves in universities, have fanned out into business, government, and the nonprofit sector, not only on the national level, where they had always been present but also in the localities. These are the individuals—called by Peter Drucker the "knowledge workers"—who constitute a group in society for which there is neither a political concept nor a political integration.[17]

"The new pluralist institutions of society are," Drucker writes, "organizations of 'knowledge workers.'" Although generally employees of organizations, they are not tied to organizations in the traditional sense, nor is their status defined by their occupation. Moving from accounting work in business, to accounting work in a hospital, to teaching accounting in a university involves no fundamental change in social or economic position. "Knowledge workers have mobility," Drucker continues. "They are 'colleagues.' They have both social and economic status. They enjoy the bargaining power that results from social equality and from becoming economically essential."[18]

Changing criteria for the success of organizations has further enhanced the importance of these individuals not merely as technical specialists, but as *intellectuals*. "The more knowledge-based an institution becomes," Drucker notes, "the more it depends on the willingness of individuals to take responsibility for contribution to the whole, for understanding the objectives, the values, the performance of the whole, and for making themselves understood by the other professionals, the other knowledge people, in the organization."[19] In other words, active intellectual commitment has become a crucial element in the effectiveness and efficiency of organizational functioning.

Drucker's analysis of the emerging "knowledge society" points to an especially important role for "the non-profit organizations of the so-called third sector."[20] Drucker believes that these organizations "are rapidly becoming creators of new bonds of community and a bridge across the widening gap between knowledge workers and the 'other half.'" He argues that they increasingly "create a sphere of effective citizenship," "spheres of personal achievement" in which the individual "exercises influence, discharges responsibility, and make decisions." "In the political culture of mainstream society," Drucker suggests, "individuals, no matter how well-educated, how successful, how achieving, or how wealthy, can only vote and pay taxes. They can only react, can only be passive. In the counterculture of the third sector, they are active citizens. This may be the most important contribution of the third sector."[21]

In contrast to the third sector's view of itself, which has tended to stress the importance of the professionalization of management and to marginalize the role of boards of trustees—which are increasingly composed of professional men and women of diverse backgrounds, rather than the WASP males who once dominated them—the vision of the possibilities of the third sector embraced by the "knowledge workers" is a far broader and more hopeful one. For the former, the purposes ("mission") of an organization is the product of efficient management; for the latter, efficiency is merely a means of realizing organizational purposes. On the face of it, the differences may seem minor. But in a setting in which the survival of society itself will depend on its ability to optimize the willing and committed participation of all relevant stakeholders, it is the difference between defining the stewardship responsibilities of trustees narrowly—as fiduciary oversight of a particular organization—or broadly—as representing the interest of society as a whole. The former leads trustees toward policies in which the organization's survival is paramount; the latter, toward policies in which the good of the organization is secondary to the good of society.[22]

The resolution of the big questions—What is the nature of private power in a democracy? Who can legitimately speak for the public?—is being proposed, not in national forums, but in the localized nooks and crannies of the institutional infrastructure. It is here, on the governing boards of the million or so nonprofit organizations now in existence, that Americans are relearning the basic skills of citizenship. Although certainly hopeful insofar as the capacity of society to engage its own increasing diversity is concerned, the involvement of the "knowledge workers" in the third sector does not, in and of itself, address the sector's capacity to take up its professed concern for the voiceless and powerless.

It may be that critical scholarship will play an important role. Grounded historical perspectives, rather than self-serving folklore and wishful thinking, may serve in a variety of ways to help nonprofits engage their greatest challenges. Most importantly, these perspectives may enable citizen volunteers to understand the full scope of their responsibilities, most especially the range of stakeholders, which needs to be considered in framing their organizations' missions and goals.[23] Fortunately, these citizens, as "knowledge workers," are better equipped to use these perspectives in the painful processes of reflection and self-evaluation than at any time in the past. These perspectives may also help the sector as a whole both to examine itself and to more effectively use its resources to serve and empower others, especially by educating Americans to the possibilities of voluntary action. Ultimately, then, this book is intended to assist in this process of leadership education.

To this end, I would have preferred to have written a connected historical narrative—a "history of the nonprofit sector." Unfortunately, it is not possible, without straying into a variety of logical (if self-serving) fallacies, to write the history of an institutional sector that only came into being in any meaningful and coherent sense within the last twenty years. The primary fallacy involved here is that of attributing significance to institutions on the basis of their subsequent development. Few Americans a century—or even a half-century—ago could have imagined the importance that charitable tax-exempt organizations would assume after 1960. Although such accounts may help to strengthen emerging institutions by solidifying a sense of collective purpose and public legitimacy, they also weaken them, by prematurely limiting their potential.

We really do not know what the potential of third-sector organizations is in the United States—and the world—of the next century. And to constrain their possibilities by overdefining them historically would be an enormous disservice. Thus, this book is intended to be no more than suggestions pointing out some of the possibilities—and the hazards—that have faced nonprofit institutions in the past.

The nine chapters of this book fall into three general categories: historical overviews of the developing institutions and ideas about the nonprofit sector (1–4); explorations of the managerial implications of historical trends (5-6); and examinations of the problems of developing and institutionalizing the idea of the nonprofit sector (7-9). The final chapter is an evaluation of the future of nonprofits, originally presented to a group of executives and board members of national health-service agencies.

1

Inventing the Nonprofit Sector

By the 1830s, foreign visitors such as Alexis de Tocqueville were describing voluntary organizations supported by private contributions as the quintessential American contribution to the democratic idea. Although such organizations had existed in one form or another since the mid-eighteenth century, they were neither ubiquitous nor universally important: in some places they were encouraged—indeed, favored—as instruments of public action, in others they were actively discouraged; to some groups in society, they were mechanisms of choice for collective action, and others preferred to act through government. Even where the organizations enjoyed public sanction and private support, their status in relation to government, in particular the question of whether they were private entities, remained unsettled for decades.

Nonprofit organizations only became a significant and ubiquitous part of the American organizational universe in the very recent past: in 1940, there were only 12,500 secular charitable tax-exempt organizations; today there are over 700,000. Most of this growth took place after 1960—and did not became significant enough to merit the compilation of regular annual statistical reports until late in that decade. The effort to treat nonprofits as an institutional sector in the National Income Accounts dates only from 1980.[1]

Under these circumstances, it is hardly surprising that historians paid little attention to nonprofits and the nonprofit sector as such, or that the existing scholarship is fragmentary and particularized, composed of examinations of particular industries and fields of activity, accounts of the development of particular institutions, and biographies of individuals prominent in nonprofit institutions or in the social and political movements that led to their establishment.

The effort to treat organizations delivering a wide variety of seemingly unrelated services—in the arts, education, health care, social welfare—as constituting a distinctive organizational sector, primarily on the basis of a set of technical criteria having to do with their status

under the federal tax code, the sources and disposition of their revenues, and their manner of governance, is part of a complex process.
On the one hand, this effort is part of the means by which organizations sharing these features are forging awareness of themselves as
distinct and coherent, particularly with regard to their legal and regulatory status. On the other hand, this effort is part of the means by
which society and governmental bodies recognize and devise mechanisms for dealing with these new entities.

The question of whether charitable tax-exempt—"nonprofit"—organizations constitute a distinctive and coherent sector is far from
settled. Some scholars argue that their reliance on direct and indirect
subsidies from government, on earned revenues, and on contributions
from business and from the wealthy points to the need to treat them
as integral with rather than distinctive from business and government.[2] Others assert that the devotion of nonprofits to "higher purposes" and, more pragmatically, to the provision of "public goods"
merits a special niche in the organizational universe.[3] These views are
framed by the contemporary debate over tax and regulatory policies
toward charitable tax-exempt organizations and are necessarily tied to
the struggle to define the ways in which these entities—and those who
support them—should be treated today and in the future.

Under these circumstances, exploring the past in order to search of
the origins of the nonprofit sector is a hazardous venture. Personal
values, as well as patronage relationships, will inevitably influence
even the most disinterested efforts to trace the origins of organizations
that, as a category, only came to advance the claim that they should
be recognized as distinctive in the very recent past. One way of avoiding this progressivist fallacy—the notion that the nonprofit sector was
immanent long before its actual emergence and that its development
was inevitable and irresistible—is to focus historical enquiries on past
debates about the standing of voluntary organizations in the polity
and in society. This perspective permits us to understand their growth
as a succession of controversies, each with proximate and ambiguous
outcomes. Within such a framework, there is no *telos* other than the
continuing debate—no ultimate resolution is assumed.

Although the existence of a nonprofit sector and the distinctiveness
of the organizations constituting it are grounded in the present, the
debate over voluntary associations and other kinds of private institutions acting in the public interest dates back to the eighteenth century
and, as such, appears to be a central part of a broader struggle to define
democratic institutions. Democratic ideals are ambiguous with regard
to how the people can best make known their will. From the beginning, Americans have argued about whether voluntary associations

threatened democracy by permitting small groups of citizens, particularly the wealthy, to exercise power disproportionate to their numbers, or whether such bodies were essential to a citizenry that, without them, would be powerless to influence the state.

Over time, the terms of the debate, as well as the institutional mechanisms of voluntary action and private initiative for public purposes, became more elaborate and concrete. By the 1870s, some were arguing that democracy attains is fullest institutional expression not through government action, but through government encouragement of private action, including grants of incorporation, tax exemptions, tax regulations providing incentives to individuals who make donations to nonprofit organizations, and the ability to set property aside in perpetuity for charitable and educational purposes. Others argued with equal passion that leaving such essential public concerns as culture, education, health, and social welfare to the discretion—or to the neglect—of the few wealthy enough to concern themselves with such issues was as dangerous to democracy as leaving the banking, transportation, and communications systems unregulated.

Recognition of the interdependence of public and private enterprise became a fundamental premise of American polity in the twentieth century. But the balance between the two was always at issue—and the status of voluntary and charitable organizations, especially those that were supported by the wealthy and that explicitly sought not only to provide services for the public but also to influence its opinions, continued to be the subject of intense, but periodic, public controversy. This became more or less continuous after 1942, when income taxation became universal through the mechanism of withholding. With government claiming a significant share of everybody's income, questions of tax equity and, in particular, the costs to taxpayers of permitting certain institutions to be classified as tax exempt and extending special tax benefits to those who supported them reinvigorated the controversy. However, once again the perennial debate was framed by a peculiar set of institutional circumstances. Although the American government grew in scale and scope after World War II, rather than creating elaborate bureaucracies to provide the cultural, educational, health, and welfare services the public demanded, it created incentives for private enterprises to do so. Because these grew incrementally in particular industries, it was decades before tax-exempt enterprises came to recognize their common stake either in the general public debate over taxing, budgeting, and regulating, or in the particular aspects of that debate which affected their interests. During the 1970s the common ground turned out to be not only highly technical issues of tax and regulatory policy but also perennial concerns about the place of private initiative in public life, which were heightened by Reaganism and its rhetorical emphasis on the evils of big government.

In the late 1980s, the need for historical understanding of nonprofit activity, however defined, was driven by a new set of concerns. The collapse of communism abroad and efforts to establish democratic governments and market economies raised fundamental questions about the place of nonprofits in modern institutional systems. Before this, scholars and policymakers could frame their concerns within a set of conditions relatively unique to American culture, in which individuals were socialized to responsible autonomy, modes of authority were geared to compliance rather than coercion, and financial and productive resources of individuals were subject to their discretionary disposal. By treating these conditions as givens, scholars and policymakers could overlook both the complex issues of interdependence and the uncomfortable issues of inequality that underlay the growth of nonprofit enterprise in the United States. But when they were faced with the task of building national institutional systems from the ground up, these questions inevitably resurfaced—reviving an awareness of the core ambiguities of democracy and capitalism.

Voluntary Associations in Early America

England's extensive use of corporations and charitable trusts in the seventeenth and eighteenth centuries had little effect on the colonies. Although the proprietary and crown colonies accepted English law and legal forms, primitive conditions, including the rarity of formal legal training, as well as limitations on the powers of colonial assemblies, particularly their inability to charter corporations, constrained the development of an American tradition of organized philanthropic and voluntary activity.[4] In New England, Puritan settlements actively rejected English law and legal forms, regarding them as instruments of oppression and corruption. The practice of law was banned as inimical to the public interest, magistrates favored arbitration of disputes over adversary proceedings, the common law was rejected in favor of clearly stated commonsensical statutes and local customs, and equity—the jurisdiction under which trusts are enforceable— was considered wholly unnecessary. The adoption of English law and legal forms did not begin in any significant way before the 1790s. And even then, it occurred in a selective fashion, framed by local and regional concerns.[5]

The situation of Harvard College, the oldest eleemosynary corporation in the colonies, illustrates well the anomalous status of all colonial corporations. Although chartered as a corporation, the college was governed by boards composed of ministers of the tax-supported Congregational church and government officials sitting ex officio. Although Harvard possessed a small endowment, given partly by benevolent colonists and partly by British friends, it was regarded as a public institution because most of its revenues came from legislative grants and from tuitions and fees.

Even after the Revolution, when merchants and lawyers began to replace clergymen on its boards and when individual gifts and bequests became more important than government funding, Harvard retained its public identity: the provisions of its charter, its professorial appointments, and even its curriculum were matters of legislative debate and concern. Not until 1865, when the senior members of the state senate ceased sitting as overseers could Harvard be considered a private nonprofit corporation in the modern sense.[6] Early business corporations in New England were similarly ambiguous in their status: their capital often consisted of combinations of public and private subscriptions; public representatives often sat on their boards; legislatures reserved the right to alter or abrogate their charters; and persuasive justifications of their public utility were necessary to obtain charters of incorporation.

The rise of voluntary organizations was rooted in powerful social, political, and economic forces, which, by the early eighteenth century, had begun to erode the authority of family, church, and government throughout the colonies. Shortages of land in older settlements, in encouraging geographical and occupational mobility, undermined the power of patriarchal families and the integrity of tightly knit communities.[7] The reintegration of the colonies into the British commercial system challenged the established order: the crown's desire to enforce its commercial regulations forced the adoption of British legal forms in places where they had been resisted; the growth of markets encouraged individual entrepreneurship and the growth of commercial interests which advocated policies that worked against those of the older elite, whose power was based on land, not money. In addition, the revival of trade also brought with it the radical political and economic ideas of the Enlightenment.[8]

By the mid-eighteenth century, upwardly mobile merchants, artisans, and commercial farmers challenged entrenched social, political, and economic elites on all fronts. The Great Awakening, which began sweeping the colonies in 1730s, was as much a social and political movement as a religious one. In seeking to alter the criteria for admission for church membership, evangelicals were also challenging the power base of older elites, because church membership was a key to political and economic influence. In New England, where the

churches were tax-supported, ecclesiastical controversies connected
with the efforts of the "Old Lights" to suppress the movement quickly
bloomed into electoral struggles, which increasingly justified themselves with the ideas and rhetoric of English radicalism.[9] Although
struggles in the middle colonies and in the South, which tolerated
religious diversity, focused on different issues— particularly questions
about alliances between royal governors and great landholders and
merchants—the overall effect was the same, moving individuals to
reassess their relation to church and state.

Benjamin Franklin (1709–1790) was also much a man of these unsettled times. Rootless, skeptical, and entrepreneurial, by the time he
was a teen-ager, he had run afoul of the authorities by writing sedi-
tious newspaper articles, rebelled against his family, and run away
from the master to whom he was apprenticed. Although rejecting the
Puritanism of his native Massachusetts, he nonetheless embodied key
elements of its ethos, particularly a penchant for calculating self-regulation. In his early twenties, he began devising "a project of arriving
at moral perfection," which would enable him "to conquer all that
natural inclination, custom, or company" might lead him into.[10] In
the absence of credible external authority, this capacity for internal
control would prove especially adaptive in the emerging market economy.

Franklin's efforts to perfect himself were closely related to his efforts
to reform society. His ideas about establishing "a united party for
virtue" or a "Society of the Free and Easy," dating from the 1730s, were
efforts to promulgate the capacity for self-reform. Directed at persuad-
ing "young and single men" to practice the methods of self-control he
had imposed on himself, Franklin's "sect" would produce a group
industrious, frugal, free from debt, and willing to advise, assist, and
promote "one anothers' interest, business, and advancement in life."[11]
"I have always thought," Franklin would later reflect, "that one man
of tolerable abilities could work great changes and accomplish great
affairs among mankind if he first forms a good plan, and, cutting off
all amusements or other employments that would divert his attention,
makes the execution of that same plan his sole study and business."[12]

The idea that fundamental social and political institutions could be
changed for the better was a radical one in a society accustomed to an
almost medieval fatalism. Popular resistance to such "perfectionism"
had been dramatically expressed in the 1720s, when Boston mobs attacked the homes of physician Zabdiel Boylston and the Reverend
Cotton Mather because of their advocacy of inoculation to prevent
smallpox. Such resistance to God's will was regarded as blasphe-
mous.[13]

As originally conceived, the efforts of Franklin drew on the only organizational models of voluntary action available in the United States at the time—the idea of the church as a covenanted body and such secular secret societies as the Freemasons, with which he had become familiar during an early sojourn in England. He used his newspaper and almanac to promote perfectionist ideas "among the common people"—much as they had been instructed by the circulation of printed sermons—but his most important initiatives centered on a group he called the Junto, "a club for mutual improvement" composed of ambitious journeymen—a scrivener, a surveyor, a shoemaker, a joiner, a merchant's clerk, a book binder, a printer, a maker of surveying instruments. The group met weekly to debate issues of morals, politics, and natural philosophy and through this experience, as Franklin noted, acquired not only "better habits of conversation" but also a capacity for self-controlled, goal-directed behavior.

This capacity did not pass unnoticed in Philadelphia: the Junto members' industriousness was "visible to our neighbors" and gave them "character and credit."[14] In addition, members sent business to one another, advancing their collective interests. Soon the Junto—and the "subordinate clubs" spun off from it—led to not only "the promotion of our particular interests in business" but also "the increase of our influence in public affairs and our power of doing good by spreading through the several clubs the sentiments of the Junto."[15]

As Franklin noted, the power of these secret societies involved both the promotion of members' economic and political interests and "the power of doing good." Self-reform through voluntary mutual-benefit associations led before long to voluntary associations directed to public benefit. These would eventually include subscription libraries, volunteer fire companies, a hospital, and an academy, the latter of which received charters of incorporation from the Pennsylvania legislature.

The associations established by Franklin and his friends in Philadelphia represented only one of several types of voluntary bodies emerging in the United States by the mid-eighteenth century. In New England, where controversies over the Great Awakening had split many parishes, dissident worshipers, unwilling to compromise with the "Standing Order" of the established church, went off and formed their own voluntarily supported congregations. Although some of these worshipers remained, at least nominally, within the fold as independent or "strict" Congregationalists, others affiliated with Baptists and Methodists, who placed an emphasis on industry, frugality, and temperance not unlike that stressed by Franklin. Overall, challenges to established churches forced the colonists to consider religion—and ultimately politics and business—as a matter of individual conviction and choice.[16] The impact of these changes was anything but uniform. Just as the Great Awakening impacted communities in different ways—with some utterly transformed and others completely unaffected—so the emergence of secular entities, such as those organized by Franklin, was isolated and idiosyncratic. Moreover, even though these voluntary bodies—religious and secular—were becoming a definable presence, the extent to which they were "private" was far from clear. As far as the handful of incorporated associations were concerned, there was little question as to their "public" nature: they justified their seeking of corporate privileges on grounds of their public utility, frequently included public officials on their governing boards, often accepted financial support from government, and subjected themselves to legislative oversight. Even such secret societies as the Masons, which had begun to spread through the leadership groups of cities and towns in the colonies after 1750, considered themselves public bodies, considering the organization to be a virtual adjunct of the church in subduing "that private selfishness, pride, and antipathy, which has such a baneful influence upon human happiness."[17]

Voluntary Associations in the New Republic

Because neither experience nor existing political theory provided a rationale for voluntary organizations, eighteenth-century Americans were profoundly uncomfortable with their implications. Even as they used such ad hoc voluntary entities as Committees of Correspondence and Sons of Liberty groups to organize resistance to the British government, they feared the consequences of unfettered individuals pursuing their private interests. This concern was underlined by the revolutionary struggle itself, which came close to failure as political factions, seizing control of state legislatures, opposed national policies, interfered with military initiatives, and schemed to advance the interests of their friends. At one point during the war, an armed mob led by the speaker of the Pennsylvania Assembly laid siege to leaders of the Continental Congress and the army.[18] And, in the economic disorders that followed the Revolution, such mob actions became more, rather than less, common. It is not surprising that voluntary associations were not mentioned in the debates of the Constitutional Convention or in the *Federalist Papers*—although the latter had a great deal to say about the threat that faction posed to republican government.

Conservative New Englanders were among those most dubious about the rise of the skeptical, self-seeking individuals. Timothy

Dwight, president of Yale College and Hartford Wit, condemned the "new fledged infidel of modern brood" who "looked up, hissed his God; his parent stung / And sold his friend, and country, for a song."[19] Ironically, the extraordinary growth of corporate activity in New England after 1780 was less an effort to extend the domain of private action than one to contain it. The charter of Connecticut Missionary Society (1798) addressed itself to

> those errors in Religion and Government, and that declention in manners, which so much prevail, and which greater endanger the well being of the State; that such is the tendency of the neglect of the Laws which have been mentioned, is forcibly illustrated by the anarchy and despotism which prevail in one of the European Nations, which miserable State has in its origin the corruption of the Christian Religion, which has been consummated by infidelity, Atheism, and the total abolition of the Sabbath, and of other institutions as serve to maintain the belief of a God and Obedience to his Laws.[20]

A similar spirit motivated Connecticut's 1792 Act of Union with Yale College, which provided the school with renewed government support, while adding to its governing board the governor, lieutenant governor, and six senior members of the legislature's upper house. "The clergy," wrote Ezra Stiles, "will have a particular & special Reason now to preach up for & recommend the Election of religious & undeistical Counsellors; & tho' now and then an unprincipled Character may get into the Council, he may be hunted down in a future Election." He concluded that the act "may be mutually beneficial by preserving a religious Magistracy & a more catholic Clergy."[21]

The economic institutions chartered in New England during this period had a similar intent. With charters granted only to politically and religiously reliable leaders and with the state reserving to itself substantial blocks of stock and appointing a number of their directors, the banks were unambiguously viewed by their supporters as public institutions and as pillars of orthodoxy.[22] The charters of many canal, turnpike, bridge, and manufacturing companies not only involved effective partnership with the state but also enjoyed the same privileges of tax exemption extended to eleemosynary institutions such as Yale College. Needless to say, there were doubters and dissenters, such as the anonymous letter writer in the *Connecticut Courant* who fretted about the "foolish and wanton" legislature parceling out the "commonwealth into little aristocracies" and thus overturning "the nature of our government without remedy."[23]

Massachusetts took the lead in establishing corporations—stockholder-owned banks, insurance companies, bridge, turnpike, and canal companies, as well as a host of nonstock corporations, such as medical societies. At the same time, the ambivalence of the state about delegating public power was evident in its reluctance to grant the courts equity jurisdiction, despite the urging of the judiciary. Although the legislature proceeded boldly, it did so without a clear awareness of the implications of empowering groups of individuals to do the public's business. In 1803, James Sullivan, who had drafted the charter of the state's first bank two decades earlier, lamented: "It is a pity that so great a variety of corporations have been formed in this country before general rules for their government had been agreed upon." Responding to an enquiry from the legislature about the duration of a particular company's charter, Sullivan had to confess that the most crucial issues affecting corporations remained utterly unsettled. "There is no legal decision, no precedent established in the government," he wrote,

> on which to predicate an opinion, or form decisive answers. The subject may eventually engage the attention and employ the learning of all the men in the commonwealth. The feelings of interest, the dictates of prudence, the calculations of policy, and even the prevelency of parties, may give the whole contest a complexion which at this time is inconceivable to anyone. The giving of a decided opinion, therefore, without a precedent or an established rule to guide my mind would be of little avail; and might afterward be considered as presumptuous and imprudent. . . . It is vain to reason upon naked principles unfortified by established rules. . . . Forensic learning is rather useless on the present occasion.[24]

However, one thing was clear to Sullivan: because the "creation of corporate interests must have a direct tendency to weaken the powers of government," attitudes toward corporations would ultimately be determined not by "naked principles," but by politics. Those confident of their ability to command electoral majorities would tend to favor strong government and to oppose corporations; in contrast, the "outs" would favor corporations in order to weaken the power of governments that their opponents controlled. And these positions would shift according to which party held power.

In the South, a forcefully expressed body of anticorporate doctrine began to emerge, largely under the tutelage of Thomas Jefferson. Although favoring the freedom of individuals to associate for common purposes, Jefferson worried that such groups, if incorporated and empowered to hold property, would become the basis for new kinds of tyranny. Viewing all organizations as containing "some trace of human weakness, some grain of corruption, which cunning will discover, and wickedness will insensibly open, cultivate, and improve," he believed that all—governmental and nongovernmental—should be restricted in their powers and privileges.[25] At the same time, he opposed the growth of the market economy, which he believed "begets subservience and veniality, suffocates the germ of virtue, and prepares fit tools for the designs of ambition."[26]

In Virginia, early grants establishing academies did not include the privileges extended to comparable institutions in New England. Academies could not receive or manage endowments, their real estate was not tax exempt, and their students and faculties were not exempt from military duty and taxation. In 1792, Virginia affirmed its unofficial policy of discouraging private eleemosynary corporations by annulling the Elizabethan Statute of Charitable Uses and seizing the endowment funds held by the Anglican church, which were turned over to county authorities.[27] One jurist would affirm the wisdom of this act by condemning "the wretched policy of permitting the whole property of society to be swallowed up in the insatiable gulph of public charities."[28] Unlike New England, where public tasks tended increasingly to be delegated to corporations—albeit ones closely controlled by the state—Virginia favored the creation of public agencies. As early as the 1770s, care for the insane was entrusted to an asylum that operated under the direct authority of the legislature.[29] Jefferson's 1779 "Act to diffuse knowledge more generally through the mass of the people" stressed the government's responsibility for education and proposed a multitiered system of state-supported schools to provide equal opportunities for acquiring the rudiments, vocational instruction, and classical education.[30] The University of Virginia, established in 1819, was a state institution, not a private one. Other southern states followed Virginia's lead.[31]

The rare charters granted to business corporations in the South treated them as strictly subservient to the state, which held substantial blocks of stock and options on all sales of shares by the original incorporators, and which reserved to itself the right to review and set prices.[32] "With respect to acts of incorporation," wrote one of Jefferson's followers, "they ought never to be passed, but in consideration of the services rendered to the public. . . . If their object is merely private or selfish; if it is detrimental to, or not promotive of, the public good, they have no adequate claim upon the legislature for privileges."[33] As late as the 1820s, the Virginia legislature was actively intervening in the affairs of the state's leading canal company—not because it was mismanaged, but because its annual dividends of 15 percent to 20 percent were considered excessive.

In Pennsylvania and New York, religious and political heterogeneity placed almost insurmountable obstacles in the way of corporations and charitable trusts. Efforts to obtain corporate charters were inevitably entangled in jealousies not only among Anglicans, Quakers, Dutch Reformed, and Presbyterians, but also between commercial and agrarian interests. Moreover, New York had repealed the Statute of Charitable Uses and had, by the establishment of the University of the State of New York (the Regents), placed the government of all charitable and educational organizations within a political structure of accountability. This hostility to private eleemosynary corporations was elaborated during the next three decades, as the state legislature passed laws that not only restricted the ability of testators to make bequests to endowed institutions but also gave the legislature the power to limit the amount of property held by such organizations.[34] Although New York City had surpassed both Boston and Philadelphia in population and wealth by 1830, its philanthropic resources were scattered among a host of competing institutions, none of them the equal of Harvard, the Boston Athenaeum, or the Massachusetts General Hospital. Not until the 1890s, after a major set of legal reforms, would the charitable and cultural organizations of New York City match its commercial ones in eminence.

The situation of nonprofit organizations in Pennsylvania in this period was similarly ambiguous. On the one hand, the new state government had encouraged the creation of incorporated and unincorporated voluntary associations. On the other hand, in depriving its courts of the equity powers necessary for the enforcement of trusts, the state government constrained the growth of these institutions.[35] Because of the diverse ethnic and religious makeup of Pennsylvania, the politics of organizations in it were invariably entangled with intense political and economic rivalries among Episcopalians, Presbyterians, Quakers, and Lutherans, between English- and German-speaking groups, and between the emergent Federalist and Democratic Republican parties. Although the state did not go so far as to establish a governmental oversight body comparable to the Regents, the effects of heterogeneity and competition were similar to those in New York, leading to a scattering, rather than a concentration, of philanthropic resources. Pennsylvania had many colleges by 1830, but none remotely comparable in wealth or influence to Harvard or Yale.[36]

The status of voluntary associations and private charities in the new states and territories west of the Appalachians reflected the conflicts in the older settlements.[37] Although the original plan of government for the Northwest Territory, which was largely drafted by New Englanders, favored private initiatives, the admixture of southerners and northerners among the settlers—each with their own ideas about the permissible extent of private power—led first to intense struggles over the chartering of corporations and, subsequently, to the emergence of organizations that were neither clearly public nor clearly private. For example, Ohio University had been originally chartered as a private corporation. However, with Jeffersonians in control of the new state, it was reorganized—with a board appointed by the governor, but with expectations that it would enjoy private support. This institution coexisted with colleges that were supported by religious denominations, as well as ones that were owned by stockholders and supported by earned income. No purely private lay-governed, privately supported college would exist in Ohio until the end of the nineteenth century.[38]

Privatizing the Voluntary Association

The establishment of the federal government created a genuinely national arena in which the advocates of divergent conceptions of public and private power could air their differences as they struggled to define republican government. Although federal precedents could never entirely resolve these differences because the status of voluntary associations, corporations, and trusts would continue to be determined in state jurisdictions, federal doctrines would constitute important models for the states, and national debates over these matters would profoundly influence thinking on the state level.

The controversy over corporations became a federal issue in 1790, when Alexander Hamilton sought a charter from Congress for a national bank. Modeled on the Bank of England, the bank was to serve as the principle depository for government funds, to act as fiscal agent for the Treasury Department, to create a circulating medium, and to exercise indirect control over the operations of state-chartered banks. On the face of it, the proposed bank differed little from those already operating in Massachusetts, Pennsylvania, and New York: its charter was not perpetual; the government would own 20 percent of its stock and appoint five of its twenty-five directors; and the bank's activities would be subject to congressional oversight.[39]

Despite this, the bank bill could scarcely have been more controversial. Secretary of State Jefferson warned that "to take a single step beyond the boundaries specifically drawn around the powers of Congress is to take possession of a boundless field of power, no longer susceptible to definition."[40] One congressman exclaimed that he would "no more be seen entering a bank than a house of ill-repute." Another denounced the bank as "an engine of corruption."[41] Even James Madison—an ardent nationalist and forceful proponent of the Constitution, despite his friendship with Jefferson—doubted that establishing a bank was within the powers of the national government. These doubts were shared by President Washington, who was only persuaded to sign the bill after protracted conferences.

Hamilton's 1791 *Report on Manufactures* stirred further debate. The report asserted that the United States could not be truly independent as long as the nation remained a supplier of raw materials for European manufacturers and a market for their finished products. Hamilton argued that true independence required economic development—development of the kind that Jefferson had a decade earlier anathematized as "a canker which soon eats to the heart" of a republic's laws and constitution. Perhaps the debate would have been less intense had Hamilton not also busied himself in organizing a corporation that would both serve these purposes and benefit handsomely from federal action. Chartered in New Jersey in December 1791, the Society for Useful Manufactures would, he hoped, serve as a model for the industrialization of the United States.[42] With extraordinary liberality, the New Jersey legislature declared the assets of the company and employees tax-exempt, granted the firm perpetual existence, gave it the power of eminent domain, and abstained from placing state officials ex officio on its board of directors. (Nevertheless, a good many elected officials held stock in the firm in their private capacities.)

Response to news of the Society for Useful Manufactures was nothing short of hysterical. "All manufacturers ought to view it as a political monster," declared one writer in the *Philadelphia Observer*, who argued that corporations were nothing less than a criminal conspiracy to defraud the public. Echoing these sentiments, "A Republican" writing in New York's *American Daily Advertiser* argued that "the present prevailing propensity for corporations and exclusive privileges [is] a system . . . well calculated to aggrandize and increase the influence of the few at the expense of the many," raising up "various bodies of men of the most influential description in the community and separating them from the mass of the people." At the same time, "by distinguishing them with peculiar marks of favor, it attaches them to the ruling powers by common ties of gratitude and self-interest, and therefore gives an additional, or rather an artificial, weight to government which our Constitution does not warrant."[43]

Enemies of the national bank and the Society for Useful Manufactures—and, more generally, of voluntary associations incorporated and empowered to hold property—did not have to stretch the truth to substantiate their charges. They had only to point to the extraordinary privileges granted the Society for Useful Manufactures and similar enterprises to demonstrate their exemption "from the common burdens placed on the rest of society." And the list of the stockholders of the society—which included two members of Washington's cabinet, seven Treasury Department officials, the American ambassador to England, and three U.S. marshals, as well as New Jersey's attorney general, three judges of the state supreme court, two mayors, and five members of the General Assembly—confirmed its enemies' suspicions of its likely political influence.

The heated controversies over the national bank and the Society for Useful Manufactures crystallized public opinion. Opponents of corporations, who grouped around Jefferson, were strengthened in their resolve to oppose them. Champions of corporations, grouped around Hamilton and concentrated in New England, viewed them more favorably. Virginia's response was to further discourage incorporation efforts and to repeal the Statute of Charitable Uses.[44] Connecticut initiated a wave of incorporations with the explicit purpose of strengthening ties between the state, the established church, and the wealthy.

The national debate over economic institutions also served as the catalyst for the emergence of a new kind of voluntary organization— the political party. Dismayed by the successes of the organized and articulate propertied interests led by Hamilton, Jefferson retired to Monticello, where he set about to mobilize a political opposition based on electoral power. Recognizing that "the people cannot assemble themselves," he set about to do so through a nationwide network of opposition newspapers and secret political clubs. These became the basis for an unlikely coalition of northern artisans, entrepreneurs, and religious dissidents with southern and western farmers.

Although retaining his convictions about the essentially undemocratic character of incorporated associations, Jefferson did not hesitate to use them as mainstays of his efforts to unseat the Federalists. Fraternal and "friendly" associations, including the Masons (many of whose lodges were taken over by Jeffersonians) and freethinking library and debating clubs (modeled on Franklin's Junto), became the recruiting grounds for the Democratic Republican state, county, and town "managers" entrusted with the task of getting out the vote in the elections of the late 1790s.[45] Although Federalists denounced these "electioneering" tactics, they were soon involved in similar organizational efforts, even if loudly denouncing them as they did so.

Jefferson's Democratic Republican party transformed the nature of democratic power itself. Before its emergence, the wealthy, learned, and respectable had ruled in the name of the people but were seldom accountable to them. Even where property qualifications did not restrict the franchise and the ability to run for office, the public had been unable to mobilize its political energies before the coming of party organizations. Their success, signaled by Jefferson's election as president in 1800, broke the ties between the state and the associations that the Federalists had been trying to forge. The proponents of incorporated associations, turned out of office and, because of the interests they represented, unlikely to regain control, began to look to the corporations they controlled—and, indeed, the corporation itself—as counterforces to the electoral power of the democratic majority. Such enterprises, formed by groups of individuals who fancied themselves "guardians of virtue" and backed by private wealth, could be the basis for redeeming the endangered Republic.

The Jeffersonians recognized the Federalists' political intentions and, between 1800 and 1819, launched a series of attacks on established incorporated associations throughout the country. In 1810, Massachusetts Federalists, fearing an upcoming Jeffersonian takeover of the legislature, revised Harvard's charter, eliminating the members of the state senate who sat ex officio on the board of overseers and specifying that all future changes in the charter must be approved by the school's governing boards. When the Jeffersonians took the statehouse in 1812, they promptly suspended these provisions and filled the restored ex officio overseers' seats with Jacobins. The struggle over the charter appeared headed for the courts when the Federalists returned to power in 1813 and restored Harvard to the hands of the faithful.[46] A similar struggle took place in Ohio, when the Jeffersonian legislature attempted to move Miami University from Oxford to Cincinnati. Although nominally a public institution, the university was supported by income from lands given by a private donor. Pointing out that Miami's charter had guaranteed that all donations would be "applied in conformity with the intention of the donor," opponents mounted a novel argument: they suggested that the charter was not merely a contingent and revocable delegation of public power; it was a contract between the donor and the trustees and, as such, constitutionally protected. If a legislature "may rightfully repeal every law passed by a former legislature," argued one champion of the university, "the whim of the moment will become the law of the land. Our country will be looked upon as a den of robbers. Every honest man will abandon our shores—and who will be found to trust the legislature of our country, when they are the first to violate their own contracts?"[47]

The most famous of the struggles over the power of legislatures to alter corporate charters involved New Hampshire's efforts to take over Dartmouth College.[48] When Jeffersonians took control of the legislature in 1816, they reorganized the college, changed its name, and replaced its twelve member self-perpetuating board with twenty-one gubernatorially appointed trustees and a board of twenty-five legislatively appointed overseers, who enjoyed veto power over the trustees. The president of the college was required to report annually to the governor on its management, and the governor and his council were empowered to inspect the college every five years and report on its condition to the legislature.

When the old board of trustees contested the action, the New Hampshire Supreme Court upheld the state, drawing on the generally accepted doctrine that corporations, as creations of the legislature, were entirely subject to its will. The old trustees appealed, and the case reached the U.S. Supreme Court in 1818. In representing the old trustees, Daniel Webster conceded that the college's charter, like that of any corporation, was an act of government. But, he suggested, individuals had been encouraged by that grant of corporate powers to make donations and bequests to trustees of the institution. Although the use was public, Webster argued that this did not diminish the private character of the donated property: the gifts were made to the trustees and, as such, constituted private contracts between the trustees and the donors. He pointed out that the Constitution specifically prohibited states from passing laws impairing contractual obligations. "The case before the court," Webster concluded, in an unabashed assertion of the concept of private guardianship of the public good,

> affects not this college only, but every college, and all literary institutions of the country. They have flourished, hitherto, and have become in a high degree respectable and useful to the community. They have all a common principle of existence—the inviolability of their charters. It will be dangerous, a most dangerous experiment, to hold these institutions subject to the rise and fall of popular parties, and the fluctuations of political opinions. If the franchise may be at any time taken away, or impaired, the property may also be taken away, or its use perverted. Benefactors will have no certainty of effecting the object of their bounty; and learned men will be deterred from devoting themselves to the service of such institutions, from the precarious title of their officers. Colleges and halls will be deserted by better spirits, and become a theater for the contention of politics. Party and faction will be cherished in places consecrated to piety and learning. The consequences are neither remote nor possible only. They are certain and immediate.[49]

By the time the Dartmouth College case reached the Supreme Court, it was clear that a definitive ruling had to be made on the status of corporations. The quarrel no longer involved mere "naked principles": fundamental rights, as well as substantial investments of property, hung in the balance. If the court decided for the state, no investment in corporate property and no charitable trust would be immune from the power of the state; legislatures, claiming to act in the name of the public, could take control of the assets of associations and put them to any use they wished. Upholding the State of New Hampshire would be nothing less than a revolution. The court, with a single dissent, accepted Webster's argument. Chief Justice Marshall asserted that the case did not involve the corporate rights of the college. If it did, the New Hampshire legislature might "act according to its own judgement, unrestrained by any limitation of its power imposed by the Constitution of the United States." Rather, the case involved the individual rights of the donors who had given property to Dartmouth's trustees. Marshall stated that the charter was not a grant of political power, an establishment "of a civil institution to be employed in the administration of government," or a matter of government funds. The charter was, rather,

> a contract to which the donors, the trustees, and the Crown (to whose rights and obligations New Hampshire succeeds) were the original parties. It is a contract made on a valuable consideration. It is a contract for the security and disposition of property. It is a contract on the faith of which real and personal estate has been conveyed to the corporation. It is then a contract within the letter of the Constitution, and within its spirit also.

As such, Marshall ruled, Dartmouth's charter could not be altered by the legislature "without violating the Constitution of the United States."[50]

Despite the outcome of the Dartmouth College case, federal doctrine on charitable corporations remained confused. Although the court had upheld the autonomy of charitable corporations, its decision in *Philadelphia Baptist Association* v. *Hart's Executors* undermined the ability of citizens to give them financial support.[51] The case involved a small bequest that Silas Hart, a citizen of Virginia, left to the Philadelphia Baptist Association, for educating young men for the ministry. Hart's executors refused to surrender the bequest to the Baptists, arguing that under Virginia law the association could not hold charitable property because it was not in existence at the time of Hart's death. In addition, Hart's executors argued that the membership of the organization was too poorly defined to constitute a legal beneficiary. Such a bequest might be legal under English law, but Virginia's repeal of the Statute of Charitable Uses rendered it void in that state. Marshall sustained the defendants.

Although the case hinged on the narrow question of whether a testator could bequeath funds in trust to an unincorporated association, the underlying issue involved the power of states to regulate the ability of voluntary associations to hold property. In its ruling, the court upheld the power of states that had abolished the Statute of Charitable Uses in order to forbid such bequests. This meant, in effect, that legislatures could not only limit the activities of voluntary associations by refusing to incorporate them (thus preventing them from receiving funds in trust), but also forbid even corporations in existence from receiving such funds without specific government approval. Thus, the substantial protections gained by incorporated associations in the Dartmouth College case were severely circumscribed in the case of *Philadelphia Baptist Association* v. *Hart's Executors,* which still left the state legislatures as the ultimate delimiters of the rights of associations.

Although the Hart decision did not affect the activities of states such as Massachusetts and Connecticut, where incorporated charitable organizations were well established in fact and in law, in New York, New Jersey, Pennsylvania, and the South—where Jefferson's political progeny, the Jacksonians, held sway—it encouraged further efforts to limit the growth and influence of private voluntary organizations. New York's 1828 revised statutes went beyond the Hart ruling, not only forbidding bequests to unincorporated associations but also restricting the proportion of estates which could be left for charitable purposes.[52] In addition, the statutes forbade eleemosynary institutions to hold property in excess of amounts specifically authorized by the legislature. The New York statutes influenced the actions of other states, particularly western ones.

Not until 1844, when the Supreme Court ruled on *Vidal* v. *Girard's Executors,* were private nonprofit corporations placed on a firm legal footing under federal law.[53] This case involved the will of Stephen Girard, an enormously wealthy Philadelphia merchant who, on his death, left $7 million for the establishment of a college for orphans in Philadelphia. Although the case raised many important issues, the central one was the status of charitable bequests in states such as Pennsylvania, which had repealed the Statute of Charitable Uses. By 1844, the quality of American legal scholarship was considerably better than it had been two decades earlier. Attorneys for the Girard estate were able to demonstrate convincingly that the Elizabethan statute had merely been the codification of a long series of previous acts and precedents and that, as a result, the status of charitable trusts were unaffected by the repeal of the 1601 statute.[54] After 1844, private charitable corporations were securely established under federal law—though this ruling did not affect the particular states that chose to limit their activities.

Antebellum Institutional Cultures

Although Tocqueville's observations on the centrality of voluntary associations to American democracy tend to be cited as definitive, readers too often overlook the distinctions he drew between civil, commerleadership—which were based on a rhetoric of public stewardship—and legitimated their accumulation of wealth—which, as their charitable actions showed, they held as stewards.[64] In the tumult of antebel-South, where "the primeval forest appears at every turn; society seems to be asleep, man to be idle, and nature alone" offering "a scene of activity and life," they were uncommon. In the "enterprising and energetic" North, where citizens regarded "temporal prosperity as the chief aim" of their existence with an "avidity in the pursuit of gain that resembles a species of heroism," they seemed to be everywhere.[55]

Tocqueville made clear, however, that voluntary associations varied in their purposes and constituencies. "The affluent classes of society," he wrote, "have no influence in political affairs. . . . They constitute a private society in the state which has its own tastes and pleasures. The rich have a hearty dislike of the democratic institutions of their country." And, deprived of direct political influence, their "chief weapons" were the newspapers and the public associations, which they used to "oppose the whole moral authority of the minority to the physical power that domineers over it."[56] Private associations of this kind differed as much from the political associations through which the majority pursued its purposes as much as those formed by "weak," "narrow-minded," and "dependent" industrial workers differed from those formed by the emergent "aristocracy of manufactures," whose members, though politically disempowered, resembled "more and more the administrator of a vast empire."[57] Had Tocqueville visited the United States in the 1850s instead of the 1820s, he would certainly have drawn the contrasts between the various kinds of associations more starkly, noting that some were unquestionably more important than others in the nation's economic and cultural development.

Two groups were especially aggressive and effective in their use of voluntary associations. Both were elements of the Federalist "Standing Order," which had been displaced by the rise of political and economic democracy after 1800. The first consisted of leaders and members of the Congregational and Presbyterian churches of the Northeast, which had been disestablished by the Jeffersonians. The churchmen, supported by Federalist merchants, professionals, and magistrates, created an "evangelical counteroffensive" whose purpose was to ensure that American democracy, both in older areas of settlement and on the made corporate organizations possible. Through their complex of organizations, evangelicals reached out to individuals, particularly the ambitious and often rootless young, educating them to modes of self-control that were particularly adaptive in a society in which external authority was largely lacking. No less important was evangelical support for these resocialized individuals, who were rewarded for their successful attainment of autonomy with responsible and remunerative places in the emerging network of private business and eleemosynary corporations. This subculture of individuals, trained to autonomy and accommodated to modes of corporate and proto-bureaucratic activity, would prove of immense importance not only in organizing the Civil War mobilization but also in creating and staffing the large-scale organizations that emerged after the war.

Paralleling the evangelical counteroffensive was a movement among the merchants of Boston, where the rise of the Jeffersonians had not only politically displaced the Federalist merchants but also economically challenged them. The traditional familial basis of business enterprise had proved extremely adaptive to colonial commercial conditions, but it handicapped those who sought to take advantage of the seemingly boundless opportunities offered by independent nationhood.[63]

The conditions of postrevolutionary commerce were dramatically different from those of the colonial period. Freed from the strictures of British mercantilist trade regulations, which had limited the growth of manufacturing and restricted the activities of American merchants in world markets, American entrepreneurs found themmerchants in world markets, American entrepreneurs found themselves possessed of boundless opportunities but lacking in both capital and organizational experience. Capital was encumbered with familial and social obligations. And new ventures, such as trade with India and China, required amounts of capital exceeding the resources of any individual family. Taking advantage of new opportunities would require joint ventures among unrelated families, as well as mobilizing the idle capital of the population as a whole. Such ventures, whether in trade or in newer corporate activities such as banking, required operatives selected for competence rather than kinship. Finally, because the postrevolutionary Boston mercantile community was remarkably heterogeneous, its leaders having come from Massachusetts' smaller towns and cities, there was a particular need for mechanisms to take the place of kinship in fostering reliability and trust.

The mercantile response was remarkably coherent and thorough. To disengage capital from familial and social obligations, the merchants began encouraging vocational diversity among their sons. Pushing sons into the professions was not a repudiation of traditional patri-

E R R A T U M

Inventing the Nonprofit Sector

by Peter Dobkin Hall

Lines 4-6 on page 32 should read:

cial, and political associations, as well as his allusions to their relative importance in different regions of the United States, and the various ways in which different social groups used them. In the slaveholding

frontier, would be tempered by the restraining influen
and education.[58]

The machinery of the evangelical counteroffensive wa
of interrelated voluntary and nonprofit organizations. At
the churches, and in close association with them was a s
nominational organizations—temperance, Bible, and trac
nationally linked network of lyceums (which presented pu
and organized debates on questions of current interest); t
stitutes, and private academies—all of which reached out to
for potential adherents. The young people who were drawr
organizations were presented with opportunities, particula
tional ones, that were lacking in society at large.[59] Evange
formed education societies that underwrote college educ
pious young men and created missionary societies, which fe
pits for those with clerical ambitions and continued the wor
ing evangelical outposts in every American community.[60] Tie
societies were a host of secular pursuits—teaching positior
public and private schools, editorships of temperance, religi
antislavery newspapers, and lyceum lectureships—which r
closely tied to evangelical purposes.[61] Even for those who
become lawyers, businessmen, or farmers after college, there v
vantages to be gained from evangelical connections, which en
the availability of credit and opened up important avenues of p
influence. Such laymen tended to assume positions of econom
litical, and cultural leadership wherever they settled.[62]

By the 1850s, evangelicals had created not only a personal a
ganizational network that embraced the nation but also a "cult
organization," a subgroup of individuals with an unusual proc
for corporate activity and voluntary action. Although a politica
nority, their influence over the central educational, charitable,
productive activities of their communities—and those of the nati
large—was astonishing. Even in western and southern states, w
the law remained hostile to private eleemosynary corporations, t
individuals often managed to insulate publicly funded cultural
welfare institutions from political control through the establishm
of relatively autonomous boards of trustees. Wherever an orphana
a library, a college, a hospital, an academy, or a professional soci
operated, it was almost invariably the work of a migrant New En
lander with evangelical connections. Much the same could be sa
about banks, telegraphs, and the major incorporated for-profit ente
prises of the mid-nineteenth century.

The evangelicals' most powerful impact was on the attitudes tha

E R R A T U M

Inventing the Nonprofit Sector

by Peter Dobkin Hall

Lines 4-6 on page 32 should read:

cial, and political associations, as well as his
allusions to their relative importance in different
regions of the United States, and the various ways
in which different social groups used them. In the
slaveholding

frontier, would be tempered by the restraining influence of religion and education.[58]

The machinery of the evangelical counteroffensive was a complex of interrelated voluntary and nonprofit organizations. At its base were the churches, and in close association with them was a set of nondenominational organizations—temperance, Bible, and tract societies; a nationally linked network of lyceums (which presented public lectures and organized debates on questions of current interest); teachers' institutes, and private academies—all of which reached out to the public for potential adherents. The young people who were drawn into these organizations were presented with opportunities, particularly educational ones, that were lacking in society at large.[59] Evangelicals also formed education societies that underwrote college educations for pious young men and created missionary societies, which found pulpits for those with clerical ambitions and continued the work of placing evangelical outposts in every American community.[60] Tied to these societies were a host of secular pursuits—teaching positions in the public and private schools, editorships of temperance, religious, and antislavery newspapers, and lyceum lectureships—which remained closely tied to evangelical purposes.[61] Even for those who chose to become lawyers, businessmen, or farmers after college, there were advantages to be gained from evangelical connections, which enhanced the availability of credit and opened up important avenues of political influence. Such laymen tended to assume positions of economic, political, and cultural leadership wherever they settled.[62]

By the 1850s, evangelicals had created not only a personal and organizational network that embraced the nation but also a "culture of organization," a subgroup of individuals with an unusual proclivity for corporate activity and voluntary action. Although a political minority, their influence over the central educational, charitable, and productive activities of their communities—and those of the nation at large—was astonishing. Even in western and southern states, where the law remained hostile to private eleemosynary corporations, these individuals often managed to insulate publicly funded cultural and welfare institutions from political control through the establishment of relatively autonomous boards of trustees. Wherever an orphanage, a library, a college, a hospital, an academy, or a professional society operated, it was almost invariably the work of a migrant New Englander with evangelical connections. Much the same could be said about banks, telegraphs, and the major incorporated for-profit enterprises of the mid-nineteenth century.

The evangelicals' most powerful impact was on the attitudes that

made corporate organizations possible. Through their complex of organizations, evangelicals reached out to individuals, particularly the
ambitious and often rootless young, educating them to modes of self-
control that were particularly adaptive in a society in which external
authority was largely lacking. No less important was evangelical support for these resocialized individuals, who were rewarded for their
successful attainment of autonomy with responsible and remunerative
places in the emerging network of private business and eleemosynary
corporations. This subculture of individuals, trained to autonomy and
accommodated to modes of corporate and proto-bureaucratic activity,
would prove of immense importance not only in organizing the Civil
War mobilization but also in creating and staffing the large-scale organizations that emerged after the war.

Paralleling the evangelical counteroffensive was a movement
among the merchants of Boston, where the rise of the Jeffersonians
had not only politically displaced the Federalist merchants but also
economically challenged them. The traditional familial basis of business enterprise had proved extremely adaptive to colonial commercial
conditions, but it handicapped those who sought to take advantage of
the seemingly boundless opportunities offered by independent nationhood.[63]

The conditions of postrevolutionary commerce were dramatically
different from those of the colonial period. Freed from the strictures
of British mercantilist trade regulations, which had limited the
growth of manufacturing and restricted the activities of American
merchants in world markets, American entrepreneurs found themselves possessed of boundless opportunities but lacking in both capital
and organizational experience. Capital was encumbered with familial
and social obligations. And new ventures, such as trade with India and
China, required amounts of capital exceeding the resources of any
individual family. Taking advantage of new opportunities would require joint ventures among unrelated families, as well as mobilizing
the idle capital of the population as a whole. Such ventures, whether
in trade or in newer corporate activities such as banking, required
operatives selected for competence rather than kinship. Finally, because the postrevolutionary Boston mercantile community was remarkably heterogeneous, its leaders having come from Massachusetts'
smaller towns and cities, there was a particular need for mechanisms
to take the place of kinship in fostering reliability and trust.

The mercantile response was remarkably coherent and thorough. To
disengage capital from familial and social obligations, the merchants
began encouraging vocational diversity among their sons. Pushing
sons into the professions was not a repudiation of traditional patri-

archalism, because the generation of fathers that encouraged this diversity assured their sons' successes (as well as exerting a continuing measure of control over them) by creating corporate organizations—for the doctors, medical societies and schools, hospitals, and infirmaries; for the lawyers, corporate directorships and testamentary and institutional trusteeships.

The mercantile strategy affected not only their own families and the institutions they funded but also society itself. Disengaging capital, the family freed it for investment in expanding markets. Institutional endowments were important as mechanisms for pooling capital and for controlling the economy, as well as facilitating the expansion of mercantile influence into noneconomic realms. These institutions not only socialized the merchants' sons but also were vehicles for the recruitment of talented outsiders.

If the evangelicals had created a nonprofit machinery that provided a foundation for the economic success of their adherents, the Bostonians had, by 1850, created a for-profit machinery in which nonprofit organizations played crucial roles as recruiters and socializers of personnel and as sources of capital. While nonprofit organizations yielded particular benefits for their creators, they were no less effective in providing crucially important services for the general public. Both merchants and evangelicals were active organizers and supporters of schools, colleges, hospitals, medical societies, orphanages, asylums, and other charitable enterprises that offered essential services that few governments or private groups were willing to undertake. The willingness of the benevolently wealthy and the evangelicals to take on these responsibilities both lent credibility to their claims for political leadership—which were based on a rhetoric of public stewardship—and legitimated their accumulation of wealth—which, as their charitable actions showed, they held as stewards.[64] In the tumult of antebellum democracy and capitalism, which had shattered official and traditional forms of authority, these two groups were distinctive in their willingness to devote their wealth to public purposes and to do so through private nonprofit corporations.

The Civil War made good the claims of evangelicals and Bostonians against those of the more doctrinaire democrats.[65] The art of public administration had stagnated under Andrew Jackson and his successors.[66] Even the army had been deprived of its most talented officers by Jacksonian hostility to professional elites. The early phases of the war effort drew on Jacksonian administrative practices, such as they were. The results were disastrous, as the Union armies were routed on every front. It was only when Lincoln—who had been profoundly influenced by Federalist-evangelical organizational activities as a young man—turned to those with significant experience in the private for-profit and nonprofit sectors that it became possible to transform the jerry-built prewar government into an effective and reasonably efficient administrative apparatus.[67]

Although the significance of the New England–based "culture of organization" was first identified by George Frederickson in his study of the United States Sanitary Commission, the private organization that took responsibility for providing medical care to the Union army, it now seems apparent that the military, logistical, and financial dimensions of the war effort also drew extensively on it.[68] College-educated New Englanders and individuals influenced by evangelical institutions were disproportionately represented in the officer corps and in key civilian positions. Institutionally, the evangelical enterprises of the antebellum period provided the bureaucratic organizational models for the mobilization, as well as being major factors in producing both the levels of expertise and the personality types necessary for the effective operation of these administrative hierarchies. The victory of the Union was seen both by its organizers and by significant elements of the general public as a legitimation of the claims of the organized private sector. By 1865, American culture had been transformed. The Jacksonian persuasion, with its prejudices against private power and the institutions and elites associated with it, was on the defensive in the face of a triumphant assertion of political nationality that identified itself with private wealth and power. But the national consolidation of private economic and cultural energies still lay in the future.

"Fighting the Wilderness, Moral and Physical": Private Institutions and the Search for Order

The outcome of the Civil War made it possible for the advocates of private power to argue that the redemption of the Union was a vindication of the private institutions, whose strength was a product of their simultaneous commitment to reason, virtue, and science. "As a people," Harvard's president Charles W. Eliot would declare in 1869, "we have but a halting faith in special training for high professional employments. The vulgar conceit that a Yankee can turn his hand to anything we insensibly carry into high places where it is preposterous and criminal. . . . Only after years of the bitterest experience, did we come to believe the professional training of a soldier to be of value in war."[69] The notion of private responsibility for the public good had been transformed by events and by social Darwinism into a scientific justification of the role of elites in America and the relation between elites and the masses. This redefinition pointed to vast new opportunities for extending the influence of private institutions.[70]

If ideology and politics suggested new tasks for the private sector, the coalescence of the two strands of private institution-building—the nationally extensive evangelical network and the urban-intensive Boston institutional hierarchy—provided the means for undertaking these tasks. From 1865 on, the advocates of private power concentrated their energies in two areas: building private business corporations capable of operating on a national scale and extending the scope, scale, and legal privileges of private eleemosynary institutions. The two efforts were necessarily related. The ability to establish and operate large-scale business organizations required new kinds of trained manpower and new technologies, as well as the ability to gather and interpret social and economic information.[71] These were needs that colleges could best supply. But to meet these needs, higher education needed the support of private wealth to expand facilities, to recruit students nationally and faculty internationally, to create new curricula, and to develop new fields for teaching and research. University administrators and reform-minded business people sought each other out, with dramatically successful results: gifts and bequests to Harvard between 1866 and 1890 amounted to $5.9 million, compared to $1.6 million for between 1841 and 1865; gifts and bequests at Yale for the same period amounted to $5.3 million, compared to $1.0 million for the previous quarter-century.[72] Businessmen became so involved with the affairs of the major universities—all of which were private—that it was hardly an exaggeration to claim, as Thorstein Veblen did, that "men of affairs have taken over direction of the pursuit of knowledge."[73] University training became essential for the pursuit of careers in larger business corporations. And businessmen were active in the founding of professional organizations such as the American Social Science Association, the American Statistical Association, and the American Economic Association, which brought together nonprofit and for-profit institution-builders in contexts of mutual concern.

It was during this period that a coherent rationale for the role of private institutions in the democratic polity was finally articulated and, more importantly, translated into legislation. In 1874, Harvard's Eliot, defending the university's tax exemption to the Massachusetts General Court, presented a detailed economic analysis of benefits the public received from private charitable institutions.[74] This analysis was so persuasive that the legislature not only raised the ceiling on the amount of charitable property that could be exempted from taxation but also increased the range of exempt institutions to include any "educational, charitable, benevolent, or religious purpose," including "any antiquarian, historical, literary, scientific, medical, artistic, monumental, or musical" purpose, to "any missionary enterprise" with either foreign or domestic objects, for organizations "encouraging athletic exercises and yachting," to libraries and reading rooms, and to "societies of Freemasons, Odd Fellows, Knights of Pythias and other charitable or social bodies of a like character and purpose."[75]

The Massachusetts law became a model for those seeking to extend the privileges of private institutions. The 1893 Connecticut Supreme Court decision upholding the exemption of Yale's real estate from taxation by the City of New Haven followed Eliot's argument almost word for word.[76] New York's charities law, revised in 1893, would also follow the Massachusetts model.[77] However, despite their successes in the Northeast, advocates of civil privatism were not unopposed.

As the New York legislature was considering the charities reform bill, Wisconsin political economist Richard Ely made a last gallant defense of the alternative, more public, institutional tradition. In a speech to the regents, Ely declared that

> Washington, the Adamses, Jefferson, and Monroe favored a national university in Washington. Were they un-American? Was Thomas Jefferson un-American when he founded the University of Virginia? What has been the practice of America? We who live in the Northwest can not admit that a few states east of Ohio and north of Virginia shall tell what is American. In the early history of this country even those states contributed taxation for the support of the university and with the exception of those few states, every state in the American Union is taxed to-day for the support of higher education. Are they not American? Is Michigan not American? Are Wisconsin, Nebraska and Missouri not American? Is the title American to be restricted to the practice of New York and Massachusetts? I cannot admit it for a moment.[78]

Ely's remarks were part of a broader challenge to the emerging relationship between big business and the growing private institutions of culture, education, and social welfare. Within the elite, the power of business was resented—and sometimes resisted—by antimodernists and avatars of "genteel culture," who believed that culture had been corrupted by its close relationships to new industrial and commercial wealth.[79] "Eliot goes about in a cab with Pierpont, hangs laurel wreaths on his nose, and gives him his papal kiss," sneered Brahmin critic John Jay Chapman. "What has Eliot got to say to the young man entering business or politics who is about to be corrupted by Morgan and his class?"[80] The effort to consolidate and rationalize the economy also met with resistance, even within the business community. In building their empires, entrepreneurs such as John D. Rockefeller and Andrew Carnegie saw themselves as standing in opposition to Wall Street—though they eventually joined forces with it. Outside the elite, intellectuals and journalists challenged the increasingly privatized economy and culture as un-American. Many of them joined forces with the alliance of northern workers and southern and western farmers to form a unified political opposition—Populism—which would, by 1896, take control of the Democratic party.

Despite opposition and criticism, the use of private nonprofit organizations grew enormously in the last decades of the nineteenth century. Big business and private wealth underwrote the growth of universities, libraries, hospitals, museums, social-welfare organizations, professional societies, and private clubs. At the same time, the middle and lower classes supported labor unions, mutual-benefit societies, fraternal organizations, volunteer fire companies, building and loan associations, and even cooperatively owned nonprofit businesses. Growing awareness of urban poverty among the middle and upper classes encouraged the establishment of charitable organizations of every sort, ranging from traditional funds for the relief of the sick, poor, and disabled to new forms of nonprofit activity, such as settlement houses and charity organization societies.[81] With the rise of the "social gospel," Protestant churches, which had until the 1860s restricted themselves primarily to spiritual matters, became active in charitable affairs and in social, economic, and political reform efforts.[82] And a host of nonpartisan organizations promoting good government, civil-service reform, and economic development became actively involved in the political process.

No less important than the private organizations directed to the reform of society was the rise of new kinds of cultural organizations whose primary constituencies were the rich. The establishment and professionalization of museums and symphony orchestras (as well as the growth of the academic specialties that legitimated their activities) played a major role in recasting the nature of urban culture, transforming the market for artistic products, and reshaping the identity of the nation's upper classes.[83] By the 1880s, charitable activity itself became subject to the trend toward rationalization, which was affecting business, as reformers attempted to make benevolence more effective through the creation of "united charities" organizations, which combined the resources of smaller enterprises, and through state charity commissions, which oversaw the administration of public and private charitable activities.[84]

As the public became more aware of violence, poverty, and disorder in the 1870s, it tended to indict foreigners and radical demagogues as sources of discontent.[85] But between the great railroad strike of 1877 and the Haymarket bombing of 1886, a fundamental shift in public perception began to take place. One of the first and most widely read products of this change, which involved a shift from seeing disorder as a problem of public and private morality to seeing it as a problem in social and economic organization, was Henry George's 1879 volume, *Progress and Poverty*.[86] In his introduction, George reviewed the optimistic expectations of most nineteenth-century Americans as they looked toward an industrial age and found them illusory: the vast increases in production and wealth brought about by industrialization had neither abolished poverty nor made people more equal. "From all part of the civilized world," George wrote,

> come complaints of industrial depression; of labor condemned to involuntary idleness; of capital masses and wasting; of pecuniary distress among businessmen; of want and suffering and anxiety among the working classes. All the dull, deadening pain, all the keen maddening anguish, that to great masses of men are involved in the words "hard times," afflict the world today. . . . It is at last becoming evident that the enormous increase in productive power which has marked the present century and is still going on with accelerating ratio, has no tendency to extirpate [poverty] or to lighten the burdens of those compelled to toil. It simply widens the gulf between dives and Lazarus, and makes the struggle for existence more intense.[87]

George was not alone in his condemnation of industrialism. Mark Twain's 1889 *Connecticut Yankee in King Arthur's Court* was a black comedy in which industry was shown to be no more than a method for enlarging on the destructive capacity of the human race. Edward Bellamy's 1886 *Looking Backward,* while anticipating an evolutionary solution to the problems of inequality, sharply condemned the contemporary industrial order.

While social and economic turbulence increased in the last quarter of the nineteenth century—and along with it criticism of business, the wealthy, and the institutions they supported, so also did the intensity of efforts by the propertied classes to deal with these problems. Although often portrayed as enemies of social and economic justice, business leaders and their allies in the professions and the universities were deeply concerned about poverty, corruption, and disorder. Very few businessmen were either hard-line social Darwinists or reactionary advocates of laissez faire.[88] Most were acutely uncomfortable with not only the contradictions between Christian social ethics that they professed and the undeniable realities of poverty and exploitation around them, but also the challenges that the concentration of wealth and industrial power posed for traditional conceptions of democracy.[89] The severest critics of business, George and Bellamy, had their greatest following among the business and professional classes.[90] Upper-class churches, led by the Episcopalians and Presbyterians, were the vanguard of socially concerned Christianity. And businessmen themselves, most notably Carnegie, wrote influential analyses of the problems of industrial order and proposed radical remedies, such as confiscatory income and estate taxation.

By the turn of the century, a paradigm for the resolution of these problems began to be articulated, laying the foundation for what would become the dominant political consensus for the next eighty years. First, as Henry Adams would note in his *Education*, it had become clear by the mid-1890s that "a capitalistic system had been adopted, and if it were to be run at all, it must be run by capital and by capitalistic methods."[91] Many believed that large bureaucratic institutions, guided by scientifically trained experts, to be the most efficient mechanisms for achieving the social, economic, and political goals of reform. Americans wishing to sustain democratic and Christian traditions—to "fulfill the Promise of American Life," as Herbert Croly would put it in 1908—were urged to become "efficient instruments" of the national purpose by accepting large hierarchical organizations, specialization, and inherent inequality of condition. These institutions would substitute for equality of condition equality of opportunity and, suffused with an ethos of service, would invest social, economic, and political life with a sense of common purpose. The new order would take the form of a moral equivalent of war, in which individuals attained their positions according to ability and talent and in which differentials of position and power, as well as high degrees of specialization and interdependence, would become recognized as essential to the pursuit of collective goals.

"Government by People outside of Government": The Private Sector Alternative, 1900–1935

Alternatives to capitalism and its legal basis, the private ownership of property, had been topics of discussion and experiment in some circles in America as early as the 1830s. But as long as socialism remained philosophical and utopian, it was not perceived as a threat to the established order. However, in the 1870s, the anticapitalist radicalisms began to be viewed in a new light, as events such as the establishment of the Paris Commune of 1871 and the emergence of radical organizations composed of farmers and urban industrial workers—capped by the great railroad strike and riots of 1877—propelled them to the forefront of public attention. Many of the more emotional journalists, academics, and politicians viewed radicalism as a moral issue. Some advocated the violent suppression of union activity, restriction of immigration (because immigrants were believed to be the vectors of socialism and anarchism), prohibition (because saloons were the centers of immigrant political activity), and restriction of the franchise. But many Americans with large business interests understood that social and political turbulence was a manifestation of fundamental problems in political, economic, and social institutions—problems that mere repression would not solve. These business leaders were also aware that leading European countries, particularly England and Germany, were beginning to respond through state action to popular demands for social and economic justice.

America's business leaders were averse to governmental solutions to social and economic problems, not so much from self-interest (neither German nor British industry suffered much from the implementation of the early social programs) as from the basic premises and historical experiences that had shaped American political culture. There was no precedent for large-scale federal action in peacetime, and even the effort to establish central control over the federal armies during the Civil War had been fiercely resisted.[92] Americans had rejected Whig programs of large-scale government scientific activity in the 1820s, and conservative opposition had stymied efforts to establish a national university in the 1880s. Although the federal government had played an important role in the building of a transcontinental railroad and telegraph, it had done so only indirectly, through providing incentives and subsidies.

Ideological opposition to big government dated from colonial times, was restated during the Revolution and in the drafting of the Constitution, and was reinforced by the pervasive, albeit largely vernacular, influence of social Darwinism. Most influential Americans saw progress as an open-ended phenomenon and feared that interference in "natural" social processes was both dangerous and, in terms of its effects on individuals, morally pernicious. Some Darwinists carried this viewpoint to extremes of laissez-faire brutalism, but most, while disapproving of government action, viewed private-sector effects on social and economic activity as acceptable. Like the capitalist marketplace, private institutions of charity and culture were voluntary, in terms of both benefactors and beneficiaries. Their survival, like that of business corporations, was determined by how efficiently they were run, not by legislative edict. And their effect, like that of markets, was on the character of individuals who, in being better enabled to compete in the struggle for existence, would move the race forward. As

Eliot had remarked to the Massachusetts legislature in advancing his argument to exempting the properties of universities and other private charities from taxation,

> the reason for treating these institutions in an exceptional manner is, that having no selfish object in view, or purpose of personal gain, they contribute to the welfare of the State. Their function is largely a public function; their work is done primarily, indeed, for individuals, but ultimately for the public good. It is not enough to say of churches and colleges that they contribute to the welfare of a State; they are necessary to the existence of a free State. They form and mold the public character; and that public character is the foundation of everything which is precious in the state, including even its material prosperity.

"The material prosperity of every improving community," Eliot continued,

> is a fruit of character; for it is energetic, honest, and sensible men that make prosperous business, and not prosperous business that make men. Who have built up the manufactures and trade of this bleak and sterile Massachusetts? A few men of singular sagacity, integrity, and courage, backed by hundreds of men and women of common intelligence, courage, and honesty. Massachusetts today owes its mental and moral characteristics, and its wealth, to eight generations of people who have loved and cherished Church, School, and College.[93]

Even if influential Americans in the last third of the nineteenth century had been able to overcome their philosophical objections to government activism, the disreputable, corrupt, and uncontrollable nature of American politics during that period would have turned them away from increasing the powers of government over private action. "How else are we to save our country if not by education in all ways and on all sides?" asked investment banker Henry Lee Higginson, Eliot's ally. "Democracy has got fast hold of the world and *will* rule. Let us see that she does it more wisely and humanely than the kings and nobles have done! Our chance is *now*—before the country is full and the struggle for bread becomes intense and bitter. Educate, and save ourselves and our families and our money from mobs!"[94]

By the 1890s, it had become quite clear to the leaders of American business, culture, and charity that the struggle between the "haves" and the "have nots" could be neither ignored nor solved by violent oppression. What was needed was a private-sector alternative to socialism. It is in this light that the paradoxes of Progressivism, which began to emerge as an organized political force in the 1890s, appear less self-contradictory. Revisionist historians of the 1950s and 1960s made much of the Progressives' curious ability to combine antibusiness rhetoric ("trust-busting") with especially close ties to big business and remarkable inaction against business combinations such as American Bell Telephone and United States Steel, which violated the spirit, if not the letter, of the Sherman and Clayton antitrust acts.[95] Others, most notably Richard Hofstadter, criticized Progressives' use of a democratic rhetoric that masked the movement's elite leadership and unrealistic and unduly moralistic concerns.[96] But, as the more recent work of Robert Weibe, Burton Bledstein, and others has suggested, Progressivism was far more than a factional movement within the Republican party.[97] It was a pervasive movement for cultural reform, whose roots, as Bledstein has shown, lie deep in the nineteenth-century history of private-sector institutions. The Progressive organizational style, with its emphasis on educated expertise and bureaucratic organization, affected both major political parties and, indeed, all realms of activity, from social work and government to business. But the common thread tying Progressivism together—leaving aside certain westerners, whose outlook owed much to Populism and who came from states with poorly developed private cultural and charitable enterprises—was the recognition that social justice should come through the actions of the private sector, assisted, but not directed by, government.

There was considerable disagreement among Progressives over the role of government. Initially some, especially literary intellectuals influenced by Populism and European radicalisms, saw the movement as a form of evolutionary socialism. Others, including the more conservative business and professional reformers, emphasized the importance of efficiency in the private sector. World War I crystallized these viewpoints. To the Left, the war revealed the oppressive power of the capitalist state. To the Right, the war mobilization, which was an experiment in public-private partnership, exposed the limitations of government bureaucratic centralization while underlining the value of planning and cooperation in the private sector.[98] As the more radical elements in the movement spun off into bohemianism and third-party politics after the armistice, the business Progressives were left free to develop a private-sector alternative to socialism.

The private-sector alternative grew out of two major sources, both within the business community. The first involved the ideas about philanthropy articulated by industrialists such as Carnegie.[99] In his 1889 essay "The Gospel of Wealth," Carnegie articulated a new doctrine of benevolence, which was based on an acknowledgment of the extent to which industrialism had altered fundamental assumptions about political and economic life. The concentration of wealth and power in the hands of a few was, in Carnegie's view, the inevitable consequence of advanced industrial development. This process, which advanced to the forefront men "with a genius for affairs," was not bad as long as the process did not become "clogged by layers of prescription."[100] If capitalism were to be self-renewing, means must be created to ensure that traditional equality of condition, which was no longer possible in the industrial setting, be replaced by equality of opportunity. This involved not only confiscatory taxation—which in ensuring that great fortunes could not be passed on, would prevent the formation of classes—but also proactive philanthropy, which would ensure the continuation of the competitive processes that underlay the progress of the race. "The best means of benefiting the community," Carnegie urged his fellow millionaires, "is to place within its reach the ladders upon which the aspiring can rise."[101] At the same time, he attacked traditional charity, which not only failed to get at the root causes of poverty, but which actually perpetuated it. "It were better for mankind that the millions of the rich were thrown into the sea," Carnegie wrote, "than so spent as to encourage the slothful, the drunken, the unworthy. Of every thousand dollars spent in so-called charity today, it is probable that nine hundred and fifty dollars is unwisely spent—so spent, indeed, as to produce the very evils which it hopes to mitigate or cure." In Carnegie's view, the responsibility for remedying the evils of the industrial economy lay with those who had created it—the "men with a genius for affairs," who, if the system were to survive, had to be willing to administer their wealth wisely, devoting it to "institutions of various kinds, which will improve the general condition of the people; in this manner returning their surplus wealth to the mass of their fellows in the forms best calculated to do them lasting good."[102]

As sensible as Carnegie's ideas seemed to many of his contemporaries, the means of carrying them out were not immediately apparent. At first, he and those he influenced, such as Rockefeller, tried parceling out their fortunes to particular kinds of institutions—libraries, churches, universities. But these rather traditional objects were not suited to addressing problems faced by American society at the turn of the century. Nor, in addition, did they solve the dilemmas of fortunes that were accumulating more quickly than they could be given away. "I am in trouble," Rockefeller told his adviser Frederick W. Gates in 1891, "the pressure of these appeals for gifts has become too great for endurance. I haven't the time or the strength, with all my heavy business responsibilities, to deal with these demands properly. I am so constituted as to be unable to give away money with any satisfaction until I have made the most careful enquiry as to the worthiness of the cause. The investigations are now taking more of my time

ıd energy than the Standard Oil itself."[103] Gates systematized Rocke-
ıeller's giving, introducing "into all his charities the principle of
scientific giving" and permitting him to lay aside "retail giving" for
"wholesale philanthropy." But even this was not enough. "Your fortune is rolling up, rolling up like an avalanche," Gates would warn
his employer. "You must distribute it faster than it grows! If you do
not, it will crush you, and your children, and your children's children."[104] Clearly some more effective instrument was needed to implement the principles of wholesale scientific giving.

Rockefeller, Carnegie, and their contemporaries proceeded cau-
tiously in moving toward the foundation form.[105] By the 1880s, the
evolution of legal doctrine in some states permitted great latitude to
the founders of charitable trusts, exempting them from many of the
constraints affecting private trusts. Rulings of the Supreme Judicial
Court of Massachusetts had stated that a trust could be considered
valid even if no particular object of charity was specified by the donor.[106] A similar vagueness of intent was permitted with regard to the
appointment and succession of trustees. Two of the earliest foundations, the Peabody Fund (established in 1869) and the John F. Slater
Fund (established in 1882), though specifically devoted to the education of southern blacks, embodied many of the features of open-ended-
ness and trustee discretion which would later characterize modern
foundations.[107] However, before the reform of charities laws in New
York in 1893, its courts had upheld more restrictive views: when corporation lawyer and former presidential candidate Samuel Tilden attempted to leave his residuary estate to a group of trustees, giving them
wide discretion as to how the funds might be used to benefit humanity
(including the establishment of "a reading room in the city of New
York"), the court ruled the bequest void for several reasons, including
the vagueness of its charitable intent.[108]

In addition to legal uncertainties, the political climate encouraged
caution with regard to the creation of new charitable instruments.
Early in this century, attacks on the wealthy and the ways in which
they used their money were a staple of mainstream journalism. David
Graham Phillips' article "The Treason of the Senate" gives a fair idea
of the setting in which the benevolently wealthy had to operate. Phillips described the 1901 marriage of John D. Rockefeller, Jr., to the
daughter to Senator Nelson Aldrich as a union between "the chief
exploiter of the American people" and the "chief schemer in the service of their exploiters."[109]

It is perhaps for this reason that credit for establishing the first
foundation of the modern type—an open-ended endowment devoted
"to the good of mankind," which carried out its charitable purposes

by giving money to institutions rather than operating them, and which entrusted decisionmaking to staffs of experts—went not to Carnegie or Rockefeller, but to Margaret Olivia Slocum Sage, the widow of Wall Street buccaneer Russell Sage.[110] A champion of women's rights and a patron of conservation and medical research, Mrs. Sage shared Carnegie's concerns about indiscriminate giving. On the advice of Robert DeForest, a corporate lawyer who had been deeply involved with reforming New York City's charities since the 1880s, Mrs. Sage decided to establish a philanthropic trust "elastic in form and method to work in different ways at different times" for "the permanent improvement of social conditions." The foundation, named in honor of her husband, was chartered by the New York State legislature in April 1907.[111]

Although Carnegie can be credited with articulating the positive rationale for foundations and for large-scale philanthropy by the new industrial elite, his own charitable ventures moved only gradually toward the foundation form. The Carnegie Hero Fund Commission, established in 1901, had the rather conventional object of giving rewards to individuals who had demonstrated conspicuous courage in assisting others. But the three other foundations he created—the Foundation for the Advancement of Teaching (1905), the Endowment for International Peace (1910), and the Carnegie Corporation of New York (1911)—were progressively more open-ended in intention and in the discretion granted trustees.[112]

The Rockefeller philanthropies followed a similar path from relatively conventional and clearly specified objects (such as John D. Rockefeller's gifts to the University of Chicago in the 1890s) toward increasingly open-ended and flexible entities. In 1903, Rockefeller endowed the Rockefeller Institute for Medical Research in New York, the first of a series of medical philanthropies.[113] In 1903, he took a major step toward flexibility with the establishment of the General Education Board. The fund was originally modeled on the Peabody and Slater funds and serving similar purposes, but by 1905 Rockefeller had expanded its endowment to $10 million and given it the mission of improving higher education on a national basis.[114] But the jewel in the crown of his benevolence was the Rockefeller Foundation, a fund of $100 million whose purpose was "the betterment of mankind."[115] Rockefeller had hoped to obtain a federal charter for the foundation—as the General Education Board had done, but the plan ran afoul of political turbulence.[116] By 1909, the political coalition sustaining progressive initiatives within the Republican party had begun to unravel in an acrimonious power struggle between Theodore Roosevelt and William Howard Taft. To complicate matters, progressives within the

Democratic party had rejected the Populism of William Jennings Bryan in favor of the more sophisticated and urbane reformism of political scientist Woodrow Wilson. The 1912 presidential race became a contest among three progressives, each trying to outdo the other as champion of the people against "the interests." Despite his close ties to big business, Roosevelt opposed the chartering of the foundations, claiming that "no amount of charity in spending such fortunes [as Rockefeller's] can compensate in any way for the misconduct in acquiring them." The conservative Taft denounced the effort as "a bill to incorporate Mr. Rockefeller." Samuel Gompers, president of the American Federation of Labor, sneered that "the one thing that the world would gratefully accept from Mr. Rockefeller now would be the establishment of a great endowment of research and education to help other people see in time how they can keep from being like him."[117] Nothing Rockefeller could do to counter charges that the foundation would serve his private interests—even offering to make the appointment of the foundation's trustees subject to government approval—was sufficient to quiet the controversy. When it became apparent that no approval would be forthcoming, he sought a charter from New York State, which was approved in 1913. The foundation's $100 million endowment made it the giant of American philanthropy.

The new foundations, particularly Russell Sage and Rockefeller, were unusual for not only the broad discretion granted their trustees but also their explicit goals of reforming social, economic, and political life. These lofty ends were to be achieved not by direct political action, but by studying conditions, making findings available to influential citizens, and mobilizing public opinion to bring about change. This relationship between academic experts, influential private groups, and government would become the paradigm of a new kind of political process—one based on policy rather than politics.[118]

It was precisely this relationship between industrial wealth and public policy that underlay the 1910–13 controversy over the chartering of the Rockefeller Foundation and the 1915–16 hearings of the Senate Commission on Industrial Relations.[119] In a general sense, the fears of those who opposed the foundations were not ungrounded. The foundations, through their ability to channel huge amounts of money toward charitable objects at will, might become major instruments through which "the interests" could influence public policy. But the fierce controversy over their existence made philanthropists extraordinarily cautious. Although a few foundations, such as Russell Sage, the Brookings Institution (1916), and the Twentieth Century Fund (1919), would address themselves fairly directly to public policy matters, most acted with greater circumspection, either by funding relatively noncontroversial activities such as health care and education or by indirectly influencing public policy through grants to intermediary organizations, such as the National Research Council, the Social Science Research Council, the American Council of Learned Societies, and the National Bureau of Economic Research.[120] Foundation grants to intermediary organizations and to universities had a profound impact on the ordering of research priorities of universities and the growth of new disciplines, particularly the social sciences.[121]

Welfare Capitalism

Philanthropy of the foundation type represented only one aspect of big business' recognition of its unique responsibilities. No less important—and, indeed, closely related—was the program of welfare capitalism that began to emerge in the 1880s. Commentators such as Stuart Brandes and Daniel Nelson have attempted to trace the origins of welfare capitalism to the mill villages of the early industrial age.[122] Although some of the welfare-capitalist efforts did involve the construction of company towns, this model of employer-employee relations was a nostalgic attempt to reconstitute an idealized but vanished social context.[123] The main thrust of welfare capitalism in both its motives and its methods was considerably more sophisticated than the crude paternalism indicted by Brandes and appears to have stemmed from the same concerns with equity, efficiency, and expertise which gave rise to the general-purpose foundations.

The key issue for welfare capitalism was not whether charity had a seat on the board of directors, but the extent to which firms could, by operating efficiently, also function more equitably. This approach necessarily involved not only improvements in technology and organization of production, particularly the introduction of statistical techniques that would permit quantitative assessments of efficiency and productivity—the practices associated with Frederick W. Taylor's "scientific management"—but also investments in human capital which would both lead the worker to identify more closely with the firm and which would, through improving his skills, make him more productive.[124] Strictly speaking, this was not philanthropy, for it was not disinterested. At the same time, the impact of welfare capitalism on the work force and on the communities affected by it—as well as the motives underlying it, which saw doing well and doing good as inextricably linked—make it necessary to consider it as a part of any overall assessment of philanthropy.

As the work of Brandes and Nelson suggests, welfare capitalism was not a clearly defined body of thought and practice. It was an uncoordinated set of managerial experiments which stemmed from a set of common concerns, but which varied enormously across the range of corporations and regions. Sometimes welfare capitalism involved direct corporate subsidies of charitable organizations, as with the massive support by the railroad industry of the Young Men's Christian Association (Y.M.C.A.). Between 1882 and 1911, the railroads contributed over $1 million for the construction of 113 Y.M.C.A. buildings and the underwriting of their operating expenses.[125] Companies also contributed to the creation of parks and playgrounds, schools, and libraries. But welfare-capitalist programs were most commonly implemented within either particular firms or the communities in which they operated. For this reason, these programs were not without shortcomings. In some of its manifestations, welfare capitalism contained an intrinsic element of paternalism, which became evident in places such as George Pullman's model community outside of Chicago, where the company exercised extraordinary social and political control over its workers and where facilities were more costly than they needed to be.[126] And, as the massacre of Carnegie's own workers at Homestead, Pennsylvania, in 1892 suggested, the freedom of the workers was sharply limited by the forbearance of their employers. Nevertheless, welfare capitalism embraced a wide variety of possibilities, ranging from the essentially exploitative company towns of the textile and mining regions, through more open-ended provisions of health care and insurance, education, pensions, and profit-sharing plans for workers and subsidization of social and cultural services for the communities in which they lived.

Welfare capitalism, especially as articulated by Carnegie in his 1886 and 1887 articles on labor relations, focused less on the company-town concept than on the relationship between corporation and community. Carnegie's establishment of public libraries and his donations for church organs pointed in this direction, but the major developers of this variant of corporate philanthropy were the entrepreneurs who operated in diversified economic contexts, many of them in smaller towns.[127] This movement had several sources. One, which developed in the troubled period between 1873 and 1896, was the board of trade movement, the association of established businesses in a given location for the purpose of encouraging economic growth—not only through promotional activities but also through programs of tax abatements, low-interest bank loans, and low-cost real estate. Often these efforts were coupled with a recognition that the attractiveness of a community for plant location depended on noneconomic factors, such as the purity of the water supply, the quality of public education, the accessibility of recreational facilities, and the character of social amenities, from housing to class relations. Given the calculable economic advantages to be gained from social investment, the business communities of many towns moved toward patterns of cooperation among business, government, and nonprofit institutions.[128] By the 1890s, these efforts gave rise to the Civic Federation movement, which sought to reconcile the diverse concerns of different interests within American communities. One of the major proponents of the civic federations was Marcus Alonzo Hanna, a most powerful figure in the Republican party nationally and a major iron and coal operator.[129]

The boards of trade and civic federations, both of which depended on business for their primary support, gave rise to the establishment of community foundations, a rationalization and centralization of the charitable resources of communities.[130] The earliest of these was established in Cleveland: in 1900, the Committee on Benevolent Associations of the Cleveland Chamber of Commerce began to specify a list of agencies permitted to solicit funds within the city; in 1913, after some years of study, the chamber organized the Federation of Charities and Philanthropy, the first Community Chest, a federated fund-raising effort that annually raised and disbursed monies to a selected list of charitable recipients.[131] Unlike the highly privatized philanthropic instruments being developed in the Northeast, the Community Chest was governed by a broadly based constituent board made up of representatives of major community groups. Energetically promoted by their creators, Community Chests spread rapidly across the United States—enjoying particular support from the business community. In 1914 Cleveland businessmen organized the first community foundation, an endowment fund administered by community representatives.[132] The foundation's organizers believed that this new kind of charitable trust would encourage givers of moderate means, as well as providing flexibility, responsiveness, and public accountability.[133]

By the end of the war, the basic elements were in place for the attempt to create a private-sector alternative to socialism. And the success of the bolshevism in the Soviet Union, the almost-successful socialist revolutions in Germany and Hungary, and a wave of radical-led strikes in the United States in 1919 made the creation of such an alternative an urgent task. Unquestionably, the central figure in the effort was Herbert Hoover, a millionaire mining engineer turned public servant, who, as administrator of European food relief during and after the war, had seen the horrors of social upheaval firsthand.

Hoover's 1922 book, *American Individualism,* which set forth his vision of a "New Era," summarized the previous half-century of social thought by business reformers.[134] Beginning with a candid acknowledgment of the "great inequalities and injustices" caused by modern

industry, Hoover sought to frame a new conception of "progressive
individualism," which would reconcile traditional democratic and
Christian values to the realities of advanced capitalism. Hoover recognized that inequality was the inevitable consequence of industrialism,
but believed that equality of opportunity, combined with an ethos of
service and cooperation which acknowledged the interdependence of
all Americans, could lead to a new social and economic order. Although there was nothing new in these ideas—which could be found
in the writings of other business reformers forty years earlier—the real
difference lay, as Hoover pointed out, in the fact that this new order
was already taking form.

One force leading to a New Era was the changing nature of business
itself. In Carnegie's time, most large firms were still owned by individuals or small groups of partners who were directly involved in their
operation. But now, Hoover argued, "domination by arbitrary individual ownership is disappearing . . . because the works of today are
steadily growing more and more beyond the resources of any one individual and steadily taxation will reduce relatively excessive individual accumulations. The number of persons in partnership through
division of ownership among many stockholders is steadily increasing—thus 100,000 to 200,000 partners in a single concern are not uncommon."[135] As ownership and management became separated, the
great enterprises would, in Hoover's view, come increasingly under the
control of managers who were "more sensitive to the more opinions
of the people" and who recognized that the "right of property not as
an object in itself." Hoover argued that these managers, "themselves
employees of . . . great groups of individual stockholders, or policy
holders, reflect a spirit of community responsibility."[136] This was not
mere idealism, but a pragmatic recognition that the success of an
economy based on mass production and distribution required economic empowerment of the masses. This depended on "organizations
for advancement of ideas in the community for mutual cooperation
and economic objectives—the chambers of commerce, trade associations, labor unions, bankers, farmers, propaganda associations, and
what not. . . . Each group is a realization of greater mutuality of interest, each contains some element of public service and each is a
school of public responsibility."[137] Organizations promoting economic cooperation worked in connection with other kinds of "voluntary
organizations for altruistic purposes"—associations for advancement
of public welfare, improvement, morals, charity, public opinion,
health, the clubs and societies for recreation and intellectual advancement—to combine self-interested pursuits with the higher values of
cooperation and public service.

A self-made man himself, Hoover repeatedly stressed that society "must stimulate leadership from its own mass." "Leadership cannot," he wrote, "be replenished by selection like queen bees, by divine right or bureaucracies, but by the free rise of ability, character, and intelligence."[138] Nonetheless, leaders, once in place, had to be free to make decisions on the basis of "intellect and progress." "Popular desires," Hoover urged, "are no criteria to the real need; they can be determined only by deliberative consideration, by education, by constructive leadership."[139]

Accepting the post of secretary of commerce from President Harding, Hoover strove through the 1920s to implement his vision of "self-government by the people outside of government." This effort, based on "voluntary co-operation within the community," extolled the best means of perfecting social organizations as caring for those in distress, advancing knowledge, scientific research, education, and, most importantly, economic life. "It is in the further development of this co-operation and a sense of its responsibility," he would later write,

> that we should find a solution for many of our complex problems, and not by the extension of government into our economic and social life. The greatest function of government is to build up that cooperation, and its most resolute action should be to deny the extension of bureaucracy. We have developed great agencies of co-operation by the assistance of the Government which promote and protect the interests of individuals and smaller units of business. The Federal Reserve System, in its strengthening and support of the smaller banks; the Home Loan banks, in mobilizing of building and loan associations and savings banks; the Federal land banks, in giving independence and strength to land mortgage associations; the great mobilization of relief to distress, the mobilization of business and industry in measures of recovery, and a score of other activities are not socialism. . . . The primary conception of this whole American system is not the regimentation of men but the cooperation of free men. It is founded upon the conception of responsibility of the individual to the community, of the responsibility of local government to the State, of the State to the national Government.[140]

In this "associative state" government would act as umpire and nexus for the exchange of information, using "promotional conferences, expert enquiries, and cooperating committees" rather than legal coercion or arbitrary controls. "Like the private groupings to which it was tied," the associative state's agencies "would be staffed by men of talent, vision, and expertise, and committed to nourishing individualism and local initiative rather than supplanting them."[141]

Hoover's efforts in the housing field epitomized his vision of public-private partnership. With the goal of relieving the national housing shortage, the Building and Housing Division of the Commerce Department strove to stabilize the construction industry, to overcome resistance to mass production and standardization, to foster city planning and zoning activities, and to promote the "spiritual values" inherent in widespread home ownership. To do this, the division worked through an organization known as Better Homes in America. Although originally a promotional activity initiated by a household magazine, the *Delineator,* Better Homes was reorganized as a public-service corporation in 1923. Operating as a "collateral arm" of the Commerce Department, Better Homes

> secured operating funds from private foundations, persuaded James Ford, a professor of social ethics at Harvard, to serve as executive director, and tied the whole apparatus to the Housing Division by having directors of that agency serve as officers in the new corporation. Working through some thirty-six hundred local committees and a host of affiliated businesses, trade associations, and schools, Better Homes carried on a massive educational campaign, which reached through some thirty-six hundred local committees and a host of affiliated groups "to provide exhibits of model homes, foster better 'household management,' promote research in the housing field, and generate a greater, steadier, and more discriminating demand for 'improved dwellings,' especially for families with 'small incomes.'"[142]

By 1932, Hoover boasted that these initiatives had led to the construction of fifteen million "new and better homes."[143]

The impressive number of businessmen who participated in New Era boards and commissions, both public and private, suggests the broad appeal of Hoover's vision of the possibility of a private-sector alternative to socialism which could promote the efficiencies of centralized planning without stifling individual initiative.[144] Typical were such leaders as General Electric's Gerard Swope and AT&T's Walter Gifford, whose careers, like that of Hoover, spanned the worlds of business, philanthropy, and government.

After graduating from MIT in 1895 (where he was a classmate of Alfred P. Sloan), Swope went to work for Western Electric in Chicago.[145] He lived in the pioneer social settlement Hull House, where he was active as a teacher and organizer. As he worked his way up through the ranks at Western Electric, he maintained his commitment to social reform. When he was transferred to Saint Louis in 1903, Swope and his wife (herself a Hull House alumna) purchased two adjoining houses in the city's most rundown district. They lived in one and created Saint Louis' first settlement house in the other.

Western Electric, like most leading manufacturing firms of the period, sold its products to other companies, rather than the public. Swope, by applying "the new mathematical equations of cost accounting to sales," discovered that "Western Electric's high-profit but low volume items, which had been credited with much of the company's success, actually lost money" and that it obtained its greatest return on high-volume, low-profit orders.[146] He urged the company to diversify its product line and to initiate a mass-marketing strategy. When his suggestions were ignored, he turned his energies to developing Western Electric's international operations, which brought him in contact with European industrial statesmen such as Walter Rathenau, whose firm, AEG, was not only a model of efficiency, innovativeness, and social responsibility but also a leading agent of broad social change.[147] In 1917, he left Western Electric to join the War Industries Board.

After the war, Swope became president of General Electric, which gave him the opportunity to develop his ideas. In short order, the company was transformed into one of the most aggressive mass-marketers in the world. Promoting the electrification of homes and the development, production, and distribution of home appliances—refrigerators, stoves, washing machines—was more than a way of making money. It provided the hardware for realizing progressive goals in regard to nutrition, sanitation, and public health. For Swope and his associates, the product itself was an instrument of social change.

Swope was also committed to more traditional kinds of welfare programs for General Electric's employees. He introduced benefit packages that included health and unemployment insurance, company-underwritten mortgages, and old-age and disability pensions. He welcomed the unionization of General Electric's plants. He also involved the firm in philanthropic activities. The C. A. Coffin Foundation, established in 1924 to underwrite graduate study in fields relating to the electrical industry, was one of the first company foundations in the United States.

Summing up his vision in a 1926 speech, "The Responsibilities of Modern Industry," Swope echoed Hoover's ideas about the role of the corporation as public servant. Swope declared that the corporation's first obligation was to provide "more things at lower cost"—to empower consumers through efficient high-volume mass production. Its second obligation was to its employees: Swope observed that well-paid workers not only were more productive but also consumed more—to the benefit of the company and the economy as a whole. The third obligation of the corporation was to itself, through exchanges of information and ideas which would lead to better, safer, and more dependable products. Swope placed the corporation's obligation to provide "a fair and uniform return" its stockholders last on his list, because, in his view, profits could be earned only if the public was served, the workers well paid, and the industry itself operated on a sound basis.[148]

At AT&T, Walter Gifford, an alumnus of Harvard and Hull House, transformed the company into a model of welfare-capitalist enterprise, enlarging its responsibilities to its workers and to the communities it served by lowering production costs and increasing its volume of business.[149] Gifford's statistical analysis of the company's operations suggested the potential of serving the consumer mass market. And with the help of progressive journalist Arthur Page, his Harvard classmate, Gifford worked to reshape AT&T's corporate image as a private company working in the public service.[150] Gifford was also attentive to the needs of his work force. Under his leadership, AT&T steadily increased wages through the 1920s, while introducing a full range of benefits, including a pension plan. Gifford was active in the associational network of philanthropic and professional organizations, serving on the boards of the Rockefeller Foundation and the National Research Fund, as well as acting as an adviser to the National Bureau of Economic Research.

Associational and welfare-capitalist activity was not restricted to top management in national firms such as General Electric and AT&T. Hoover's associational network of trade associations and government agencies saw local communities as the primary arenas of action. Thus, in cities such as Cleveland and Allentown, Pennsylvania, businessmen fostered cooperative enterprises with perhaps greater enthusiasm and thoroughness than national leaders.[151] Working through chambers of commerce, trade associations, and service clubs, businessmen organized charities, and local institutions of higher education underwrote surveys of local economic and social problems. These surveys in turn became the bases for proactive policies that involved not only business activity but also public-private partnerships and philanthropic initiatives in such fundamental areas of public life as education, recreation, and city planning. Private and community foundations, as well as federations of charities, played important roles in these cooperative initiatives.

On the national level, Hoover's vision of the central role of the private sectors in shaping the nation's future appears to have been widely accepted in both the business and professional communities. This acceptance was reflected in the emergence of a remarkably coordinated network of private organizations, which included progressively managed corporations, corporate and independent foundations, policy institutes, private universities, and intermediary bodies, including trade associations and scholarly bodies such as the National Bureau of Economic Research, the American Council of Learned Societies, and the Social Science Research Council. Among the more important efforts of these linked organizations were the National Research Fund, which involved a $10 million commitment from major corporations to underwrite basic scientific research in universities, and the President's Research Committee on Social Trends, which was a comprehensive attempt, using scholarly teamwork, to accurately assess the present and future direction of American life in the twentieth century.[152] Although a federally sponsored effort, the committee's work was funded by the Rockefeller Foundation and staffed by the Social Science Research Council.

The real measure of the ubiquity of Hoover's ideas, however, was the extent to which they formed the basis for the first phase of the New Deal. The centerpiece of Roosevelt's first-term program was the National Recovery Administration (N.R.A.). In its essentials, it was a formalization of the private-sector alternative that Hoover had been building during the 1920s. Designed to revive industrial and business activity and to reduce unemployment, the N.R.A. was based on the principle of industrial self-regulation, operating under government supervision through a system of fair-competition codes. Based on the fair-trade codes that had been developed by associationists under Hoover's leadership, these collective security arrangements were designed to prevent wage- and price-cutting, which in turn would enable corporations to maintain employment levels, intrafirm benefits packages, and support for nonprofit welfare agencies. Although Hoover himself denounced the N.R.A., it was not only a direct offshoot of his ideas and the programs he had fostered during the 1920s, but it also owed much to the ideas of his colleagues in the business world. The Swope Plan of 1931, for example, anticipated many of the N.R.A.'s essentials and constituted the intellectual and institutional bridge between the private-sector emphasis of the New Era and the more statist tendencies of the New Deal.[153] In many respects the N.R.A. was little more than a formalization of the private-sector alternative, through which the private for-profit sector and the nonprofits that depended on it would be guaranteed stability, which would enable it to not only generate employment and deliver the social services that had provided under their welfare-capitalist programs, but also continue their philanthropic activities in society at large.

From Welfare Capitalism
to Corporate Liberalism, 1929–1950

For over fifty years, business and the private nonprofit organizations that it sustained had taken the lead in working toward a private-sector alternative to socialism. Contrary to conventional wisdom, nonprofit organizations were not broadly supported by Americans in the early twentieth century. A 1909 survey by the Cleveland Chamber of Commerce showed that in this city of over 600,000 people, the $500,000 collected by its charities in that year was contributed by only 5,386 donors. Of these (800 of which were businesses), 55 percent came from 54 individual contributors, and 90 percent from 1,066.[154] This basis of charitable support led to efforts to broaden the base of charitable giving, through increasingly sophisticated fund-raising efforts by Community Chests, Y.M.C.A.'s, hospital funds, and university fund drives. Nevertheless, the basis of charitable support remained narrow: for example, in the Yale capital campaign of 1926-28, 63 individuals—constituting .003 percent of 22,123 contributors, gave over one-half of the $21 million subscribed.[155] Similarly, of the total annual gifts to Harvard in 1925, 35 percent came from large business firms and their top managers.[156] Thus, ironically, as the number and importance of private nonprofit organizations grew in the 1920s, so also did their dependence on support from business and the wealthy.

Although government figures on charitable giving are generally reliable after 1917, when the charitable deduction for individual givers was incorporated into the tax code, it is difficult to obtain exact figures on the level of corporate contributions before 1936, when firms were allowed the same privilege. Nevertheless, the fragmentary evidence that exists is suggestive of its importance. For example, between 1920 and 1929 thirty-five thousand corporations gave over $300 million to Community Chests in 129 American cities.[157] During the same period, corporate contributions to Y.M.C.A./Y.W.C.A., hospital, and other welfare-service building funds in 37 cities amounted to $6.5 million. The proportion of corporate contributions to the totals raised in these fund drives ranged as high as 47 percent, with an average of nearly 20 percent.[158] Although there was no tax incentive for charitable giving by corporations, and under the law in many states such giving was illegal, the practice continued on a surprisingly large scale.

It was true, however, that even with the N.R.A. the resources of the private sector were inadequate to the massive challenges of the Great Depression. The economic crisis of the 1930s was national and international in scope, whereas most foundations and private social-welfare agencies operated on a local level. In the end, their dependence on business proved a handicap rather than an advantage, because the role business of the corporations was to make money. When pressed, welfare and benefits programs were often the first areas in which savings were sought by cost-cutters. Some firms, most notably AT&T, acted very quickly both to curtail benefits programs and to lay off workers.[159] Others, such as General Electric and Bethlehem and United States Steel, struggled to maintain their commitments to employees.[160] But ultimately, as Bethlehem Steel's Charles Schwab admitted, "None of us can escape the inexorable law of the balance sheet." In any event, because welfare capitalism was based on voluntary compliance, it was effective only in the most centralized industries, such as steel, communications, and electrical equipment manufacturing. Many industrial sectors were relatively unaffected by trade associations. And many workers labored in small enterprises that stood entirely outside the associationist system. But this did not always matter. For example, in Allentown cooperative relationships between businesses and among the for-profit, nonprofit, and public sectors worked so well that the impact of unemployment and deflation were minimized.[161] The city actually had more plants in operation by 1939 than it had in 1929. But overall, the private-sector alternative did not withstand the Depression.

The death blow to the N.R.A. was the 1935 Supreme Court decision on *Schecter* v. *the United States*.[162] This case did not address itself to the trade associations and other collective security arrangements that had made welfare capitalism possible. The case was concerned with the ability of Congress to delegate legislative power to the executive branch, the power on which the government had based its ability to write and enforce the N.R.A. codes. But without federal authority, the codes were meaningless. And with the demise of the N.R.A., all hope for the private-sector alternative was lost, for even massive increases in individual giving could not compensate for the loss of business support.

Deprived of a consolidated private sector on which it could depend for the delivery of basic social and cultural services, the federal government had no choice but to turn to direct action. From the standpoint of Roosevelt's electoral constituency—which was, in effect, an alliance of populist southern and western farmers and urban workers who had always opposed big business—turning away from the private sector and toward public action was politically advantageous. It enabled Roosevelt to cast off his ties to the business community and commit his administration to a rhetoric and a set of policies which had profound appeal to these groups. This strategy yielded immediate political benefits, even if they did not succeed in bringing about recovery.

However, over the long-term it fundamentally altered the relation of business and nonprofit organizations to government, making the latter the senior member of the public-private partnership that had been assembled by the Progressives and affirmed by Hoover's New Era policies.

Roosevelt did not entirely rule out a charitable role for big business. His 1936 tax act for the first time permitted corporations to deduct charitable contributions from their federal income taxes. (He originally opposed the deduction, but finally accepted it after intensive lobbying by the Community Chest.)[163] The increased tax burden both for corporations and for individuals in upper-income brackets created major incentives for large-scale giving.

It is difficult to assess the impact of Roosevelt's post-1935 redistributional tax policies. Their impact on individual givers taken as a group was minimal: between after 1935 and the war, taxpayers never donated more than an average of 2 percent of their gross income to charity.[164] For most Americans, these changes in the tax laws made little difference, because rates were high enough before the introduction of universal withholding in 1943 to exclude all but the wealthiest taxpayers. Of these, only those earning $300,000 or more increased their level of giving substantially after 1935.[165] Because the government did not gather statistics about business giving before 1936, we can only speculate about the impact of the corporate charitable deduction. F. Emerson Andrews' figures on the corporate share of contributions to Community Chests between 1920 and 1951 show surprisingly little change in giving levels until World War II, when a combination of patriotism and high excess-profits taxes undoubtedly encouraged firms to give more than they had in the past.[166] The level of corporation giving in support of research in the natural sciences actually fell after 1936, despite the deductibility of this kind of giving: between 1930 and 1935, industry contributed between 60 percent and 75 percent of all funds devoted to scientific research; by 1940, contributions from industry dropped to less than 20 percent.[167] The response to tax incentives appears to have been pronounced only as it affected foundations, whose rate of formation increased dramatically. The number of foundations more than doubled between 1930 and 1939.[168]

These figures suggest that, except with regard to the establishment of foundations, coercive tax legislation may actually have had a negative impact on charitable giving. Certainly it altered the rationale for giving from a positive one in which individuals and firms gave because they believed in a cause or an institution to a negative one of tax avoidance. Further, as Roosevelt's rhetoric and policies became more stridently opposed to business and private wealth, corporate activities became subject to intensive critical scrutiny by congressional committees, regulatory agencies, labor unions, and profit-starved stockholders. This scrutiny discouraged even the most idealistic managers from straying far from the most conventional kinds of charitable activities. In this atmosphere of distrust, corporate social and cultural investment—which involved active efforts by companies to affect the environments in which it operated—became a relatively bland and unimaginative "corporate philanthropy." Despite tax regulations permitting corporations to deduct up to 5 percent of pretax income for charitable gifts, business giving during the 1936–80 period never reached the 2 percent level.[169]

It is interesting to speculate on what giving patterns would have been without a public-policy emphasis on tax coercion. Unfortunately, virtually all nonprofits scholarship has emphasized the negative. Thus, Andrews would write, in 1967,

> that the extraordinary variations [in corporate foundation formation] are clearly related to corporate tax chronology. Excess-profits tax, when combined with normal tax increases, began to rise sharply from 1940, reaching very high levels by 1945 [172 corporate foundations were formed between 1942 and 1945; only 36 had been formed in all previous years], at the close of which excess-profits taxes were rescinded. They were again put into effect during the Korean War, from July 1, 1950, through 1953, at the close of which the combined tax rate for affected corporations was 82 percent. More than 42 percent of these foundations were established during those four years.[170]

Although these increases may be accounted for solely in terms of tax chronology, it is worth noting that there were other powerful forces influencing corporate givers after 1940, and particularly between 1947 and 1955. One force was the increasing conviction in the business community that the growth of federal power could be checked only by a concerted effort to marshal the financial and cultural resources of the private sector against the further growth of federal power. The Arthur Page Papers, which contain correspondence between Page—who was the leading figure in American corporate public relations between 1930 and 1950—and a host of major foundation and corporation executives, reflect this concern. The first efforts to coordinate and consolidate business support for higher education (movements in which Page played a leading role) occurred during this period.[171] It is also worth noting that the major challenge to the legal restrictions on corporation giving was mounted by the group of which Page was a part and that its language reflected their concerns. As the chief justice of the

New Jersey Supreme Court noted in his endorsement of a broader mandate for business philanthropy,

> I am strongly persuaded by the evidence that the only hope for the survival of the privately supported American college and university lies in the willingness of corporate wealth to furnish in moderation some support to institutions which are so essential to public welfare. . . . I cannot conceive of any greater benefit to corporations in this country than to build and continue to build, respect for and adherence to a system of free enterprise and democratic government, the serious impairment of either of which may well spell the destruction of all corporate enterprise.[172]

The effort to counter the socialist tendencies that men such as Page and his associates saw in the growth of federal power after 1936 was ultimately limited. These men had been the first generation of progressive business managers—the avatars of the private-sector alternative. By the late 1940s and early 1950s, they were dying out or passing the reins of power to younger men. Their successors were men for whom (if Hays and Abernathy are to be believed) management was more a matter of technique than of vision.[173] They were more than willing to accommodate themselves to the welfare state. Allen Matusow said these corporate liberals "were not reactionary champions of laissez-faire, as myth would have it, but sophisticated managers seeking to secure their hegemony with governmental assistance."[174] The result was a set of attitudes about corporation giving which mirrored the new managerial outlook. Just as the new managerial approach emphasized short-term over long-term returns on investment, tax avoidance, and public relations, the dispensing of corporate charity as an executive prerequisite became the dominant characteristic of corporate giving.[175]

Nonprofits and the Welfare State, 1950–1990

Although much of the postwar rhetoric about nonprofits suggests that they grew as a counterpoise to the expanding scale and scope of the federal government, there is persuasive evidence that government policies played a major role in fueling the explosive growth in the number of charitable tax-exempt organizations. Numbering only 12,500 in 1940 and 50,000 in 1950, by 1967, there were 309,000, by 1977, 790,000, and by 1989, just under one million—an eightyfold increase in forty years.[176] By contrast, the number of business corporations during the same period increased from 473,000 to three million—a mere sevenfold increase.[177] Government policies played a crucial role in the growth, not only indirectly through creating incentives to individuals and firms for contributing to private organizations serving governmental ends, but also directly, through grants and contracts.[178] By the 1970s, it was estimated that direct government support to charitable tax-exempt organizations ranged from 35 percent to 55 percent of total annual revenues.[179] In retrospect, it seems quite clear that the American welfare state, rather than involving the elaboration of a vast bureaucracy concerned with delivering cultural, educational, health, and social services, encouraged the development of a private infrastructure to implement its purposes.

The interplay of forces in the creation of this distinctly Americanized version of the welfare state was extraordinarily complex. Changes in foreign policy, economic philosophy, tax and budgeting practices, legal doctrines, conceptions of the social role of corporations, and demographic factors all played important roles. First, the war and postwar years internationalized the outlook of Americans, not only bringing into sharp focus the confrontation between the capitalist democracies and totalitarianism, but also underlining the need for altering the ways in which the nation would find the revenues to sustain its role as the free world's political and economic leader. Traditionally—except in wartime— government spending had been limited by the amount of available revenues.

The urgent tasks of maintaining international security, domestic economic stability, and keeping the country poised for military mobilization altered this relationship. As policy commitments replaced available revenues as the foundation of the federal budgetary process, Keynesian economic theory pointed to the ways in which taxing, spending, and borrowing could be used to influence the economic activities from which government drew its revenues. The highly progressive tax rates of the postwar years were accompanied by loopholes that encouraged the transfer of private resources into activities—for-profit and nonprofit—that government economic planners deemed necessary to the national purpose.

The introduction of tax policies designed to channel the enormous postwar increases in individual and corporate income into savings, investment, and charitable giving coincided with the aging of the founders of many of the United States' great twentieth-century industrial fortunes. This produced an enormous increase in the number and importance of foundations. There were only 203 foundations with assets exceeding $1 million in 1929, but 2,058 by 1959—with the vast majority of these established within the decade. In 1929, their assets represented only 10.7 percent of the total property controlled by charitable tax-exempt organizations; by 1973, their share was 21.7 percent.[180] Most obviously, this growth was a response to steeply progressive income and estate taxes. Foundations enabled the wealthy to avoid taxation while maintaining control of their enterprises.[181] Thus, for example, when Henry Ford died in 1947, stock in his closely held company was divided into two classes. The voting stock was retained by the family, while the nonvoting securities were given to the Ford Foundation, which sold them at an immense profit.[182] The family was able to pass control of the Ford Motor Company to the next generation without paying a penny in taxes. At the same time, the family was able to vastly increase its influence on American politics, culture, and society—because the Ford Foundation, with its aggressive mandate for social change, was also the wealthiest of all American foundations. While Ford and many other foundations established by wealthy families after the war undoubtedly performed valuable services, some politicians and journalists wondered whether the increasingly tax-sensitive public would regard as genuinely charitable the overt use of tax-exempt foundations to help the wealthy avoid taxes and concentrate wealth to promote liberal policy agendas with which they were not in sympathy.[183]

The growing importance of foundations established by business wealth was accompanied by changes in the understanding of corporations about their place in the polity. Despite the business community's estrangement from the Roosevelt administration's domestic policies in the late 1930s, the important elements of big business and Roosevelt shared an understanding of the extent to which America's interests were threatened by the rise of fascism and, more distantly, by the power of the Soviet Union. Nonprofit lobbying and public-information organizations such as the Foreign Policy Association, the Council on Foreign Relations, and the Committee to Defend America by Aiding the Allies, as well as the foundations themselves, played a key role in preparing the public to accept the inevitability of American involvement in world conflict.[184] And as the nation began to prepare for war, Roosevelt shifted his rhetorical gears and welcomed major business figures (John Foster Dulles, James Forrestal, Henry Stimson, and others) back into his administration. As in World War I, individuals from private corporations, foundations, and universities proved essential in organizing the war effort and in planning the postwar world order.

But unlike World War I, from which business leaders emerged disenchanted with big government, World War II encouraged closer ties between the two. Despite some wariness, especially among older business progressives, the prospect of the United States as the dominant world power appears to have sustained in the postwar era the public-private partnership that developed during the war. Surely a major factor in this partnership was the parallel growth of foreign-policy activism in government and the internationalist orientation of business. The growing influence of Keynesian economic thought also helped business and government leaders to recognize their common stake in national and international economic stability. Pax America transformed the federal government into not only the largest single consumer of goods and services in the nation, but also the undisputed controller of its economic life—facts that could not be ignored by managers concerned with stability and reliable short-term returns on investment. Government's assumption of a central role in national economic, social, and political stabilization—the planning function that had previously been assumed by a coalition of private groups— proved increasingly acceptable to the business community, as it became apparent that the United States' struggle with the Soviet Union would be a long-term commitment requiring a high degree of national unity and as Dwight David Eisenhower's probusiness administration allayed fears about Washington's leftward drift. The acceptability of the enlarged federal role was further enhanced by the fact that it remained dependent on universities, foundations, think tanks, and business groups such as the Business Advisory Council, the Conference Board, the Committee for Economic Development, and the Business Roundtable. These organizations, which promoted active public service by business managers and academic experts, became the basis for a privatized policy establishment.[185]

The close ties of the federal government to big business were mirrored by its connections to nonprofit enterprise, as the government became the largest source of financial support for charitable tax-exempt organizations in the fields of culture, education, health, and social welfare. Beginning in the early 1940s, when basic and applied research became crucial to the war effort, government became the largest single contributor to the incomes of private universities. This role became permanent in the postwar effort to defend the peace and with the establishment of the National Science Foundation and the National Institutes of Health, both of which gave massive grants to private hospitals and universities. The passage of the G.I. Bill in 1944 and its renewal in 1952, together with the 1958 National Defense Education Act, provided massive indirect subsidies to private institutions through federal underwriting of student aid. The Hospital Construction Act of 1945 and the postwar encouragement of the growth of private nonprofit health-insurance plans transformed the federal government into a major actor in the health-care field, though still acting largely through the organizations of the private sector.[186] Federal funding of charitable tax-exempt institutions grew still further in the

1960s, with the intensification of international rivalries in arms and space exploration and with the War on Poverty.

Inventing the Nonprofit Sector, 1950–1990

As early as the 1930s, radical journalists and social critics such as Harold Laski, Eduard Lindemann, Horace Coon, William H. Allen, and Ferdinand Lundberg had begun to question the power of foundations and other endowed private institutions.[187] Although foundations escaped the attention of the Temporary National Economic Committee investigations of corporate and private wealth, which sharply questioned the humanitarian intentions of the welfare capitalists, some in the world of philanthropy had already begun to worry about their political vulnerability. In 1938, Frederick W. Keppel, president of the Carnegie Corporation, had deplored

> the large number of foundations which make no public record of their activities whatsoever—thereby failing to recognize their responsibility to the public as organizations enjoying exemption from taxation, a privilege shared with religious, educational, and charitable institutions. The instances in which it seems impossible to obtain pertinent information is disquietingly large. The question is not whether the funds of these silent trusts are put to useful purposes—indeed, some of the so-called family foundations are to the writer's knowledge making their grants with intelligence and discretion—it is rather whether public confidence in the foundation as a social instrument, a confidence which is in no small degree based upon the policy of complete publicity adopted by the better known foundations, may not be endangered.[188]

Ultimately, the threat came from the Right, as part of the broad realignment of political loyalties during World War II. As early as 1940, many isolationists had already identified what they saw as an internationalist conspiracy to draw the United States into the war and had begun to question the role of foundations and a variety of tax-exempt interest groups which advocated American intervention in Europe. However, these charges did not find legislative expression until 1944, when, in the context of a Senate debate over tax legislation, John A. Danahar of Connecticut proposed an amendment to restrict the amount of losses from secondary businesses which could be allowed as deductions.[189] On the face of it, the amendment was aimed at wealthy individuals who used expensive money-losing businesses to avoid taxation. But as the debate proceeded, it became clear that it was aimed at the activities of Marshall Field III, one of the nation's richest and most politically liberal businessmen and philanthropists. On the eve of the war, Field had recognized the problems that isolationist control of the press (by men such as Hearst and Robert McCormick) posed for internationalist efforts to prepare the nation for the inevitability of war. To combat the isolationists, he established two newspapers, *New York PM* the *Chicago Sun-Times*. Although both newspapers consistently lost money, they were widely read and effectively promoted internationalism. But as the war drew to a close, the isolationist coalition, a curious alliance of Irish-Americans and native-born Americans with populist roots, began to sharpen its knives. The former group, mostly Democrats, had never forgiven Roosevelt for coming to the aid of the British. The latter, mostly Republicans, had never forgiven the internationalists for depriving their candidate, Robert Taft, of the party's presidential nominations in 1940 and 1944.

Rather than attacking the charitable deduction, which would have aroused opposition from a wide range of charitable organizations, as well as wealthy conservatives, the isolationist coalition pursued a more politically viable strategy. That the real intention of those favoring the Danahar amendment was to strike out at liberal internationalists such as Field, rather than to eliminate special privileges for the wealthy, was made unmistakably clear as the debate proceeded. (Although there was a close historical association between the kind of populist sentiment that favored "soaking the rich" and isolationism.)[190] The proposal was ultimately defeated, not because Field's friends rallied to his cause, but because the amendment would have had a particularly severe impact on livestock breeders.

The start of the Cold War, the breakup of wartime domestic and international political alliances, and the death of the nation's leading internationalists, Roosevelt and Wendell Willkie opened the door to an assault, which was cloaked in anti-Communist rhetoric, against liberal internationalism. The antisubversive movement, which included the activities of the House Committee on Un-American Activities and the Senate Internal Security Sub-Committee under Senator Joseph McCarthy, was directed in large part against the policy elites, as well as the private universities and foundations with which they were closely associated. The antisuberversives' animus represented a continuation of the old Populist hostility against eastern big business, which had been rekindled by factional struggles within the Republican party over its commitment to internationalism. Thus, it was no coincidence that Alger Hiss, a primary target of the antisubversives, was the president of the Carnegie Endowment for International Peace.

In April 1952, the Select (Cox) Committee of the House of Representatives began an investigation of "educational and philanthropic foundations and other comparable organizations which are exempt

from federal taxation to determine whether they were using their resources for the purposes for which they were established, and especially to determine which such foundations and organizations are using
their resources for un-American and subversive activities or for purposes not in the interest or tradition of the United States."[191] According to Andrews, the foundations were able to use their influence to
install Chicago corporate lawyer Harold M. Keele, rather than a professional redbaiter, as the committee's chief counsel. From the beginning, Keele made it clear that his would be no grandstanding inquisi-
torial performance, but would proceed "in the temper of a British
royal investigating commission" to "look at all the facts and to arrive
at a balanced conclusion."[192]

Keele began his work by meeting privately with the heads of the
largest foundations and urging their cooperation with the committee's
work. This they agreed to do. In fall 1952, all foundations with assets
of $10 million or more received a questionnaire covering virtually
every aspect of their operations. Responses ran to book-length—for
example, the Guggenheim Foundation's ran to over three hundred
pages. As it turned out, the foundations' willingness to cooperate was
generously rewarded. Keele allowed the foundations and their friends
to present their case first—which they did with extraordinary effectiveness and vigor. By the time Paul Hoffman, president of the Ford Foundation, had finished his lyrical presentation on foundations as an
integral part of "what we have here in America," even Chairman
Eugene E. Cox, the Georgia firebrand whose charges had sparked the
investigation, was ready to throw in the towel. "You have made a very
fine case for the Ford Foundation," he conceded. "As a matter of fact,
you have made a fine case for all the foundations."[193] After two weeks
of hearing testimony from such notables as Henry Ford II, John D.
Rockefeller 3rd, Alfred P. Sloan, and Vannevar Bush—as well as a
handful of professional anti-Communists—the committee completed
its work. Its final report, submitted to Congress in January 1953, ring-
ingly endorsed the loyalty of the foundations. "So far as we can ascer-
tain," it declared, "there is little basis for the belief expressed in some
quarters that foundation funds are being diverted from their intended
use."[194] The report concluded by recommending better public reporting and a reexamination of pertinent tax laws to encourage private
individuals to make greater gifts to "these meritorious institutions."

Unhappy with the Cox Committee's conclusions, Congressman B.
Carroll Reece pushed for a continuation of its work. In April 1954, the
House authorized a Special Committee to Investigate Tax-Exempt
Foundations and Comparable Organizations (the Reece Committee).
Unlike its predecessor, which limited its attention to generalities, the

Reece Committee mounted a comprehensive enquiry into both the motives for establishing foundations and their influence on public life. Areas of interest included the use of foundations as mechanisms of tax avoidance and dynastic control, their influence on the social sciences, their power to influence public opinion and policy through selective patronage of academic research, their failures of fiduciary responsibility, their bureaucrats' rising power, their influence on the press and broadcasting, and, last but not least, their role in promoting internationalist foreign policy and supporting subversive activities. The Reece Committee, after lengthy proceedings, found philanthropy blameless of supporting communism, but it challenged traditional American institutions in a more profound and disturbing way: vast private fortunes, preserved by being incorporated as perpetual charitable trusts and in which donors retained considerable control, were administered by a "guild" of managers—the "philanthropoids"—who used their power to control research, education, and the media. Their influence over government included control not only of the fund of information on which the public and politicians based their actions, but also of the experts who advised and implemented public policy. Although the promotion of internationalism and moral relativism by foundations concerned the committee, it saw their concentrated power as the more central threat. Even if benign, this power posed a threat to democratic government.[195]

The Reece Committee's report, submitted in the midst of the ultimately successful efforts to censure McCarthy, failed to attract much attention. McCarthy's fall led to a discrediting of all efforts that smacked of redbaiting. Once again, the foundations and the other organizations of the growing tax-exempt universe had a fortunate escape. Nevertheless, their vulnerability had been underscored—and their leaders set about to prepare for future congressional assaults by trying to create a public record of their activities.[196] Initiatives took several forms. In 1955, the Ford Foundation made its first grants to encourage scholarly investigations of the role of philanthropy in American life. In the same year, the Carnegie Corporation and the Russell Sage Foundation began planning the establishment of "a new organization [that] would be a strategic gathering place for knowledge about foundations"—the Foundation Library Center. The center's activities, which included the publication of a comprehensive directory of foundations and a bimonthly magazine, *Foundation News.*[197]

Interestingly, these modest efforts, underwritten by the Carnegie Corporation on groundwork laid by the Russell Sage Foundation, encountered broad resistance in the philanthropic community. Other big foundations dragged their feet about contributing to the center's support. And smaller ones viewed efforts to gather information about their assets and activities with suspicion. Despite resistance, the center would serve as an institutional basis for the growth of self-awareness among charitable tax-exempt organizations, enabling them not only to more effectively defend themselves but also to thoroughly reconceptualize their place in the democratic polity.

These efforts came none too soon. In July 1959, the Senate Finance Committee recommended a liberalization of tax-code provisions affecting unlimited deductions for charitable contributions. A minority on the committee—which included senators Russell Long, Albert Gore, Eugene McCarthy, and Clinton Anderson—issued a sharply worded minority report, which charged that "this bill is designed specifically to encourage a proliferation of foundations which would be established by individuals and families." "The tax base is being dangerously eroded by many forces," the minority warned, "among them tax-exempt trusts and foundations. Not only is the tax base being eroded, but even more harmful social and political consequences may result from concentrating, and holding in a few hands and in perpetuity, control over large fortunes and business enterprises. The attendant inequities resulting from the tax treatment of contributions, particularly in the form of capital, to foundations are being magnified daily." Noting that 87 percent of the thirteen thousand foundations had been created since 1940 and that approximately twelve hundred new ones were being created every year, the minority report warned that "at present rates of establishment, substantial control of our economy may soon rest in the 'dead hands' of such organizations." The minority report urged that "the social, political, and economic implications of the growth of foundations should be thoroughly studied," underlining the dangers of wealth "removed from ostensible ownership and from the free choices presented by the marketplace and by the democratic processes of a free government, free economy, and a free society."[198]

In May 1961, Texas Congressman Wright Patman took up the challenge suggested by the minority report, using the floor of the House to deliver a series of speeches on foundations and other tax-exempt organizations.[199] He began with "A Fresh Look at Tax Exempt Foundations," which had as its theme the "disproportionately rapid growth of foundations."[200] On subsequent days, he addressed the "Power and Influence of Large Foundations," "Foundations Fail to Give Adequate Financial Reports," and "IRS Needs Sharper Tools."[201] On August 7, Patman delivered a lengthy speech, which was published in the *Congressional Record* under the title "Lid Lifted on Information about Tax-Exempt Foundations." Briefly stated, Patman concluded:

I am at present concerned with first, foundation-controlled business competing with small businessmen; second the economic effect of great
amounts of wealth accumulating in privately controlled, tax-exempt
foundations; third, the problem of control of that capital for an undeter-
mined period—in some cases in perpetuity—by a few individuals or their
self-appointed successors; and fourth, the foundations' power to interlock
and knit together through investments, a network of commercial alliances, which assures harmonious action whenever they have a common
interest.[202]

He promised to continue examining "the economic consequences of
the granting of tax exemption to privately controlled foundations"
and to report "from time to time" to the House.

Patman's efforts over the next decade, conducted under the auspices
of the Small Business Committee, focused not on subversion, but on
economic issues, particularly the favorable treatment that philanthropy brought the very wealthy and the power of philanthropy over
the economy.[203] Patman's well-publicized findings, which received
wide attention both in the press and in such volumes as Ferdinand
Lundberg's 1968 best-seller, *The Rich and the Super-Rich*, were expressions of growing discontent with the inequities of the tax system.[204]
These concerns were coming to be shared by a number of economists
and tax-policy experts in the Treasury Department, who were beginning to question unexamined assumptions about the efficiency of the
current tax system, particularly with regard to the charitable deduction.[205] The department's report on foundations, issued in 1965,
recommended major changes in the rules governing foundations,
including prohibitions on business dealings between donors and
foundations, limits on foundation ownership of voting control of
businesses, restrictions on the deductibility of donor-controlled gifts,
and regulation of the number of years donors and their families
could sit on governing boards.[206] Although dramatic proposals, they
were far less radical than those being put forward by Patman, who
urged a moratorium on the creation of tax-exempt organizations, limiting the life of foundations to twenty-five years, a 20 percent tax on
foundation incomes, a prohibition on borrowing or lending money,
and a requirement that all contributions and capital gains be spent as
income.

Patman's persistence, combined with rising taxes and inflation,
which increased the tax sensitivity of the public, stimulated a rising
demand for tax reform. In February 1969, the House Ways and Means
Committee began hearings on the subject. The lead-off witness was
Patman, who railed against the ways in which the foundations had
"perverted" philanthropy, transforming "one of mankind's more

noble instincts" into "a vehicle for institutionalized, deliberate eva-
sion of fiscal and moral responsibility."[207]

Although they faced a common threat, the defenders of charitable
tax-exempt organizations were remarkably ununified in their efforts to
defend themselves. In September 1964, Rockefeller family associate
Ray LaMontagne surveyed the disarray, in a memorandum addressed
to John D. Rockefeller 3rd regarding the possibility of creating a "National Association of Foundations."[208] Although numerous organizations sought leadership in the field, none of them, LaMontagne noted,
completely filled the bill: the Foundation Library Center was limited
by its primary function as an information-gathering organization; the
Council on Foundations, at that time only a few months old (having
been created out of a reorganization of the National Council of Community Foundations), lacked "sufficient stature and adequate resources to be an effective and influential force"; the National Information Bureau was narrowly concerned with philanthropic standards;
the New York University Conference on Charitable Foundations and
other "periodic" and "regional" conferences were mere forums for
"persons who are interested in charitable foundations." LaMontagne
believed that what was needed was a national association of foundations which would work to establish and improve standards, policies,
and procedures—up to and including a formal accrediting process.
The association would not only provide technical support, public
relations, and lobbying services but also help "foundations gain a
keener awareness of their opportunities and responsibilities" and
"stimulate studies to discover new ways by which foundations could
be of greater service to society in this changing world."[209] LaMontagne
also implicitly acknowledged the obstacles standing in the way of such
an association, due to the diverse interests of the foundations, intermediary associations, and donee elements of the tax-exempt universe.

LaMontagne's suggestion was utopian, given the state of foundations in the mid-1960s. Even relatively well-institutionalized agencies
such as the Foundation Center and the newly organized Council on
Foundations, despite their calls for "stronger internal discipline and
evaluation" and "friendly encouragement from government," were
unable to present specific legislative recommendations when asked to
so by the House Ways and Means Committee in 1965, because of lack
of agreement among their members.[210]

Things had not much improved by 1969, when Congress began
hearing testimony on proposed sweeping revisions in the tax code.
Former Foundation Center president F. Emerson Andrews testified as
a "private citizen and foundation watcher." He was alone in favoring
the recommendations of the 1965 Treasury Department report on

foundations, which he praised as "judicious" and "carefully factual" in its efforts to correct abuses.[211] But the leaders of big foundations were unanimous in their opposition to any form of increased regulation.[212] The Carnegie Corporation's Alan Pifer defended the "honored place" of foundations and warned that "governmental control" of the sort embodied in the proposed tax reforms would "have far-reaching and extremely dangerous consequences for the American pluralistic system." The Ford Foundations's McGeorge Bundy echoed this theme, pointing out that the growing role of government increased the need for private philanthropy, which fostered diversity and pluralism. George Harrar and Dana Creel, representing the Rockefeller philanthropies, defended their institutions and urged against the passage of any regulations that would "act as dis-incentives for the creation and growth of foundations" or that would "discourage individual charitable giving."

The unyielding stance of the foundations won them few friends on the Hill. Bundy's testimony, described by some as arrogant, was marked by sharp exchanges with the committee over the foundation's political activities, including funding voter-registration drives and "fellowships" given to former members of Robert F. Kennedy's staff. By the time the hearings concluded, it was quite clear that Patman's charges had been largely accepted at face value and that major changes in regulations governing foundations and favoring their wealthy donors were inevitable.

The 1969 Tax Reform Act, as finally passed, proved to be far less draconian than many had feared. On the whole, it followed the lines of the 1965 Treasury Department report—with the major addition being restrictions on political activities. Foundations succeeded in winning concessions in the enforcement area: organizations found in violation would suffer financial penalties and be given opportunities for self-correction rather than facing loss of their tax-exempt status. Although comprehensive, the act was also unclear in many areas. It would take several years for Congress, the Treasury Department, and officials of tax-exempt organizations to negotiate what the provisions of the bill really meant and how they were to be applied.[213] Although the 1969 Tax Reform Act turned out to be less than a disaster for philanthropy, it once again underlined the vulnerability of the charitable tax-exempt universe.[214] Quite clearly, quoting Tocqueville to Congress would no longer serve as an effective defense. Future efforts would have to rely on the technical language of law and economics that had come to frame the creation of tax policy by the late 1960s.

One of the few figures to recognize how significantly philanthropy had changed since the war was John D. Rockefeller 3rd. His statements contrasted sharply with those of foundation executives, who, according to one congressman, expressed an "all or nothing" attitude, felt entitled to act outside the tax system, and left Congress no middle ground.[215] Rockefeller urged philanthropy and government to work together to reevaluate the place of foundations in modern society.[216] Rockefeller's call for a public-private partnership in the drafting policies affecting "private initiative in the public interest" acknowledged the complexities and uncertainties of the relationship between government and the private sectors that had developed since the war. On the most fundamental level, as the role of government grew, some in Congress wondered whether private philanthropy was needed anymore. Others were concerned about government support for private institutions whose policies on race and gender ran counter to public policy.

The current of hostility to foundations and other tax-exempt organizations did not end with the passage of the 1969 Tax Reform Act. Patman and other congressional leaders had watched with dismay as the act's provisions were progressively watered down by the I.R.S. In June 1972, Patman wrote to leading foundations demanding that they demonstrate their compliance with various sections of the act.[217] In spring 1973, the Treasury Department proposed further toughening of tax-law provisions affecting foundations and large donors.[218] And by the fall, the Subcommittee on Foundations of the Senate Finance Committee, chaired by Indiana's Vance Hartke, began a series of panel discussions on the issue.[219] Hartke was outspokenly hostile and disdainful to foundation representatives. His only positive comments came in response to the suggestion that a "National Commission on Philanthropy" be formed to father reliable information about foundations. After witnessing these interchanges, journalist Henry Suhrke concluded that "the outlines of what must be done is fairly clear. Someone, somehow, must gather statistics so that we will have an idea of what is going on in the foundation world."[220]

Unknown to Suhrke and most of the foundation world, steps were already underway to do just this—and then some. Such an effort dated back to the months before the hearings on the 1969 Tax Reform Act started, when John D. Rockefeller 3rd had convened a blue-ribbon panel, the Commission on Foundations and Private Philanthropy. Made up of individuals prominent in business, education, law, and the arts, the Peterson Commission, as it came to be known (after its chairman, Pete Peterson, president of Bell and Howell), set itself the task of studying "all relevant matters bearing on foundations and private philanthropy" in order to make "long-term policy recommendations." Its report, based on literature surveys, questionnaires, and interviews, was a pioneering effort to go beyond merely descriptive characterizations of the role of philanthropy and polemical assertions of its indispensability.[221]

The Peterson Commission report failed to have the desired impact, because not only was it completed after the passage of the 1969 Tax Reform Act but also little of the information it gathered was really new. The commission's most important contribution was to recognize the domain of philanthropy beyond the donor community, including not only grant makers but also a broad range of voluntary groups supported by a mix of public and private funds. To the government, this was hardly a startling insight: tax law treated all charitable tax-exempt organizations, donors and donees, as a unified class, even though it made increasingly elaborate regulatory distinctions between different types of nonprofits. But to the foundation world, this expanded view of its concerns was very new indeed.

No sooner had the Peterson Commission disbanded than Rockefeller and his associates initiated conversations with Ways and Means Committee Chairman Wilbur Mills, Treasury Department officials, and others with regard to convening "a group of knowledgeable and concerned individuals to review and make recommendations in regard to tax incentives in the philanthropic field" and other matters relating to the well-bring of "the whole private nonprofit sector."[222] With Mills' affirmative response, the effort to organize what was then called the Committee on Tax Incentives began in earnest, under the direction of Leonard Silverstein and Rockefeller's associates Howard Bolton and Datus Smith.[223] What had been conceived of as a relatively modest effort took on greater urgency and importance with the new year—the year of Watergate. One of the revelations in the impeachment hearings was a memorandum by presidential aide Pat Buchanan which laid out strategies for combating "the institutionalized power of the Left concentrated in the foundations that succor the Democratic party," mentioning the need for "a strong fellow running the Internal Revenue Division . . . and an especially friendly fellow with a friendly staff in the Tax-Exempt office."[224] This, combined with the Hartke hearings and the increasingly restrictive proposals from the Nixon administration, made it clear that philanthropy's best defense was to seize the policy initiative.

Patronage of scholarship played a crucial role in allowing philanthropy to shift the basis for advancing its claims for special status under the tax code. In the early 1960s, the 501(c)(3) Group, a loose network of tax lawyers and top officials of national donee organizations, had begun exchanging information about the technical dimensions of the tax code as it affected charitable tax-exempt organizations.[225] The group had been troubled about the ineffectiveness of pluralist rhetoric in the 1969 hearings and—with an eye to the emerging econometric literature on tax policy—were alarmed by the emergence of a scholarly literature that seemed to suggest there was no economic justification for such things as the charitable deduction.[226] "We all felt intuitively that taxes influenced giving," Hayden W. Smith, then chair of the group, later recollected. "But none of the available scholarship supported our viewpoint. We cast a net looking for economists who might look into this for us."[227] After rejecting various Washington-based economists as biased, the group learned of the work of Harvard economist Martin S. Feldstein, who had done important work in the 1960s on the economics of health care. Smith met with Feldstein, who, in January 1973, made a formal proposal for a research project on the effects of deductibility on charitable contributions and, more broadly, to produce "a more general analysis of the rationale and effects of the current tax treatment."[228] These studies would be directed to professional economists, tax lawyers, and government officials.

Members of the 501(c)(3) Group were ambivalent about Feldstein's proposal.[229] On the one hand, they earnestly desired to strengthen the rationale for the favorable treatment of charitable tax-exempt organizations. On the other hand, they feared that if Feldstein's studies ended up buttressing the existing literature, which uniformly discredited such treatment, their cause would be weakened. Some group members were so anxious about this that they sought to have Feldstein agree to suppress his findings if they failed to support their views. Feldstein resisted this suggestion. Ultimately, the impasse was broken through the secret intervention of the Rockefeller family office, which not only supplied the bulk of the funding but also, acting through group members Lindsley Kimball and David Freeman, persuaded their colleagues that they had nothing to lose by backing Feldstein's work.[230] If Feldstein came up with the wrong results, his efforts would simply confirm the existing literature. However, the right results would alter academic debate on tax policy and, more importantly, by transforming the tax-policy debate on charitable organizations into a technical econometric question, would effectively depoliticize it, removing it from congressional hearing rooms and placing it in the more rarefied arena of high economic policy.

Feldstein began his study in February 1973, having agreed to keep the 501(c)(3) Group appraised of his preliminary findings. Within months, it became clear that his analysis strongly supported philanthropy—and he was given the go-ahead to complete the study, which he completed by December 1973. The importance of Feldstein's work, which created a compelling and academically credible rationale for the tax treatment of nonprofits, was suggested by the language of the *Philanthropy Monthly*'s "Outstanding Service Award" for 1974." "The research of Dr. Martin Feldstein is so pertinent to the debate as to the future of charitable contributions that its significance cannot be over-estimated. . . . He has shown us that the charitable deduction works—it is effective in producing more revenues for charity than is 'lost' by government. This finding is all the more important because it reverses the presumptions held as a result of earlier studies."[231]

Feldstein's exciting findings put the work of Rockefeller's Commit-tee on Tax Incentives into high gear. By May 1973, the committee, now renamed the Advisory Group on Private Philanthropy, had become a top priority with both the Rockefeller group and the Treasury Depart-ment, now led by William Simon.[232] By the end of the summer, a prestigious group—exquisitely balanced by geography, party, gender, race, occupation, and religious denomination—had been recruited un-der the chairmanship of John Filer, a corporate lawyer and the chief executive officer of the Aetna Insurance Company.[233] The joint effort of Congress, the Treasury Department, and the private sector would be "aided by a distinguished panel of experts including economists, sociologists, tax attorneys, and specialists in nongovernmental organi-zations." The commission's broad mandate would include considera-tion of: "(1) policy considerations respecting the present system of incentives to private philanthropic giving; (2) specific considerations relating to the present treatment of private contributors; (3) specific considerations relating to the present method of supervising, regulat-ing, and classifying charitable institutions; and (4) alternative means of achieving the results sought by [the] present structure of private philanthropy in the United States."

The foundation world was kept completely in the dark about these maneuvers. And the announcement of the formation of the "Citizens' Commission on Private Philanthropy and Public Needs" by Secretary of Treasury George Schultz and Mills—only weeks after the bruising encounters with Senator Hartke—came as a complete and not entirely welcome surprise.[234] One gets some sense of the shock to organized philanthropy in a hastily scrawled memorandum from Robert F. Go-heen, president of the Council on Foundations, to one of his staffers, Eugene Struckhoff. "*big* problem!!" Goheen wrote. "I am not at *all* sure that *this* committee with mostly *lawyers* and highly institution-alized establishment types are the best qualified—without some leav-ening—to decide all of these issues important to others that approach the matter from a different perspective. Has charity become all *law*? Is it irrecoverably committed to lawyers instead of its traditional prac-titioners?"[235]

The willingness of Rockefeller and top government officials to keep the foundations in the dark about the formation of the Filer Commission—and to keep them at arm's-length once its establishment was announced—was indicative of the deep split that had emerged in the foundation world after the passage of the 1969 Tax Reform Act. One group, primarily consisting of top foundation executives and loosely grouped around John Gardner, believed that philanthropy's defense should be based on more effective public-relations initiatives—and stoutly resisted any and all efforts to promote either internal or external policing.[236] The other faction—far less unified and gathered around several centers, including the Rockefeller family office, the leadership of the Foundation Center, and the members of the 501(c)(3) Group—was deeply troubled about the direction of American philanthropy, particularly its increasing insularity, self-servingness, and lack of responsiveness to social change.[237] When the Gardner group proved more politically adept—at least within the confines of the foundation trade associations—those favoring a more candid approach to philanthropy's problems had little choice but to join forces behind the Filer Commission.[238]

The results of the Filer Commission's work were published by the Treasury Department in six weighty volumes in 1977.[239] This comprehensive multidisciplinary survey of every aspect of charitable tax-exempt organizations described and analyzed the role of nonprofits as employers, as sources of essential health, educational, welfare, and cultural services, and as forces in political life. The work also carefully considered the regulatory and tax issues affecting these organizations' well-being. Most importantly, the work gave substance to what, up to then, had been only an idea: that charitable tax-exempt organizations composed a coherent and cohesive "sector" of American political, economic, and social life. This unified conception of nonprofits as part of a "third," "independent," or "nonprofit"—or, as the commission preferred to call it, "voluntary"—sector lay the groundwork for establishing organizations that could give its common interests unified expression.

Initially, the majority and the commission had hoped to establish a permanent quasi-governmental agency—modeled on the British Charity Commission—within the Treasury Department. But hopes for this were dashed by the Carter administration, which not only questioned the propriety of such an industry presence within a government department, but also was engaged more broadly in a sweeping review of the regulatory process.[240]

Because the Filer Commission had failed in its main task—the creation of an agency that would have effectively removed public policy toward philanthropy from the political process—those in sympathy with the commission's recommendations had to try to devise alternate means of bringing the diverse and discordant elements of the tax-exempt universe—the third sector—into harmony. This would not be easy. Even within the commission there had been sharp differences over the major policy recommendations and how best to implement them.[241] And though most elements in the world of philanthropy had, despite their initial resistance, ended up cooperating with the commission, resentments and rivalries—some personal, some institutional—still remained. As the commission tried to sort out its impasse, a variety of groups—chiefly the National Council on Philanthropy (NCOP) and the Coalition of National Voluntary Organizations (CONVO)—began actively vying to assume leadership of the now nearly united sector.[242]

Conciliating these interests took almost four years. And even when agreement on a unified organization to serve all elements of the nonprofit sector was finally reached, it was in effect an agreement to disagree. Repeatedly reminding itself of the diversity of the sector and its key role in preserving pluralism in American society, the new entity, Independent Sector (IS), pledged itself to address its mission "only by working through the vast network of organizations already extant," understanding that "the extent to which the new organization tries to overreach these groups and build separately, it will have neither an impact nor a future."[243] In considering the long-term dangers IS faced, organizers listed first and foremost "the danger of slipping into a spokesperson role. To do so not only will be a disservice to the sector and society, but will bring the wrath of the sector down on the organization. There are very few issues where the sector will ever speak with one voice or tolerate one voice speaking in its behalf."[244] Organizers also warned of the hazards of developing "a trade association reputation. If we find ourselves responding only to issues relating to the financial and organization needs of the sector, we will gain a reputation as an organization concerned only with institutional interests and not with the public good."[245] As originally envisioned, IS was to be a loosely coordinated organization: "the distinct majority" of its members "definitely want decentralization rather than centralization of planning and decisionmaking," organizers noted. "Up to now, we have resisted even the suggestion of a program committee. However, a committee of some such names might be put in place. . . . The committee's responsibility would not be as a central planner of all programming, but rather as a help to renew new suggestions in relation to existing resources and priorities."[246] Rather than serving as a spokesman, IS would, its organizers hoped, be a "common meeting ground" for all elements and all viewpoints within the charitable universe.

Nonprofits in the Reagan Era

The formation of IS coincided with the election of Ronald Reagan. The new president, who had proclaimed himself a friend of philanthropy and voluntarism, set about not only to increase its responsibilities—by cutting back federal spending and allowing localities and private charities to "take up the slack"—but also to highlight the need for greater support for nonprofits. To stimulate higher levels of voluntary effort, the president convened a Task Force on Private Sector Initiatives, chaired by industrialist William Verity and directed by E. B. Knauft, chief of corporate contributions at Aetna and a former Filer Commission staffer.[247] After months of meetings, the commission failed to reach agreement on whether the private sector was up to the task—a point brought home by the unwillingness of many major corporations to commit themselves to giving at even the 2 percent level (much less the 10 percent that was permitted under the new administration's tax legislation).[248] The most serious blow to the president's efforts came from policy analysts Lester Salamon and Alan Abramson of the Urban Institute, whose analysis of the Reagan budget proposals suggested that the nonprofit sector, by then so dependent on public funding, would be crippled by cutbacks in federal spending—which the scholars demonstrated as constituting between one-third and one-half of nonprofit revenues.[249]

Over the past decade, neither the government nor philanthropy's defenders have managed to articulate coherent policies toward the nonprofit sector. The Reagan and Bush administrations, though rhetorically supporting private initiative, have promoted tax proposals that would eliminate or reduce incentives to charitable donors. At the same time, conservative efforts to privatize public services, often through contracting them out to nonprofits, have encouraged the continuing growth in the number of nonprofit organizations.[250] This combination of threatened cutbacks in direct and indirect federal support for nonprofits and privatization has encouraged nonprofits to become far more entrepreneurial, reducing uncertainty by broadening their financial bases beyond charitable contributions to include a mix of grants, contracts, donations, and sales of services. Nonprofits responded by encouraging the professionalization of management, with skills in marketing, accounting, and planning, as well as in reinterpreting organizational missions to fit the new circumstances.[251] The professionalization of nonprofits management, the increasingly active presence of businesspeople on boards of trustees, and unprecedentedly high levels of corporate giving were the Reagan era's chief legacy to the nonprofit sector.[252]

As nonprofits achieved an influence and visibility in the 1980s that would have been unimaginable even a decade earlier, groups such as IS and the Council on Foundations found themselves increasingly stymied by changes in the sector. These national organizations were not geared to deal with local and regional organizations—the arenas in which most of the growth was taking place. Further, their commitment to the rhetoric of nonprofits as an "independent" sector made less and less sense in a world in which the nonprofit form was not only increasingly hybridized—and, as such, harder to distinguish from for-profit organizations—but also more closely tied to government at all levels. Moreover, services that had once been more or less the exclusive preserve of nonprofits—the arts, culture, education, health, and welfare—were, by the late 1980s, being delivered by for-profit and government agencies as well, sometimes in competition, sometimes cooperatively. Nevertheless, nonprofits industry spokespeople had difficult acknowledging these changes because doing so would have required abandoning their belief in the nonprofit sector's distinctiveness.

Certainly the greatest changes in the nonprofit world have involved both vastly greater numbers of organizations and vastly broader public participation and support.[253] Mutual-benefit and advocacy organizations (including churches) aside, most nonprofits had been a relatively unruffled preserve of primarily Protestant community elites—people who knew one another, who shared the same values and goals, and who tended to dominate the major social and economic institutions of their communities. The mass availability of higher education and economic growth in the decades following World War II moved new elements—particularly people of non–Northern European and non-Protestant background—into positions of leadership in the private sectors. They brought with them a variety of new perspectives on communities, as well as their needs and how best to meet them.

By the end of the 1980s, charities such as the United Way were compelled to make major changes in their policies to accommodate the increasingly pluralistic nature of American communities and their leadership.[254] The increasing diversity of backgrounds and viewpoints of community leaders has found its most compelling expression in growing conflict among board members and between boards and managers over organizational missions, goals, and strategies. This conflict has led to growing attention to the broad issues of community leadership and how it should be recruited and trained.[255] These have strained conventional conceptions of the nonprofit sector as a private domain, because much voluntary activity involves service in public-sector arenas, such as municipal and regional boards and commissions.

Conclusion

The debate continues over how a democracy can best do the public's business. Despite the growing recognition of nonprofits as a centrally important part of American life, doubts still remain about the wisdom of delegating public tasks to private groups. Some commentators, pointing out how few of the organizations enjoying tax exemption are actually concerned with benefiting the needy, have urged a thorough overhaul of tax laws. Others have pointed to the ways in which philanthropy, despite the strictures of the 1969 Tax Reform Act, continues to serve the purposes of the wealthy far more than it does those of the population as a whole.

Perhaps the most significant shift in the debate has involved the Rights's decreasing hostility to nonprofit activity. As conservatives became a unified political force in the 1980s, they depended more and more on their own network of think tanks, foundations, and sympathetic academics. This influential counterestablishment, combined with the growing importance of foundations outside the Northeast, has helped to broaden the profile of philanthropy, making it less the creature of a small group of like-minded cosmopolitans with liberal proclivities.[256]

At times, the coexistence of Right and Left has been less than peaceful. In the early 1980s, efforts of the Council on Foundations to compel its members to adopt affirmative-action guidelines and other policies involving greater public responsiveness led to outspoken protests by conservative grant makers.[257] Liberals and conservatives went head to head again in the Buck Trust case, in which Buck attempted to alter the terms of a charitable trust to benefit a more obviously needy population than the residents of affluent Marin County, California.[258] Despite these conflicts over philanthropic goals, there has been broad agreement on means—and on the need to defend and if possible extend the privileges accorded nonprofits generally.

Accompanying the current broad acceptance of the activity of nonprofits has been a growth in concerns about their global dimensions.[259] On the one hand, American nonprofits are increasingly seeking support from overseas corporations, while foreign corporations doing business in the United States are increasingly eager to be good "corporate citizens." On the other hand, the collapse of communism and consequent efforts to put free-market economies and democratic polities in its place has, necessarily, suggested the need for third-sector organizations abroad as well. Despite forceful arguments in favor of establishing nonprofit sectors abroad, questions remain about what forms they might take.

The lack of unanimity on these issues, as well as the continuing debate over the mission, goals, and mechanisms of philanthropic, voluntary, and nonprofit organizations, has been disheartening to some. For others, the debate is an exciting intellectual adventure involving fundamental questions about the nature of human institutions, the possibilities of political, economic, and social organization, and the quality of our values and moral imagination.

2

Reflections on the Nonprofit Sector in the Postliberal Era

Like Scripture and statistics, few literatures have been more conscientiously misconstrued than Alexis de Tocqueville's pronouncements on the fundamental institutions of the United States in *Democracy in America*. Defenders of the independency of the nonprofit sector, in particular, have delighted in citing Tocqueville's dictum on voluntary associations:

> Americans of all ages, all conditions, and all dispositions constantly form associations. They have not only commercial and manufacturing companies, in which all take part, but associations of a thousand other kinds, religious, moral, serious, futile, general, or restricted, enormous or diminutive. The Americans make associations to give entertainments, to found seminaries, to build inns, to construct churches, to diffuse books, to send missionaries to the antipodes; in this manner they found hospitals, prisons, and schools. If it is proposed to inculcate some truth or to foster some feeling by the encouragement of a great example, they form a society. Wherever at the head of some new undertaking you see the government in France, or a man of rank in England, in the United States you will be sure to find an association.[1]

This characterization strikes up delightful Binghamesque images of barn raisings and volunteer fire companies, of randomized democratic diversity and a bounty of organizational possibilities as rich as the American land. It also—as used—ignores the larger conceptual framework of Tocqueville's analysis of American society. For, as he implied in the last sentence of this passage, Tocqueville did not view private voluntarism as an amusing carnival midway of private intentions, but as a fundamental part of a national power system. To be sure, voluntarism displayed a certain amount of randomness, but at its core there was, as he observed, "a natural and perhaps a necessary connection" between the civil associations and the political associations through which citizens combined to influence the state.[2] And this connection was of no small significance. First, it was the basis for organizing *political* opposition to the power of elected officials:

> In the United States, as soon as a party has become dominant, all public authority passes into its hands; its private supporters occupy all the offices and have all the force of the administration at their disposal. As the most distinguished members of the opposite party cannot surmount the barrier that excludes them from power, they must establish themselves outside of it and oppose the whole moral authority of the minority to the physical power that domineers over it.[3]

Second, this connection was the basis for formulating the conceptual agenda on which political opposition necessarily had to be based. Tocqueville's belief that the ability of an organized political opposition to diminish the moral authority of the majority came not from its numerical strength, but from the peculiar relation of political and civil associations, through which "those arguments that are most fitted to act on the majority" are discovered in the hope of ultimately "drawing over the majority to their own side, and then controlling the supreme power in its name."[4]

Can we regard this organizational process, which is clearly so central to the exercise of power in a democratic society, as being "independent" in any meaningful sense? Clearly we can. In the mid-1970s, when one of the first major scholarly investigations of the private nonprofit sector was being designed out, the title of the project description was "Proposal for a Study of Independent Institutions." Its rhetoric echoed the narrow construction of Tocqueville, defining as its topic a "third sector," which took up the social tasks that we assigned to neither governmental nor business establishments:

> To many or most citizens, the non-profit world appears to reflect and to advance several of our most precious values. This sector is viewed as the place where public purposes are pursued through a congeries of private initiatives. It is here that social and cultural experimentation can be conducted by a multitude of free agents, in a testing process analogous both to the commercial marketplace and the First Amendment's marketplace of ideas. Here too, citizens can give expression to their concern for humanity and for beauty through their gifts of time, energy and funds. By banding together to pursue common goals, the millions of participants in voluntary organizations contribute to the social integration, the sense of community, of the larger society. As a result of these virtues, the non-profit sector contributes immeasurably and incomparably to the quality and vitality of life in the United States.[5]

Interestingly, these scholars, all of whom possessed wide practical and theoretical knowledge of nonprofit organizations, never seriously questioned the independence of the third sector. Even when citing dissent from their essentially positive view of nonprofits, they took its autonomy for granted: "Some, from a majoritarian perspective, condemn non-profit groups, or at least many categories of them, as elitist and non-'accountable'; some believe the voluntary sector to be insufficiently responsive to social needs; others think it borrows some of the worst habits of the neighboring worlds of business and government: predation, corruption, and sloth, aggravated by bigness and power."[6]

This unexamined assumption regarding the independence of the sector was carried over into the proposed program's research agenda. While "function" and "accountability" were to be the concepts giving "direction to the entire research program," the investigation of function was to be focused *not* on the place of nonprofits in the total organizational universe (from which they were assumed to be largely independent) but, rather, on the efficiency and effectiveness of nonprofits in the various fields in which they operated.

Pseudo-Tocquevillian assumptions about the independence of the nonprofit sector were also fundamental premises of the work of the Filer Commission (the Commission on Private Philanthropy and Public Needs) as it launched its ambitious multivolume study of independent institutions in 1973:

> Few aspects of American society are more characteristically, more famously American than the nation's array of voluntary organizations, and the support in both time and money that is given to them by its citizens. Our country has been decisively different in this regard, historian Daniel Boorstin observes, "from the beginning." As the country settled, "communities existed before governments were there to care for public needs." The result, Boorstin says, was that "voluntary collaborative activities" were set up to provide basic social services. Government followed later.[7]

This viewpoint permeated the commission's research agenda, which, while acknowledging the importance of government regulation and the tax code as environmental factors affecting the nonprofit sector, never seriously addressed the question of its independence. The commission assumed that "voluntary collaborative activities" were a fixed—if endangered—feature of American life.

It is only within the last five years that this view of private nonprofit organizations has begun to be seriously challenged. And the challenge has come not from the traditional "majoritarian" (i.e., populist) critics of the sector or from leftist scholars (who tended to assert a necessary but usually unexamined connection between organizational sectors), but from scholars who were on the whole committed to the survival of the sector and whose approach was influenced by a set of overlapping crises in public policy, nonprofits management, and scholarly perception. This chapter examines these crises and their impact on the emerging revision of our understanding of the place of the nonprofit sector in American life.

Reaganism and the Crisis of the Nonprofit Sector

The election of Reagan in 1980 promised a fundamental reordering of institutions comparable only to the administrative revolutions mounted by Andrew Jackson and Franklin Delano Roosevelt. The Reagan revolution took two major forms. The first involved a strident rhetoric that characterized the federal government as a parasitic usurper of the private sector: Reagan promised to return government to the states and localities, to deregulate the economy, and to reduce the federal social role. The second, more concrete, form involved a series of proposed budget cuts which would impact with particular severity on federal programs concerned with social welfare, health, education, environment, and culture.

The Reagan revolution remains incomplete. Like other presidents who were swept into office promising radical changes, Reagan discovered both the unwieldiness of representative government and the differences between the freedom of the office-seeker and the institutional constraints on the officeholder. Alexander Hamilton wrote of Thomas Jefferson, privately evaluating the revolutionary potential of the new Democratic-Republican regime:

> Nor is it true that Jefferson is zealot enough to do anything in pursuance of his principles which will contravene his popularity or interest. He is as likely as any man I know to temporize, to calculate what will be likely to promote his own reputation and advantage; and the probable result of such a temper is the preservation of systems, though originally opposed, which, being once established, could not be overturned without danger to the person who did it. To my mind, a true estimate of Mr. Jefferson's character warrants the expectation of a temporizing rather than a violent system.[8]

That the Reagan revolution should remain incomplete is no more surprising than the ultimate willingness of Jefferson (despite his anti-statist campaign rhetoric) to expand the powers of central government far beyond anything attempted by his Federalist predecessors.

As with the Jeffersonian revolution, the real significance of the Reagan revolution may reside less in its success in translating campaign rhetoric into legislative reality than in its impact on certain institutions and interest groups in American society, which, in re-

sponding to the new administration's rhetoric and budgetary proposals, changed their own perceptions of their place in the polity. The
Jefferson revolution of 1800 displaced a long-established social, political, and economic establishment.

The displaced Federalist elite, after taking stock of its unpromising
future electoral prospects, acted on that awareness by creating a body
of legal and political theory which differentiated public and private
spheres of action. And this elite created within the latter a set of voluntary corporate organizations claiming immunity from state interference—an immunity that was ultimately affirmed in 1819 in the Dartmouth College case.[9]

Although the roots of the perceptual and institutional revolution of
the 1980s lie deep in crises of liberal institutions and intellectual life
which can be dated back to the 1940s, this chapter argues that the
election of Reagan crystallized disparate political, institutional, and
intellectual concerns and moved them toward a common resolution.
Specifically, I argue that both the supporters and administrators of
private nonprofit organizations and the scholars of American organizational life were unusually sensitive to the implications of Reaganism. And out of this sensitivity came a revolution in thought, which
may, in turn, lead to significant changes in American institutions.

The new administration believed that nonprofits—in combination
with an economic recovery that would reduce unemployment—could
fill the gaps in services created by its proposed spending cutbacks. This
viewpoint led to the creation in 1981 of the president's Task Force on
Private Sector Initiatives. After months of well-publicized meetings,
the task force failed to formulate a coherent program for the private
sector. Although the administration increased the deductibility of corporate charitable contributions from 5 percent to 10 percent in its 1981
tax package, in the uncertain economic climate few corporations were
willing to commit themselves to even a 2 percent level of giving.
Further, as Lester Salamon and Alan Abramson pointed out in their
1981 paper "The Federal Budget and the Nonprofit Sector: Implications of the Reagan Budget Proposals," the administration had failed
to appreciate the extent to which federal funds had become a crucial
component in the revenues of the nonprofit sector and that, without
such funds, nonprofits were unlikely to maintain even their current
levels of service.[10] Finally, the administration failed to formulate a
coherent overall policy on the role of nonprofits. On the one hand, it
continued to pare federal social and cultural expenditure and rhetorically support private voluntarism. On the other hand, it attempted
to eliminate or reduce many of the tax incentives that ensured reasonable levels of private support for the sector. Similarly, its education

policy, while appearing to favor private institutions through such devices as tuition tax credits, simultaneously advocated cuts in student-loan programs, research support, and direct institutional aid, threatening to make the elite private institutions that historically have constituted the apex of the American educational system accessible only to the wealthy.

Despite the Right's deep-seated hostility to private philanthropy, it seems unlikely that the president set out to destroy or weaken the nonprofit sector. Rather, the rhetorical emphasis on voluntarism by the administration suggests that its understanding of the place of the sector in the American institutional system was clouded by a folkloric pseudo-Tocquevillianism. The central irony of the impact of Reaganism on the nonprofit sector, as Salamon has pointed out, is that its budget proposals "inadvertently posed a serious threat to the viability of the . . . sector in pursuit of an effort to get government out of the sector's way."[11]

Professionalization, Entrepreneurship, and the Crisis within the Third Sector

The Reagan administration's redefinition of the federal social role was only one dimension of the crisis of public policy regarding the nonprofit sector. Equally important was the political response of the nonprofit sector as it reacted to the Reagan administration's initiatives. Although nonprofits presented a remarkably united front in the face of efforts by tax reformers in the administration to remove the charitable deduction from the federal tax code, their apparent institutional unity obscured serious differences within the sector. These differences interfered with its ability to clearly formulate its own future role in the American polity.

The most important of these areas of dispute had to do with the professionalization of nonprofit organizations. Although efforts to make both charitable giving and the delivery of welfare, health, education, and cultural services more disinterested and hence more effective date back to the nineteenth century, attempts to professionalize nonprofits management through the delineation of standards of behavior, the creation of a body of literature on nonprofits management, and the establishment of training programs for those wishing to work in the nonprofits world date only from the early 1970s. The movement was both a specific response to the regulations contained in the 1969 Tax Reform Act and a general response to broad public criticism of the performance of private nonprofit organizations. While this act was aimed specifically at foundations, its provisions affected the entire nonprofit sector both directly and indirectly. By enhancing the vigilance of the IRS in its oversight of foundations and other nonprofits, both in the granting of tax-exempt status and in policing fiscal procedures, the act raised managerial standards. Compliance with the law increasingly required expertise, rather than the "methodless enthusiasm" that once sufficed to keep small nonprofits going. Further, as the foundations were forced to comply with complex reporting requirements, tax and distribution regulations, and funding restrictions, it was to their advantage to bring in professional managers. But their doing so increased the formality and the complexity of the grantor-grantee relationship: applicant organizations had to be able to demonstrate degrees of financial responsibility and generate fiscal information of a kind that had been, heretofore, beyond the ability of volunteer-operated entities. Finally, because the 1969 act coincided with the economic crisis of the 1970s—a catastrophic inflation that increased institutional costs and a downward trend in charitable giving—nonprofits were forced to look beyond their traditional constituencies and to become entrepreneurial in order to survive.

The 1969 Tax Reform Act brought about important reforms: the rationalization of the investment and giving policies of nonprofits was praiseworthy, given the egregious abuses of the public trust by certain foundations. And on the face of it, professionalization was a good thing. It increased the efficiency, accessibility, and accountability of nonprofits. In many instances, it dramatically improved the quality of services offered. But it was seen by some—and not without good reason—to be a sort of Trojan horse.

Historically, managerial professionalization has tended to reduce the policy role of governing boards in favor of staff control. As staffs become more professionalized, institutional activities tend to reflect the priorities of their managers rather than their boards. Because professional managers tend to share common outlooks and to apply to the managerial task the same set of standards, their dominance in organizations promotes institutional homogenization. In any other organizational sector, this isomorphism might be acceptable. In the nonprofit sector, which has been traditionally looked to as a fundamental source of social and cultural diversity, it is problematic.

One of the strongest arguments for the existence of perpetual endowments has been their relative freedom from public accountability—to either electorates or markets. This freedom has permitted individuals to fund the enormously diverse range of charitable, educational, and social-welfare activities covered by the language of the Elizabethan Statute of Charitable Uses and the acts governing the establishment of charitable trusts in the states that repealed the statute.[12] Since the eighteenth century, statutes and court decisions have established a legal basis for a remarkable freedom in underwriting an enormously diverse range of activities. Whether the wealthy and charitable have availed themselves of this freedom is another matter.

A number of early commentators on philanthropy regarded this freedom as a danger. Samuel Atkins Eliot, writing on the charities of Boston in 1845, recognized that the multiplicity of "institutions of benevolence" within the city could have the positive effect of stimulating and increasing the scale of giving so "one man's example becomes the impulse to another, till the pulsation is quickened throughout the whole community."[13] However, he was more concerned that "the multiplicity of objects" would "diminish the resources of each." Eliot therefore recommended that "those . . . who are disposed to deeds of charity, can perhaps do more good by contributing to the funds of an existing institution, than by starting a new project that may divert a portion of their means from establishments that need more."[14] Eliot's fears were echoed a generation later by Andrew Carnegie, who, in his 1889 essay "Wealth," harshly criticized "indiscriminate charity" and urged the wealthy to devote its surplus wealth to those objects that place new opportunities within the reach of the masses.[15]

Once philanthropy began to follow the lead of corporations and government in consolidating and rationalizing its resources, fears of too much diversity were replaced by fears of conventionality. As early as 1936, well before the professionalization of nonprofits management had begun, the extraordinary conventionality of charitable giving had become the subject of critical debate. This problem was a central concern of Eduard Lindeman's pioneering 1936 study of foundations:

In a dynamic civilization, where cultural values become flexible by reason of the impact of science, technology, and industry, these so-called "good" people [the caretakers of charitable wealth] become frequently the most formidable barriers impeding the attainment of the better. Curiously enough, it is more often than not this very group which takes advantage of and exploits the instruments of science and technology; but they utilize these tools, not as a basis for exploring and anticipating the cultural future but rather for purposes of maintaining the cultural status quo. Those who administer the great reservoirs of vested wealth in this country are predominantly of this type. Foundations and trusts, considered as aggregates of social control, represent primarily the pattern of conventionality.[16]

Although the number of large private foundations had increased from about four hundred in Lindeman's time to over three thousand in 1972, when Waldemar A. Nielsen conducted his study *The Big Foundations*, complaints about the conventionality of large-scale philanthropy had, with the magnitude of the sector, grown louder. Nielsen noted that

> the enormous prestige of the Rockefeller Foundation, with its proclaimed objectives of getting at the causes of human problems rather than treating merely the symptoms and of advancing the frontiers of knowledge, has helped to create the impression that its lofty standards characterize the larger foundations as a group. Similarly, some of the better and more articulate foundations . . . have frequently spoken of "mounting systematic attacks on major problems," "mapping out long-term program strategies," and "exploring through creative experimentation and demonstration new solutions to the critical dilemmas of our society," thereby reinforcing a common impression that the large foundations in general are sophisticated, energetic and innovative. Unfortunately, they are not. The majority are unprofessional, passive, ameliorative institutions: they basically offer the multitude of useful nonprofit organizations in American life which depend on contributions "another door to knock on" in meeting their current operating needs and capital requirements.[17]

To date, no serious effort has been made to actually assess the role of nonprofits as a source of innovation. I suspect that critics such as Nielsen are victims of the "quantitative fallacy," the tendency to judge significance as a function of quantity. Although the grants of the Rockefeller Foundation to such enterprises as the National Bureau of Economic Research, the President's Research Committee on Recent Social Trends, and, in the 1940s and 1950s, to the Alfred Kinsey's research on sexual behavior, undoubtedly composed only a tiny proportion of its total grants, the impact of the research produced by these organizations and individuals has been incalculable. Similarly, the small amounts granted by the Carnegie Corporation to support Gunnar Myrdal's *American Dilemma* and by the Stern and Taconic foundations to support voter registration drives in the South had disproportionately great effects. The diversity and innovativeness of nonprofits, especially foundations, needs to be examined. However, such an investigation should be informed by an awareness that most foundation giving is devoted to operating budgets and capital expenditures rather than special projects.

While the extent of conventionality in the nonprofit sector remains to be assessed, the professionalization of the sector is likely to increase it. Since the passage of the 1969 Tax Reform Act, the management of foundations and other nonprofit organizations has become steadily more professionalized. Led by schools of public health, which by the 1960s were attempting to upgrade and standardize hospital administration, the movement has spread to business schools, which have initiated programs in nonprofit management, as well as to the humanities, where courses in museum management, public history, and the administrative aspects of historic preservation are rapidly becoming standard fare.

This movement has brought with it many benefits. Supporters of nonprofits enjoy an unprecedented degree of accountability, as professionalized managers have learned to subject their organizations to the financial accounting standards of corporate businesses. Further, professional managers, trained in the techniques of marketing and fundraising, have been able to substantially increase the revenue bases and public exposure of their organizations. Finally, the quality of services in many nonprofit organizations has been dramatically increased. (Nowhere has this been more evident than in the field of historical organizations. Two decades ago, most were dingy and unvisited shrines celebrating the achievements of the wealthy and powerful. They are now far more sensitive to the diverse populations of communities, presenting their historical roles with the latest and most effective exhibition media.)

Although professionalization has certainly rationalized philanthropy, the question of whether it has increased its diversity remains unanswered. There is good reason to believe that it has not. First, as the 1985 study of foundation careers by Terry Odendahl and her associates suggests, professionalization has in practical terms meant that an increasing number of foundation executives are being recruited from within the foundation world.[18] If, as Lindeman asserted, "fixed responsibilities of administration, especially administration of wealth, tend invariably to develop in executives habits of conservatism and conventionality"—and he was writing of trustees, most of whom were laypeople—one would suppose that staff professionalization, whether in the form of sector inbreeding or academic training in nonprofit management, would only increase this tendency.[19] Indeed, if the outcomes of professional business management criticized by William J. Abernathy and Robert H. Hayes, James Fallows, and other commentators have any validity, the long-term consequence of philanthropic professionalization will be a further narrowing of the sector's outlook and activities.[20]

Another problem stemming from professionalization is what some commentators have identified as its implicit political agenda. The leading promoter of philanthropic professionalization has been the

Council on Foundations, an umbrella group that gathers and disseminates information on organized philanthropy and frequently represents the interests of foundations in legislative forums. In the wake of the Reagan administration's vows to drastically curtail social-welfare expenditures and affirmative-action efforts, the council began to move in a direction that some conservatives found profoundly disturbing:

> The Council is intended to function as a representative organization, encompassing the diverse perspectives of its nearly 1,000 members. But in recent years, it has become increasingly narrow, systematically excluding opposing points of view from its meetings, programs, and publications as it proselytizes for its own orthodoxies.
>
> At annual meetings, the need for balance has been abandoned in selecting panels for discussion of controversial topics. The Council's official publication, *Foundation News,* is now edited by a journalist previously employed by the Environmental Defense Fund, runs laudatory articles on the anti-nuclear movement and other favored "progressive" causes. And this year, for the first time ever, the Council requested members to sign a statement of "principles and practices" upon renewing their membership, committing themselves to the principle of affirmative action, etc.
>
> Soon, the Council will inaugurate a training program, for foundation and corporate contributions staffers, which will address not only "how to" issues, but "the broader philosophical and ethical concerns of grantmakers."[21]

Because council president James A. Joseph had publicly defined these concerns in terms of the empowerment of the poor and minorities, it is hardly surprising that the conservative foundation community regarded professionalization with intense suspicion.[22]

That professionalism carried with it a potential for politicization was nothing new. By the 1970s, prominent businessmen such as William E. Simon, David Packard, and Henry Ford II were warning corporations and foundations not to support institutions whose programs were detrimental to the interests of the free-enterprise system. As Ford said when he resigned from the board of the Ford Foundation in 1977, "the Foundation is a creature of capitalism [but] it is hard to discern recognition of this fact in anything the Foundation does. It is even more difficult to find an understanding of this in many of the institutions, particularly the universities, that are beneficiaries of the Foundation's grant programs."[23] All suggested that the misdirection of philanthropy and its organizational beneficiaries was due to the power of professionalized staffers, whom Simon in 1980 identified with a "new class of reformers" who were seeking "to reshape the future along collectivist lines."[24]

Even when political agendas are not the issue, managerial professionals may often reshape organizational policies in ways that run counter to the interests and desires of donors and trustees. Over the past five years, nonprofits management journals such as *Museum News* have been full of articles on the stages of organizational development. Interestingly, the major factor in institutional transformation is identified as the introduction of professional managers and its impact on the board of directors.[25] Conflicts between professional managers and boards seldom involve politics. More often, they focus on the definition and implementation of organizational goals, as well as adherence to standards of fiscal and curatorial responsibility. Nevertheless, the prevalence of such conflicts suggests a significant and largely unnoticed struggle for institutional control, which, in terms of the debate over diversity in the nonprofit sector, may be of considerable significance.[26]

Even when not concerned with empowerment and social justice, these struggles between boards and managerial professions are in a certain sense political in nature. Traditionally, small nonprofits reflected the interests of members, donors, and charismatic amateurs capable of mobilizing the resources of communities of interest. To the extent that the nonprofessional management of these organizations was accountable to anyone, it was only to the individuals who composed them. The activities of the organization, whether of good, bad, or middling quality, were really of concern to no one else. The addition of professional management greatly increased the complexity of the organization. While technically subservient to the wishes of boards and members, professional managers defined their goals in terms of their professional career interests. Thus, they sought to shape their organizations' activities to please both their boards and their professional peers. (While one would expect the members of a small museum to be delighted by the "professionalization" of the institution's offerings, this has not always been the case, for the purposes of such organizations are generally more complex than their charter purposes suggest).

Another factor in the professionalization of nonprofits management which has led to conflict among managers, boards, and donors is the freedom of the manager to cultivate and recruit new organizational constituencies. Whether taking the form of new funding sources, new members, or entrepreneurial strategies that enable the organization to be independent of board largess, this freedom gives the professional manager substantial autonomy to fundamentally alter the direction of an institution, the composition of its board, and the nature of its membership.

Whatever benefits may accompany professionalization—and it is still too early to evaluate its impact—it may also bring with it serious problems. First, it may decrease incentives for large-scale charitable giving because, as nonprofits become more professionalized, the relationship between big givers and managers becomes increasingly impersonal. Historically, there has been a close relationship between large-scale giving and the likelihood that an organization would maintain the interests of donors, their families, their businesses, and—in a more attenuated sense, their world-view and their class interests. Traditionally nonprofits, especially in the fields of education and culture, have been inordinately dependent on small groups of large donors.[27] Managerial techniques that reshape the market for nonprofits, by identifying new donor and consumer constituencies, decrease the dependence of organizations on these small groups. As professionally managed nonprofits become more market-oriented, they may create disincentives for giving by large donors. As nonprofits become more responsive to the desires of consumers, they become in a certain sense more democratic, but at a cost to pluralism, innovation, and excellence.[28]

The desirability of institutional democracy and rationality is a moot point. However, it does present one of the most difficult policy choices about the future of private philanthropy. Because we are a democracy, we are necessarily uncomfortable with the idea of enormous accumulations of private wealth devoted in perpetuity to public purposes, but operating without public accountability. From the Walsh investigations of the Progressive years, through the writings of Horace Coon (1938), Ferdinand Lundberg (1968), and Nielsen (1972), critics of private philanthropy have scored the irrationality, self-serving tendencies, and undue public influence of such entities.[29] At the same time, these features of private philanthropy are precisely the ones most productive of diversity, innovation, and pluralism—its most valuable contribution to the quality of American life. As Tocqueville noted with regard to the *ancien régime,* the very irrationality of its institutions "had the effect of maintaining in the minds of Frenchmen a spirit of independence and encouraging them to make a stand against abuses of authority."[30] In America, private nonprofit organizations came into being precisely for that purpose. But in the heyday of twentieth-century liberalism, the power of private wealth was more feared than the professionally administered central state, which, because its powers were untried, could still be regarded as the people's agent. However, the experience of the past two decades has shown that the establishment of a healthy, well-ordered freedom may be a more complex matter than one of institutional rationality and professionalism. Although not without its hazards, institutional *irrationality* may also have its benefits.

The Crisis in Nonprofits Scholarship

The rationalization of philanthropy was a good idea—but one that was based on fundamental misconceptions about the structure and function of the nonprofit sector. The first misconception involved the premise of sectoral independence, the belief following from it that the professionalized administration of large accumulations of private wealth in the public interest would ensure that nonprofits acted as a third force independent of, and standing between, government and business. The independence of the nonprofit sector was to be assured by the professionalism of its personnel and by government regulation.

This conception was appropriate to the years between 1945 and 1980, when the most obvious threats to the nonprofit sector appeared to be the rise of the welfare state and the "majoritarian" populisms of the Right and Left. These led both to increasing federal regulation and, with the rise of the Great Society, to the attachment of strings (such as affirmative-action guidelines) to federal aid. No one imagined that the *real* threat to the sector was not attacks on its independence, but that its independence was largely illusory.

As early as 1960, the illusory independence of the third sector began to be uncovered with the publication of *Education in the Forming of American Society,* Bernard Bailyn's historiographical work. Bailyn's critique of the relation between the history of education and the mainstream of historical scholarship is extraordinarily resonant in the context of the broader issue of nonprofits. Bailyn began by pointing out that the historiographical problem was not a lack of educational scholarship. "The field of study," Bailyn wrote,

> has not suffered from neglect, which firm direction and energetic research might repair, but from the opposite, from an excess of writing along certain lines and an almost undue clarity of direction. The number of books and articles on the schools and colleges of the colonial period, on methods of teaching, on the curriculum, school books, and teachers is astonishingly large; and since at least the end of the nineteenth century the lines of interpenetration and framework of ideas have been unmistakable. And yet, for all of this, the role of education in American history is obscure. We have almost no historical leverage on the problems of American education. The facts, or at least a great quantity of them, are there, but they lie inert; they form no significant pattern.

"What is needed," Bailyn continued, "is not so much a projecting of new studies as a critique of the old and, more important, an attempt to bring the available facts into relation with a general understanding of the course of American development." "In other words," Bailyn concluded, "the problem was not an absence of research, but the failure to pursue historical research within a theoretical framework that demonstrated the structural and functional relationship between education and other sectors of social, economic, political, and intellectual activity."[31]

The larger part of *Education in the Forming of American Society* is taken up with an effort to suggest the centrality of education to American society, but the most interesting and pointed part of the book deals with the question of why educational historiography had turned out to be so prolific and at the same time so theoretically sterile. He located the problem in the process of educational professionalization:

> The development of this historical field took place . . . in a special atmosphere of professional purpose. It grew in almost total isolation from the major influences and shaping minds of twentieth-century historiography; and its isolation proved to be self-intensifying: the more parochial the subject became, the less capable it was of attracting the kinds of scholars who could give it broad relevance and bring it back into the public domain. It soon displayed the weakness and extravagance of emphasis that are the typical results of sustained in-breeding.[32]

The main emphasis and ultimately the main weakness of the histories written by the educational missionaries of the turn of the century derived directly from their professional interests. Seeking to demonstrate the immemorial importance and evolution of theories and procedures of the work in which they were engaged, they directed their attention almost exclusively to the part of the educational process carried on in formal institutions of instruction. They spoke of schools as self-contained entities whose development had followed an inner logic and an innate propulsion. From their own professional work, they knew enough of the elaborate involvement of school and society to relate instruction somehow to the environment, but by limiting education to formal instruction they lost their capacity to see it in its full context and hence to assess the variety and magnitude of the burdens it had borne and to judge its historical importance.

Ironically, although Bailyn's book inspired a generation of historians to explore the social and intellectual basis of education, only a handful attempted to link the evolution of educational institutions to such fundamental structures as family, profession, and bureaucracy.

The range of scholarly interest remained surprisingly circumscribed. Only one scholar, John S. Whitehead,[33] attempted to explore the role of colleges in the process through which public and private sectors became differentiated. Only one scholar, Colin Burke, was willing to undertake a nationally focused, quantitative organizational survey of the emergence of colleges in the nineteenth century.[34] And the largest and most important historical issues—of financial support, governance constituencies, and the recruitment and distribution of college graduates—remain virtually unexplored.[35]

It was only when the Reagan administration turned to the nonprofit sector to provide those welfare and cultural services that it had always claimed as its particular province—while promising to massively reduce public spending in these areas—that the issues brought forth by Bailyn in 1960 began to be more generally perceived as significant. And this perception only happened because policy-oriented social scientists became aware, as they analyzed the likely effects of Reagan's budgetary measures, of the degree of the private nonprofit sector's dependence on federal revenues.

Certainly the most influential recognition of this fact came in 1981, when the Urban Institute published Salamon and Abramson's "The Federal Government and the Nonprofit Sector: Implications of the Reagan Budget Proposals."[36] This work was composed of detailed studies of federal spending in program areas of concern to nonprofits, the estimated impact of proposed federal budget cuts on nonprofit organizations, and the implications of those cuts for private giving and the future of the nonprofit sector. The work projected an alarming scenario in which the administration's proposed spending cuts would fall hardest on education, social welfare, and the arts—areas of particular concern to the sector. These areas were, moreover, particularly dependent on public funding. The work concluded with a grim assessment, based on past trends, of the likely inability of private giving to fill the revenue gap created by reductions in federal spending.

Salamon and Abramson's summary of principal findings began with this surprising assertion:

> The proposed Reagan budget cuts, if enacted, would significantly reduce the revenues available to a wide assortment of private, nonprofit organizations, ranging from symphony societies to social welfare agencies, from private colleges to local community organizations. These impacts result from the fact that nonprofit organizations have become active partners with the federal government in a broad range of public purposes. Because adequate data on the extent of this involvement are virtually nonexistent, however, the true impact of the proposed cuts on the nonprofit sector has been difficult to ascertain.[37]

This recognition of the interdependence of public and nonprofit sectors was couched in relatively ahistorical terms, because Salamon and Abramson evidently assumed that the public-private partnership they described was of fairly recent origin.

By 1985, Salamon had come to recognize that the relationship between government and the nonprofit sector was of considerable historical depth. His 1986 paper "Partners in Public Service: Government and the Nonprofit Sector in Theory and Practice" begins by citing a turn-of-the-century commentary on the role of public funding in the realm of private charity: When Alexander Fleisher pointed out in 1914 that no problem of social policy is "more harassing, more complex and perennial than that of determining the proper relation of the state to privately managed charities within its border," he was calling attention to a point that current observers of American society have tended to ignore: the "welfare state" has taken a peculiar form in the American context, a form that involves not only the expansion of the state but also an extensive pattern of government reliance on private, nonprofit groups to carry out public purposes. In a number of fields, government has turned more of the responsibility for delivering publicly financed services over to nonprofit organizations than they have retained for themselves. In the process, government has become the single most important source of income for most types of nonprofit agencies, outdistancing private charity by a factor of two to one. What Fleisher termed "the sore thumb of public administrative policy" has thus become the core of the nation's human-services delivery system and the financial mainstay of the nation's private, nonprofit sector.[38]

Salamon argues that the failure of scholars and policymakers to acknowledge the interpenetration of government and the private nonprofit sector is a product "not simply of an absence of research, but more fundamentally a weakness of theory":

> Both the theory of the "welfare state" and the theory of the voluntary sector have been deficient—the former because of its failure to differentiate between government's role as a provider of funds and its role as a deliverer of services; and the latter because of its tendency to justify the voluntary sector in terms of failures of government and market, and thus to make involvement by these other sectors in the world of nonprofits appear suspect at best.[39]

Perhaps because he is not an intellectual historian, Salamon does not pursue the question of why the "pervasive partnership" has remained unexamined. His interest is solely in tracing its policy implications and in demonstrating the extent to which Reagan's budgetary policies "inadvertently posed a threat to the viability of the sector in the pursuit on an effort to get government out of the sector's way."

Whereas Salamon's work has concentrated on the fiscal features of sectoral overlap, research in other areas is suggesting further dimensions of government-onprofit sector interpenetration. For example, it appears that the career patterns of policymakers have tended increasingly not only to cross sectoral lines but also, especially at the higher levels, to serially or simultaneously occupy strategically important positions in all three sectors.[40] Typical of such individuals was John Gardner, whose career led from university teaching (1936-42) to the Federal Communications Commission (1942-43)—and from government to the Carnegie Corporation of New York (1946-65), of which he became president in 1955. He also served as the president of the Carnegie Endowment for the Advancement of Teaching (1955-65). President Johnson tapped Gardner to be secretary of Health, Education, and Welfare (1965-68). After stepping down, he headed the Urban Coalition (1968-70) and Common Cause (1970-75), and was also one of the founders of Independent Sector (1980), the most important of the nonprofits trade associations. He served as a trustee of the New York School of Social Work (1949-55), the Metropolitan Museum of Art (1957-65), and Stanford University (1968-), and he also taught at Harvard's Kennedy School and MIT (1968-69) and served on a variety of government boards and commissions. Similarly, McGeorge Bundy's career path led from the Council on Foreign Relations (1948-49), to professorships and deanships at Harvard (1949-61), to the White House as President Johnson's national security adviser (1961-66), to the presidency of the Ford Foundation (1966-1979), and to an endowed professorship at New York University. Gardner and Bundy's contemporary Robert S. McNamara moved from a professorship at the Harvard Business School (1940-43) to the Ford Motor Company (1943-61), to the Defense Department (1961-68), and to the presidency of the World Bank (1968). He also served as a director of the Ford Foundation, the Brookings Institution, and the California Institute of Technology. Although career lines of this sort are part of the folklore of the scholarly Left, only recently have they begun to be systematically examined in a more disinterested way. John S. Stanfield's work on philanthropy and social science in the first half of the twentieth century delineates a useful paradigm of the intersectoral configuration as a network of patronage and personal relationships.

There has been a tendency for giving institutional elites to recruit keepers and appropriators of their funds from the same sociological generation. That is, people who become foundation officers and government agency administrators may not be of the same biological age range, but they share experiences in the same historical milieu which shapes the definition of science. Since giving institutional elites have a vested interest in employing those most knowledgeable about the newest paradigms, then drawing from the most contemporary sociological generation makes sense. To do otherwise would ultimately waste funds and lead to the development of outmoded programs which would become an embarrassment to the giving institution.[41]

Stanfield further argues that, as giving shifted from individuals to organizations, there has been a need both for philanthropic managers and for a coordination of institutional giving patterns. These, he asserts, serve the essentially economic purpose of reducing funding overlap and duplication. However, they also have cultural consequences:

> The need to coordinate giving on an organizational level has contributed to a generation affect. Although certainly there is a great diversity in personal values, world views, and organizational resources, the coordination of giving produces a network which standardizes procedures and general giving philosophies. It creates, in the anthropological sense, a culture of giving in which its participants adhere to similar traditions, values, and norms. This culture is structured in an organizational field which identifies the keeping and appropriating of funds as a career line. This last point is seen in the ease by which administrators of giving institutions exchange personnel. Although in the process of shifting from foundation to foundation or foundation to government agency an individual must make the necessary institutional adjustments, he/she will at least still be participating in the same organizational field, and therefore will know the routines of the giving.[42]

The work of Terry Odendahl and her associates, which focuses on the contemporary foundation scene, also emphasizes the intersectoral character of philanthropic career patterns.[43]

If the nonprofit sector is tied structurally to government and business as sources of revenue and personnel, as well as serving as a conduit for services essential to both, it is also substantively connected. Few have noted that one of the greatest ironies of the expansion of the welfare state between 1933 and 1980 was its remarkable dependence of government on the private sector—particularly private universities, foundations, and research institutes—as a source of policy formulation.[44]

There is hardly an area of federal activity—foreign affairs, race relations, economic policy—in which the primary intellectual paradigms and consensus-building activities have not originated in the private nonprofit sector. For example, in the years leading up to American involvement in World War II, the government, for obvious political reasons stemming from the strength of isolationist sentiment, was remarkably passive. Creating a bipartisan political consensus and shaping public attitudes in favor of American intervention fell entirely to a cluster of private voluntary organizations.[45] They handled the immediate tasks of coordinating leadership and public information and, more importantly, had, through the isolationist 1920s and 1930s, fostered the study of international affairs in the universities and brought together academics and policymakers. Similarly, public policy on race relations was influenced by the close relationship among a handful of foundations (the Rosenwald Fund, the Laura Spelman Rockefeller Memorial Foundation, and the Carnegie Corporation), private universities, and, once the federal government became seriously concerned about the "Negro Problem" after World War II, the government agencies whose task it was to translate privately generated research into workable legislation.

Finally, some organizational theorists have come to acknowledge the interdependence of the sectors as a matter worthy of attention. In 1982, Paul J. DiMaggio and Walter W. Powell published "The Iron Cage Revisited: Conformity and Diversity in Organizational Fields."[46] Their argument was addressed to the phenomenon of organizational homogenization—the tendency of organizations, whatever their purpose, to become more similar over time. Contrary to the conventions of organization theory, which posit a "diverse and differentiated world of organizations" and explain institutional change in terms of rational responses to a variety of forces (competition, innovation, public demand, and government policy), DiMaggio and Powell asserted that the world of organizations was surprisingly homogeneous and that the sources of homogeneity have less to do with rational efforts to realize institutional goals than with nonrational efforts to attain stability and reduce unpredictability through the introduction of organizational routine. More significant than their focus on nonrational factors in organizational change was their suggestion that the unit of analysis for studying institutional isomorphism was the "organizational field." By this they meant

> those organizations in a population that, in the aggregate, are responsible for a definable area of institutional life. In an organizational field, we would include key suppliers, resource and product consumers, and regulatory agencies, as well as other organizations that produce a similar service or product. The virtue of this unit of analysis is that it directs our attention not imply to competing units, as does the population approach of Hannan and Freeman (1977) and Aldrich (1979), or to networks of organizations that actually interact, as does the interorganizational network approach of Laumann et al. (1978) and Galaskiewicz (1978), but to the totality of relevant actors.[47]

As DiMaggio and Powell recognized, their viewpoint represented a considerable departure from the conventions of the social sciences. It not only focused on nonrational factors but also ignored the sectoral boundaries so central to most studies of institutional activity. Most interestingly, its central insights were derived not from the usual comparative and cross-sectional approach to organizations. Instead, like Salamon's recent work, it drew extensively on historical studies of institutional development.

The "new" nonprofits scholarship is still embryonic. Nevertheless, it appears to represent a powerful new direction of enquiry. This power stems from a number of sources. The scholarship draws on an intellectual discontent with unidisciplinary rationalism, whose roots go back to the early 1950s.[48] This discontent was given added impetus in the 1970s, as it appeared that the economic and sociological models on which the policies of the welfare state had been based were misguided. The rise of massive social dislocation, political violence, and runaway inflation belied the confident promises of a half-century of social engineering.[49] These two forces, one proceeding from intellectual enquiry, the other from public events, combined to give an urgency to efforts to look at the world in new ways. Within the field of history, a handful of scholars became aware that a focus on organizations could provide an integrated approach to the diversity of American life, tying together sectors, as well as facilitating multidisciplinary approaches to complex developmental patterns.[50] Within sociology, political science, and anthropology, small groups of scholars came to see both the importance of organizational studies as common disciplinary referent and the particular value of historical enquiry.[51]

The Reagan revolution brought about the final crystallization of the new approach to nonprofits. Its neo-Federalist rhetoric notwithstanding, Reaganism represented the naked rise of state power, purely politicized and uncloaked—as the liberal version had been—by a rhetoric of benevolence. Scholars who had been inclined to view the nonprofit sector somewhat cynically (when they looked at it at all), as part of the institutional system of corporate liberalism, came to realize after 1980 not only that the sector was genuinely endangered but also the possible consequences of its extinction.

It was not enough to perceive that the sector was at risk; more important was the need to understand the conditions necessary for its survival. To gain this understanding requires, as Salamon notes, not merely an increase in the quantity of scholarship, but major changes in the theoretical framework through which we view organizations. The interpenetration of sectors is an established fact. The epistemological problem is to devise methods that will enable us to grasp its extent and significance.

Theory and Policy

If the patterns of sectoral hybridization described by Salamon, Galaskiewicz, Odendahl, Stanfield, and others are as important as they appear, the pervasive characterization of the nonprofit sector as an independent one is not only misleading but also destructive. For at a time such as the present, in which the fundamental public policies that will determine the future of the sector are under active consideration, brave but misled scholarship could—and, as this chapter suggests, already has—work against the best interests of nonprofit enterprise.

The starting point for any serious consideration of the place of nonprofits in the American polity is to accept the policy implications of the scholarly recognition of sectoral interpenetration: that the nonprofit sector is a dependent sector, not an independent one. The choices that lie before it—and before the public as it seeks to redefine the role of government and its relation to the universe of private institutions—have primarily to do with the types and consequences of various kinds of dependency.

Dependency can be narrowly or broadly construed. Broadly, it involves fundamental positive conceptions of how states and societies should be organized: the boundaries between public and private spheres of action (sovereignty); the just distribution of resources and influence; and the accountability of corporate bodies public and private. Narrowly, dependency involves normative issues: sources of institutional revenue, governance mechanisms and constituencies, and the powers of regulatory agencies. The Tax Reform Act of 1969 focused on the normative issues of dependency. Its major provisions dealt with taxation on investment income and income from ownership of unrelated business, distribution of income requirements, self-dealing, excess business holdings, disclosure and reporting, and advocacy activities. However, the positive issues were left largely unexamined, primarily because both the congressional critics, led by Patman, and "responsible" spokesmen from the foundation community fundamentally agreed that the nonprofit sector could and should be an independent one. To be sure, the foundation world was deeply troubled by the series of investigations leading up to the 1969 Tax Reform Act. Many viewed the act itself as an unwarranted intrusion of government into the private sector.[52] But differences over strategy and rhetoric aside, both Congress and the foundations shared the set of positive premises about the sector and sought to devise normative mechanisms that would assure its independence.

The 1969 Tax Reform Act promoted important and long-needed reforms. But it also appears to have had distinctly negative effects on the nonprofit sector as a whole. Some of these effects did not become obvious until Salamon and Abramson's 1982 paper, which pointed out the dependency of the sector on government. Assessing the act's impact on the relations among business, private wealth, and nonprofits is a more complex matter. Some critics of the act argue that it has slowed the rate of foundation formation since 1970.[53] Others assert that the result of the act was that public support for charitable organizations of all kinds—including educational, medical, welfare, and cultural ones—was beginning to erode and that one of this nation's most precious assets, the concept of private initiative for the public good, was in serious danger.[54] Whatever the final verdict on the 1969 Tax Reform Act, it is doubtful that anyone will conclude that it encouraged diversity or innovativeness in the nonprofit sector, even it has left its growth unimpaired. Whatever gains the sector may have made over the last decade and a half will have been despite rather than because of the act.

The 1969 Tax Act was predicated on the false assumption that nonprofits were—or should be—an autonomous sector in which reforms could be instituted without regard to the social, political, and economic infrastructure on which they depended. The reality is that most nonprofits (churches aside) depend for their survival on revenues supplied by private wealth, corporate and private. Thus, meaningful legislation affecting nonprofits necessarily has to take into account the variety of reciprocal and mutually beneficial relationships between donors and recipient institutions that constitute a major, though by no means the only, incentive for their support.

A related misconception—shared by both legislators and nonprofits—bears on another aspect of the motives of charitable donors. Because so little has been known of the history of charitable giving before the late 1930s, with the introduction of steeply progressive income-tax legislation and the corporate charitable deduction, it has been generally assumed that tax avoidance has been a major incentive for individual and corporate philanthropy. F. Emerson Andrews, at one time considered the leading authority on philanthropy in the United States, went as far as to write that the dramatic changes in foundation formation and corporation giving after 1940 could be entirely explained by tax chronology.[55] Although the federal tax code undoubtedly played a major role in influencing giving patterns, there is reason to believe that its importance has been vastly overstated.[56] Its importance is belied not only by the long history of large-scale charitable giving which preceded the existence of a federal income tax, but also by the fact that, once tax legislation containing incentives for giving was in place, levels of donations seldom approached the maximum permitted by the code. The use of tax legislation to promote charitable giving constituted a negative incentive: people were encouraged to give not because they believed in an institution or a cause, but because such giving was rewarded by a reduction in monies owed the government. The force of this negative incentive over time appears to have eroded the capacity of donors to formulate positive rationales for giving—with unfortunate effects on both the amount and imaginativeness of giving. The recent survey by Yankelovich, Skelly, and White of the attitudes of top business managers toward corporate contributions gives abundant testimony to limited conception of this activity that prevails today.[57] Whereas once corporations made major investments in the welfare of their workers, in basic research and product development, and in their communities without any tax incentives for doing so, corporations today view contributions programs primarily as tax avoidance and public-relations devices—and support them accordingly. The need to encourage the development of positive rationales for individual and corporate giving constitutes one of the major challenges facing the nonprofit sector today. But, once again, this need requires a frank appraisal of the relation between private wealth and public power and an understanding of the essential dependency of the nonprofit sector.

Finally, recent developments in the field of health care have raised important questions about the efficiency of nonprofits as an organizational form. The rapid growth of the proprietary sector in health care, though increasing the fiscal effectiveness of health-care delivery, has, some have argued, distorted medical priorities, improving services for well-to-do consumers while reducing them for the poor, emphasizing spectacular surgical feats in favor of preventative programs that serve greater numbers of people, and replacing medical judgments on courses of therapy with actuarial mandates.

The health-care issue raises in its clearest form the importance of moving the debate over nonprofits policy away from emotionally charged rhetoric and false definitions toward a more dispassionate conception of the institutional universe as it has actually developed. As it existed before World War II, the largely private health-care system in the United States reflected primarily the interests of the medical professionals who ran it.[58] Medical care is decentralized and dependent for its revenues on fees, charitable giving, and endowment income, and both its quality and its accessibility varied enormously from place to place. Federal involvement in health care began after the war, with the underwriting of hospital construction and encouragement of the growth of private nonprofit medical-insurance plans. Because of the political power of organized medicine, the equitable distribution of health services remained a problem. Only with the creation of Medicare and Medicaid in the 1960s did quality health services become widely available. But the federal-reimbursement system introduced serious fiscal distortions into the system, inflating health-care costs, favoring certain medical specialties over others, and unjustly enriching dishonest practitioners. Finally, in the 1970s, fueled by the enormous federal and corporate outlays for health-care costs and a rising tide of neoconservative political sentiment, hospitals began to reorganize themselves on a for-profit basis. By the early 1980s, as the growth of federal spending on health slowed, medical treatment became unavailable in many places for the indigent and the uninsured.

Which institutional configuration was the more equitable? Which was the more efficient? The fundamental problem in each configuration stemmed not from whether health care was organized on a for-profit, public, or nonprofit basis, but on the relation between the health-care-delivery agency and the organizational field of which it was a part. Each pattern of dependency brought with it definable sets of advantages and disadvantages. None represented a golden age of either fiscal or moral perfection. However, a consideration of the alternatives suggests that the real issue is not the relative advantages of for-profits over nonprofits, but the consequences of particular institutional configurations and, in particular, the relations between different institutional sectors. The health-care problem presents in its clearest form the hazards of considering any organizational sector as freestanding, as well as the consequences of making policy as if it were.

The History and Theory of Organizations, Public Policy, and the Need for an Intermediate Synthesis

Certainly one of the most important lessons to be drawn from the tumultuous history of the modern world is that ideas matter. Although the optimistic efforts of twentieth-century social and economic planners to base public policy on the social sciences may have been premature, the impact of broad intellectual constructs about the possibilities and purposes of nations has been undeniable. And in times of social reconstruction, ideas take on particular importance in shaping events.

The shortcomings of the social sciences have stemmed primarily from their ahistoricity and their tendency to fragment and thereby distort the continuum of collective action. The shortcomings of history have stemmed from its narrow preoccupation with politics and individual personalities, its resistance to the analysis of collective behavior and normative patterns, and its adherence to rationalistic models of explanation.

Over the last thirty years, the social sciences and history have been converging in both interests and methods. It is a convergence with particularly important policy implications, because contemporary social policy, if it is to work effectively, has to be based both on serious appraisals of the capacities and resources of groups of individuals and institutions and on an understanding of how they have behaved over time. The issue is no longer one of the superiority of facts over theory, but a recognition of the interaction between the two and their mutual grounding in the continuous nature of the social process.

Any really adequate reappraisal of the nonprofit sector, therefore, is inevitably tied to the broader effort to reconstruct the enterprise of social understanding and to tie it more usefully to the formulation of public policy. This effort, appropriately enough, has focused on the history and theory of organizations, because those are both the entities most immediately affected by policy, as well as the aggregations of collective action most easily studied. It is not coincidental that the effort to reform ideas about society should focus to so large an extent on the institutions most centrally important to the generation and propagation of ideas. For, as the historical record shows, the process of social change often has more to do with changes in the institutional contexts in which activities are carried on than in the activities themselves. (This is the central lesson to be learned from the work of revisionist scholars David Rothman and Michael Katz.)[59]

When *Education in the Forming of American Society* appeared thirty years ago, Bailyn and other scholars in the avant garde of American history were concerned about the discipline's narrow preoccupation with political issues. Bailyn's book was an effort both to rescue the history of education from the educators, who had turned it into an exercise in self-justification, and to place at the center of scholarly awareness a concern with the crucial importance of the infrastructure of cultural institutions in the unfolding of the historical process. Bailyn's book focused only on education. But the same set of concerns might have been expressed about any one of the institutional activities in the fields of charity, welfare, health care, and culture, none of which had received significant scholarly attention. Fortunately, Bailyn's book was not idiosyncratic; it was symptomatic of a deeper concern within his field. And between 1960 and the present, some of the most interesting work in American history has been done by scholars who, in investigating the evolution of American society, have illuminated the development of cultural institutions— education, the professions, hospitals, museums, foundations—as well as the philanthropic activities that made their growth possible.

The burgeoning of these subfields has added immeasurably to the richness and variety of American historical scholarship. But, ironically, there has been little effort to synthesize this diversity. To be sure, some monographs made important linkages between the developing bodies of specialized knowledge: David F. Allmendinger's *Paupers and Scholars* (1973) connected the demographic crisis of nineteenth-century New England to the growth of educational institutions; Thomas Haskell's *The Emergence of Professional Social Science* (1977) tied the evolution of the social sciences to the general crisis of authority in postbellum America; and David F. Noble's *America by Design* (1977) firmly, though polemically, established the important relationships among business, the universities, and the natural sciences.[60] But true efforts at synthesis have been few and far between. Louis Galambos, the dean of the historians of organization, has made an important effort to delineate an institutional universe encompassing both for-profit and nonprofit entities.[61] And Burton J. Bledstein's *The Culture of Professionalism* (1976) attempted a premature but nevertheless important overview of the relation between bureaucratic organizations and class development.[62]

One of the most interesting dimensions of the movement in historiography toward a consideration of institutional universes is the accompanying recognition that, rather than borrowing from social theory, historians were making it. This awareness grew out of criticism of the ways in which some historians of the 1950s and 1960s had misused sociological and psychoanalytic theory. The most devastating of these critics was political scientist Michael Paul Rogin, whose *The Intellectuals and McCarthy* (1967) took to task pluralist historians such as Richard Hofstadter.[63]

The main thrust of Hofstadter's work had been to use the theories of mass politics developed by the Frankfort School as a basis for analyzing American political life. Rogin pointed out that Hofstadter's dichotomizing of politics into an ideological tradition, which was based on the irrational impulses of status groups, and a pragmatic tradition, rational by virtue of its links to concrete class and market interests, was both inaccurate and self-serving. Rogin's detailed political analysis showed that McCarthy's major electoral support came not from the projective rationalizations of old agrarian radicals, but from immigrant and other groups motivated by more tangible concerns. Rogin also suggested that the pluralist analysis had distorted the facts of American political and institutional life in order to legitimate the political role of academic intellectuals.

Another major source of the shift toward theoretical self-consciousness among American historians stemmed from the new interest in social history. Whatever the theoretical shortcomings of the pluralists, they succeeded in moving a generation of graduate students away from a narrow concentration on the history of articulate elites toward the study of the collective behavior of groups. Although most of this work was not theoretically focused, taking Weberian and Parsonian models of social transformation for granted, by the mid-1970s detailed examinations of the "modernization" of several dozen American communities raised questions about the adequacy of social theory.

In 1978, Thomas Bender published an unusually thoughtful critique of the use and misuse of social theory by American historians, *Community and Social Change in America*.[64] He pointed out not only the inability of theory to explain the complex processes that social historians were finding, but also the extent to which the oversimplifying tendencies of social theory were in large part due to the defective historical materials on which early sociologists such as Weber had been dependent in formulating their constructs.

American historical scholarship has followed no clear direction since the 1970s, though it has been profoundly affected by the political currents of the past decade. Reflecting the rise of neoconservatism, there has been an effort to abandon social analysis in favor of narrative. However, a handful of scholars has responded to the lure of theory and has directed its interests to exploring both the social context of organizational development and the rise of organizational systems.[65] Intellectually, the bridge between these theoretically oriented historians and the social science of organizational behavior has been through economic history. Although the work of William Miller and others in the 1950s had suggested the importance of organizational and social structural issues in economic behavior, the issue did not receive major attention until 1977, when Alfred D. Chandler's monumental *The Visible Hand* was published.[66] Chandler's book demonstrated not only the extent to which organizational and managerial issues had been overlooked by most historians, but also the theoretical impoverishment of organizational history even at its best. Although Chandler cast an impressively wide net, his delineation of the history of management was not only ultimately an exercise in technological determinism, dependent on dubious economic conception of economic rationality, but it also studiously ignored the extent to which the managerial revolutionaries and the institutions they created were dependent on a noneconomic infrastructure of law and internalized values. Because *The Visible Hand* was published at a time in which both the overall direction of economic policy and the specific performance of American managers had become a matter of public debate, the responses to the book brought together historians with theoretical concerns and social scientists who had come to recognize the extent to which their theoretical concerns could be illuminated by historical research.

These concerns only began to intersect with the policy debate over the future of the private nonprofit sector with the beginning of the Reagan revolution in 1981. At this point, analyses of the consequences of the proposed budget cuts of the president, his folkloric conceptions of the roles of family, corporation, community, and private voluntarism in American life, and his challenge to the positive assumptions of twentieth-century liberalism about the relation of public and private activity not only fostered a convergence of scholarly concerns but also highlighted the policy implications of scholarship.

The consequences of crisis and convergence for nonprofits scholarship seem clear. First, we are forced by political and economic realities to abandon the rhetoric of sectoral independence and philanthropy and to investigate those sensitive and often obscure regions of sectoral interdependence and interpenetration. Doing this requires in turn an abandonment of unidisciplinary approaches to organizational behavior, for such approaches invariably contain implicit premises about organizational and individual rationality which have little bearing on the realities of institutional life. These alterations in the normative dimensions of scholarship will necessarily have an impact on its positive content. For when scholars become conscious of the extent to which values are implicit in methods (and, consequently, the extent to which methods dictate outcomes), the importance of deliberate values choices is highlighted. Viewed from this perspective, scholarship becomes an active exercise of the moral imagination rather than a passive, mechanical, positivistic venture in the gathering of facts. The implications of this degree of scholarly responsibility are disturbing. But, as the current crisis in the nonprofit sector, in organizational scholarship, and in political life indicates, they present an unavoidable challenge.

3

"A Bridge Founded upon Justice and Built of Human Hearts": Reflections on Religion and Philanthropy

- Of the 916 projects listed in the 1986-87 compendium of research-in-progress compiled by Independent Sector, only 43 (4.7 percent) dealt specifically with religion.
- Of the 130 working papers produced by the "flagship" nonprofits research enterprise, only 2 (1.5 percent) specifically addressed religion or religious organizations. Of these 2, only 1 dealt with American religious organizations—and that with the technical question of how churches were treated under the federal tax code.
- Of the 2,195 books and articles listed in Daphne Layton's *Philanthropy and Voluntarism: An Annotated Biography* (1987), only 57 (2.1 percent) specifically dealt with religion.[1]

The scholarship of philanthropy has given religion remarkably short shrift. This deficiency is particularly striking in view of the fact that churches and denominationally tied institutions command nearly two-thirds of all the contributions, 34 percent of all volunteer labor, 19 percent of all the wage earners, and 10 percent of all wages and salaries in the nonprofit sector.[2]

This oversight is curious, not only because of the quantitative significance of religious organizations but also because of a number of compelling qualitative reasons for them as a part of the nonprofit sector: as organizations they share many processual and structural similarities with secular nonprofits, in particular a strong mission orientation; historically, secular and religious nonprofits have been closely associated; and, in the contemporary setting, there is suggestive evidence that churches play an important role in stimulating nonreligious voluntarism, whose impact is community-wide.

Why has religion been overlooked in efforts to understand voluntarism and philanthropy? Part of the answer may be that few scholars are likely to possess firsthand knowledge of what churches do and how they do it. The nature of funding for nonprofits research may also play a role, because less than 2 percent of foundation grants are awarded to religious organizations and, of these, only a minuscule proportion for studying religion.[3] The organization of nonprofits as an industry may also play a role in diminishing attention to the role of religious nonprofits: of the six hundred members of Independent Sector (IS) in 1985, only twenty-five (4 percent) were identifiable as religious organizations, including ten nondenominational but religiously oriented agencies, five Jewish, four Catholic, four Lutheran, and one each from the Methodists, Evangelicals, Churches of Christ, and Seventh Day Adventists.[4] Notably absent were such major denominations as Baptist (the nation's third-largest denomination), United Church of Christ (fifth-largest), Mormon (seventh-largest), Eastern Orthodox (eighth-largest), and Episcopalian (ninth-largest).[5] Interestingly, the amount of research devoted to religious nonprofits is roughly proportional to the representation of religious organizations in IS and to the number of foundations having religion as a field of interest.

Although it is clear that the mainline nonprofits have had little interest in religion, it is equally evident that religion had little interest in the mainline nonprofits. When the great circling of the wagons of nonprofitdom began in the 1960s, the churches, on the whole, stayed clear of the trade-association impulse. Some may have believed themselves immune from the sanctions that were being imposed on foundations. Others may have found the trade associations' stands in favor of such things as affirmative action, participatory governance, and public accountability incompatible with their own convictions. Whatever the cause, the aloofness of religious organizations complimented secular scholarship's indifference to the role of religion in American philanthropy and voluntarism.

The Origins of Modern Philanthropy

The wariness with which organized religion and organized philanthropy regard each other today has deep historical roots. These involve not only the contention of religious and secular institutions for "the high moral ground" but also, more fundamentally, differences of conviction and outlook. In order to grasp these differences, it is necessary to briefly review the origins of organized American philanthropy and its relation to organized religion.

Modern American philanthropy came into being in the last third of the nineteenth century, when the dislocations caused by rapid industrialization and urbanization outstripped the capacity of existing institutions to care for the poor and dependent. In particular, the rising tide of crime, violence, and social disorder between 1877 and 1893 led many Americans to think seriously about the ties between progress and poverty.

To some, it seemed quite clear that traditional forms of charity and almsgiving were not only inadequate to the task of alleviating misery but also actually aggravated it. The strongest proponents of this viewpoint were those influenced by Darwinist social theories, especially those of the British political economist Herbert Spencer. Spencer's leading American spokesman also happened to be the nation's wealthiest industrialist, Andrew Carnegie. Carnegie gave clearest expression to the modern conception of "scientific" philanthropy in his famous 1889 essay "Wealth." "Those who would administer [wealth] wisely," wrote Carnegie,

> must indeed be wise; for one of the serious obstacles to the improvement of our race is indiscriminate charity. It were better for mankind that the millions of the rich were thrown into the sea than so spent as to encourage the slothful, the drunken, the unworthy. Of every thousand dollars spent in so-called charity today, it is probably that nine hundred and fifty dollars is unwisely spent—so spent, indeed, as to produce the very evils which it hopes to mitigate or cure.[6]

"The best means of benefiting the community," he continued,

> is to place within its reach the ladders upon which the aspiring can rise— free libraries, parks, and means of recreation, by which men are helped in body and mind; works of art, certain to give pleasure and improve the public taste; and public institutions of various kinds, which will improve the general condition of the people; in this manner returning their surplus wealth to the mass of their fellows in the forms best calculated to do them lasting good.[7]

Carnegie's radical scheme called for nothing less than the use of private wealth to attack the causes of poverty and dependency rather than merely using it to alleviate their symptoms.

Carnegie's proposals were based on a carefully reasoned Darwinist reinterpretation of society and the place and purposes of the individual within it. As a Darwinist, Carnegie viewed the life of the community as a collective phenomenon, in which the struggle for existence, more than merely ensuring the survival of the fittest, created a hierarchy of relationships of mutual dependency. The "men of affairs," as he referred to the administrators of industry and its wealth, were inevitably dependent on their employees, as their employees were dependent on them.[8] In this setting, "the life of the race"—the good of the community—involved society's capacity for continuous self-renewal, through the preservation of conditions that encouraged individual initiative to continuously create and re-create enterprises. In this process, philanthropy played a vitally important role, not only by "placing within their reach ladders upon which the aspiring can rise," but also by continuously redistributing wealth. Carnegie's comment that "he who dies rich dies disgraced" was more than an injunction to charity—it was a pragmatic acknowledgment of the extent to which economic and social progress depended on the circulation of wealth, and he took it seriously enough to suggest the imposition of confiscatory inheritance taxes and progressive income taxation.

Carnegie's view of society—which was the framework that shaped his ideas about philanthropy—rested on quantitatively based concepts of efficiency.[9] Just as in his business he had pioneered cost accounting, so in looking to the larger problems of society he sought to relate calculable inputs to calculable outputs. From this economistic approach followed a number of significant departures from traditional charitable practice. Because the value of philanthropic investments was to be calculated in terms of the measurable effectiveness of investments, philanthropists must, of necessity, shift their attention from the symptoms of poverty and dependency (suffering) to their causes. This shift required that they turn their attention from alleviating the sufferings of individuals to impersonal and abstract problems, systems, and institutions. Finally, scientific philanthropy involved a shift from attending to the subjectively defined *needs* of individuals to the *eligibility* of individuals for assistance: Were they "worthy" or "unworthy"? Were they potentially good investment vehicles?

Despite their radicalism, Carnegie's ideas were, on the whole, well-received. This acceptance doubtlessly stemmed from the extent to which they meshed with the thinking of those who, by the 1880s, had given the greatest attention to the problems of maintaining social and economic order in this especially turbulent period. Certainly the most important of these groups were the "charity organization societies," which, beginning in the late 1870s, were striving to rationalize charitable services and promote cooperation among charitable agencies.

Although influenced by social Darwinism, this movement's preoccupation with "lavish, uninformed, and aimless" charity, which "encouraged pauperism and imposture," was actually an outgrowth of the secularized social-reform activities of the antebellum decades.[10] These activities had originated in a religious movement, the second Great Awakening, which had sought to redeem America from "those Errors in matters of Religion and Government, and that declension in manners, which so much prevail, and which greatly endanger the well-being of the State."[11] Over time, these efforts had become increasingly secular in emphasis, focusing less on religion than on character formation. Bible, tract, moral, missionary, and Sabbatarian societies of the 1820s gave rise to nondenominational temperance, abolitionist, and young men's associations, as well as more focused activities directed to the poor and disabled, to public health, and to the abolition of slavery.[12] Despite this secular shift, the central theme of antebellum reform remained moralistic: poverty, dependency, and ill health were products of defective character, failures of "moral prophylaxis." Because democratic government was, by definition, incapable of exercising a moral influence, the role of voluntary associations was to supply the moral dimension that would otherwise be lacking.

By the 1850s, voluntary charitable efforts were so ubiquitous that reformers had begun to worry about inefficiency, waste, and duplication of effort.[13] However, underlying this economistic rhetoric was a more profound anxiety about the charitable elite's failure to stem the tide of democracy.[14] The United States Sanitary Commission, a private organization to which the government in 1862 entrusted coordination of relief, sanitary inspection of army camps, and provision of nurses, hospitals, and ambulance services, became the paradigm for the reformulation of charitable activities in the postwar period.

Drawing its members from among "men brought up in luxury, with all the advantages of high and generous culture," the commission was less concerned with the alleviation of suffering than with reducing war costs for the taxpayer and preserving the soldier, or "producer," when he "returned to the industrial pursuits of civil life."[15] Even more important than this, the members of the commission regarded their work as "a matter of teaching order and discipline:"

Men such as Henry Bellows, George Templeton Strong, and Charles Stille welcomed the sufferings and sacrifices of the hour because they believed they served the cause of discipline in a broader sense than that demanded by purely military requirements. An unruly society, devoted to individual freedom, might be in the process of learning that discipline and subordination were good in themselves, and the commissioners wanted to play their role in teaching this lesson.[16] In line with this, the commission

> regarded the spontaneous benevolence of the American people, not as something embodied and expressed in their own work, but as a great danger to the discipline of the army which it was their business to limit and control. The desire of people at home to bring comfort and relief to the soldiers was regarded by the conservatives on the commission in much the way they had regarded the reform impulse before the war. If not limited and controlled, it would be a danger to established institutions.[17]

The charity organization societies were based on the same rationale as the Sanitary Commission and, in many cases, were set up by its veterans. Like its wartime predecessor, a charity organization society was

> a semi-official body of prominent citizens who inspected public institutions such as poor houses and work houses—much in the way the Sanitary Commissioners had inspected the camps—and made recommendations, based on "scientific" principles. Like the commission, it placed members of the upper classes in positions of influence which were immune from the pressures of democratic politics. If the Sanitary Commission had been devoted to military efficiency at the expense of purely humanitarian ends, the State Charities Aid Association was apparently more interested in the efficiency of the labor force than in the relief of suffering. It opposed public relief as "undermining the self-respect of recipients, fostering a spirit of dependence opposed to self-support, and interfering with the laws governing wages and labor.[18]

Not surprisingly, charity organizers found social Darwinism a congenial doctrine—and it became the common ground for alliances with pragmatic "men of affairs" such as Carnegie, whose vast wealth could be harnessed to higher purposes than mere conspicuous consumption.

The third strand of modern American philanthropy led from the thought of the classic political economists of the late-eighteenth and early-nineteenth centuries. Beginning with Malthus' "Essay on Population" (1798), English social thinkers had devoted considerable attention to the problems of poor relief, the need for reforming the Elizabethan poor law, and the conditions of industrial labor. Although political economists, who upheld free trade and abhorred government interference, and philanthropists, who advocated government action to protect factory operatives, were at loggerheads for decades, by the 1870s the spokesmen for "the dismal science" and the "humanity mongers" had drawn together.[19] Once again, social Darwinism was the medium of accommodation between these two seemingly incompatible viewpoints. The communitarian and perfectionist concerns of the philanthropists meshed with the Darwinists' interests in the "life of the race" and evolution. Their particular meeting ground was the process of selection, which, in human societies, was clearly subject to rational control. Both agreed that natural selection was "not only a harsh, but an expensive way of improving the species"; and both came to agree that, by rationally ordering the environment, the process of selection could become more efficient and less costly.[20]

The significance of this accommodation was more institutional than intellectual. In the 1860s, political economy was the concern of only a handful of academics. Essentially a deductive philosophical enterprise, the field had languished, in large part because of the resistance of college benefactors, many of whom were staunch advocates of tariff protection of American industry, to its free-trade doctrines.[21] Social Darwinism, in providing a rationale for empirical and inductive social and economic research, created an opportunity for academic careerists; the economic and social crises of the 1870s underlined the importance of this shift of emphasis. The formation of the American Social Science Association in 1868 was the first tangible sign of the eagerness of political economists to make themselves indispensable in "fighting the wilderness, physical and moral," which Americans found themselves facing in the decades following the Civil War.[22] The creation of this cadre of highly trained, university-based professional specialists was the cornerstone in the foundation of "scientific" philanthropy.

When social Darwinist ideology, industrial wealth, and academic expertise came together in the 1890s, modern American philanthropy was born. Underwritten by the millionocracy and guided by the academic enterprise that industrialists so generously funded, philanthropy was part and parcel of the broader movement that one historian has called "the corporate reorganization of American life."[23] Although employing a rhetoric of benevolence, "scientific" philanthropy's desire to put charity on a businesslike basis was anything but humanitarian. Philanthropy was far more concerned with efficiency and "race progress" than with alleviating suffering, and Amos Warner, one leading writer on philanthropic subjects, commented that

the most obvious result of charity as a selective force has been to lengthen the lives of the individuals cared for. There are many who believe it to be in and of itself a uniformly desirable result. They hold that no spark of human life can be extinguished without greater indirect loss than the direct gain which comes in freedom from the necessity of supporting the individual. They would care with all tenderness for the most misshapen, physically and morally, until death could no longer be postponed. As the author has stood by the beds of consumptive or syphilitic children, he has wondered if it was a kindness to keep life in the pain-racked body. Cure was out of the question so far as medical science now knows, and one wonders why days of pain should be added to days of pain. The same questions recur as one passes through the incurable wards of an almshouse, especially as one studies the cases of cancer patients. The answer of religion to such questions is easy, and it seems very sure that without religious incentive we should not have entertained our present views regarding the sanctity of human life.[24]

According to Warner, because religion stood in the way of putting the unfit out of their misery, the only alternatives to extermination as a cure for pauperism were "preventative measures in proportion as the burden of the dependent has increased and the standard of care risen, the search has spread from symptoms to causes, from causes to conditions of poverty, and culminated in a concerted demand for prevention rather than relief."[25] Such preventative measures included forbidding the marriage of insane and idiotic persons, those afflicted with syphilis and gonorrhea, and epileptics. The writer also urged the castration and "permanent isolation" of the "essentially unfit:"

> The movement to establish philanthropic monasteries and nunneries for the feeble-minded is becoming the substitute for natural selection. The prevention of marriage of the unfit, the sterilization of criminals, and the custodial care of the imbecile are initial steps in prevention—that the unfit may cease to be produced and to produce. . . . Certain it is, that while charity may not cease to shield the children of misfortune, it must, to an ever increasing extent, reckon with the laws of heredity, and do what it can to check the spreading curse of race deterioration.[26]

Although the rise of fascism made this kind of thinking unfashionable, it is important to remember that, through the 1930s, this kind of social Darwinist brutalism remained perfectly respectable and continued to dominate the thinking of many grant makers and the charities that benefited from their largess.

Religion and Philanthropy

Warner's ill-concealed contempt for "the unfit" and for those who would care for "the most misshapen, physically and morally" expressed the sentiments of not only the emerging cadre of secular philanthropists but also a Protestant mainstream. As early as the 1850s, a vigorous pamphlet battle had been waged between churchmen who favored institutionally based "scientific" approaches to social problems and those who argued that "the work of the real disciples of Christ must be performed by them individually, and not by the church. The love for men which ought to glow in the bosom of individual Christians could never dwell in a corporation or ecclesiastical organization."[27]

The institutionalists of the 1850s became the Sanitary Commission boosters of the 1860s, who, by the 1870s, were setting up charity organization societies and arguing, as did Henry Ward Beecher, that any workingman unable to support his family on a dollar a day was morally deficient and that railroad strikers should be subdued with "bullets and bayonets, canister and grape."[28] Anti-institutionalism never really achieved any large-scale organizational expression; it merely remained as a persistent but troubling reminder that the mission of the church might not be as easily translatable into programs of social action in the world as some seemed to believe.

To say that this spiritual emphasis did not achieve organizational expression is not to argue that it was without significance. The younger clergy—those entering pulpits during the turbulent period between the panics of 1873 and 1893—as well as many in the laity, responded to the tide of suffering and disorder as a distinctly spiritual challenge. Walter Rauschenbusch, who served an immigrant congregation in New York's Hell's Kitchen in the 1890s, described the impact of seeing "good men go into disreputable lines of employment and respectable widows consent to live with men who would support them and their children. One could hear human virtue cracking and crumbling all around."[29] Confronting suffering as an immediate human issue rather than as a set of textbook abstractions or newspaper alarms forced ministers such as Rauschenbusch to rethink their theology, to ponder the meaning of charity, and to recast the role of the church and its ministry as a social force.

Certainly one of the most touching and widely read accounts of this process is the Charles M. Shelton's novel *In His Steps* (1897).[30] Its protagonist, the Reverend Henry Maxwell, presides over a wealthy downtown church. In the midst of a Sunday service, a "dusty, worn, shabby-looking young man" appeared in Maxwell's church:

> There was nothing offensive in the man's manner or tone. He was not excited, and he spoke in a low but distinct voice. "I'm not an ordinary tramp, though I don't know of any teaching of Jesus that makes one kind of a tramp less worth saving than another. Do you?" He put the question as naturally as if the whole congregation had been a small Bible class. He paused a moment and coughed painfully. Then he went on.
>
> "I lost my job ten months ago. I am a printer by trade. The new linotype machines are beautiful specimens of invention, but I know six men who have committed suicide inside of the year because of these machines. Of course, I don't blame the newspapers for getting the machines. Meanwhile, what can a man do? I know I have only learned one trade, and that's all I can do. I've tramped all over the country trying to find something. There are many others like me. I'm not complaining, am I? Just stating the facts.
>
> "But I was wondering, as I sat there under the gallery, if what you call following Jesus is the same thing as what He taught. What did he mean

when He said: 'Follow me!'" Here the man turned about and looked up at the pulpit. "The minister said that it is necessary for the disciples of Jesus to follow His steps, and he said these steps are obedience, faith, love, and imitation. But I did not hear him tell you what that meant, especially the last step. What do you Christians mean by following the steps of Jesus?

"I've tramped through this city for three days trying to find a job. In all that time I've not had a word of sympathy or comfort. . . . What I feel puzzled about is—what is meant by following Jesus? What do you mean when you sing 'I'll go with Him, with Him, all the Way?' Do you mean that you are suffering and denying yourselves? Are you trying to save lost and suffering humanity as I understand Jesus did? What do you mean by it?

". . . somehow I get puzzled when I see so many Christians living in luxury and singing 'Jesus, I my cross have taken, all to leave and follow Thee,' and remember how my wife died in a tenement in New York City, gasping for air and asking God to take the little girl too. Of course I don't expect you people can prevent everyone from dying of starvation, lack of proper nourishment, and tenement air. But what does following Jesus mean? I understand that Christian people own a good many of the tenement houses. A member of the church was the owner of the one where my wife died, and I have wondered if following Jesus all the way was true in his case?"[31]

The tramp then fell forward and died on the communion table while everyone stood in horrified silence. As Shelton noted, this event was destined to make "a remarkable change" in the "definition of Christian discipleship" for Maxwell and certain members of his congregation—as well as for the community in which they lived.

Although this immensely popular book proceeded to spin a rather fantastic millenarian tale in which businessmen, newspaper editors, lawyers, and doctors began putting their Christian principles into practice and ultimately reforming American society, there was nothing imaginary about its starting point—the stark confrontation between Christian ideals and the realities of suffering. As Shelton took pains to point out, the moralistic pronouncements of the social Darwinists and the advocates of charity organization societies simply did not apply to the immediate human realities of suffering. Blaming the poor for their poverty in an economy in which human destinies were so profoundly affected by technological change and global markets simply did not make sense. Explaining the causes of poverty "scientifically" and formulating programs for its eradication did not did nothing to alleviate the hunger, fear, and humiliation of those who suffered from it.

A minister with a background in social work, Shelton directly challenged the social Darwinism of philanthropists such as Carnegie and Warner, whose *American Charities* had appeared three years before *In His Steps*. Serving as minister of a Congregational Church in Topeka, Kansas, a state where the catastrophic decline of commodity prices after 1873 had impoverished a once staunchly Republican farming population and converted it into a bulwark of Populism, Shelton knew that poverty and dependency were more than a matter of moral deficiency.[32] For Shelton, as for many others who knew the facts of poverty firsthand, the impersonal and parsimonious solutions of Warner and the other "scientific" philanthropists made no sense in terms of the facts of poverty.

More to the point, Shelton and others found it difficult to reconcile the "scientific" philanthropists' view of the "essentially unfit" to their reading of Scripture. Nowhere was this clearer than in regard to texts such as Luke 10:25–37, which narrates the parable of the Good Samaritan:

And behold, a certain lawyer stood up, and tempted him, saying, Master, what shall I do to inherit eternal life? He said unto him, What is written in the law? how readest thou?

And he answering said, Thou shalt love the Lord they God with all thy heart, and with all thy soul, and with all they strength, and with all thy mind; and thy neighbor as thyself.

And he said unto him, Thou hast answered right: this do, and thou shalt live.

But he, willing to justify himself, said to Jesus, And who is my neighbor?

And Jesus answering, said, a certain man went down from Jerusalem to Jericho, and fell among thieves, which stripped him of his raiment, and wounded him, and departed, leaving him half dead.

And by chance there came down a certain priest that way; and when he saw him, he passed by on the other side.

And likewise a Levite, when he was at the place, came and looked on him, and passed by on the other side.

But a certain Samaritan, as he journeyed, came to where he was: and when he saw him, he had compassion on him.

And went to him, and bound up his wounds, pouring in oil and wine, and set him on his own beast, and brought him to an inn, and took care of him.

And on the morrow, when he departed, he took out two pence, and gave them to the host, and said unto him, Take care of him: and whatsoever thou spendest more, when I come again, I will repay thee.

Which of these three, thinkest thou, was the neighbor unto him that fell among the thieves?

And he said, He that showed mercy upon him. Then said Jesus unto him, Go, and do thou likewise.

Here and in other texts, Christ demanded a kind of brotherly love that did not calculate, that did not draw distinctions between the "worthy" and the "unworthy," the "fit" and the "unfit." Love of one's neighbor, like one's love of God, had to be absolute and unconditional.

This reading of Scripture had a number of rather startling implications. On the practical side, it implied that one could not separate one's work in the world from one's beliefs. This was precisely the point that Christ seemed to be making in Mark 10:17–30, when he drew a distinction between obeying the Ten Commandments, a merely legal exercise, and faith:

And when he was gone forth into the way, there came one running, and kneeled to him, and asked him, Good Master, what shall I do that I may inherit eternal life?

And Jesus said unto him, Why callest thou me good? There is none good, but one, that is God.

Thou knowest the commandments, Do not commit adultery, Do not kill, Do not steal, Do not bear false witness, Defraud not, Honour thy father and mother.

And he answered and said unto him, Master, all these things have I observed from my youth.

Then Jesus beholding him loved him, and said unto him, One thing thou lackest: go thy way, sell whatever thou hast, and give to the poor, and thou shalt have treasure in heaven; and come, take up the cross and follow me.

And he was sad at that saying, and went away grieved: for he had great possessions.

And Jesus looked around about, and saith unto his disciples, How hardly shall they that have riches enter into the kingdom of God!

And the disciples were astonished at his words. But Jesus answereth them, Children, how hard it is for them that trust in riches to enter into the kingdom of God!

It is easier for a camel to go through the eye of a needle, than for a rich man to enter into the kingdom of God.

And they were astonished out of measure, saying among themselves, Who then can be saved?

And Jesus looking upon them, saith, With men it is impossible, but not with God: for with God all things are possible.

Then Peter began to say unto him, Lo, we have left all, and have followed thee.

And Jesus answered and said, Verily I say unto you, There is no man that hath left house, or brethren, or sisters, or fathers, and children, and lands, for my sake, and the gospels,

But he shall receive an hundred-fold now in this time, houses, and brethren, and sisters, and mothers, and children, and lands, with persecutions; and in the world to come, eternal life.

Shelton, Rauschenbusch, and their contemporaries were sophisticated enough to understand that Christ was not merely condemning wealth and urging the virtues of poverty. Rather, he was asserting the primacy of spiritual over worldly obligations. More importantly, he was challenging his questioner to make a choice between one and the other—and, as the subsequent discussion with the disciples indicates, it was the capacity to make that choice, to truly love both God and one's neighbor, that constituted the core of "walking in his steps." This was, of course, the very choice that confronted Shelton's protagonist, the Reverend Henry Maxwell.

Shelton, Rauschenbusch, and the other ministers who rejected "scientific" philanthropy were not alone in believing that Christian charity involved far more than the economical provision of services. As important, if not more so, was the creation of a community of feeling, a set of human bonds, which was, in itself, perhaps more valuable than the services themselves. Jane Addams suggested as much in her 1892 essay "The Subjective Necessity for Social Settlements":

The impulse to share the lives of the poor, the desire to make social service, irrespective of propaganda, express the spirit of Christ, is as old as Christianity itself. We have no proof that the early Roman Christians, who strained their simple art to the point of grotesqueness in their eagerness to record a "good news" on the walls of the catacombs, considered this good news a religion. Jesus had no set of truths labeled Religious. On the contrary, his doctrine was that all truth is one, that the appropriation of it is freedom. His teaching had no dogma to mark it off from truth and action in general. He himself called it a revelation—a life. These early Roman Christians received the Gospel message, a command to love all men, with a certain joyous simplicity. . . . The Christians looked for the continuous revelation, but believed what Jesus said, that this revelation, to be retained and made manifest, must be put into terms of action; that action is the only medium man has for receiving and appropriating the truth. . . .

That Christianity has to be revealed and embodied in the line of social progress is a corollary to the simple proposition that man's action is found in his social relationships in the way in which he connects with his fellows; that his motives for action are the zeal and affection with which he regards his fellows. By this simple process was created a deep enthusiasm for humanity, which regarded man as at once the organ and the object of revelation; and by this process came about the wonderful fellowship, the true democracy of the early Church, that so captivates the imagination. The early Christians were pre-eminently nonresistant. They believed in love as a cosmic force. . . . The spectacle of the Christians loving all men was the most astounding Rome had ever seen. They were eager to sacrifice themselves for the weak, for children, and for the aged; they identified themselves with slaves and did not avoid the plague; they longed to share the common lot that they might receive constant revelation. It was a new treasure which the early Christians added to the sum of all treasures, a joy hitherto unknown in the world—the joy of finding the Christ which lieth in each man, but which no man can unfold save in fellowship. . . .

I believe that this turning, this renaissance of the early Christian humanitarianism, is going on in America, in Chicago, if you please, without leaders who write or philosophize, without much speaking, but with a bent to express in social service and in terms of action the spirit of Christ.[33]

It is difficult to imagine Addams accommodating herself to the economistic motives and methods of "scientific" philanthropy. She described her attempts at cooperation with Chicago's newly organized Bureau of Organized Charities in the bitterest terms, telling how, in attempting to conform to its "carefully received instructions," she had refused relief to a shipping clerk who had lost his job.[34] A white-collar worker forced to work outside in the winter as a manual laborer, the man contracted pneumonia and died. "I have never lost trace of the two little children he left behind him," Addams wrote, "though I cannot see them without a bitter consciousness that it was at their expense I learned that life cannot be administered by definite rules and regulations; that wisdom to deal with a man's difficulties comes only through some knowledge of his life and habits as a whole; and that to treat an isolated episode is almost sure to invite blundering."[35]

Despite this experience, Addams could never wholly reject the ideas of the "scientific" philanthropists, because the sheer magnitude of the problems she faced seemed to require a wholesale rather than a retail approach to charity. As Henry Steele Commager so artfully put it, "more and more she came to feel like Alice with the Red Queen: no matter how fast she ran, she was still in the same place; the poverty, the slums, the crime and vice, the misgovernment, the illiteracy, the exploitation, the inhumanity of man to man—all these were still there."[36] Overwhelmed, she persuaded herself that "scientific" philanthropy could be humanized—and the union of the two traditions were symbolized in 1905, with her election as president of the National Conference on Charities and Corrections and the merger of the journals of charity-organization and settlement-house movements into *Charity and the Commons.*

Although Addams never ceased to believe that "scientific" philanthropy could be humanized, in her eagerness to be politically and organizationally effective she may have traded away those aspects of her work which made it so distinctive. As welfare historian Michael B. Katz points out, in exchange for the Progressives' adoption of a social-legislation plank authored by Addams (who also seconded the nomination of Theodore Roosevelt as the party's presidential candidate), "Addams and her colleagues decided to swallow their liberal convictions and accepted the convention's refusal to seat black delegates, and they set aside their pacifism when they failed to protest the platform's calls for rearmament."[37] Later efforts to reassert these moral claims came too late—by the 1920s, "social work" as a profession carried on in the framework of public bureaucracies and privately funded universities and social-service agencies had supplanted personal and religious commitment as the basis for charitable activity.

Although the rhetoric of social-welfare work owed much to Addams, in practice, as it emerged in the 1920s, it was more firmly rooted in the economistic than the religious traditions of charity. This is especially clear in volumes such as *Recent Social Trends in the United States,* the 1933 compendium that, among other things, sought to summarize the social-welfare achievements of the previous three decades. The chapter on "privately supported social work," by Sydnor H. Walker of the Rockefeller Foundation, was sharply critical of charity in the 1890s for its "marked obtuseness to the existence of any personal feelings or of a defined personality among the recipients of social work."[38] While asserting that "the private social agencies were approaching the old problems of poverty and delinquency in a new positive spirit," Walker's use of a humanized rhetoric fails to mask the fact that the old economism was alive and well: the chapter devotes most of its attention to standards, coordination, centralization, and other professional issues.

By the 1930s, it was quite clear that the religious spirit that had informed much of the charity of the 1890s had succumbed to mere fact-finding. "In the end," Katz wrote of this, "the reformers' path to professionalism tied the management of social change to the development of their own careers. Along with university-based social scientists, who had faced similar career problems a few decades earlier, they made the trip from 'advocacy to objectivity' by resting the case for their authority and importance on the capacity of neutral experts to find technical solutions to complex problems. Somehow, those neutral technical solutions usually supported whomever it was that paid the bill."[39]

Religion and Philanthropy in the Postliberal Era

The gradual assumption of social-welfare responsibilities by government which began with the Progressive movement of the early twentieth century obscured the differences between religion and philanthropy which so concerned Americans a century ago. Christian conceptions of brotherly love and secular conceptions of charity and philanthropy have become almost indistinguishable. And yet, beneath the rhetoric, tensions have remained: the absence of scholarly attention to religion referred to at the beginning of this chapter is only one symptom of a far more fundamental unease, which, in recent years, has begun to reemerge.

In the 1960s, an increasing federal commitment to social welfare and health-care services, combined with the use of private nonprofit vehicles for providing services, fueled demands for greater efficiency and effectiveness and the elimination of waste, duplication, and overlap. The spiraling inflation of the 1970s and the budgetary austerity of the 1980s forced caregiving agencies to not only do more with less, but also justify their programs, procedures, and policies to an increasingly competitive array of public and private funders. On the organizational level, evaluation and assessment, strategic analysis and planning, managerial professionalization, and sophisticated accounting systems were put in place in the hope of making philanthropy more business-like. On the system level, ambitious plans were drafted to encourage cooperation, cost and facilities sharing, and a rational division of funding, labor, and markets in the hope of eliminating duplication and waste.

Although few failed to give lip service to efficiency and effectiveness as ideals, efforts to restructure voluntary organizations have been less than successful, often bringing about a rediscovery of the long-buried differences between "scientific" and religious philanthropy.[40] Rationalization, whether on the system or the organizational level, has been especially problematic for denominationally tied social-service and health-care agencies, in which commitment to services has always been more important than budgetary considerations and in which quality of service has tended to be defined in less than calculable ways. The supporters of one Pennsylvania hospital that bowed out of efforts to create a regional health-care system a decade ago succinctly summarized the issue:

To Sacred Heart doctors and nurses, however, medical philosophy included more than higher degrees, a sharp scalpel and a sharp mind. It included TLC—tender loving care. And the hospital became known for it. No matter what a patient's faith, a nun was supposed to visit every patient every day. Staffers saw the atmosphere as homey. Doctors, nurses, staff and patients were "a family."

"This hospital was known for tender loving care," said one Sacred Heart doctor. That view meshed with Sacred Heart's religion. The hospital had "the Guardian Angel flying over the building," said one doctor. And Sacred Heart loyalists said that faith in God was what made for better medicine. At Sacred Heart, Msgr. Fink wrote, "Faith and Science walked strongly forward." Each was as important as the other.[41]

Although this debate over the qualitative distinctiveness of religious caregiving was first perceived as an essentially political effort by the denominations to maintain control of their institutions, it now seems increasingly clear that it was really a reiteration of the old debate between "scientific" philanthropy, with its economistic concerns and its preoccupation with the "worthiness" of clients, and religious philanthropy, which wanted to relieve suffering first—and ask questions later. This conflict became apparent as unhappiness with management professionalization and organizational and system restructuring spread from religiously affiliated organizations to other kinds, particularly neighborhood and community-based voluntary agencies, that placed mission over methods.

Although nonprofits scholarship has been dominated by economistic concerns with efficiency and effectiveness, an important literature has begun to emerge which gives serious attention to the qualitative dimensions of philanthropy and voluntarism. Although not explicitly addressing itself to the religious aspects of helping and caregiving, this work legitimates the religious contention that "brotherly love" and the building of community and identity among both caregivers and the cared-for are as important as the services provided. Interestingly, this body of literature has not developed merely in response to contemporary tensions between marketing and mission, but has emerged from the effort to create a case-based theoretical understanding of organizations. Tracing its roots to Chester Barnard's 1939 classic, *The Functions of the Executive,* this enterprise offers a view of organizations which is both richer and more complex than that offered by the economists and more compatible with the view of human behavior as ethically governed.[42]

The purpose of organization theory was not to criticize the inefficiency of organizations, but to point out that what had been considered inefficiencies were really central to their activities and might even constitute their raison d'tre. However, only recently has organization theory begun to reconnect itself to more traditional concerns about social ethics and purposes, specifically addressing itself to contemporary efforts to make voluntary organizations more effective and efficient.

Few have been more eloquent than sociologist Carl Milofsky, who underlined the creation of community values and social bonds as a positive and desirable outcome of voluntary action. "Community is an ideology or abstraction that does not automatically develop in an area," Milofsky wrote, "it is a sense of identification with and commitment to a place, and must be constructed through the efforts of individual actors and organizations."[43] More than merely articulating this broadened viewpoint, he sought its historical antecedents, pointing out the extent to which social-welfare pioneers such as Addams dissented from the narrow economism of the "scientific" philanthropists of her own time. And Milofsky discerned the bureaucratic and community-based models of voluntary organizations as distinct and possibly incompatible ethical traditions:

> Roland Warren once argued that when thinking about social change people orient themselves toward one of two general values, which he characterized as "truth" and "love." The truth orientation, he explained, refers to "the impassioned conviction of the zealot, the person who is convinced that he has come upon some fundamental moral value and wishes to see it embedded in the warp and woof of events." The love orientation, in contrast, is used "roughly in the sense of the Latin *caritas* and the Greek *agape*, and 1 Corinthians. I am using it not in the affective sense, but in the appreciative sense as a relationship of infinite appreciation and respect, perhaps best expressed by Stoic and Jew and Christian alike in the concept that men are all brothers, being children of the same loving Father." Warren claimed that, in their purest form, these values tend to conflict with each other.[44]

"Pragmatism, as opposed to truth and love," Milofsky wrote, "tends to produce certain distinctive organizational structures that close off broad-based participation and crystallize a division of labor in a way that reifies expertise."[45]

Conclusion

Where does this debate leave us? It does seem clear that "scientific" philanthropy, both public and private, did little more than sequester poverty and suffering, putting them out of sight and out of mind, and propagate the illusion that delegating the tasks of caregiving to specialists and institutions absolved us of personal responsibility for the poor and dependent. But now the hungry, the homeless, and the incurably ill confront us daily, literally demanding that we respond personally to their evident needs. More jails and more police will not help. Nor can we expect that AIDS will solve the problem of poverty by exterminating the "unworthy" and "essentially unfit."

In pondering the problem of bridging the steadily widening chasm between the haves and the have-nots and the inadequacies of our methods, we would do well to consider the words with which Jacob Riis concluded *How the Other Half Lives:*

> The sea of a mighty population, help in galling fetters, heaves uneasily in the tenements. . . . The gap between the classes in which it surges, unseen, unsuspected by the thoughtless, is widening day by day. No tardy enactment of law, no political expedient, can close it. Against all other dangers our system of government may offer defense and shelter; against this not. I know of but one bridge that will carry us over safe, a bridge founded upon justice and built of human hearts.[46]

The courage—the foolhardiness—needed for this was not then and is not now within the capacity of the calculating. Without discovering its religious roots, American philanthropy is unlikely to play a significant role in the building of such a bridge.

4

Cultures of Trusteeship in the United States

Scholars may see trusteeship as a problem in organizational behavior and group process, as a problem in law and public policy, as a set of ethical issues, as a set of irreducibly unique historical instances, or in a variety of other ways, according to their disciplinary frameworks, their personal experiences on or with boards, or their political ideology. Board members themselves—as well as those affected by their actions—also may understand the term in a variety of ways. They may see themselves as acting for their family, community, class, nation, or conscience.

Can trusteeship be understood as independent of the historical and social settings in which it has existed—or, indeed, of the settings and viewpoints from which scholars seek to understand it? Does trusteeship have a universal and autonomous meaning—or it is, like any other fact or artifact, a social construction, the outcome of a negotiated process through which individuals structure the collective meanings on which they base their behavior?

The ways in which we answer these questions have a profound bearing not only on our own approach to trusteeship but also on the expectations that trustees bring to their tasks and, ultimately, on the public policies that frame and constrain the process of governance.

This chapter does not seek to be definitive: it seeks to be provocative and exploratory. It begins by considering the broad setting in which contemporary trusteeship is situated, suggesting not only some of the factors that have lead to changes in values, behaviors, and expectations of trustees and participants in the organizations for which they have formal responsibility, but also the ways in which these changes have led scholars to look at trusteeship as a phenomenon worthy of attention. This chapter then explores four cultures of trusteeship—four distinct, but nevertheless overlapping and interpenetrating, ways in which trustees themselves understand trusteeship. The chapter concludes with an assessment of the implications of this way of viewing trusteeship for consultants, scholars, and policymakers.

Changing Dimensions of Trusteeship: An Overview

Contemporary scholarship, particularly that focusing on the nonprofit sector, tends to obscure certain important facts about trusteeship. The most important of these is the diversity and complexity of the legal and institutional cultures of which trusteeship is a component. Only within the last thirty years, with the adoption of model legal codes by most states, has there been any degree of formal uniformity in the definition of nonprofit corporations or unincorporated charities. Before that, each state had its own set of statutes and court decisions setting forth the duties and powers of trustees. Even with the advent of legal standardization, there apparently remains considerable disagreement among states as to the place of charitable tax-exempt organizations in society and, consequently, as to the rights, powers, and obligations of trustees.[1]

Increasingly stringent state and federal regulatory oversight of charitable tax-exempt organizations, while directed at institutions rather than trustees, has also significantly altered the trustee role, particularly by altering the nature and extent of trustee liability and setting forth a variety of limitations on what trustees may or may not do.[2] Even such familiar legal doctrines as the Prudent Man Rule have been turned on their heads. This rule was originally meant as a mechanism for expanding the discretion of trustees in investing funds—and, in particular, freeing them from accountability to beneficiaries. For example, if a trustee chose to invest funds to maintain family control of an enterprise or to tie charities to the economic enterprises of a particular community, the courts were unlikely to intervene as long as such investment did not work to the obvious disadvantage of the trust or the private aggrandizement of the trustee. However, recent court decisions have favored an interpretation of the rule requiring that trustees invest in ways that favor maximum short-range return—including sell-offs of closely held firms and portfolio diversification.[3] These decisions have been reinforced by the provisions of the 1969 Tax Reform Act regulating "excess business holdings" by charitable tax-exempt organizations. The decisions have diminished the discretion of trustees, transforming them, in effect, into mere investment managers.[4]

Accompanying changes in the legal and regulatory environment have been significant shifts in organizational demography. These have had incalculable impacts on the meaning of trusteeship, on its social function, and on recruitment into trusteeship ranks. In 1940, the IRS estimated that the number of charitable tax-exempt organizations in the United States totaled about twelve thousand.[5] Today the number exceeds 1.2 million. In the 1950s and 1960s, the IRS received an average of seven thousand applications for tax-exempt status annually; by 1985, this number had increased to fifty-nine thousand.[6]

The reasons for this astounding increase in the number of charitable tax-exempt organizations is related to their changing purposes. The growth of the welfare state in the post–World War II decades did not require a commensurate expansion in a federal bureaucracy concerned with direct delivery of health, welfare, education, and cultural services. Rather, the growth occurred through a tax system that encouraged the development of private agencies to carry out the public purpose. Although in many cases these agencies received government grants and contracts, the federal government also used the tax system to provide incentives (deductions) for fund transfers (donations) between taxpayers and organizations certified as serving certain public purposes (charitable tax-exempt organizations). Viewed from this perspective, Lester Salamon's finding that one-third to one-half of all nonreligious nonprofit revenues come directly from government—with the remainder coming in the form of donations from individuals, foundations, and corporations, which are, in effect, subsidized by the tax system—is hardly surprising.[7]

Accompanying this explosion in the number of charitable tax-exempt entities is an enormous proliferation in their purposes. The range of activities in which nonprofits now engage is not only largely coextensive within those carried out by government and business, but for that reason render the term *charitable* as applied to them largely a misnomer.[8]

Under these circumstances, trusteeship takes on a very different meaning than it once had. The specialized nature of the services provided by nonprofits, as well as intensified competition for funding, contracts, and clientage, has raised the level of expertise needed by trustees. At the same time, the dramatically increased number of nonprofits has created an enormous demand for competent trustees—a demand that far exceeds the population of those with either trustee experience or an understanding of traditional trusteeship values.

To further complicate matters, the vast expansion in the number of nonprofit organizations has been accompanied by a segmentation in their markets. Some operate with a national focus, other emphasize state, regional, or local level activities. Although this differentiation of scope is in a certain sense not new, in the past the various levels of organizations were only loosely coupled—if they were coupled at all. Now, however, with increasing overlap in their programmatic concerns, competition for common resources and clients, and their tendency to draw from the same body of credentialed professionals for staff, nonprofit organizations tend to interact, interpenetrate, and overlap. One outcome of this situation appears to be a hierarchical structuration of the nonprofit domain. And this itself is part of a broader structuration—allocation of resources, status, and division of tasks—among public, for-profit, and nonprofit organizations.

Needless to say, the implications of these phenomena are considerable for what trustees are in a formal sense, how they understand their roles, from what backgrounds they are likely to be recruited, and what bodies of special information they are likely to bring to their tasks. More to the point, because different settings for trusteeship coexist and to some degree overlap, trustees may be subject to cross-pressures as to what kinds of values, expertise, and roles are appropriate to which kinds of organizations. Some organizations may require boards to be proactive and entrepreneurial, not only in raising funds but also in delineating missions and designing programs; others may require boards to be supportive but deferential. And these demands may vary within organizations over time.

These changes in the demography of charitable tax-exempt organizations have not taken place in a stable environment. The funding environment, in terms of available resources and of tax and regulatory factors, has been highly uncertain. The rise—and subsequent decline—of federal funding for nonprofits, changing patterns of foundation funding, increasing dependence on earned income, and the rising importance of corporate grant-making (which by 1984 had eclipsed outlays from independent foundations) have created a financial setting that demands of trustees not only high levels of managerial competence but also a capacity to balance market efficiency against organizational missions.

Over the past forty years, the increase in the numbers of nonprofit organizations serving broader and more diverse constituencies has transformed patterns of trustee recruitment. More women, ethnics, and minorities, particularly representatives of client groups, have joined the ranks of trustees. In addition, since the 1970s, business executives have become far more involved with nonprofit boards. Unlike the past, when board service by businesspeople was largely ceremonial and in general reserved for those from top management, trustees are increasingly being recruited from the ranks of middle management. Indeed, there are indications of emerging ties between voluntary service and the building of successful corporate careers. However, this pattern of greater executive involvement is complicated by the fact that business trustees are less likely to have community roots (indeed, for them voluntary service is a way of becoming rooted)—so the values and expectations they bring to boards are likely to be of a very different sort than those borne by their predecessors.[9]

For a variety of reasons, there appears to have been a fundamental alteration in the composition of boards of trustees. And the participation of new groups has brought new values, expectations, and patterns of behavior to the boardroom. However, once again it is important to remember that this change as not been pervasive: the new board cultures have not supplanted the older ones—they coexist with them, sometimes interinstitutionally, sometimes intra-institutionally.

More competitive environments, intensified regulatory demands, and public expectations of more and better quality service have led to fundamental changes in relations between trustees and staffs. In particular, staffs have become more professionally oriented, both in terms of their possession of credentialed technical competence in the areas in which organizations operate and in terms of specifically managerial competence. Each kind of professionalization produces different kinds of tensions and potential conflicts with boards. The core of this conflict involves the question of who is best fit to act as steward for the public interest—and, indeed, what the public interest (or the public) is. Academically oriented professional staffs claim to represent the public interest, pointing to issues of standards and accreditation, whereas trustees may insist that the public interest should be defined in terms of what is best for the community (which is represented by trustees). Managerially trained professional staffs may even challenge the fiduciary role of trustees, arguing for greater authority on the basis of greater expertise with regard to financial management.

In describing these changes, I run a risk of evoking an image of a golden age of trusteeship, in which charitable organizations were disinterestedly run by a small group of community leaders, who attained their positions only after a long apprenticeship. This image parallels much of the commentary in the financial press about ethical decline in the securities markets, as old-school WASPs have been pushed out by brashly unscrupulous ethnics. In fact, commercial morality as we know it was socially constructed in the early years of this century by men who understood the political hazards of buccaneering—and this awareness came only after a long period of turbulence. Similarly, a stable culture (or, more accurately, cultures) of charitable trusteeship—the one that we tend to look back to—was a negotiated solution, the product of the desire of community leaders in certain places and at certain times to maintain civic culture as "an ordered platform bounded by rules." (Intrinsically ethnocentric and paternalistic, this civic order had its shortcomings, as well as its advantages).

To further muddy the waters, even when the WASP model appears to be the dominant one, it is not. Organizational life in American communities has always been far richer and more complex than scholarship has admitted. Because historiography almost invariably attempts to "explain" the present, it selects from the past artificial liniarities of development. However, in the real world the development process is always a matter of multiple outcomes. The failure of some forms to become dominant does not rule out their significance— they continue to exist within their niches, serving their clients, enlisting loyalties, forming and molding viewpoints and values—only emerging later, under altered circumstances, as important factors.

Cultures of trusteeship parallel cultures of philanthropy and voluntarism. And these, in turn, parallel cultures of economic and political life. Because the same individuals who serve on nonprofit boards may also serve in governmental and business capacities, we need to understand the broad setting of organizational culture, of which charitable trusteeship is only a part. These cultures may vary from place to place, according to the social, economic, political, and juridical configurations in which voluntary action takes place. But such cultures may also coexist in particular settings, sometimes operating in conflict with one another and sometimes complementing one another. In our own time, the most notable feature seems to be convergence—with a consequent need to recognize and consciously articulate the way in which they relate to one another.

Cultures of Trusteeship: Grassroots Organizations

When Tocqueville wrote of the American propensity to form "associations of a thousand kinds," one of the kinds of organizations foremost in his thinking was the grassroots voluntary organization— the mutual-benefit, single issue/single interest, based in the goals of ethnic, neighborhood, denominational, political, aesthetic (and sometimes athletic) interests. Although undoubtedly the most common kinds of nonprofit, these are the organizations we know the least about. Because they are frequently informal, unincorporated, and transient, they have generally not captured the interest of scholars of American organizational life.[10] The very informality of these organizations precludes conventional notions of trusteeship: they seldom have either formal structures or assets to administer. Moreover, because they seldom presume to represent themselves as speaking for the good of the community as a whole, they elude conventional notions of stewardship.

Although perhaps inconsiderable in themselves, these organizations are important from the standpoint of trusteeship because of the part they have played in molding the values and expectations of those who, in our own time, are assuming roles within more formal trusteeship settings. (Just as Tocqueville suggested that the playground was the schoolroom of democracy, so grassroots organizations may have served as the training grounds for many of those now sitting on nonprofits boards).

It is difficult to deal with these organizations in all their bewildering diversity. However, they cannot be ignored, because though most appear and vanish without ever achieving formal institutional status, others constitute the first stage for entities that do succeed in establishing themselves. Understanding these primordial forms may well shed light on characteristics of trusteeship which might be overlooked in examining more fully elaborated institutions.

Furthermore, evidence suggests not only that virtually all American voluntary associations emerged from such a primordial broth, but also that the process of emergence was and is an ongoing one. In addition, there appear to be important interactive effects involving those organizations that merged early in the development of the associational domain and those emerging later.

The first voluntary organizations in the United States were created to empower groups of individuals, sometimes as agents of the state, sometimes as a counterpoise to the power of the state. Almost invariably, established organizations, whether quasi-public or private, viewed newly emerging associations as threats to public order and more often than not sought to crush them. In the early nineteenth century, "mechanics societies" were organized to politically, socially, and economically empower craftsmen and small businessmen who had been, up to that point, virtual strangers to formal modes of organizational activity.

We do not know whether the adoption of these modes represented an acceptance of the values of socially superior groups or if these small holders carried with them into the institutional realm expectations and modes of behavior from the informal relations of craft culture. Mary P. Ryan's important study of associations in antebellum Oneida County, New York, suggests that these organizations fundamentally altered informal groups, forging common bonds, empowering them as *groups,* and redirecting and focusing individual energies to common purposes. This process, she suggests, created the basis for what became the dominant Protestant middle-class identity.[11]

Voluntary associations seem to have similar impacts on immigrant groups, most fundamentally transforming them from groups of individuals who had identified themselves primarily in terms of kinship and town of origin into "the Irish," "the Italians," and so on. These identities served as bases for economic empowerment—through trade unions, mutual-benefit societies, and ethnic businesses—and for the emergence of an informal leadership structure based on wealth, political power, or both.[12]

Adopting the organizational modalities of the dominant Protestants, however, did not necessarily lead to acceptance or assimilation. The institutional domain of the ethnics often operated in parallel with that of the WASPs. Was this failure to integrate a function of WASP prejudice? Or did ethnics view and use voluntary associations in ways that differed significantly from those of the Protestant overclass? For example, did ethnics lack broad civic sensibility? Were they too focused on special interests?

There are no simple answers to these questions. Indeed, the answer seems to depend on the group, as well as on the place. For example, the Jewish charities of Allentown, Pennsylvania, during the depression of the 1870s, were the first to acknowledge the dimensions of the economic crisis and the first to organize relief efforts on a community-wide basis. The city's other ethnic groups were either passive or self-serving: the dominant one, the Pennsylvania Germans, generally eschewed institutional action of any kind, preferring to work through family networks; the English and Irish ironworkers helped each other as national groups; but none reached out to the community as a whole. In Allentown, at least, the preferences of particular ethnic groups for particular kinds of organized collective action seems quite evident.[13]

Such preferences may have had a good deal to with the frequently successful mobility of Jews into community leadership in Allentown and elsewhere. The prominence of Jews on the governing boards of New York City's cultural organizations—the Kahns at the Metropolitan Opera, the Lehmans at the Metropolitan Museum of Art, the Paleys at the Museum of Modern Art—is suggestive.[14] An orientation to organized philanthropy and, more broadly, to corporate activity is fundamental to Jewish institutional culture—indeed, in Judaism the congregation itself is viewed as a voluntary body. And, Max Weber notwithstanding, the ethic of work in the world as a form of service, as an essentially religious activity, did not originate with the Protestants![15]

Scholars have given little attention to ethnic cultures and their organizational values. However, there is evidence that the WASPs, the Germans, and Irish differed in their preferences. For example, the 1878 Worcester, Massachusetts, *City Directory* shows that of the city's seventy-eight voluntary associations, only nine were identifiably ethnic. Of these, five (6 percent) were Irish groups—though the Irish constituted 20 percent of the total population—and three were German, though the city's 325 ethnic Germans comprised less than 1 percent of its population! The groups thus ranked themselves in terms of voluntary organizations per capita: Germans: 1:108; WASPS, 1:420; and Irish, 1:1,676.[16] The Irish, at this point at least, appear to have preferred channeling their collective activities through church and political organizations, and trade unions, rather than through lay-controlled charitable organizations.

Although I run the hazard of stereotyping ethnic groups, it does appear that "national" traditions (in the sense of familiarity with particular technologies of collective action) have a good deal to do with where particular groups locate themselves in the polity—and, of course, with their propensity to occupy formal trusteeship roles. To say this is not to suggest that the political, church, and union activities evidently favored by Catholic immigrants are any less voluntaristic than the associational forms favored by the Germans and the WASPs. However, activities favored by Catholic immigrants were less likely to give rise to a recognizable trusteeship traditions, in part because the issue of moral oversight, so central to the stewardship dimension of traditional trusteeship, tended to be left to ecclesiastical authorities in Catholic communities. (However, it is interesting to contrast Jewish and Irish associational patterns: though the Jews were notably active in politics and trade-union activity, they also created a wide range of other kinds of voluntary bodies, whereas the Irish seldom did.)

It does appear that by the 1920s some Irish and Italians, especially the more occupationally mobile, were joining forces through voluntary associations for common purposes. The rise of the Knights of Columbus and other cross-ethnic Catholic fraternal organizations had begun by the early 1880s. By the turn of the century, Catholic hospitals were being organized, often as a response by Catholic physicians to their exclusion from being able to attend at Protestant-controlled institutions.[17] Although apparently analogs to mainstream lay-controlled community institutions, questions remain as to the degree of control exercised by the laity. Some of the literature on efforts to rationalize the health-care system in the 1970s suggests that, despite formal trusteeship control by wealthy and prominent Catholic laymen, the influence of the church in setting policy remained decisive.[18]

It seems quite clear, even from this highly circumstantial and fragmentary evidence, that trusteeship may have had different meaning for different ethnic groups. These differences may have persisted even as, by the 1970s, boundaries among the ethnic communities appeared to be breaking down, with ethnics joining mainstream boards in large numbers. The meaning of these differences needs to be explored. Did familial, religious, or political loyalties remain more important for ethnics than for WASPs? (Or do we merely tend to confuse WASP forms of loyalty with civic sensibility?) Were higher education and mobility so thoroughgoing in their effect that what Miriam Wood has called a MAPs (Middle-Aged Professional) orientation became predominant? Was the MAPs orientation a way of building a common set of organizational concerns in order to bridge the gaps among the more particularist values associated with ethnicity? The answers to these questions may have significant bearing on the meaning of trusteeship and on the behavior of trustees: one set of conditions may create pressures for trustees to see themselves as representatives of particular constituencies; another set may diminish the significance of particularities and make "objective" standards of organizational performance the common ground among trustees from different backgrounds.[19]

Finally, it is difficult to make general statements about ethnic traditions of voluntary action, giving, and trusteeship because of the evidence suggesting that the organizational values and orientations of ethnic groups varied from place to place according to the underlying institutional cultures that surrounded them. Places with powerful and inclusive federationist civic cultures, such as Cleveland and Allentown, may have encouraged the development of lay associations and patterns of lay trusteeship far earlier than cities and regions where ethnics were excluded from central economic, cultural, and political activities. Thus, ethnic trustees in inclusive civic cultures may be more similar to their WASP counterparts than ethnic trustees in less inclusive and more conflicted settings. To complicate matters further, there may be ethnocentric counterforces in inclusive settings, protective responses to the apparent ease of assimilation, which may act to keep ethnics outside of the mainstream of institutional life.[20]

The issue of grassroots trusteeship raises far more questions than can possibly be answered under present circumstances. That we know so little about the issue indicates how narrowly we have focused our inquiries. WASP/elite/civil privatist models have so dominated our thinking about philanthropy and voluntarism that we have tended to overlook other alternatives.

Cultures of Trusteeship: Midwestern Federationism

"Wherever at the head of some new undertaking you see government in France, or a man of rank in England," wrote Tocqueville, "in the United States you will be sure to find an association."[21] While the Frenchman was correct in citing the ubiquity of associations, he failed to note how much they varied in form and function from place to place within the new nation. The model of civil privatism that he had in mind was peculiar to the Northeast—and almost unknown elsewhere.

Midwestern political economist Richard T. Ely took note of this fact in an 1893 address to the regents of the University of the State of New York:

I have heard someone here today say that state aid [for universities] was un-American. . . . What has been the practice of America? We who live in the northwest can not admit that a few states east of Ohio and North of Virginia shall tell what is American. In the early history of this country even those states contributed for the support of the university and with the exception of a few states, every state in the union is taxed today for the support of higher education. Are they not American? Is Michigan not American? Are Wisconsin, Nebraska and Missouri not American? Is the title American to be restricted to the practice of New York and Massachusetts?[22]

Ely asserted that the state university "is here to stay." And he urged that private benevolence should be extended to public institutions:

The great evil at the present time in the United States is that the forces of good are too split up. There is in our country always a desire on the part of the majority for good government, but there is little unity among those who constitute the majority. . . . The great trouble with us is that the state does not receive our affections. Our treasure is elsewhere and where our treasure is there is also our heart. Our interests are too diverse. We are engaged in various business enterprises . . . which have interests by no means identical with those of the public, and even in education we have erected a means of division in the denominational college. We win money in industries which must fight the state and then give money to sectarian institutions which continue to fight the state. What kind of a public life have we a right to expect under such circumstances? The measure I propose would tend to strengthen public institutions, to induce men and women to make generous gifts and thus bring to the state that feeling, that warm affection, which the noblest patriots have ever cherished.[23]

Ely concluded his remarks by contrasting the civic spirit of communities in which citizens depended on private philanthropy to do for them what they would not do for themselves with those in which public and private resources worked together for the common good:

I would like, if there were time, to say something about what constitutes paternalism. Is the state something apart from us, over us, doing things for us or do we ourselves act through the state? Where do the resources

of the state come from and who determine its activity? If we ourselves act
through the state I consider it a noble kind of self-help. This is paternalism, when the people have no trust in themselves; when they fold their
arms and say we are not good nor wise nor competent enough to establish
our own educational institutions and we hope some kind of millionaire
will do it for us. In the meantime we fold our arms and wait for somebody
to help us. That is paternalism and a very bad kind of paternalism. . . .
Let us not rely simply on rich men, but rather help ourselves and then
if rich men will help us to help ourselves that is desirable.

Through a mistaken policy, private sectarian foundations have been
brought into existence resulting in the educational chaos from which we
are struggling to emerge. We must recognize the situation. We cannot
make a *tabula rasa* and begin from the beginning, but we must build on
foundations already laid and I urge the hearty cooperation of the best
private and denominational schools with public educational institutions
for the attainment of common ends.[24]

Although the northeastern champions of a privatized civic culture
may have viewed Ely as a radical, he was doing little more than describing the fundamental characteristics of associational culture in the
Midwest. There, as late as the turn of the century, purely private institutions were oddities. Institutional hybrids, which combined government and private funding and governance modes, were common-
place. Out of these hybrids grew the region's distinctive contributions
to American philanthropy and voluntarism, the Community Chest/
United Way (federated fund-raising), the community trust (federated
endowments), and community charity federations. Not surprisingly,
this alternative institutional culture produced modes of trusteeship
which were considerably different from those prevalent in the Northeast—and that have, subsequently, been viewed as the classic model.

The national political, economic, and cultural systems emerging at
the end of the nineteenth century were far more selective in their
impact than generally believed. Although some cities and towns did
become mere satellites of national metropolitan interests, others were
able to develop civic cultures, sets of civic institutions, and modes of
economic activity which enabled them to fully participate in national
arenas while simultaneously maintaining effective sovereignty over
their own affairs. Federations and associations played a key role in this
process, permitting business and government to confront the problems
of economic turbulence and political diversity collectively and cooperatively rather than adversarially. Although public life in the United
States generally became more privatized during this period, civic institutions of the Midwest, where federative and associational modes
were especially important, retained a degree of public control and

participation which made them quite different from the forms of private control characteristic of the Northeast.

Although the stresses of industrial and urban growth prompted the emergence of a distinctive civic culture in Cleveland and other midwestern cities, the character of that response was rooted in a set of institutional values which had been formed nearly a century earlier. The trans-Appalachian region, in particular that part which would be included within the Northwest Territory (Ohio, Illinois, Indiana, Wisconsin, Michigan, and Minnesota), had, from the very beginning of settlement, been subjected to cultural cross-pressures. These profoundly affected the ways in which such fundamental issues as the power and responsibilities of government, distinctions between public and private domains, and the role of private corporations, for-profit and nonprofit, were resolved.

To begin with, it is essential to understand that, at the time this region was being settled, these issues were among the most fiercely contested public questions. Even in New England, where legislatures were notably willing to "parcel out the commonwealth into little aristocracies," as one critic labeled chartered corporations, the status of these entities was far from clear.[25] Massachusetts Attorney General James Sullivan summed up the situation in "On the Life of Corporations," an 1802 opinion written in response to a query from the general court:

> There is no legal decision, no precedent established in the government, on which to predicate an opinion or form decisive answers [with regard to the powers of corporations]. This subject may eventually engage the attention, and employ the learning of all the men in the Commonwealth. The feelings of interest, the dictates of prudence, the calculations of policy, and even the prevalency of parties, may give the whole contest a complexion which is at this time inconceivable to any one. . . . It is vain to reason upon naked principles unfortified by established rules.[26]

Sullivan was prescient. For the next two decades, the question of corporations would engage the attention of legislatures in every state. New England's ultimate resolution to encourage the growth of private corporations should not be mistaken for unanimity on the subject: after all, it was the action of the New Hampshire legislature to revise Dartmouth College's charter that led to the Dartmouth College case of 1819. Even those New Englanders who favored corporations shifted positions on their relationship to the state as political power passed from the Federalists to the Democratic Republicans. In the South, the situation was no less ambiguous and confused: though Jefferson and his followers generally opposed corporations, they permitted the

chartering of a variety of public-service companies—academies, turn-
pikes, and canals—under terms that tied them closely to the will of the
legislature. National policy was similarly unclear. The Supreme
Court decided the Dartmouth College case in favor of corporate autonomy, but in the same session it also ruled to restrict the powers of
corporations to receive charitable trusts. And, of course, the struggle
over the Bank of the United States, which centered on the question of
a private entity doing the public's business, still lay ahead.

The Midwest was not merely a passive observer of these struggles,
nor did their resolution in the older states have any binding impact
on the new settlements. Even when, as in the case of Ohio's Western
Reserve, the majority of the inhabitants came from Connecticut,
which would be among the most enthusiastic promoters of incorporation, they were far from being of one mind on the question. They
merely brought with them—along with the rest of their impedimen-
ta—the ambivalence and irresolution of their native political cultures.
In some cases, the migration process operated selectively to encourage
westward movement by those who were opposed to and oppressed by
the procorporate Standing Order.

Ohio's resolution of the corporate question came only after a protracted struggle, which, as in other places, centered on the status of
colleges. The state's earliest colleges had been chartered as public institutions—that is, as institutions whose governing boards were appointed by the legislature and whose support was to come from public
grants of land. However, when these proved inadequate, institutions
such as Ohio University and Miami University turned first to the legislature for funding and, when this failed, to private donations. Even
before the Dartmouth College decision, which defined the New Hampshire institution as private because it had been privately supported,
James McBride and other Ohio politicians were advancing similar
arguments with regard to the state's supposedly public universities.[27]

The key factor in Ohio's ultimate acceptance of corporations—and,
by implication, of the capacity of private entities to operate in the
public interest—was not determined by any clear-cut political victory
of the friends of corporations over their enemies. Rather, the acceptance was a product of "domestication": private support for both older
and newer colleges (as well as other corporations) tended to come from
groups that were intensely committed to *local* interests. Within this
framework, the "aristocratic" or class interests so feared by the Jeffersonians and Jacksonians seemed irrelevant. The promotion of local
interests—and, in particular, a common appreciation for the role of
"public" institutions in promoting economic growth—rendered political divisions inconsequential. Although many of the colleges

founded after 1830 were denominationally affiliated—often in the hope of encouraging coreligionists in the East to offer support—the disappointment of these expectations led, once again, to their transformation into community-supported entities with important ties to local economic development.

One gets some sense of the *mentalité* of Ohio's institution-builders from this 1824 speech by Robert Hamilton Bishop, Miami University president:

> The Miami country, and a vast tract of land to the west and the north of this district, is rich, and is to be rich for ages in producing human and immortal beings, as well as in producing all that is necessary for the support of animal life. And the soil is to be cultivated by lords of the soil and by their children. We could name the father of a family in this district, who has prepared all his sons for college, and who has supported some of these sons at college, by making his sons at once farmers and scholars. The sons have had, from their boyhood to their maturity, their study and their laboring hours; their study and their laboring weeks; and, while attending college, their study and their laboring months; and in this way, the mind and the body have been mutually invigorated and supported. An independence of mind, and an independence of fortune, and a strength and vigor of mind and body, have thus been cherished, and secured, and perfected; compared with which the largest hereditary states among the lordships and dukedoms of Europe are perfect insignificance. Now, with but very little exertion, but with a combined and well directed exertion, the whole country from which the Miami University is to derive its chief resources, may be filled with such noblemen of nature. Every family and every neighborhood, has entirely at its own command the means of preparing any given number of sons for entering the regular classes of the university. And in this way a healthy and virtuous, and really learned population, may be continued till the end of time.[28]

This statement indicates the early emergence of a set of institutional ideals which, in effect, strove to reconcile the conflicting views of corporations that still sharply divided Ohioans: Miami University's function was to create "lords of the soil," learned and virtuous farmers, not a professional aristocracy; higher education should be accessible to anyone willing to work for it—and working for it was itself a part of the process of education; education was of particular value to the people in the locality of the university and hinted at its potential contribution to the region's growth. These ideals presented quite a contrast to "The Yale Report of 1828," which defined Yale's educational task as serving national rather than local needs and in supplying merchants, lawyers, ministers, and statesmen rather than farmers "with the discipline and furniture of the mind."[29]

The importance of this contrast is suggested by Colin B. Burke's 1982 study of American collegiate populations, in which he argued against the traditional view of midwestern colleges as "small, inefficient, and inflexible" products of local boosterism and religious parochialism. He suggested that they differed from the elite institutions of the Northeast not because they were the inferior products of small minds, but because they were created to serve regions whose needs were considerably different from those of the increasingly urban and industrialized Northeast:

> The new colleges of the period were oriented to educating students who were much less likely to have come from an elite background and who had different occupational goals than those who entered the established colleges. The character of the institutions was shaped by the backgrounds and objectives of their students. . . . The careers of their students indicate that the colleges were enrolling young men who were aggressive, mobile, involved in the development of the American society and economy. The students, if they did form an elite, formed a working elite. They entered science, business, and the professions and made significant contributions in all of those fields. They were involved in politics and government at levels far above expectation and they contributed leadership and expertise to the growth of American industry.[30]

Bishop's ideas, as well as the overall pattern of institutional development in the first half of the nineteenth century, support the hypothesis that the bifurcation of educational traditions foreshadows a more profound divergence in American culture between national and regional institutions and networks. Although recent historiography has suggested that the split of "island communities" from the national culture was due to local resistance—often irrational and self-defeating—to the emergence of large-scale economic organizations and the "new middle class" of university-trained experts and professional managers, which ultimately supplanted and subsumed regions and localities, it appears that the divergence of institutional patterns was more than reactive and vital as the national culture.

What emerges here is a version of cultural and economic nationality which—rather than being a crudely Darwinist hierarchy of actors differentiated according to their efficiency in responding to opportunities—presents a more complex problem in population ecology in which competing organizations with different missions operate in a common-resource environment, locating niches that enable them to survive and serve the needs of their constituents. This process leads to an organizational universe that is diverse and functionally differentiated rather than hierarchical. Viewed from this perspective, midwesterners, rather than vainly resisting modernization and becoming ultimately subordinated to the more advanced Northeast, developed organizations that, though sharing many of their values and willing to use many of their organizational techniques—whether corporation in the antebellum period or bureaucracy at the turn of the century— did so with a regional focus.

Within this regional culture, conceptions of the relations between public and private domains were drawn very differently than in the Northeast, whose pattern became the model for national organizations, for-profit and nonprofit. The latter moved early toward a strictly private form. Although state representatives remained on the governing boards of Harvard and Yale until well into the mid-nineteenth century, they were a minority and neither exercised significant influence over the policies of those institutions nor brought with them any financial support.

Ohio and other parts of the Old Northwest moved toward a mixed institutional economy, characterized by organizational fields in which public, nonprofit, and proprietary entities participated, and in which distinctions between public and private institutions were not clearly drawn. Of the thirty-nine colleges and universities operating in Ohio at the end of the nineteenth century, only one, Ohio State, was a public institution in any clear-cut sense—"unlike all others," wrote a contemporary, "it is not a corporation. Its trustees, seven in number, are appointed by the governor, for a term of seven years, and appointed by the Senate. Their powers and duties are all prescribed by law. . . . They may not incur an indebtedness except by the consent of the legislature and as provided by law. The ownership of the property is vested in the state of Ohio."[31] "There are," the writer noted in a manner that suggested the novelty of the form—then less than twenty-five years old—

> advantages and disadvantages in this method. It insures a conservative management and expenditure of funds. This is important to state institutions of all kinds. Inasmuch as all appropriations must be provided by the legislature the university is held to a careful regard for the intelligent public opinion of the state. There being no corporate rights to be forfeited the legislature might, at any time, change the character, alter the methods, or entirely abolish the institution. On the other hand, the limitations of the State University are such as to hinder it from meeting emergencies as they arise, or devising plans looking into the future. There is a limit to the resources available from the state, and this limits as well what may be undertaken.[32]

The state's other institutions took a variety of forms. For example, the University of Cincinnati was a "city university." Organized as a

corporation, with a "board of directors" appointed by the superior
court, the university was supported by a combination of municipal tax
revenues and private benevolence. (Between 1889 and 1900, the latter
amounted to nearly $300,000—and the institution held endowments of
more than $1 million.)[33] Miami University, whose mixed constitution
of publicly appointed trustees and private support originated in its
1809 charter, struggled along until 1873, when the latter proved insufficient to keep its doors open.[34] In 1885, the university reopened,
sustained by a combination of private funding and an annual appropriation from the state. In 1902, the state doubled its annual appropriation to Miami University, at the same time establishing a normal
school, which was placed under the control of the university's trustees.
Despite the large amount of state support and the fact that the trustees
were appointed by the governor, James J. Burns, in his 1905 survey of
Ohio's educational history, seemed uncertain as to how to characterize
Miami University: he classed both it and the University of Cincinnati
as public institutions, but took pains to distinguish the former from
the purely public Ohio State University.

Burns' uncertainty is evident in his description of Ohio University—which, like Miami University, had a mixed constitution from its
founding (in 1804).[35] Burns classed Ohio University as a private institution, though its trustees continued to be appointed by the governor,
and it had begun receiving regular state support as early as 1838 and
by 1847 was granted the right to fund its debts through the issuance
of tax-exempt bonds. By 1902, it was operating a state normal school
and, evidently, receiving substantial state as well as private support.
Edward Alanson Miller's 1918 study of nineteenth-century educational
legislation in the state came to this curious conclusion about the status
of Ohio University: "The appointment of trustees, the requirement of
reports [regarding its finances and methods], and certain general requirements specified in the charter include all of the control or
guidance on the educational side. It is evident that the institution was
not regarded in any true sense as a state university, if by that term is
meant an institution supported by the state and governed by policies
of state initiation."[36] Although not public in the sense that Ohio State
was, Ohio University was clearly not private by the standards of northeastern institutions such as Harvard!

It is interesting that in a state notable for the number of colleges
established—twenty-seven alone by 1860—Cleveland, one of its most
important commercial centers, possessed no institution of higher
education before 1880. This is curious in view of the extraordinary
activity of other kinds of private associations devoted to improving
the public in the nineteenth century. It may be that the city's older

families were so accustomed to sending their sons to Yale and other New England colleges that they simply did not see establishing a local institution as a worthwhile investment.[37] It is also possible that the anti-institutionalism of this "wilderness of Whiggery," which ran so deep as to prevent Whigs from ever organizing themselves as an effective political force, precluded the kind of major long-term commitments that building up a college represented.[38] It is also likely that, by the time Congregationalist-Presbyterian Western Reserve College opened its doors in rural Hudson in 1826, denominational politics had become so complex as to preclude any kind of concerted support. And by midcentury, as Cleveland became industrialized, the increasingly secular orientation of the city's elite proved an obstacle to any outpouring of support.[39]

Cleveland finally did decide that institutions of higher education would be an ornament to the city. In 1881, philanthropist Leonard Case donated $1 million toward the establishment of a school of applied science. For income, Case directed that the income from his downtown properties—a major block on the public square—be diverted to support the new school.[40] Interestingly, city officials had hoped that the childless multimillionaire would leave his real estate to the city. As it was, the city was given two hundred acres to be used for industrial plants and railroad rights-of-way—which became Cleveland's first planned industrial district.

That Case chose to make a private institution, the School of Applied Science, his major beneficiary in no sense suggests a significant departure from the mixed public/private themes of the region's institutional culture. For one thing, the technological orientation of the new school assured that it would become a catalyst for the benevolence of other businessmen, to whom the practical applications of mathematics, science, engineering, and chemistry were of immediate and growing interest. (Indeed, it is worth noting that though Cleveland continued to send young men to Yale, very few attended its Sheffield Scientific School—those who might have, it seems fair to assume, were sent to Case.)[41] In this sense, Case's endowing a private institution served a crucially important public purpose, by directing the attention of the city's commercial and industrial leadership to areas in which cooperation rather than competition was preeminently important. In addition, the fact that Case chose to place the endowment in the relatively inflexible form of strategically situated real estate suggests that he may have had in mind the ultimate use of this property as the nucleus for some sort of planned development.[42] (The Case block became the site of the public library in 1921, and the main post office in 1902.) Thus, even the corpus of the Case endowment ended up serving a public purpose—though the city government did not happen to be the agency through which this was done.

Cleveland's second institution of higher education, Western Reserve University, was put together by financier Amasa Stone in a manner not unlike the way he or his contemporaries might have consolidated a collection of smaller railroads or manufactories into a single enterprise.[43] One component, tiny Congregational Western Reserve College, was induced—on the promise of a half-million-dollar endowment—to relocate from rural Hudson, to change its name to Adelbert College, to cut its denominational ties, and to abandon its commitment to educating women. Another component, the quasi-proprietary Cleveland Medical College, had been established in 1843. Between 1888 and 1915, other units were added, including a college for women and schools of law, dental medicine, library science, pharmacy, and applied social science.

This effort to create "the only privately owned and financed urban university in Ohio"—a private institution on the northeastern model—proved largely unsuccessful.[44] By 1906, the Dental School was losing so much money that the university sold it to the owner of a dental-supply company. Although remaining in name a part of the university, the Dental School was run as a proprietary diploma mill for ten years—until university trustees repurchased it in 1916. The university's graduate school did so poorly that in 1921, nearly thirty years after its founding, it had never granted a doctorate and had attracted so few students that the trustees closed it down. The School of Applied Social Science was plagued by financial difficulties, questions about its validity, and the curious tendency of Cleveland elite to look beyond itself for expertise to advise its social experiments. Despite this, the school managed to survive. The Library School, though persistently a money-loser, attracted enough public support (from the Cleveland Public Library) and private donations (including a $100,000 gift from Andrew Carnegie) to survive until 1986. The Depression very nearly finished off Western Reserve University: between 1930 and the end of World War II, when enrollments were swelled because returning GIs were being educated at public expense, the school teetered on the edge of bankruptcy.[45]

If one were to judge Cleveland's private sector from the history of Western Reserve University, one would have to conclude that philanthropy—at least in the pure form of disinterested private initiatives in the public interest—was a failure there. To conclude this would, of course, be erroneous, because it is not particularly useful to measure one culture by the standards of another. To understand Cleveland, we must grasp the distinctively communitarian patterns that had been developing in the Old Northwest since the early nineteenth century, for these profoundly shaped the city's institutional response to industrial and urban problems.

Nineteenth-century America presented communities with a range of choices. The public, private, and mixed forms of collective action available in the educational sphere were also available in the domain of economic activity. The early phases of industrialization had been accepted passively because community leaders did not understand that economic development led to qualitative changes in social and political life. But with the depression of the 1870s, community leaders began to devise ways of reducing their vulnerability to the business cycle—and at the same time to regain control of their localities. Diversification seemed the most promising strategy for making local economies "panic proof."[46]

Although boards of trade had been established in considerable numbers in the Midwest in the 1840s and 1850s, they had tended to be dominated by commercial interests rather than industrial ones. However, in the 1880s boards of trade broadened their efforts, focusing particularly on economic diversification through attracting new industries. To be successful, diversification required cooperation—not only among businessmen who controlled their communities' capital and real estate, but also between business and government. Improving and expanding municipal services was viewed as essential in to attracting new firms: streets, schools, parks, police, fire, and sanitation, as well as the development of privately owned electric, water, transportation, and communications systems, required cooperation and coordination between municipal government and business. In cities such as Cleveland, the Board of Trade, which reconstituted itself as the Chamber of Commerce in 1893, became the central agency for mediating this relationship.[47]

To understand why Cleveland's business community became the most important element in reforming the city's institutions, as well as why the Chamber of Commerce became the primary arena for mobilizing private resources for public purposes, we must review the ways in which the city's leaders understood the economic, political, and cultural events between 1870 and 1900. We are fortunate in that Cleveland produced numerous outstandingly important and articulate individuals whose writings and actions permit us a remarkably clear view of the business leaders' evolving understanding of their civic role.

The first of these individuals was John Hay.[48] A native of Salem, Indiana, Hay had served as one of President Lincoln's secretaries. After the Civil War, Hay served in the diplomatic corps, then joined the staff of the *New York Tribune,* then run by Whitlaw Reid, Horace Greeley's protégé. In the course of covering the presidential campaign of 1872, Hay met and fell in love with Clara, daughter of Cleveland industrialist Amasa Stone, whom he married in 1874. (Stone's younger daughter Flora married Samuel Mather in 1881. Mather would succeed his father-in-law as the city's preeminent industrial and philanthropic leader). Hay made Cleveland his home and became deeply involved in Amasa Stone's business interests. By 1877, Hay had become sufficiently competent to assume control of Stone's enterprises while his father-in-law traveled in Europe. Thus, Hay was on the front lines during the great railroad strike and civil disorders in the summer of that year, when he reported to Stone that

> since last week the country has been at the mercy of the mob, and on the whole the mob has behaved rather better than the country. The shameful truth is now clear, that the government is utterly helpless and powerless in the face of an unarmed rebellion of foreign workingmen, mostly Irish. There is nowhere any firm nucleus of authority—nothing to fall back on as a last resort. The Army has been destroyed by the dirty politicians, and the State militia is utterly inefficient. Any hour the mob chooses, it can destroy any city in the country—that is the simple truth.[49]

Hay's experiences led to his writing what is now considered to be the first American "social realist" novel—the anonymously published *Breadwinners—A Social Study*, which appeared in 1883. Set in Cleveland (which he called "Buffland"), the novel depicted the political impotence of the wealthy, learned, and respectable, who, despite their commitment to improving their communities, were frustrated by an electorate predominantly consisting of immigrants efficiently led by unscrupulous politicians. Arthur Farnham, Hay's protagonist,

> and his friends had attempted a movement . . . to rescue the city from the control of what they considered a corrupt combination of politicians. They had began, as such men always do, too late, and without any adequate organization, and the regular workers had beaten them with ridiculous ease. In Farnham's own ward, where he possessed two-thirds of the real estate, the candidates favored by him and his friends received not quite one tenth of the votes cast. The leader of the opposing forces was a butcher, one Jacob Metzger, who was not a bad man so far as his lights extended. He sold meat carcass; and he conducted his political operations in the same way. He made his bargains with aspirants and office holders and kept them religiously.[50]

Like so many in the 1870s, Hay operated under the comfortable assumption that American conditions—equal opportunity, high wages, equal laws, and the ballot box—would prevent a war between labor and capital. The riots of 1877, "blew such vaporing away." According to his biographer, Hay believed,

> as did many of his contemporaries, that the assaults on Property were inspired by demagogues who used as their tools the loafers, the criminals, the vicious,—society's dregs who have been ready at all times to rise against laws and government. That you have property yourself is proof of industry on your part or your father's; that you have nothing, is a judgment on your laziness and vices, or on your improvidence. The world is a moral world; which it would not be if virtue and vice received the same rewards.
>
> This summary, though confessedly crude, may help, if it be not pressed too close, to define John Hay's position. The property you own—be it a tiny cottage or a palace—means so much more than the tangible object! With it are bound up whatever in historic times has stood for civilization. So an attack on Property becomes an attack on Civilization.[51]

Although Hay mentioned the existence of railroads and factories in *The Breadwinners—A Social Study,* he completely failed to understand their significance. He continued to view industrial workers as though they were autonomous craftsmen and so was unable to see the increasingly turbulent relations between labor and capital as anything but a crisis of political morality.

Hay called attention to the elite's political "impasse," but his failure to grasp the significance of industrialization left him powerless to overcome it. Others would be more successful in recognizing that economic and technological changes were tied to fundamental and thoroughgoing shifts in social and political relations. They would believe themselves to have a large measure of control in designing the institutional response to these developments.

It was Andrew Carnegie, from nearby Pittsburgh, who most clearly and compellingly articulated these ideas in his 1886–87 essays on the labor question and his 1889 essay on the administration of surplus wealth.[52] In these, Carnegie sought to reconcile the increasingly unequal distribution of wealth and power resulting from industrialism with traditional democratic and Christian ideals. His solution was based on a vision of the industrial enterprise and the society in which it operated which emphasized their overall unity and interdependence. Although modern industry, with its specialized and hierarchically ordered labor force, precluded traditional kinds of equality of condition, it offered new possibilities based on equality of opportunity. However, these required organizational mediation, in particular "associations and conferences" of employees—trade unions. These not only served to "educate workingmen" and "give them a truer conception of the relations of capital and labor," but also "permitted the ablest and best workmen to come to the front." "The right of the working-men to combine and form trades-unions," Carnegie declared, "is not less sacred than the right of the manufacturer to enter into associations and conferences with his fellows."[53] These forms of organization in turn permitted the formation of the kinds of "partnership between the employers and the employed" essential to peaceful labor relations and continuing economic progress.

In a manner that proved especially compelling to the leaders of industrial Cleveland, Carnegie stressed the role of "practical men," "men of affairs," in the process of socializing the industrial order. He was profoundly and outspokenly distrustful of "those doctrinaires who sit in their cozy studies and spin theories concerning the relations between capital and labor."[54] It was up to the "men entrusted with the management of great properties" to search "out the causes of disaffection among their employees, and, where any exist," to "meet the men more than half-way in the endeavor to allay them."[55] Accessibility and open-mindedness constituted only one dimension of this kind of industrial leadership. Equally important was the capacity to recognize the connections between working conditions, productivity, and profitability. In effect, Carnegie was suggesting that the workplace, rather than the realm of politics, was an appropriate arena for resolving the struggle between labor and capital—and that enlightened business managers would be the primary actors in the process.

Carnegie's 1889 essay on philanthropy, "The Gospel of Wealth," built on these assumptions. Charity in the industrial setting was not merely to alleviate suffering, but to place within the community's reach "the ladders upon which the aspiring can rise."[56] True philanthropy involved economic empowerment: "The individual administrator of surplus wealth has as his charge the industrious and ambitious; not those who need everything done for them, but who, being most anxious and able to help themselves, deserve and will be benefitted by help from others and by the extension of their opportunities by the aid of the philanthropic rich."[57]

Not coincidentally, Carnegie assigned government an especially important role in the reallocation of surplus wealth from its creators to its beneficiaries: he praised confiscatory inheritance taxes and progressive income taxes as "salutary," urging that "nations should go much further" to use their power to ensure that "the surplus wealth of the few will become, in the best sense, the property of the many, because administered for the common good."[58] He expressed considerable doubt about the value of purely private endowments, viewing "the best gift which can be given to a community" as one that the "community will accept and maintain as a public institution, as much a part of the city property as its public schools." An endowed institution "is liable to become the prey of a clique. The public ceases to take an interest in it, or rather, never acquires an interest in it. The rule has been violated which requires the recipients to help themselves. Everything has been done for them community instead of its only being helped to help itself, and good results rarely ensue."[59]

Carnegie did not regard philanthropy as a pursuit suitable only for the rich: "It is not the privilege, however, of millionaires alone to work for or aid measures which are certain to benefit the community. Everyone who has but a small surplus above his moderate wants may share this privilege with his richer brothers, and those without surplus can give at least a part of their time, which is usually as important as funds, and often more so."[60] Carnegie concluded with an evocation of the importance of diversity: "It is not expected, nor is it desirable, that there should be general concurrence as to the best possible use of surplus wealth. For different men and different localities there are different uses. What commends itself most highly to the judgment of the administrator is the best use for him, for his heart should be in the work."[61]

The meanings that readers drew from the essays of Carnegie depended on where they were situated. The essays themselves were ambiguous—reflecting the his own ambivalent relationship to the national economy.[62] Read from the perspective of a leader in a city such as Cleveland (or Pittsburgh or Chicago), Carnegie's injunctions did not constitute a blueprint for nationality. Rather, they constituted a paradigm for social reform in a local setting, in which business played the leading role and in which economic empowerment was the primary goal. Government was to serve as both regulator and partner in pursuing these ends. What Cleveland eventually did hewed remarkably close to the recommendations of Carnegie—more closely, indeed, than he ultimately did as a philanthropist. (But by the time Carnegie began setting up his foundations, more than a decade after writing "Wealth," he sold his steel company to the Morgan interests and, as a capitalist rather than a manufacturer, took on a more national—and international—outlook.)

One of those who took Carnegie's ideas particularly to heart was Cleveland businessman Marcus Alonzo Hanna, who would, perhaps more than any other American of his time, translate them into the new kinds of political instruments.[63] Because Hanna was an active businessman, he did not, like Hay and other "writers of the closet," partake of the hysteria that followed the labor troubles of the 1870s. Hanna understood that limiting the franchise would only intensify and protract the struggle between workers and employers. Moreover, he believed that the demands of organized labor were not incompatible with the desires of organized capital. Beginning in the early 1870s, he had personally met with groups of dissatisfied employees to settle disputes. In 1876, during the general strike in Ohio's Massillon coal district, his company was the first to "recognize the cardinal principle of arbitration in the settlement of wages, disputes, and also the first to recognize the 'Miners' National Association.'"[64] (Interestingly, representing the miners in this dispute was a young lawyer from Canton, Ohio, named William McKinley.)

Hanna's experience as an employer led him to accept as self-evident Carnegie's suggestions that the solution to the struggle between labor and capital depended on the rapprochement among organized interests. Thus, Hanna was immediately interested when his attention was called to Chicago's Civic Federation—a group that, beginning in 1893, had brought together representatives of labor, capital, and the general public to discuss questions of public policy, that favored arbitration of labor disputes, and that used methods such as surveys to investigate problems and to suggest possible solutions.[65] In 1900, Daniel R., Hanna's son, played an important role in organizing the National Civic Federation and in bringing its resources—and his father's influence—to bear on settling strikes in the coal and steel industries. As Herbert Croly, the biographer of Hanna, would reflect many years later, his ideas implied

> the organization of both employers and employees, a definite theory of economic relations between them and of the social and economic issues involved in their disputes. . . . He was one of the first of our public men to understand that the organization of capital necessarily implied some corresponding kind of labor organization. He clearly saw that the large corporations could not survive in case their behavior toward their employees was oppressive, and that they would in the end strengthen themselves by recognizing union labor. Derived as the two forms of organization were from analogous sources, the future of both depended partly upon their ability to find some basis of mutual accommodation and cooperation, not incompatible with the public interest. In grasping this connection, and in insisting upon it, Mr. Hanna traveled far ahead of prevailing business and political opinion.[66]

Hanna recognized that workers were not

> satisfied with the share of the product which they received under competitive conditions; and he came to realize that they were right in not being satisfied. . . . By proclaiming that capitalists had systematically exploited

their employees and that in their dealing with labor a humane motive should be substituted for the ordinary economic motive—in assuming such an attitude he was showing once again how clearly he could read and profit by the lessons of his experience. His whole plane of political and economic thought was raised to a higher level. He had liberated and made articulate the underlying humanity of his own personal feeling towards the mass of his fellow-countrymen.[67]

More importantly, he carried his views to the public: "He became a reformer, dedicated consciously to the task of converting other people to a better way of dealing with a fundamental problem; and the best of it was that his public appearance as a labor reformer was the natural, although fortuitous, expression of his lifelong personal feelings and behavior."[68] Had Croly been less of a nationalist, he would have been more appreciative of the extent to which events in Cleveland during the 1890s shaped Hanna's reformism. Croly might have also looked into the ways in which Hanna's views encouraged the progressive activism of the city's business community after 1900.

Hanna was by no means the only Cleveland businessman to become a reformer in the 1890s, nor was his "better way" the only way of dealing with the problems of industrialism. Tom L. Johnson, who became the dominant figure in Cleveland's municipal politics in the first decade of the twentieth century, had undergone a similar conversion experience—but the agencies of his transformation from millionaire traction promoter and steel manufacturer to progressive reformer were Henry George's *Social Problems* and *Progress and Poverty*. Although Democrat Johnson's political views diverged sharply from Republican Hanna's with regard to matters such as the protective tariff, regulation of monopolies, and private ownership of public utilities, their convictions about the especially important role of business leadership in the reform process, as well as the need for institutions to promote community development through associational and federative means, seem very similar.[69] Thus, though Cleveland reformism included a wide spectrum of belief, the leaders of both right- and left-wings were businesspeople who were willing to work with or through private-sector entities such as the Chamber of Commerce to define the public interest and through municipal government to implement their goals.

The *mentalité* of Cleveland's business community after 1890 is evident in the activities of the Chamber of Commerce, which joined to its promotion of economic diversification a widening set of reform issues. It took an active role in the debate over reforming the city's charter—which eventually led its municipal committee to hive off into a separate entity, the Municipal Association, which maintained an ongoing interest in questions of city administration and which was the strongest advocate of the 1912 "home rule" charter and the 1921 adoption of the city-manager form of government.

By the late 1890s, the Chamber of Commerce had begun to concern itself with land-use questions. Significantly, these efforts focused on promoting public-private cooperation, acting through quasi-public bodies that coordinated public and private resources. Thus, the chamber's Committee on Public Buildings, established in 1899, had within a year evolved into the City Plan Commission, which worked with reformist Mayor Tom Johnson to create the Group Plan for the Mall. Obviously, the chamber's political and financial backing for the construction of the new city hall, public library, and other public buildings was a crucial factor in the implementation of this plan. Without the business community's willingness to invest in such municipal improvements—through underwriting bond issues, shouldering an increased tax burden, and making available key pieces of real estate such as the Case city block, which had remained in the hands of the Case estate—the redevelopment of the city's center never could have taken place. The chamber played a similarly crucial role in the establishment of the Metropolitan Park Commission, which, like the Group Plan, had a quasi-public character and was based on coordinating public and private resources to develop recreational resources.

Housing issues were inseparable from the larger concerns of city planning—and here also the Chamber of Commerce took the lead, urging the passage of a municipally administered housing code (1914) and tenement code (1916), as well as financing individual home ownership through the establishment of "limited dividend corporations" during the 1920s. Among the most important and enduring contributions of the chamber to city planning was its role in organizing the University Improvement Company in 1919, which was instrumental in creating University Circle, Cleveland's unique "complex of cultural, educational, religious, and social service institutions in a parklike setting."[70] University Circle—and adjacent University Heights—had their origins in the mid-1880s, when Jephtha Wade gave the city a substantial parcel of land adjoining the Case Institute and Western Reserve University campuses. Subsequent donations by prominent businessmen, purchases of land by the institute and the university (on whose boards the businessmen sat), and a willingness to coordinate private development activity led to the creation of a planned urban environment, which became a national model.

Cleveland's Chamber of Commerce was no less active in the area of social welfare—and it is here that the differences between the northeastern and midwestern models of civil society are most evident. To begin with, the chamber, a business organization, was far more likely to be the seedbed of reform proposals than a foundation or a private university. Moreover, these proposals were far more likely to be carried out through quasi-public bodies than through purely private philanthropic entities. The city's two pioneering ventures in cooperative charity, the Federation for Charity and Philanthropy (the ancestor of the Community Chest and the United Way) and the Cleveland Foundation (the first community foundation).

In 1900, the Chamber of Commerce formed a Committee on Benevolent Associations to investigate the increasing number of causes making appeals in the city and to distinguish between fraudulent and worthy solicitors.[71] Subsequently, the committee began to respond to complaints from established charities about the difficulties of fundraising, particularly those due to competition for the attention of a limited pool of donors. In 1909, the committee launched a full-scale investigation of the problem, inviting seventy-three charities to submit their lists of donors and donations for analysis. The results were astonishing:

> Out of a city of over 600,000 people, it was found that the whole charitable enterprise, receiving current contributions of $500,000 was supported by only 5386 separate contributors of $5 or more—less than one per cent. of the population. Of these, furthermore, more than 800 were commercial firms and corporations. Moreover, of the 5386 contributors 54 were giving 55 per cent. of the total contributed, while 1066 individuals and firms were contributing 90 per cent. of the total.[72]

The committee immediately not only expressed concern about the need to make fund-raising more effective and efficient, but also particularly emphasized the need to broaden the base for charity by educating small givers.

In 1913, the Chamber of Commerce created a new organization, the Cleveland Federation for Charity and Philanthropy, which brought together fifty-three charitable organizations endorsed as legitimate by the Chamber of Commerce's Committee on Benevolent Organizations. These donees elected ten of their number to serve on the Federation's thirty-member governing board. Of the twenty remaining members, ten were elected by "the city's larger givers" and the rest were "selected to represent the city at large by the president and directors of the Chamber of Commerce."[73] The federation planned to make a coordinated appeal that would permit donors either to designate particular organizations as beneficiaries or to place their gifts for distribution at the discretion of the governing board. The federation's first campaign,

conducted between October 1912 and February 1913, was conspicuously successful, bringing in $300,000 from four thousand donors—
which constituted two-thirds of the city's annual "benevolent
budget."[74] Subsequent efforts proved even more successful, not only
increasing the total funds raised but also broadening the basis of participation. "In a single year," noted one correspondent for a national
magazine in the mid-1920s, "nearly half the inhabitants, man, woman,
and child—$458,000, to be exact—contributed to the Community
Chest."[75]

For all of its obvious benefits, the Cleveland Federation only dealt
with one aspect of charity: the problem of meeting the current needs
of participating organizations through annual gifts. The federation
did not address the desire of some donors to create charitable trusts,
which would yield income for benevolent purposes in perpetuity. Nor
did the federation deal with the "dead hand"—the problem of assuring
that future needs would be met by such perpetual trusts. The open-
ended grant-making foundations that began to appear in the first
decade of the new century were one way of dealing with the "dead
hand"—but the idea of allowing a self-perpetuating board of trustees
to decide what constituted "the benefit of mankind" or the good of the
community was inimical to the institutional traditions of Cleveland
and other cities of the Old Northwest.

The community trust idea developed in 1913 by Frederick H. Goff,
president of the Cleveland Trust Company, constituted a nearly perfect
expression of this institutional ethos: a foundation would be set up
to receive charitable trust funds, which—as under the federation
scheme—their donors could either designate for particular purposes or
leave to the discretion of the foundation for distribution; the actual
tasks of administering the funds would be delegated to commercial
banks; their distribution would be overseen by a distribution committee of public and private officials—as originally established, by two
directors of the Cleveland Trust Company, the mayor of Cleveland, the
senior probate judge of Cuyahoga County, and the senior presiding
judge of the U.S. District Court for the Northern District of Ohio.[76]
This arrangement (which became common in the Midwest, but less so
in the Northeast) made the Cleveland Foundation a quasi-public body
in the mold of many other entities created in Cleveland during this
period.[77] The purpose of the foundation was the same as that of the
federation; it was as much to make philanthropy more efficient as it
was to increase levels of public involvement. As Goff noted, the foundation appealed not only to the wealthy but also

to men and women of moderate means whose surplus (after caring for children and relatives) would not be great enough to endow a chair or a charity or accomplish any other notable purpose. By the combining of many small funds a large income is provided with which work of real significance to the community may be accomplished. It makes appeal to the possessors of wealth, large or small. Men of great wealth have in the past created private foundations, but no a way has been provided by which even greater foundations may be created out of the contributions of many citizens.[78]

The Cleveland Foundation would more than justify the hopes of its founder. It played a key role in rationalizing and professionalizing other private voluntary and philanthropic efforts in the city and, perhaps more importantly, profoundly influenced public policy through its sponsorship of studies and surveys and in its capacity to leverage both public and private funds to achieve particular goals.

As important as the Federation for Charity and Philanthropy and the Cleveland Foundation may be as national models, we must recognize that, from the local standpoint, they were merely adjuncts of a broader and more complex set of commitments to cooperative community action, which centered on the interconnection of business and government. This interconnection was in marked contrast to the situation in the Northeast, where private nonprofit institutions—particularly foundations and universities—occupied the central position in delineating public policy.

The contrast among the different styles of civil society at the turn of the century is captured by the confrontation between George F. Baer, spokesman for the anthracite operators during the national coal strike of 1902, and Cleveland's Marc Hanna, who played a leading role in its mediated settlement. "The rights and interests of the laboring man," Baer declared, "will be protected and cared for—not by the labor agitators, but by the Christian men to whom God in His infinite wisdom has given control of the property interests of this country, and upon the successful Management of which so much depends."[79] Hanna's terse response, that "any man who doesn't meet his men halfway is a damned fool," was more than just a blunt assertion of common sense—it summed up three decades of his struggle to come to terms with the new kinds of responsibilities business carried in the industrial age. More importantly, his response encapsulated the difference between the classic and the midwestern view of trusteeship. While both Baer and Hanna saw themselves as stewards acting in the public interest, the northeastern or civil-privatist model placed the "guardianship of virtue" outside political and economic processes.

The midwestern or federationist model did not crudely define the public interest as a political product; rather, it viewed the public interest as emerging from negotiated understandings between public and private interests.

To be effective, such a mode of proceeding had to be inclusive. And such an inclusive system required widespread support and participation. There is suggestive, but far from conclusive, evidence that civic participation was far more widespread in the Midwest than the Northeast. A comparison of turn-of-the-century graduates of Harvard and Yale is illuminating in this regard. It is worth noting that Yale graduates of the class of 1905 still living twenty-five years later were approximately twice as likely to have served as directors or trustees than their Harvard contemporaries (Yale: 182/237; Harvard: 173/605).[80] This overall pattern is replicated in the patterns of civic participation by graduates of both institutions in particular settings: of the seven-member class of 1905 Yale graduates resident in Cleveland in 1930, six had served as directors or trustees (four as directors only, one as trustee only, and one in both capacities). In contrast, of the thirteen-member class of 1905 Harvard graduates resident in Cleveland in 1930, only four had served as trustees or directors. Interestingly, all of the Yale graduate directors or trustees had been born in or near Cleveland and returned there to pursue their careers after graduation. This was true of only seven of the thirteen Harvard graduates.

The most interesting observations, however, involve the careers of graduates born in Cleveland, regardless of whether they attended Yale or Harvard. Clevelanders were far more likely to return to their native city than other graduates born in Ohio: of the twenty-six-member class of 1905 Yale graduates born in the state, eleven (45 percent) returned to the state—versus six of the seven born in Cleveland (85 percent); of the twenty-nine Ohio natives in Harvard's class of 1905, thirteen (45 percent) returned to the state—versus five of the nine (56 percent) Cleveland natives.

These figures suggest that Cleveland's civic culture was unusually vital, offering opportunities to young men who could easily have gravitated to more exciting metropolitan centers. Indeed, Oliver Wendell Holmes defines a true metropolis as one that "drains off" talent, capital, and beauty from cities and towns within its "suction range."[81] By this definition, civic vitality can be defined in terms of the ability of a city to retain its talented and ambitious young people. An inclusive civic life appears to be an important component of this kind of pattern, because mobility into positions of community leadership constitutes an important dimension of opportunity. Cleveland evidently possessed this characteristic.

On the eve of World War I, alternatives to the northeastern model of civil privatism were still being discussed—most notably in a published exchange of views between *Harper's Weekly* editor Norman Hapgood and Chicago businessman Julius Rosenwald, both of whom came out of the midwestern civic tradition (Hapgood was from Indianapolis, Rosenwald was from Chicago). Introducing a series on modern charity, Hapgood briefly recounted the evolution of philanthropy. "Once charity was personal," he wrote,

> giving a cent to a beggar, visiting the needy in the neighborhood, being personally open to individual appeal, exhausted the prevailing conception of help for the suffering. . . . But when man began to organize society on a far more complex basis he found hand-to-hand charity insufficient. He had harnessed steam. He had invented machines, forces of nature, to do his work. Organization was everywhere. Organization came into charity. . . . With organization came investigation. Earnest, efficient citizens supported it, because they believed it was scientific, effective, and they desired knowledge and brains as well as heart-throb behind their efforts.[82]

But Hapgood believed that scientifically informed, efficiently organized charity was not without its shortcomings:

> Organized industry has brought new evils along with benefits. So also organized charity has its faults, and these are seen by many who devote their lives to the work, fully as clearly as by indiscriminate barkers. Nevertheless we all tend to defend our activities, the things we know, and to oppose what supplants them. Therefore organized charity leaders, in formidable numbers, fight the inevitable next step. They see that the individual effort had to admit the private organization. They do not see that the private organization must be supplemented by the whole community—by institutions of the city, state, nation, aimed to remove the evil at an earlier stage. They oppose minimum wage, widow's compensation, municipal, state, or federal industrial enterprises related to unemployment, public insurance against old age, disease, or lack of work. They cannot see the writing on the wall. They would have history stand still.[83]

Hapgood's critique elicited a defense of midwestern charitable forms which, though based on Chicago's experience, could just as well have been written about Cleveland. Appropriately, the respondent was Rosenwald, one of the city's leading businessmen.[84] The Sears Roebuck chairman proceeded to point out that the United Charities of Chicago "has taken a stand unequivocally in favor of minimum wage legislation," that "the citizens and social experts directly connected with the United Charities, the Associated Charities and other friends of organized charity" had been the strongest advocates of state-funded pensions for widows, and that these organizations had been steadfast in their efforts "to relieve unemployment through public agencies. Instead of opposing efforts for social legislation," Rosenwald declared, "our leaders of organized charity have urged public officials that they undertake service that obviously they can better carry on than can private charities, as, for instance, open air schools, care of dependent children, care of the tuberculous, infant welfare work, playground extension, ample provision to meet the problem of the homeless man and many other items. I hold no brief for organized charity leaders, here or elsewhere," he concluded,

> but my personal hope is that more and more the greater governmental units, like the county, city, state, and nation, will take over and operate tried and true social agencies for the betterment of mankind that have been originated by private initiative and funds. This is no new thing. It is only history repeating itself. We, in Chicago, know that history is not going to stand still. In fact, our leaders in charity are trying aggressively to help make social history.[85]

Rosenwald's description of the relationship between private and public agencies—though one that is generally accepted now— differed significantly from the northeastern pattern, in which private institutions sought to retain, wherever possible, their monopoly of eleemosynary activities—if necessary with public funds.[86] In the District of Columbia at the turn of the century, almost one-half of the funds allocated for aid to the poor went to private agencies; in New York State, this figure approached 60 percent.[87] Yale and MIT, both private institutions, controlled federal Morrell Act moneys until after the turn of the century. It is important to understand the difference between government taking direct responsibility for delivering services in areas pioneered by private agencies (Rosenwald's model) and government underwriting the activities of private institutions.

One final point with regard to the midwestern or federationist institutional system has to do with how inclusive it really was. By the late 1920s, Cleveland had become a national model of civic enlightenment. "It has combined," wrote R. L. Duffus in the *New Republic,* "unmitigated materialism with a degree of something resembling civilization."[88] What made the city different was its "sense of civic responsibility," the "habit of giving back to the public a part of what had been taken away," which "early became respectable among Cleveland's rich men." "If there is such a thing as a capitalistic system," Duffus declared, "it has been strengthened and bolstered up by the application of the Cleveland Idea."

Out of the thunderous smoke of the valley of the Cuyahoga, out of flames and fumes, out of sweat and sorrow, Cleveland has begun to build a twentieth-century fairyland. . . . It is a dwelling place with a bathroom, a bit of sun and even, if he listens to what the children learn in their art classes at schools, some elementals of good taste. But he also has a share in the community dwelling places, in a great art museum lovelier than the palace of almost any king; in a vast civic auditorium where any one may hear Bach fugues on the organ, attend a Shriners' convention or hear a President nominated; in a library in which the patrons are actually treated as citizens and equals rather than as convicts, in a lofty new railway station, fruit of the labors of the brothers Van Sweringen, in the Mall, which will presently become a wide pleasure ground running grandly to the lake, in a lovely series of parks. The public buildings and spaces of Cleveland are imposing. They satisfy the eye. They create a sense of citizenship comparable, however remotely . . . with that which the Athenians must have derived from the edifices upon the Acropolis.

Although he admired Cleveland's achievements, Duffus also found the city profoundly disquieting. "Never," he wrote, has

a community been compelled to contemplate, with such scientific and unoriental intensity, its own navel. . . . Cleveland would cooperate even if it had to be genteelly clubbed into doing it. Cleveland would be neighborly, Cleveland would give til it hurt. The agencies of publicity which had been devoted to developing national patriotism were directed toward stirring up community patriotism, and with much the same systems of pains, penalties and rewards. . . . This ballyhooing for cooperation has its tyrannies and its Freudian suppressions. . . .

Underneath the Nordic veneer, there is, certainly, a non-Nordic restlessness and discontent. . . . In 1924, it may be recalled, the voters of Cleveland rejected the stainless Calvin in favor of the hell-roaring La Follette. This, clearly, was not the work of the Cleveland Foundation or of the Community Chest. It was, from the Republican point of view, something less than cooperative. Did it bespeak a proletarian dissatisfaction with the art galleries, libraries, parks, schools, little theaters and scientific charity? Was it a revolt against the whole theory of municipal grandmothering?

"Man does not live by bread alone," Duffus concluded, "nor by parks, nor by model tenements, nor by low tax rates, nor even by art galleries; he lives, if at all, by adventure."

Was the expertly managed cooperative benevolence of Cleveland—its perfected corporatism—really a matter of the "approximately 30 percent of the population who are native-born whites of native parentage" dominating the rest of the city's population? Although it is undoubtedly true that WASPs controlled more than their share of Cleveland's wealth, evidence for the inclusiveness of the leadership structure is fairly persuasive. The Cleveland—or, more broadly, the midwestern—model did not wither away with the Depression. It has persisted and remains an important alternative to the models of civil privatism and trusteeship offered by the most influential elements in organized philanthropy.

Cultures of Trusteeship:
Boston, the Classic Model of Civil Privatism

No American city conveys an impression of stability and continuity more than Boston. Nor—perhaps not coincidentally—is any city more closely identified with the concept of trusteeship than "the Hub." The "Boston trustee" is a legendary figure, not only as prudent fiduciary for the descendants of the city's Brahmin families, but also as steward of community values and interests, usually in his capacity as board member of a long-established and well-endowed private charitable institution.[89] And it was out of the efforts of the city's economic and cultural leaders to institutionalize those values that the Prudent Man Rule, the first application of the Rule Against Perpetuities, and other fundamentals of the theory and practice of trusteeship in the United States arose.

The relative antiquity of Boston trusteeship should not blind us to the fact that it was very much a social construction produced to serve the needs of a particular group of individuals in a particular place at a particular time. It took many years for the private trusteed institution to gain acceptance even in its birthplace—and many more years before it was accepted as a model in other parts of the United States.

Most of the families whose names we instantly identify as bastions of proper Boston were, until the 1780s, not Bostonians at all. The Cabots were in Salem; the Lowells, in Newburyport; the Adamses, in Braintree; the Peabodys and Lawrences, in rural Essex and Middlesex counties.[90] When they came to Boston after the Revolution to fill the vacuum left by the departure of the old Tory elite, they did not find a city of old established private institutions. There were no banks, no insurance companies, and indeed no corporations of any kind—except for Harvard College.[91] And Harvard, though venerable even then, was essentially a public school: the bulk of its revenues came from the state, and its major governing board, the overseers, consisted of the governor, deputy governor, the governor's council, and the entire membership of the State Senate—along with the ministers of the towns adjoining Cambridge (who, inasmuch as the churches were tax-supported and the minister was elected by their congregations, could also be viewed as public officials).[92]

Testamentary trusteeship was as unknown as institutional trustee-ship in late-eighteenth-century Boston. As late as 1804, efforts to create trusts under wills were frustrated by the courts. As the Supreme Judicial Court noted in its decision in the case of *Prescott v. Tarbell*, "if the conveyance was in trust, this court could not have compelled the execution of it; and, until the legislature shall think proper to give us further powers, we can do nothing upon subjects of *that* nature."[93] In 1810, in the case of *Parsons v. Winslow*, the court again pointed to its inability to compel the enforcement of trusts because the legislature had not granted it equity powers.[94]

Yet within a generation, the whole apparatus of trusteeship—testamentary and institutional and in its fiduciary as well its stewardship dimensions—had been put in place.[95] The apparatus did not gradually evolve over centuries, nor was it a wholesale appropriation of English equity jurisprudence and trust practice—which by this point were both highly developed. Although English precedents proved important, Bostonians seem to have selected only those that served their needs (such as the distinction between charitable and noncharitable trusts), rejected others (such as the role of ecclesiastical courts in regulating charitable trusts), and innovating when they thought it necessary (as in the Prudent Man Rule, which set forth the "sound discretion" of "men of prudence" in the management of their own affairs as the standard for fiduciaries—thus freeing trust capital for investment in the state's growing industries).[96]

A number of factors pushed the entrepreneurs of postrevolutionary Boston toward the use of the trust as a device for regulating society, institutions, and families. Political turbulence was undoubtedly important. The decade following the Revolution was punctuated by violence and disorder. Mobs seized courthouses in rural districts. By the 1790s, inspired by French revolutionaries, American artisans and farmers were breaking away from the established church and resisting deference to their "natural leaders." As the "ignorant and vicious" became politically empowered, the "wealthy, learned, and respectable" merchants, ministers, and magistrates began to understand the uncertainty of merely political power.[97]

Although the state's conservative constitution, which favored the wealthy over the poor and urban interests over rural ones, could be counted on to temper the force of democratic revolution, the organization of a national political opposition to Federalism in the mid-1890s clearly numbered its days. Conservatives began to cast about for alternatives to political power—and one area of particular interest was the law, especially laws that permitted individuals and groups to act in the name of the public without being directly accountable to the public.[98]

Not surprisingly, Harvard College became the catalyst for this effort. There were two reasons for this, one strategic, the other pragmatic. Strategically, Harvard was an important power base because it not only controlled significant endowment funds (it was a major source of commercial credit in this period) but also controlled access to the learned professions, the law, and the clergy. The leading role of these groups in fomenting public sentiment during the Revolution had made clear how influential such credentialed groups could be. Thus, even at this early date, conservatives understood the potential power of the college in manipulating knowledge and legitimacy to their advantage.[99]

Pragmatically, even though Harvard had been regarded as a public institution, its charter offered unusual possibilities for private control. One of its governing boards, the self-perpetuating group of seven fellows, was already under the control of conservative laymen. While the overseers remained nominally a public body by virtue of the numerical dominance of members of the State Senate, for the time, at least, it could be counted on to favor the conservative viewpoint, because the state constitution limited seats in the State Senate to those with considerable property.[100] However, open conflict with the democratic opposition broke out in 1810 when, fearing their displacement in the coming elections, Federalists voted to alter the composition of the overseers:

> By eliminating the State Senate, the *ex officio* members were reduced to eleven, and the clerical members were limited to fifteen, keeping existing ministers (all "men of correct principles") in office until death or removal; fifteen new laymen were to be elected by the Board itself; and the new Board, thus constituted, would fill future vacancies by cooptation. The first lay members elected by the Board were all Federalists, of the same type as the Fellows—indeed it would seem that the one purpose of this Act was to make the Overseers a sort of "waiting club" for the Corporation.[101]

When the Jeffersonians took power in 1811, they immediately repealed this act. But when the legislature was returned to the Federalists a year later, the 1810 statute was reenacted. A compromise statute was finally passed in 1814, which balanced the number of ex officio public representatives against the co-opted laymen—thus avoiding a court battle which could have made the famous Dartmouth College case the Harvard College case.[102] (The central issue in the two situations was substantially the same, both having to do with the legislature's power to alter the provisions of corporate charters. However,

New Hampshire's Jeffersonians proved less accommodating than those of Massachusetts).

The privatization of Harvard in the second decade of the nineteenth century set a precedent that encouraged wealthy Bostonians to establish a range of other private institutions with public purposes. This wave of institution-building really took off after 1819, when the legislature granted equity powers—jurisdiction over trusts—to the Supreme Judicial Court.[103] In rapid succession, on a case-by-case basis, the courts, which were dominated by conservatives, resolved the major ambiguities regarding the power of testamentary and institutional trustees, giving them virtual immunity from the claims of third parties, the demands of beneficiaries, and the public interest as defined by any elected body.[104]

The evolution of institutional and testamentary trusteeship in Massachusetts was closely intertwined not only because both partook of the same body of English precedents but also because the same group of wealthy merchants and, by the 1820s, industrialists had vital interests in the creation of new instruments for controlling and conveying wealth. Those who had profited from the opportunities of the post-revolutionary decades understood, as Holmes noted, that "it is in the nature of large fortunes to diminish rapidly, when subdivided and distributed," as was the universal New England practice. "A million," Holmes continued,

> is the unit of wealth, now and here in America. It splits into four handsome properties; each of these into four good inheritances; these, again, into scanty competences for four ancient maidens,—with whom it is best that the family dies out, unless it can begin again as its great-grandfather did. Now a million is a kind of golden cheese, which represents in a compendious form the summer's growth of a fat meadow of craft or commerce; and as this kind of meadow rarely bears more than one crop, it is pretty certain that sons and grandsons will not get another golden cheese out of it, whether they milk the same cows or turn in new ones. In other words, the millionocracy, considered in a large way, is not at all an affair of persons or families, but a perpetual fact of money with a variable human element.[105]

Bostonians were concerned about their capacity to pass their fortunes intact to future generations, and testamentary trusteeship—which made it possible to maintain their capital intact, while adhering to traditions of partible inheritance by dividing the income it yielded— answered those concerns. But mere possession of wealth was not enough. Bostonians had other things in mind as well.

The most immediate of these things came up long before the question of estate planning and bore on the problem of making their fortunes. The ambitious merchants from the provincial ports quickly discovered the limitations of traditional forms of business organization to exploit the opportunities offered by commerce beyond the protected confines of the British mercantile system. The capital and the range of talent available in family partnerships was insufficient to the risks and the challenges. One way of increasing their capital base was to reduce or alter their sons' claims on family capital—which they could do by encouraging some of their sons to enter the professions rather than their fathers' counting houses. (A professional education was far less costly than giving a son the capital to start his own business.)[106]

To make the professions attractive, the prestige of occupational alternatives was enhanced by turning them into learned professions— a status that neither law nor medicine had fully achieved at the end of the eighteenth century. Creating endowments for professional schools, which the merchants began to do by the 1780s, had an added advantage. The capital, though nominally under institutional control, was not lost to their commercial interests because, to yield income, it had to be invested. Before the 1820s, the most common form of investment took the form of secured loans to merchants. Later, as merchants moved into textile manufacturing and railroading, endowments were moved into stocks. Doing this, of course, gave the merchants an added incentive to become involved in institutions as trustees—who, of course, were in a position to control the investment of these funds.[107]

The creation of endowment funds served to free up family capital for more purely economic purposes while actually increasing the amount of capital available to civic-minded merchants and industrialists. In addition, by diverting the sons of these wealthy families into the law, medicine, the clergy, and teaching—and later engineering, architecture, and other specialized pursuits—the endowed institution and the testamentary trust served to extend the influence of these wealthy families beyond the commercial domain and into every aspect of social and cultural activity.

The testamentary trust and endowed institution served other important purposes as well. Reducing the number of sons in family firms was only one component of increasing their available capital. Equally important was the admission of nonrelated individuals as partners. Although these individuals frequently brought with them capital, knowledge, experience, and valuable commercial contacts and although their commercial involvement was almost invariably cemented by marriage (often multiple marriages between the partners' families), merchants could protect themselves against possible fortune hunters with testamentary trusts that protected their daughters' inheritances from their husbands. At the same time, endowed institutions, Harvard in particular, became increasingly important as a means of recruiting and socially credentialing prospective husbands and business associates.[108]

"Boston is just like other places of its size," wrote Holmes, posing in the 1850s as the Autocrat of the Breakfast Table,

> only perhaps, considering its excellent fish-market, paid fire department, superior monthly publications, and correct habit of spelling the English language, it has some right to look down on the mob of cities. I'll tell you, though, if you want to know it, what is the real offense of Boston. It drains a large watershed of intellect, and will not itself be drained. If only it would send away its first-rate men, instead of its second-rate ones, (no offense to the well-known exceptions, of which we are always proud,) we should be spared such epigrammatic remarks as that which the gentleman has quoted [that the Boston State House is the hub of the solar system]. There can never be a real metropolis in this country, until the biggest center can drain the lesser ones of their talent and wealth. —I have observed, by the way, that the people who really live in two great cities are by no means as jealous of each other, as are those of smaller cities situated within the intellectual basin, or *suction-range*, of the large one, or the pretensions of any other. Don't you see why? Because their promising young author and rising lawyer and large capitalist have been drained off to the neighboring big city, —their prettiest girl has been exported to the same market; all their ambition points there, and all their thin gilding of glory comes from there.[109]

What made Boston a center that drained "a large watershed" of wealth, talent, and beauty were its endowed private institutions and, in a larger sense, its distinctive concept of trusteeship—of private responsibility for the quality of civic life. By the 1840s, the city had become the home to an extraordinary range of privately supported and governed institutions. Writing in the *North American Review* in 1845, Samuel Atkins Eliot, treasurer of Harvard University listed institutions that had received nearly $3 million in private support since 1830:[110]

Boston Athenaeum
Humane Society
Boston Dispensary
Massachusetts General Hospital
Massachusetts Charitable Society
Boston Penitent Female Refuge Society
Boston Fragment Society
Boston Mechanics Institution

Boston Eye and Ear Infirmary
Boston Female Asylum
Boston Society for the Diffusion of Useful Knowledge
Boston Society for the Religious and Moral Instruction of the Poor
Charitable Mechanic Association
Boston Asylum for Indigent Boys
Fatherless and Widows' Society
Charitable Fund
Massachusetts Congregational Charitable Society
Seamen's Friend Society
American Education Society
Bible Society
Harvard College Boston Society of Natural History
Mercantile Library Association
Mechanic Apprentices Library Association
Massachusetts Agricultural Society
Massachusetts Horticultural Society
Boston Asylum for Indigent Boys
Howard Benevolent Society
Boston Lying-in Hospital
Boston Port Society
Boston Society for Employment of the Female Poor
Boston Orthopedic Institution
Boston Episcopal Charitable Society
Charitable Association of the Boston Fire Department
Prison Discipline Society
Society for the Prevention of Pauperism

Underlying this extraordinary organizational diversity, however,
were a number of fundamental unities. The wealthiest and best-sup-
ported institutions were tightly interlocked, not only with one another
but also with the central economic enterprises of the region. The economic importance of these ties is suggested by the failure patterns of
banks during the depression of 1837–42: of the forty-three commercial
banks operating in Boston in 1836, only twenty-four survived the
crisis; of these, twenty-one were linked to endowed charitable organizations through directors and trustees. Of the ten banks that failed,
nine had no such connections.[111] Analogously, the Massachusetts Hospital Life Insurance Company, a for-profit subsidiary of the Massachusetts General Hospital, was not only the largest single source of investment capital in New England before the Civil War, but also tightly
interlocked with the textile industry and the promoters of real-estate
development and western railroads.[112] Quite clearly, charitable endow-

ments served as capital pools, sustaining Brahmin organizations in times of crisis and supplying them in boom times with capital to sustain growth and expansion.

The significance of these linkages was far more than economic. To be sure, the charities, like the business corporations, represented an effort to collectivize family capital and to place it under the "rational" (or at least prudent) control of testamentary and corporate trustees. But the economic relationships were merely an analog to a more profound collectivizing of the socialization process. The Brahmins, acutely concerned with the problems of establishing and maintaining leadership (and being worthy of it), had created a network of educational and cultural institutions whose purpose was to train, test, and sort out the young, promoting the most able to preeminent positions as trustees of the central organizations that defined the Brahmins as a class.[113] As Ronald Story has so ably shown, the Brahmin institutional system did not spring into being overnight. Through the first half of the nineteenth century, it operated so informally that men such as Henry Adams could write that Harvard in the 1850s

> was a mild and liberal school, which sent young men into the world with all they needed to make respectable citizens, and something of what they wanted to make useful ones. Leaders of men it never tried to make. Its ideals were altogether different. The Unitarian clergy had given to the College a character of moderation, balance, judgment, restraint, what the French called *mesure;* excellent traits, which the college attained with singular success, so that its graduates could commonly be recognized by the stamp, but such a type of character rarely lent itself to autobiography. In effect, the school created a type, but not a will. Four years of Harvard College, if successful, resulted in an autobiographical blank, a mind on which only a water-mark had been stamped.[114]

Adams was, as usual, being ironic. An institution that, even in its apparent doldrums, could educate the most influential historian of the nineteenth century (Adams himself, who graduated in 1858), the most important legal thinker (Justice Oliver Wendell Holmes, class of 1861), the most important educational reformer (Charles W. Eliot, class of 1853), the most important economic thinker (Henry's older brother, Charles Francis Adams, class of 1856), and a pioneer of modern investment banking (Henry Lee Higginson, class of 1858) was doing a good deal more than producing "a type but not a will." As Adams himself acknowledges, "the College Catalogue for the years 1854 to 1861 shows a list of names rather distinguished in their time."[115]

Eliot, Adams' contemporary, both institutionalized the informal system of leadership production and most clearly articulated its goals and methods. Although Eliot is generally seen as a radical educational reformer—and, if one views him only through the lens of education as it was before 1869, he certainly was—what he was actually doing was internalizing within the university a set of activities which had, heretofore, taken place outside of it. (The process was parallel to what business corporations were doing as they moved from being single-unit family-owned enterprises to being integrated multidivisional managed enterprises.) Eliot's reforms involved both backward and forward integration—backward into taking control of the recruitment and preparation processes through the creation of standardized admissions testing and participation in efforts to reshape secondary schools; and forward into professional training and interaction with the occupational structure through the reform of graduate and professional education (which now took place at Harvard itself, rather than abroad or in semiproprietary schools) and through involving officers of the corporations that would be hiring Harvard graduates in molding the university's curriculum.[116]

Eliot's famous 1869 essay "The New Education" made sense to Boston's leaders not because of its novelty, but because it formalized patterns of education, socialization, and leadership selection that had existed for decades in the network of families which composed the Brahmin class. "We do not apply to mental activities the principle of division of labor," Eliot declared in 1869, "and we have but a halting faith in special training for high professional employments. . . . Only after years of the bitterest experience did we come to believe the professional training of a soldier to be of value in war." "The civilization of a people," he continued, "may be inferred from the variety of its tools. . . . As tools multiply, each is more ingeniously adapted to its own exclusive purpose. So with the men that make the State. For the individual, concentration, and the highest development of his own peculiar faculty, is the only prudence. But for the State, it is variety, not uniformity of the intellectual product, which is needful."[117]

The basis for adapting higher education to the needs of an economy and a polity that required a wide range of specialized skills and a general managerial capacity to oversee the whole posed a problem not unlike that faced by the Bostonians three generations earlier, when they sought to direct their sons into a broader spectrum of occupations: they wanted sons with business ability to become businessmen, while permitting those with other interests to pursue them. One source from this period suggests the familial setting in which this happened:

[Father] had desired that each of his boys should follow a profession of his own selecting, and both the customs of the period and the needs of the day impelled to an early choice. . . . By the time they were ten years old, James began to be dubbed "the doctor" and Harry "the Commodore:" for the latter had determined, when a mere boy, to seek his fortunes on the sea. Robert, the oldest son, and, as James thinks, his mother's favorite, decided to throw in his lot with the merchants, and Charles with the lawyers. Patrick, the youngest, was likewise to be trained for a business life.[118]

Significantly, guarantees of success were attached to none of these choices, and they did not lead automatically to more generalized positions of community or institutional leadership. Each occupation presented an arena in which the young were taught and tested. Some succeeded, others failed. In this particular family, of the three brothers who entered commerce, only the youngest, Patrick, became successful—first as a merchant and, subsequently, as a founder of the textile industry with his cousin Francis Cabot Lowell. Patrick also gravitated beyond commerce into more generalized positions of community leadership as a director and trustee. The brothers who entered law and medicine both became outstanding members of their professions—and by virtue of that moved into the leadership orbit as directors and trustees. Money and connections were not crucial determinants of their success. Nor, in itself, were the careers they choose. They were, after all, competing with young men who were no less monied and well-connected—as well as with the talented and ambitious outlanders who gravitated to Harvard and to Boston's commercial and cultural institutions.[119]

The collective nature of the city's institutions tended on the whole to minimize the significance of family favoritism, and the young and striving tended to be assessed on the basis of performance rather than pedigree. This emphasis of ability over breeding was, as a number of public controversies of the 1830s and 1840s suggest, not always easy for families to accept.[120] And, indeed, when Eliot proposed formalizing this system and placing it under the control of the university, he was fiercely opposed—not only by those who disdained the talented but base-born "cheap material" that he proposed to attract to the university, but also by elements in the professions, particularly medicine and the clergy, who stood to loose stature and income if his plans were implemented.[121]

For Eliot, as for his forebears, the starting point of the educational system was recognizing that talent and ability (what he called "faculties," the "natural bent" that proved to be the basis of a calling) were not given by God impartially,—to each round soul a little of each power, as if the soul were a pill, which must contain its due proportion of many various ingredients. To reason about the average human mind as if it were a globe, to be expanded symmetrically from a center outward, is to be betrayed by the metaphor. A cutting tool, a drill, or auger would be a juster symbol of the mind. The natural bent and peculiar quality of every boy's mind should be sacredly regarded in his education; the division of mental labor, which is essential in civilized communities in order that knowledge may grow and society improve, demands this regard in the peculiar constitution of each mind, as much as does the happiness of the individual concerned. . . . To make a good engineer, chemist, or architect, the only sure way is to make first, or at least simultaneously, an observant, reflecting and sensible man, whose mind is not only well stored, but well trained also to see, compare, reason, and decide.

"A boy's course of study," Eliot continued,

> should be representative; it should be selected as to reveal to him, or at least to his parents and teachers, his capacities and tastes before he is seventeen years old. Teachers are apt not to believe much in natural bents. They observe that the boy who is fond of mathematics is generally good in the classics also; that the boy who takes kindly to language is generally respectable in all other subjects. . . . But this general fact does not invalidate the fundamental proposition, that a man will be productive and happy in his life work in just proportion to his natural fitness for it. The teacher, mother, or father can do nothing better for a boy than to find out, or help him to find out, this innate aptitude. . . . [A] boy's training up to sixteen years of age has not been right if it has not made possible for them all careers which start at or near that point.[122]

For Eliot, the undergraduate course was the arena in which each boy would finally encounter the "revelation of his own peculiar taste and capacity." He suggested that the successful undergraduate education consisted less of the subjects offered than how they were framed. "The whole tone and spirit of a good college," he asserted, "ought to be different in kind from that of a good polytechnic or scientific school. In the college, the desire for the broadest culture, for the best formation and information of the mind, the enthusiastic study of subjects for the love of them without any ulterior objects, the love of learning and research for their own sake, should be the dominant ideas."[123]

"The elective system," Eliot argued, "gives free play to natural preferences and inborn aptitudes, makes possible enthusiasm for a chosen work."[124] This process of "following one's nose," making choices and discovering the consequences of doing so, led a young man to discover his natural bent—his vocation. "Let him reverently give it welcome, thank God, and take courage," Eliot urged. "Thereafter he knows his way to happy enthusiastic work, and, God willing, to usefulness and success."[125]

Of course, knowing what one wanted to become and becoming it were, in Eliot's system, two very different things. While the undergraduate years were ones in which individuals discovered themselves, they were also ones in which they were ranked and judged. Eliot placed great emphasis on the novel practice of *grading*—the use of objective standards to assess and rank the performance of individuals. The undergraduate years were (as Henry Adams knew all too well) also preparation for true education—the education that came from experience. Eliot considered completely erroneous the "notion that young men can be made competent at any school, no matter how good, to take up immediately the charge of great enterprises."[126] Those with professional ambitions would go on to postgraduate study to acquire specific technical proficiency. But even this was not enough. Competency ultimately required experience:

> If well organized [postgraduate education] can convert a boy of fair abilities and intentions into an observant, judicious man, well informed in the sciences which bear upon his profession; so trained, the graduate will rapidly master the principles and details of any actual works, and he will rise rapidly through the grades of employment. . . . After the school, a longer or shorter term of apprenticeship . . . will be found essential.[127]

Even then, of course, nothing was assured. The best that educators could do was to "train and arm" young men for "fighting the wilderness, physical and moral."[128] Their ultimate success depended on their own actions in the struggle for existence.

It is important to emphasize that Eliot expected the individuals shaped by the "New Education" to be not only technically proficient but also "observant, reflecting, and sensible men." He conceived of the undergraduate experience as one that permitted a student to discover his *calling*—an essentially religious core of personal and spiritual commitment, which established the student's future educational and occupational direction in the sense of pursuing particular proficiencies and experiences, but which also framed those activities in an ethos of service to self, community, and God. The "New Education" was more than vocational, it was professional in the highest sense of the term.

As Herbert Croly, a product on Eliot's system and chief architect of the progressive ideology, would later say, an individual who became a professional in this sense was more than a "better instrument for the practice of some serviceable art"; he became a "moral instrument" for the reorganization of the nation's "economic, political, and social institutions and ideas."[129] In effect, the professional became a trustee of his own talent, improving and building on it for its own sake, but also for the communities of which he was a part. To the extent that the conception of the professional embraces the capacity for independent and disinterested judgment, professionalism is a form of trusteeship— by not only analogy but also intention. The desire of elite Bostonians to create an alternative to electoral authority, one that defined a place for an aristocracy of virtue in a democratic polity, found its ultimate expression in institutionally created and mediated professionalism.

Creating professionals in this sense, however, was only one dimension of Eliot's vision of the reconstruction of society. It was not enough to "train and arm" such men to fight the "wilderness, physical and moral." It was also necessary to articulate the institutional settings in which such "men of character" might exercise their leadership. Eliot located their primary influence not in public life, as office holders (though he did not exclude this as a possibility, remote as it may have seemed in the political setting of the late nineteenth century), but in what we would call the private sector—in economic and cultural institutions. In defending Harvard's tax-exempt status before the Massachusetts legislature in 1874, Eliot described "the material prosperity of every improving community" as a "fruit of character," which was, in turn, the product of the state's privatized institutional culture:

> It is energetic, honest, and sensible men that make prosperous business, and not prosperous business that makes men. Who have built up the manufactures and trade of this bleak and sterile Massachusetts? A few men of singular sagacity, integrity, courage, backed by hundreds of thousands of men and women of common intelligence, courage, and honesty. The roots of the prosperity are in the intelligence, courage, and honesty. Massachusetts today owes its mental and moral characteristics, and its wealth, to eight generations of people who have loved and cherished Church, School, and College.[130]

If "energetic, honest, and sensible men" make "prosperous business," what makes the "few men of singular sagacity, integrity, and courage"? Eliot believed they were the products of "Church, School, and College"—most of all the latter.

Eliot's description of "the heart of the University," the board that "holds the funds, makes appointments, fixes salaries, and has, by right, the initiative in all changes of the organic law of the University," seems to describe it in terms identical to those he uses to characterize the state's economic leadership. First, the board should have "a steady aim, and a prevailing spirit which is independent of individuals and transmissible from generation to generation."[131] The board should have a "catholic spirit," "intellectual honesty," and "independence of mind." Second, the spirit of the board "must be a spirit of fidelity—fidelity to the many and various trusts reposed in them by the hundreds of persons who have given money . . . in the beautiful hope of doing some perpetual good upon this earth." Board members must, in other words, be prudent fiduciaries. Third, the board "should always be filled with the spirit of enterprise": "It should be eager, sleepless, and untiring, never wasting a moment in counting laurels won, ever prompt to apply the liberality of the community, and liking no prospect as well as that of difficulties to be overcome and labors to be done in the cause of learning and public virtue." He concluded: "The picture I have drawn in thus delineating the true spirit of the Corporation of the College" constitutes "the noble quintessence of the New England character—that character which has made us a free and enlightened people; that character which, please God, shall yet do a great work in the world for the lifting up of humanity."[132]

Eliot's comments on Harvard's second governing board, the overseers, are worth noting. Although by 1866 the overseers were elected by the alumni, Eliot believed they constituted a form of "public supervision":

> The real function of the Board of Overseers is to stimulate and watch the President and Fellows. Without the Overseers, the President and Fellows would be a board of private trustees, self-perpetuated and self-controlled. Provided as it is with two governing boards, the University enjoys that principle safeguard of all American governments—the natural antagonism between two bodies of different constitution, powers, and privileges. While having with the Corporation a common interest of the deepest kind in the welfare of the University and the advancement of learning, the Overseers should always hold towards the Corporation an attitude of suspicious vigilance. They ought always to be pushing and prying. . . . Our main hope for the permanence and ever-widening usefulness of the University must rest upon this double-headed organization.[133]

In making his point, Eliot pointed to the situation of endowed institutions in England:

> The English practice of setting up a single body of private trustees to carry on a school or charity according to the personal instructions of some founder or founders has certainly proved a lamentably bad one. . . . These schools were generally managed by close corporations, self-elected, self-controlled, without motive for activity, and destitute of external stimulus and aid. Such bodies are too irresponsible for human nature. . . . These corporations were often hampered by founders' wills and statutory provisions which could not be executed, and yet stood in the way of organic improvements. There was no systematic provision for thorough inspections and public reports thereon. We cannot flatter ourselves that under

like circumstances we should always be secure against like dangers. Pro-
voked by crying abuses, some of the best friends of education in England
have gone the length of maintain that all these school endowments ought
to be destroyed, and the future creation of such trusts rendered impossible.
French law practically prohibits the creation of such trusts by private
persons.[134]

Carried along by the force of Eliot's sentiments, we may easily miss
the point that if the overseers represent the public, it is the public in
a very special sense. Certainly Eliot is not referring here to oversight
by government or by elected public officials, as had been the case at
Harvard before 1866, when the board had been dominated by state
senators. The overseers to which he refers are individuals elected by the
alumni—a very special portion of the public. And the overseers' role
as pushers and priers, as challengers of the wisdom of the self-perpetuating fellows (the corporation), is exercised not as public representatives, but as stakeholders in the organization. Much as Eliot had
internalized so many other functions in transforming Harvard into an
integrated multidivisional enterprise, the reconstituted overseers were,
in effect, an internalization of public accountability.

By being internalized in this way, could it really be said, in any
meaningful way, that the overseers represented the public? The answer
is certainly not—unless one accepts the peculiar assumptions of the
civil privatists that the will and interest of the public are something
other than what it expresses through government and elected representatives. A generation earlier, Eliot's father, in writing of Boston's charities, had argued that "the exclusive ambition for political distinction,
which is a sort of contagious mania among us, must subside," to be
replaced by "other objects, such as science, theology, and law. Power,
we know, will always be the object of ambition; but, we trust, not
necessarily or exclusively political power."[135] The object of these other
kinds of power were to extend "personal self-control, as a principle to
guide our public and private conduct." Sufficiently extended through
charitable institutions, the time would come, he predicted, when "all
the powers of the human mind shall be so appropriately and adequate-
ly cultivated, as to make them subservient to a virtuous will"—the
higher good of the community as interpreted by its leaders.[136] (This
all sounds like an anticipation of mid-twentieth pluralism, which in
a similar fashion emphasized the significance of organized groups as
an antidote to majoritarian mass movements.)

For Charles W. Eliot, his father's hope was fast becoming an institutional reality. The "men of character" who loved and cherished
"Church, School, and College" had built not only prosperous business
but also a powerful infrastructure of private institutions. These insti-

tutions had the unique capacity to systematically and broadly recruit, train, test, and provide opportunities for future leaders. Although Eliot was reticent about the political role of such "men of character," he did not doubt the place that they would assume in the nongovernmental dimensions of public life. Still, he could hardly have been surprised when, beginning in the 1890s, his graduates began to assume key roles in forming the progressive movement—whose fundamental ideals were little more than Eliot's beliefs writ large and which was spearheaded by the educated, the most notable of them, including Theodore Roosevelt, graduates of Harvard.

We should not let the national political prominence of people such as Roosevelt distract us from the fact that progressivism (and by this I mean not the Republican splinter movement of 1912, but the broad nonpartisan movement of bureaucratically oriented professionals into national leadership that began in the 1890s) was merely one aspect of what one historian has called "the corporate reconstruction of American life."[137] An important subtext of this reconstruction was the privatization of important dimensions of institutional life. The spread of the concepts and institutions of Bostonian civil privatism to other places, particularly to New York City, which had become the nation's financial center by the 1890s, was a crucial component in the process.

In the late 1860s and early 1870s, the Boston institutional paradigm was unique; neither New York City nor Philadelphia had anything like it.[138] Indeed, both more resembled Ohio to the extent that legislatures had severely restricted the ability of individuals to establish and endow private institutions and that those that were established were subject, especially in New York State, to stringent oversight and regulation. It was not easy to overcome these limitations on private power. Historical accounts that describe the revision (or, more accurately, the Bostonization) of New York State's charities laws in 1893 as a broad and spontaneous public response to the defeat of the Tilden Trust— and that suggest that the case suddenly made New Yorkers aware of the survival of irrational Jacksonian restrictions on private benevolence—are less than accurate.[139] The decision in the Tilden case should have come as no surprise to anyone because New York State courts had regularly upheld the state's charities laws in case after case.[140] Further, a reading of his will makes clear that the trust Tilden proposed was no ordinary charity. The "public reading room" was merely a suggestion to the trustees of his $3 million residuary estate. He had empowered them to use his bequest for any purpose they deemed suitable. The trust was an open-ended charity of a kind virtually unknown at the time—even in charitable Boston.[141]

The effort to revise and liberalize New York's charities laws after the defeat of the Tilden Trust was no more spontaneous than anything else that transpired in that state's machine-dominated political process. Liberalization occurred only after a carefully orchestrated campaign supported by financier-philanthropists such as J. P. Morgan (who was also, not coincidentally, a major benefactor of Harvard) and led by such men as James Barr Ames, dean of Harvard Law School.[142] And, as James Wooten's study of the privatization of legal training in the state during the 1890s suggests, the Bostonization of charities laws was only one front of this effort to reshape New York City's institutions.[143]

Finally, it is important to point out that the Bostonization of New York City's cultural and educational institutions did not—and could not—lead to a replication of Boston's unique characteristics. At best, the translation was a very imperfect one because, even in its elite financial circles, New York City was infinitely more heterogeneous.[144] The factionalization of the economic elite by religion, ethnic origin, age of wealth, and other factors—combined with the extraordinary and continuing influx of the newly wealthy into the city from other places (such as Carnegie and Frick from Pittsburgh, and the Rockefellers, Whitneys, and Harknesses from Cleveland)—precluded unified institutional effort. Civil privatism in New York City was important to the extent that its central cultural institutions—the Metropolitan Museum, the Museum of Natural History, the Metropolitan Opera, the New York Philharmonic, Columbia University—helped to define the interests of a particularly wealthy and influential group. However broadly these institutions may have affected public life in the city and region, they never dominated it in the way that the Massachusetts General Hospital, Harvard, Boston Symphony, and Museum of Fine Arts complex dominated Boston.

In New York City, civil privatists were only one of several competing elites. Although they were sufficiently influential to be able to persuade the legislature to liberalize charities laws sufficiently to permit Boston models of institutional trusteeship, these models coexisted with others. Even in the field of legal training, in which the regents had bent over backward to favor the more exclusive forms of professional training, testing, and licensing, proprietary institutions continued to flourish. Only gradually was elite patronage able to differentiate the prestige firms and prestige schools that supplied them with clerks and partners.[145] But even elite patronage did not drive competitors out of the market. Nonelite for-profit and public enterprises remained similarly viable in the domain of cultural activity. Even the nonprofit cultural domain became an arena for competition between the old and the new rich.[146]

The uniqueness of New York City as a locality may help explain the peculiar patterns of trusteeship and directorship found among Yale and Harvard graduates who lived in the city. Unlike those who settled in Cleveland and other midwestern cities, almost all of whom served as directors and trustees at some point in their careers, very few New Yorker graduates did. Moreover, the few who served as trustees and directors tended to hold a great many positions. It appears that board service was distinctively associated with elite status in New York City in a way that it was not elsewhere—even in Boston. It may be that New York's City's institutional environment was relatively impoverished: because the city's traditions of civil privatism were new and weak, people did not look to voluntary action as a meaningful activity and, as a result, neither formed nor participated in voluntary organizations to the extent that people did elsewhere.[147]

For an impressionistic examination of this point, it is worth comparing three more or less contemporary popular novels about life in New York *(Life with Father)*, Boston *(The Late George Apley)*, and the Midwest *(Babbitt)*. Clarence Day's father, a prosperous stockbroker, apparently participated in no voluntary organizations other than the church—and that, as his son points out, with the greatest conceivable reluctance. However, the lives of Apley the Bostonian and Babbitt the midwesterner were almost entirely defined by organizational activities of one sort or another.[148]

Charity and Dynasty: Trusteeship and the Very Rich

Ironically, New York City's civil privatist elite (which, as noted, was only one of the city's elite factions) came to have far more influence nationally than locally. The city itself was not even sufficiently civic-minded to have a Community Chest—and yet by the 1920s it was notable for its concentration of new forms of charitable wealth, the grant-making foundations. These could battle hookworm in the South and transform professional education across the country, but their influence on the city itself was negligible.

In terms of the cultures of trusteeship which we have been considering, foundations are notable in two respects. First, they had a special relationship to the professional and managerial elites produced by the "New Education." By the 1920s, the foundations helped to tie together the system of government bureaus, private social-service agencies, universities, trade associations, and professional societies that composed the backbone of Hoover's associationist vision.[149] Thus, foundations played a key role in actualizing the public dimension of professionalism as a form of trusteeship. Second, they also constituted an important aspect of the dynastic process for the possessors of the vast fortunes created at the close of the nineteenth century. It is this issue—the model of trusteeship developed (or not developed) by these inconceivably wealthy families—to which the final portion of this chapter is devoted.

The immensity of the wealth accumulated by the men popularly denoted as robber barons in the years following the Civil War presented a unique and unprecedented problem, both for society and for themselves. No one really knew what to make of it because the conditions that facilitated such accumulations—new technologies of production, distribution, and communication, combined with the creation of a truly national economy—had not existed before the 1870s.

The creators of the first great fortunes, the Astors and the Vanderbilts, despite the size of these fortunes, seem to have given curiously little thought to their meaning. They were evidently oblivious to the broader issues of stewardship or to the potential public function of enormous wealth. They dealt with transmitting these fortunes effectively but unimaginatively—through a modified form of primogeniture. Their charitable giving, though generous, was also singularly unimaginative: they founded no great or new institutions. (Perhaps if Vanderbilt factotum Chauncey DePew had been a graduate of Harvard rather than Yale, things would have turned out differently!) The degeneration of these families, with their ostentatious public displays of useless luxury, their conspicuous immorality, and their unconcealed lack of interest in public life, served as an object lesson to others who possessed enormous wealth.[150]

It may not be insignificant that these fortunes were made before the mounting of major political challenges to industrial capitalism, which began in the mid-1880s. It certainly seems more than coincidental that Andrew Carnegie, the first of the robber barons to acknowledge that the kind of wealth he possessed differed in more than quantity from earlier fortunes, did so after investing considerable effort in analyzing the implications of the labor struggles and violence of 1886.

Carnegie's essay "Wealth" gave a great deal of attention to the question of stewardship, but disregarded dynastic concerns. (Perhaps if he had had sons, he might have felt differently.) Similarly, the childless Olivia Sage, who created the first modern American foundation, did not concern herself with issues of family continuity. One family that did so was the Rockefeller family—and it did so in a way that not only profoundly shaped the theory and practice of trusteeship in the United States but also linked, in curious ways, the classic civil privatist model of Boston and the more inclusive midwestern model of civic responsibility.

It cannot have been insignificant that John D. Rockefeller, Sr., was from Cleveland.[151] He grew up there and laid the foundations for his vast fortune there. In many ways, his style as a businessman remained rooted in there. As Alfred Chandler has pointed out, Standard Oil never—at least as "Senior" remained active in its management—developed a "single, highly centralized administrative structure."[152] The Standard Oil Trust remained a loose collection of committees that depended on "the advice and assistance of a permanent staff housed at the trust's central offices at 26 Broadway." This relatively informal style, which emphasized essentially horizontal relationships between "associates" rather than hierarchical ones between "officers," owed more to the institutional ideologies of the Cleveland business community than to those of the northeastern metropolis.

The midwestern roots of "Senior" also seem to have played a key role in shaping his philanthropic vision. In 1902, when he set up the first of his independent grant-making institutions, the General Education Board, rather than incorporating it in a state friendly to civil privatism, he sought a federal charter—thus risking the scrutiny and criticism of a public that, even at that point, regarded him with suspicion and hostility. Rather than establishing a perpetuity, he permitted the board to be self-liquidating, capable of spending both income and principle. (It spent itself out of existence by 1960, having distributed over $324 million.)[153] In 1909, when he sought a federal charter for an open-ended grant-making entity, the $100 million Rockefeller Foundation. He agreed, in addition to the federal charter and clauses permitting the foundation's ultimate liquidations, to provisions for an ex officio board (consisting of the president of the United States, the chief justice of the Supreme Court, the president of the Senate, the speaker of the House, and the presidents of Harvard, Yale, Columbia, Johns Hopkins, and the University of Chicago), as well as limitations on the foundation's ability to accumulate income and to invest in the securities of any one corporation. What underlay these extraordinary provisions was Rockefeller's conviction that the foundation was a direct gift "to the whole American people" and should be, for that reason, "forever subject to the control of their elected representatives."[154] This concept of a charitable trust as a distinctly public one was part and parcel of the midwestern institutional ethos.

The proposed charter for the Rockefeller Foundation created a political firestorm for reasons having little to do with the foundation or its purposes. Despite the pleas of Rockefeller spokesman Jerome Greene, who stated that the defeat of the bill "will not prevent the establishment of the Foundation," but would merely "prevent Congress from exercising any control over it," the proposal was finally withdrawn.[155]

Rockefeller had no trouble obtaining a charter from the New York State legislature. But a state charter forced him to abandon almost all of the public features that he had originally proposed. For example, it was senseless to have an ex officio board composed of New York State officials. Besides the notable lack of distinction of New York officialdom, their parochialism would be unsuited to an organization that proposed to operate "for the benefit of mankind" on a national and international basis. A self-perpetuating board composed of prominent individuals would clearly be better equipped to define the foundation's broad purposes. By the time the foundation was finally in operation, the only remaining artifact of its midwestern origins was the provision of its charter which empowered the trustees to liquidate the foundation if they deemed it wise to do.[156]

Significantly, neither board was dominated by either the founding family or its associates. Of the eleven members of the original General Education board, only three—Wallace Buttrick, John W. Gates, and John D. Rockefeller, Jr.—were closely tied to family interests. The other nine were widely experienced, nationally known, and independent-minded professionals and businessmen: W. H. Baldwin, a railroad president; D. C. Gilman, president of the Johns Hopkins University; Morris K. Jesup, the international jurist; banker and philanthropist George Peabody; department-store executive R. C. Ogden; educator J. L. M. Curry; and editors Albert Shaw and Walter Hines Page (Charles W. Eliot would join the group in 1908). The initial Rockefeller Foundation board was family-dominated (including John D. Rockefeller, Sr., John D. Rockefeller, Jr., and associates Fred Gates, Charles Heydt, and Starr Murphy, as well as quasi-outsiders Simon Flexner, Jerome Greene, and Wickcliffe Rose, all of whom were connected to the General Education board, and President Harry Pratt Judson of the University of Chicago, a major Rockefeller beneficiary). But by 1920, this was no longer the case: the board, now expanded to fourteen, included only six family members or associates (John D. Rockefeller, Sr., John D. Rockefeller, Jr., Buttrick, Flexner, Murphy, and Judson). Their influence was counterbalanced by legal luminaries such as A. Barton Hepburn and Charles Evans Hughes and wealthy philanthropists and businessmen such as Julius Rosenwald, Martin Ryerson, and Frederick Strauss.[157] This propensity for recruiting independent-minded associates rather than yes men seems to have been a carryover from the corporate culture of the Standard Trust, which was an extension of the midwestern corporate style.

Despite the essentially nonfamilial character of these boards, they seem to have played an important part in the dynastic process in the Rockefeller family. The fact that John D. Rockefeller, Jr., was placed on the General Education board when only six years out of college and lacking any significant business or professional experience suggests that his father expected contact with such independent-minded men of national and international reputation to play a role in training him to accept the responsibilities attached to possessing the world's largest private fortune.

John D. Rockefeller, Jr., may well have had the same idea in mind when he put his eldest son, John D. Rockefeller 3rd, on the General Education board and Rockefeller Foundation board when he was just out of college—and long before he was permitted to sit on any outside boards (despite many invitations to do so). As John D. Rockefeller 3rd's biographers note, "he remained acutely aware of his junior status, content for years to merely get to know the outstanding men among his fellow directors and to observe the fascinating flow of work within the foundation."[158] Just how independent-minded senior trustees and staff could be was quickly brought home to John D. Rockefeller 3rd. He had been appointed as secretary to the trustees of the China Medical Board, which was related to the Rockefeller Foundation board. In June 1932, he met with the board for the first time. Apparently Roger Greene, the chief executive of the operation, bridled at young Rockefeller's presence and told him off. His exact words have not been recorded, but it is safe to assume that they had to do with his lack of qualifications as a trustee.[159] "It had been my assumption," Rockefeller wrote to Raymond Fosdick, president of the Rockefeller Foundation board,

> that it was up to me as secretary to present the docket to the Board. However, it would seem that this is completely up to the director. Naturally it was irritating to him when I assumed this function and responsibility. However, this in no way justifies what he said to me.
>
> At the meeting of the Board Monday morning I am going to ask the directors exactly what they desire my function as secretary to be. According to the by-laws my duties are entirely mechanical. While this is perfectly satisfactory to me I just want to be sure exactly where I stand and what is expected of me.[160]

The day following the blow-up, young Rockefeller tried to make his position clear to Greene, with whom he had crossed swords:

> I have just received a note from Mr. Fosdick concerning the telephone conversation which you and I had yesterday afternoon. It is a genuine relief to me to realize that you did not mean all that you said.

> With the future well-being of the College in mind it seems to me that
> there are three courses open to us: that I resign as secretary of the CMB,
> that you resign as acting director of the College, or that you and I work
> out some common basis of understanding which will make it possible for
> us to work together in the future. This last course is the one that appeals
> to me most.[161]

Evidently the last course was not the one that appealed to the prickly
executive, for on June 28 John D. Rockefeller 3rd had resigned from
the board, believing that it was "much more appropriate" for a ste-
nographer to serve in the position "under the by-laws as they now
stand."[162] In the battle between the senior outsider and the junior
family representative, the outsider won.

This contretemps is interesting because it not only demonstrates
how little deference the Rockefellers could count on in the organizations that had created, but also led Fosdick to articulate with unusual
clarity the special associational culture of the Rockefeller organizational complex and to hint at its dynastic implications. Commenting
on John D. Rockefeller 3rd's letter of June 23 to Greene, Fosdick
praised the young man's tact:

> I thought your letter admirable in every respect. In fact, I was very proud
> of it. It reminded me of your father's characteristic attitude of forbearance.
> In the twenty years in which I have been associated with him, I have come
> to admire—perhaps more than any other quality—his gentleness and tol-
> erance of human frailty. I have seen him in situations where the average
> man would be exasperated and justifiably angry. Always he has kept his
> poise and serenity. He has always overlooked the unpleasant aspects in
> order to get at the good in other people. Perhaps this is a quality that he
> inherited from his father. Your grandfather surrounded himself with very
> vigorous and forthright associates, and I have heard that sometimes they
> were not very pleasant or agreeable. But your grandfather took them for
> the good they had in them and overlooked the other part. Simon Flexner
> does the same thing with the prima donnas he works with up at the
> [Rockefeller] Institute. And this same creed we try to live up to down at
> 61 [at the Rockefeller Foundation].[163]

It is especially telling that through all this John D. Rockefeller 3rd did
not appeal to his father, nor did his father, who surely knew what was
going on, intervene in any way. If working on family-related boards
was to serve effectively as training for service in the world beyond the
family, it was clearly essential for John D. Rockefeller, Jr., to avoid
intervening on his son's behalf.

The family-created philanthropies were quite clearly regarded as
training grounds for nonfamilial responsibilities. During his first four

years in the family office, John D. Rockefeller 3rd restricted his board service to organizations in which his father had an interest—the Dunbar National Bank (a black bank), the Bureau of Social Hygiene, the New York International House, the Industrial Relations Counselors, the China Medical Board, the Riverside Church, the General Education board, and the Rockefeller Foundation—turning down the many invitations to become a director of both for-profit and nonprofit corporations. However, in 1933 he was approached about becoming a trustee of the American Museum of Natural History. His father opposed the idea, feeling that such commitments should be avoided unless the young man were prepared to give the time and the money expected of trustees. After "an agonizing period of indecision," John D. Rockefeller 3rd "made a minor declaration of independence and accepted the bid."[164] Shortly afterward, Henry Fairfield Osborn, the museum's director, wrote to John D. Rockefeller, Jr.:

> Your son is a most welcome new member of our Board of Trustees. Every one is impressed with his personality and his obvious intention to thoroughly master the various problems that come before the Board. It was a pleasure to see him among the fine group of young men who are now taking on their shoulders our wonderful institution. The difficulties of the present time will off them an opportunity for splendid training. It is their baptism by fire—to use a Napoleonic expression.[165]

Still, in December 1934, after a half-decade in the family office, the memorandum John D. Rockefeller 3rd addressed to his father outlining his work was grouped under three headings: first, twenty "Boards and Committees on which I am serving because of your interest in them"; second, six "Special Responsibilities and Duties other than Boards and Committees which I have assumed because of your interests" (all of these were family-related); and third, five "Activities unrelated to your interests." The last and smallest group included the Museum of Natural History Board, the Boy's Bureau Committee, the Home Mortgage Advisory Board (which by this point in the depths of the Depression was no longer active), One Beekman Place Corporation Board (this was the co-op in which John D. Rockefeller 3rd lived), and the Special Work, Inc., Board (this was a partnership formed with his brother Nelson to recruit tenants for Rockefeller Center).[166]

The hesitancy of John D. Rockefeller, Jr., about his son's becoming involved with outside groups did not diminish significantly over the years. In 1936, when John D. Rockefeller 3rd was thirty, he was invited by Stuart M. Crocker, a vice-president of International General Electric, to "join a number of men whom I think you know to get together for a bit of refreshment and a brief chat about our voluntary hospitals."[167] Well aware of his father's concerns, young Rockefeller had the invitation reviewed by Packard, whose response was characteristic:

> My impression is that this invitation, like all the other different types of approach which are being made to you, has as its primary objective the enlistment of your personal interest in the problem of voluntary hospitals. . . . For you to accept might be a nice gesture, but any gesture toward the hospital situation, apart from your contribution, must be considered in relation to the amount of resistance which you wish to be called upon to exercise in avoiding more personal involvements in the problem.
>
> I have been impressed with the spirit and seriousness of purpose with which the group of younger men are trying to take hold of this hospital situation, and it is my belief that they should be encouraged in such ways as are wisely possible. The problem for you, however, is to translate your good wishes and encouragement in ways that will not be construed as a readiness on your part to shoulder more of the load than you are disposed to do.
>
> In short, my advice is of a rather split character. I think it would be an interesting experience for you, as well as helpful to those who were wrestling with the hospital problem, to show some interest and encouragement of a personal character. On the other hand, I don't quite see how you can do that through attendance at meetings without incurring a greater involvement than I believe you wish.[168]

It appears that John D. Rockefeller, Jr.'s policy, as articulated by Packard, involved more than a crude oedipal effort to put Johnny in his place. What Packard was saying, in effect, was that the young man should only become involved with groups whose work *genuinely* interested him. He should not commit himself simply because he felt that he ought to.

The problem for John D. Rockefeller 3rd, as for so many other men born into family dynasties, was discovering these interests. Undoubtedly, John D. Rockefeller, Jr., had hoped that in addition to helping his sons develop mature judgment, serving on the broad spectrum of family boards would, as with Eliot's elective system, permit them to discover their "natural bents"—and that this would permit them to build their interests beyond the family complex. But this was no easy task. In December 1934, John D. Rockefeller 3rd wrote to family legal adviser Thomas Debevoise about his efforts to take control of his life. In this letter, he described a conversation with his father in which they had hashed out how he would divide his responsibilities between the Rockefeller Foundation (with which his father said "it had been suggested that I might become more closely associated") and the newly completed Rockefeller Center. He was unwilling to become more involved with the former because "any relationship I might have with the Foundation would almost by necessity be two or three times removed from what was actually being accomplished by its grants." However, while Rockefeller Center was more appealing to him because it promised greater "hands-on" involvement, he felt ill-equipped to deal with a major business responsibility. "Last night," he concluded,

> Blanchette [his wife] and I spent some time going over my personal activities as listed in my letter to Father. We had specifically two thoughts in mind in so doing: first, to determine those duties or projects where I actually had individual responsibility rather than as one of a group, and second, to ascertain where I had responsibility through leadership if not through decision. As to the former, we singled out the management of the New York office and of the Pocantico Estate as the main items. Insofar as the latter is concerned, I am Chairman of several sub-committees and have, of course, taken considerable initiative in connection with the Theater Committee [of Rockefeller Center]. Blanchette suggested that from the point of view of experience, it might be desirable if I were to serve as chairman of certain other committees, and possibly of smaller boards. Now that I think of it, I am inclined to feel that she is entirely right, although it really had not occurred to me before. As a matter of fact, *I have hardly done any presiding at meetings of any kind* [emphasis added].[169]

Despite John D. Rockefeller 3rd's determination to actualize himself through exercising leadership on the boards and committees on which he served, the list of "interests" which he compiled in May 1941 was not substantially different from the one he had assembled seven years earlier. Although the list was not broken down into family and non-family categories, the predominance of the former (nineteen out of twenty-five) was nonetheless clear. In addition to the Museum of Natural History board, which had joined in 1933, nonfamily responsibilities now included the board his alma mater, Princeton, and two Pocantico area charities, a local church and hospital. Clearly, he had come no closer to his goal of exercising leadership on any of them— he rather plaintively noted with reference to his vice-chairmanship of the Davidson Fund, one of his father's personal foundations, that he "can act as ex-officio member in absence of chairman."[170]

It would take John D. Rockefeller 3rd another twenty years before he discovered his "natural bent" and began fully developing his own institutional interests. In the interim, he would continue to search for himself within the family complex and, as a result, to experience repeated humiliations at the hands of his father, his father's associates, and the professional administrators who ran the foundations his family had established. (His brothers Laurence, Nelson, Winthrop, and David followed somewhat more independent courses.) Only in the 1960s—after the death of his father—would he finally assume the kind of leadership he had always yearned for, as founder of the Population Council, chief fund-raiser for Lincoln Center and Japan House, and, most notably, through his efforts to help American philanthropy to organize and understand itself. There was a certain appropriate irony in the latter: because philanthropy had been so crucial to forming his personal identity, his role as organizer of the Peterson and Filer Commissions, which so thoroughly redefined our understanding philanthropy (and did so in ways clearly not to the liking of many philanthropoids), may be seen in important respects as an effort to come to terms with, and take control of, his adult identity.[171]

Stepping back from the process through which John D. Rockefeller 3rd and his brothers were trained for their responsibilities as leaders to examine the nature of the leadership itself presents an interesting contrast to the kind of leadership commonly associated with the civil privatist model. For example, in Boston an individual would move from less prestigious charitable and business boards to more prestigious ones, assuming in the process greater and greater responsibility to—and identification with—the class of which he was a part. Mere money and pedigree counted for little, as Godfrey Lowell Cabot learned in his frustrated attempts to get on to the board of the New York, New Haven, and Hartford Railroad in the days when it was considered to be the most exclusive men's club in the Northeast. Cabot, for all his wealth, was simply not clubbable in the sense that he did not display those traits of character deemed by his contemporaries as needed for real leadership. Although he was unquestionably community-minded, his civic labors tended to take somewhat eccentric forms, such as being a leading light in the Boston Watch and Ward Society.[172]

The incentive structure for the Rockefellers was almost the inverse of that seen in civil privatism. In December 1934, John D. Rockefeller, Jr., wrote to John D. Rockefeller 3rd describing the sizable trusts he had set up for each of his children:

> As you know, Grandfather and I have always been keenly alive to the responsibilities inherent in the possession of wealth. He believes, as I do, that these responsibilities and the opportunities which they bring for useful living and unselfish service to mankind, should be shared with those of the next generation when and as soon as those of the next generation have reached such an age and attained maturity as justifies their being entrusted with them. Of the sincerity of our belief in this policy the dispositions of property which Grandfather and I have made in the past have given concrete evidence.

The "1934 Trusts" were "spendthrift trusts," managed by a committee of trustees composed of John D. Rockefeller, Jr.'s associates, a group that enjoyed complete discretion as to if and when either the income or the principal of these funds should be disbursed. As John D. Rockefeller, Jr., would note, "the men I have selected to serve on the Committee of the trust are men of matured judgment and in sympathy with our family policies. They know my hopes with respect to you and I feel sure you can rely upon them to act in accordance with what they believe to be your best interests." Access to the family fortune, in other words, was contingent on demonstrating competency and maturity in terms of "family policies." "It is my hope," John D. Rockefeller, Jr., continued,

> that the Committee . . . will deem it wise to pay to you from the outset a substantial proportion of the income, if not the entire amount, and that as you handle with wisdom these added responsibilities, the Committee may soon see fit to place at your disposal from time to time substantial parts of the principal until it is all entrusted to you. As your funds are thus increased, I should hope that you would be disposed to continue to devote any surplus over and above what may be reasonably necessary for your current living expenses and to enable you to meet the obligations, social, civic and philanthropic, properly falling upon one in your walk of life, to building up for yourself a principal fund adequate to meet the larger responsibilities of life that will come to you as the years go by.[173]

Rather than integrating the young Rockefellers into a broader social group beyond the family, this arrangement had the effect of progressively isolating them from the society around them. In civil privatist leadership culture, which was directed to integrating a group of wealthy families into a coherent and cohesive class, those who demonstrated judgment and maturity were granted more responsibility *for others* through trusteeships of institutions such as Harvard, which were central to the entire class of which they were a part. The dynastic culture rewarded the young Rockefellers' maturity and judgment with increasing responsibility over themselves and over their share of the family fortune. This arrangement effectively narrowed rather than broadened their relationships to groups beyond the family.

Although the Rockefeller brothers would serve on a great many boards, both family- and nonfamily-related, their activities were characterized by an almost obsessive solicitude for the family and its collective concerns—by the need, as Packard said, to consider their involvement "in relation to the amount of resistance which you wish to be called upon to exercise in avoiding more personal involvements in the problem." As trustees, the Rockefellers were always outsiders who were peculiarly detached from the ongoing group processes of the boards on which they sat. Memoranda and telephone logs make clear that almost nothing involving board service was left to chance: the family office was used to investigate every aspect of every organization before a brother committed himself to it; no meeting was attended without a full office-prepared briefing of the relevant issues; and incredible amount of time was devoted to behind-the-scenes politicking and consensus-building. In one sense, these preparations can be seen as consummately responsible boardmanship. In another sense, it displays a distinctive fearfulness and aversion to the uncertainties of the interpersonal dimension of the board process.[174]

Some of this can be attributed to the peculiarities of the Rockefeller experience. The Rockefellers were, after all, unique. The immensity of their wealth and the avidity with which they were pursued by those who wanted some of it gave them good reason to be cautious. At the same time, there is good reason to believe that such caution has normative significance as well and that the stance and family office/associate system they developed constitutes a distinctive trusteeship culture in and of itself. This is suggested by anthropologist George Marcus, who contrasted the "merely comfortable old money families" who compose the major constituency of the civil privatist institutions of the northeastern metropolitan upper classes with dynasts such as the Rockefellers, "for whom really complicated wealth structures, trusts and the like, are very animated and intrusive ancestral dead hands upon the living."[175] In reference to the such dynasts, Marcus points to "the mystified construction of great abstract wealth across generations by experts such as lawyers and advisers of various sorts,"

> through whom both fortune and family identity become gradually more autonomous from the control of the family and inherently more dynasty-minded than the descendants who in effect become clients, or a wholly owned subsidiary, of the fortune and its administration. So, the formal corporate qualities of their families . . . are constructed for descendants by literally incorporating external agents (not ancestors, but lawyers, bankers, and other advisers), and these do provide a basis of continuity and discipline for persons who as they age as adults becomes more unruly in their imposed collective family life.[176]

The Rockefellers were neither the only immensely wealthy American family to develop an integrated complex of philanthropic and business interests nor were they alone in using charitable trusteeship as an educational component of the dynastic process. As Marcus suggests, large fortunes generally have family offices that attempt to centralize and keep control of the fortune's diverse manifestations in the larger worlds of law, finance, and corporate business, as well as look back towards the family and do various welfare services for descendants. . . . These days, such offices either turn into ramifying bureaucracies themselves, represented coherently only by the mythic order of the organizational flow chart or, given their conservative and conserving nature, cannot really manage effectively the fortunes interests in the risk environments of investment markets and farm out functions, sharing the power to manage and reinvent the descendants with external expert agencies.[177]

Thanks to extraordinary facilities such as the Rockefeller Archive Center, we are able to discover a great deal about the inner workings of this one family—but we know next to nothing about the Fords, the Fields, the Mellons, the DuPonts, the Lillys, and other contemporary families of great wealth.[178] Given the nature of our legal culture, as well as the extent to which these families seem to have looked to one another for guidance in formulating dynastic policies, it seems likely that their trusteeship values and practices, as well as their methods of coordinating their business, social, civic, and philanthropic interests, followed a family-office form similar to that devised by the Rockefellers. If so, the families do indeed constitute a distinct trusteeship culture and one with broad implications for trusteeship as a whole because of the presence of dynastic descendants or their representatives on nonprofit boards throughout the country.[179]

Trusteeship in a Pluralist Society: The Intersection and Overlap of Cultures

The civil privatist seeks to optimize the interests and identity of his social class; the dynast, the interests and identity of himself and his family; the midwestern federationist, the identity and interests of the community as a whole; the grassroots leader, the interests and identity of his neighborhood, ethnic group, or special cause. And these orientations to trusteeship hardly exhaust the possibilities. For example, Harvard and Yale classbooks suggest the existence of a trusteeship culture within the learned professions, which, rather than asserting the interests of particular professions, emphasizes those of professionals as professionals. And there are undoubtedly other trusteeship cultures as well, some regionally rooted, others grounded in other kinds of significant collectively self-conscious social groupings, including, most notably, business.

Each of these trusteeship cultures is discrete and coherent in the sense of representing particular bodies of values and practices with regard to the technologies of administering resources for the benefit of third parties. Although the trusteeship cultures can be traced to particular localities in terms of their historical development, they constitute more than a simple problem of interregional variation in institutional cultures. In any event, institutional cultures—the values, expectations, and technology of organizations—are not an attribute of places, but of the people who inhabit them. They are portable and are borne along from place to place by the people who share them. Thus, we may find midwestern federationist systems elaborated in places other than the Midwest—in Allentown, Pennsylvania, or Oakland, California—or civil privatism taking root in New York City or Philadelphia.

To complicate matters further, organizational values and technology can detach themselves from groups of individuals who have shared backgrounds and historical experiences and assume autonomy as ideas. The spread of civil privatism in the 1890s and of federationism in the 1920s present good examples of this.[180] Who is receptive to these ideas and how they translate these ideas into action poses an interesting problem. For example, it is quite clear that Clevelanders drew very different lessons from Carnegie's "The Gospel of Wealth" than New Yorkers: for the former, the Great Ironmaster's ideas catalyzed an underlying set of community values into an institutional culture that emphasized horizontality and inclusion and that located leadership of the polity in the business community; for the latter, Carnegie's ideas, intersecting with civil privatism and enormous accumulations of wealth, led to the charitable foundation and increasingly hierarchical institutional relationships in which professionals rather than businessmen assumed authority.

Finally, because these trusteeship cultures are mobile, whether moving in connection with groups of individuals or as ideas detached from the experience of the groups who originated them, they have neither remained pristine nor blended together into an overall all-encompassing institutional culture. Rather, they coexist, compete, overlap, and intersect in various ways and in various settings as individuals who view trusteeship in different ways serve as trustees of nonprofit organizations.

A half-century ago, this complexity would have been unimaginable. In 1940, there were only twelve thousand or so charitable tax-exempt corporations in the United States (not counting churches). These very likely were primarily institutional vehicles for old-line community leaders—civil privatist and dynastic elites, with a smattering of parallel ethnic and religious charitable corporations.

Three factors served to change this situation: (1) the mass assimilation of ethnic minorities into the ranks of professional and economic leadership (thanks to postwar prosperity and the G.I. Bill); (2) the rise of a welfare state that implemented its programs through grants and contracts to private sector, unusually nonprofit, agencies and through tax policies that encouraged funds transfers to these agencies; and (3) a legal and regulatory environment that regarded these private tax-exempt entities as formally accountable to governmentally set standards of serving the public interest.

The assimilation of ethnic minorities meant that individuals whose prospects were once largely constrained by the boundaries of the groups into which they had been born could now seek—and reasonably expect to achieve—places in the overall leadership structure of city, state, and nation. Thus, boards of central community institutions—hospitals, museums, libraries, symphony orchestra—which had once been the exclusive preserve of WASP civil privatists were opened up to people whose backgrounds, values, expectations, and understanding of the trusteeship role were quite different. To some degree the entry of these new leaders was welcomed, for they brought with them new wealth, new audiences, and undeniable executive talent. But to some degree the entry was forced: public accountability, especially the ability to credibly sustain claims of serving the public interest, required a broadening of board membership; at the same time, tax regulations, especially those imposed by the 1969 Tax Reform Act, required the separation of charitable organizations from donors and their families.

The situation involved far more than the entry of new groups into old organizations. Federal encouragement, combined with the desire of ethnic groups and others to pursue their interests through formal organizations, led to an incredible proliferation of nonprofits, many of which competed with established organizations. Competitive pressures forced both older and newer organizations to recruit trustees more inclusively—with the result that boards were even more likely to be composed of people whose backgrounds, experiences, and expectations differed from one anothers'. To further complicate matters, a combination of competitive pressures and the increasingly complex regulatory environment transformed many nonprofits into professionally staffed entities—adding yet another set of outlooks to boards, inasmuch as top staffers often sat as trustees in the organizations that they ran.

We hear a good deal these days about a "leadership crisis" in nonprofits. Most frequently, this crisis is articulated as one involving boards of trustees: not enough good people are willing to serve on boards; those who serve on boards do not do so effectively; and there are destructive conflicts between boards and staffs. Various efforts have been mounted to deal with the crisis, primarily through community-based efforts to recruit and train would-be trustees and to provide consultative interventions with the boards of troubled organizations.[181] To serve these efforts, an enormous amount of prescriptive literature has been created, some of it for the use of particular organizations, some of it addressing itself to the issue of trusteeship in general.[182]

All of these efforts, both written and participatory, have proceeded with a combination of good intentions—and an astonishing lack of understanding of unconsciousness of organizational process and setting. The efforts relentlessly assume that individual and organizational processes are rational and orderly. In this, the trusteeship/leadership efforts differ strikingly from the evolving literature on the management of nonprofits, directed primarily to professional administrators. This literature, which has developed out of critical studies of management in business and government agencies, has focused on the irrationality and complexity of group processes in organizations. However, these studies have not suggested that organizational processes are uncontrollable, but rather that there are particular procedures that need to be followed if they are to be understood and managed.[183]

Ironically—or perhaps appropriately—little of the management literature has focused on trusteeship. Nor have those promoting the education of trustees shown much of an interest in developing a critical literature for themselves. The reluctance of academic management scholarship to engage the problem of trusteeship is easy to understand. Unlike managerial roles, which can be examined and discussed with reference to a particular organization or kind of organization, trusteeship is essentially extraorganizational. As boundary-spanners, trustees are driven by externalities that are difficult to observe and account for (such as the overall allocation of power within the community in which organizations operate). Further, because management scholarship has generally evolved in tandem with managerial professionalization, it has tended to treat the nonprofessional dimensions of organizations, trusteeship in particular, as being of secondary importance.[184]

The critical unconsciousness of trustees and their would-be educators is a bit more difficult to understand. However, it may stem from what trusteeship represents in our time in terms of power, position, privilege, and—most of all—as a symbol of achievement. Here the historical association of trusteeship with elite and dynastic authority assumes significance. Inevitably, trusteeship connotes broader and higher kinds of leadership, of the sort once exercised by these vanishing elites. The contemporary prescriptive trusteeship literature is replete with nostalgic references of a time—not so long ago—when, as Frederick T. Miller said in a recent essay in the *Chronicle of Philanthropy*, "prior to and immediately following World War II, a highly motivated volunteer spirit dominated the values and attitudes of many Americans who fulfilled their needs for affiliation and sense of community in fraternal lodges, churches, and other voluntary organizations. Those organizations hired few paid staff members, thus assuring community ownership of the organization." These "traditional leaders" born before 1938 "experienced the tragedies of the Depression, and personal and family security became paramount in their concern. They became highly skilled in making more out of less, and know from personal experience the importance of caring for others."[185] Miller contrasted these "traditional leaders" with "new leaders" born after 1947, who "put themselves before the needs of society" and whose "personal needs and aspirations were often ranked above the community."

Judith Huggins Balfe expressed similar nostalgia in a recent essay on the baby-boom generation as arts patrons. "Generally," she asserts, "baby boomers give less volunteer time and less money to all charities than do their elders, even when income, education, occupation, and religious behavior are held constant."[186] Noting that elites have historically patronized the arts "in order to establish strong boundaries between themselves and the masses," Balfe suggests

> it is likely that such needs are bound to be felt more acutely as they become more difficult to achieve. . . . The need for such status assertion and boundary maintenance surely exists among baby boomers to an even greater degree than among earlier cohorts: the competitive Yuppies need to try to distinguish themselves from their more numerous peers upon *some* grounds, and acquiring expertise in High Art can serve as well as acquiring expertise in High Tech. Accordingly, some baby-boomers become patrons of arts organizations to provide evidence of being knowledgeable.

Despite these incentives, Balfe concludes that although some baby boomers support the arts, they volunteer neither time nor money in amounts comparable to their elders—no more than they do to any other area of philanthropy.[187]

Balfe's indictment of the baby boomers shares with Miller's analysis the curious absence of an historical dimension. Both authors control for income, education, occupation, and religion in comparing "traditional" and "new" leadership, but neither, curiously, controls for age—a not insignificant factor given that the behavior of any cohort at midcareer is likely to be considerably different from its behavior at middle age. And we have no data on trusteeship, patronage, or other forms of institutional participation for earlier cohorts.[188]

Balfe, Miller, and others, moreover, also fail to take into account the drastically altered institutional settings for participation, especially the astonishing increase in the number of nonprofit organizations in every field. There is, of course, a reason for this increase. Virtually all of the data to which they refer has been gathered at the behest of established institutions, which are bound to look askance at the proliferation of new organizations and the alternative forms of the goods and services these new entities produce.

The subtext of these lamentations on the baby boomers, like that contained in the abundant literature on the decline of ethical behavior in the business world, involves nostalgic evocations of a lost golden age of civic-mindedness, which is inevitably associated, sometimes with disturbing explicitness, with the eclipse of traditional WASP community and institutional leadership.[189]

If this chapter has accomplished nothing else, it should have shown that "traditional leadership" in the sense of a single, coherent, unchallenged instrumentality for managing and allocating collective resources never existed. The dominance of civil privatism—which most contemporary commentators view as the "one best way"—was brief and partial: to the extent that it was dominant at all, it held sway for little more than a half-century outside of Massachusetts; and in most places outside the Northeast it never took root.

Certain scholars of organizations have observed that "a solution is a product looking for a problem." Viewed from this perspective, many "leadership training" efforts may be viewed as efforts to impose on a complex and pluralistic society prescriptive conceptions based on ahistorical, mythic, and oversimplified notions of trusteeship. If the evidence offered in this chapter is correct, these efforts are bound to fail—indeed, there is already considerable evidence that they have failed in the sense that recruitment and training efforts have in many cases intensified conflicts within boards and between boards and staffs.[190]

To say that interventions have created rather than solved problems is not, however, to suggest that leadership education and consultant involvement in board processes are in themselves useless. But the time may have come for these efforts to move away from rigid prescriptiveness, to take cognizance of the pluralism that has brought together various cultures of trusteeship in the settings of particular organizations, and to begin working to facilitate negotiated common understandings of the trustee role, based not only on the formal fiduciary frameworks that define it but also on the host of informal and often unarticulated assumptions about who trustees are and what they do.[191]

Although we have tended to treat trusteeship as an expression of rationality, as a product of a rule-governed legal order, this only captures a portion of its meaning. Trusteeship may be seen as a central element in the folklore of our secular elites, in which the ability—or possession of the authority—to impose order and regularity on future acts (and this, from a legal standpoint, is the most distinctive aspect of the equitable conceptions that frame trusteeship), as well as being central to the identity of the groups who wield this mysterious capacity. The formal and rational dimensions of trusteeship may have a folkloric component—spiritual, typological, encoding a shared inner world of symbols, encompassing a cosmology that permits us to view the universe and, in particular, the chaos and uncertainty of a pluralistic and perpetually changing democratic capitalism as orderly and meaningful. Whatever else it does, trusteeship may involve a way of reassembling the universe in other words, through the collective unifying power of sacred symbols.

In this sense, trusteeship may share another important characteristic with folk culture in that it can be *created,* much as American folk culture was created in the first half of the nineteenth century through the negotiated blending of Anglo-Celtic and Afro-American elements.[192] This process created a realm of collective meaning, of shared imaginary experience. It seems likely that institutional cultures have undergone—and continue to undergo—a similar process.

The American institutional landscape is like the American streetscape. Certain architectural styles may predominate in certain neighborhoods; other neighborhoods may be an amazing stylistic jumble. But the issue is not as simple as purity and eclecticism, homogeneity and heterogeneity. Structures that appear the same may have very different meanings to different people. For example, a New England migrant to Cleveland might have built a Greek Revival house not only because the style, which was new in the 1820s, permitted him to identify with national democratic ideals, but also because the floor plan in such a structure, permitting as it did degrees of individual privacy not possible with traditional architectural forms, allowed him to actualize those ideals. The same house, built by an antebellum migrant from the South, might have a very different set of meanings: the privatized floor plan was nothing new for southerners, but the civic and commercial orientation implied by the Greek Revival style was. Again, the same house might have been built at the end of the nineteenth century by someone interested in "colonial revival" styles—and for this person the style might have connoted an antidemocratic and anticommercial sensibility, a rebellion against materialism. Again, the same house built by a Tracy Kidder or some other postmodernist do-it-yourselfer carries with it yet another set of meanings.[193]

If the structure as a physical artifact is the same in each case, does it really matter that it meant different things to different people? Is it the same house? If we accept our task merely as one of cataloging materials, dimensions, and methods of construction, I suppose it is. If we accept our task as one of understanding the relationship between the physical structure and the people who use it, it most definitely is not.

In the field of historic preservation, there has been a long-running battle between those who believe that historic buildings should be returned to their original condition and that stylistically incongruous structures and additions should be removed and those who believe that the evolution of structures reflects the transformation of the communities that produced them and, for that reason, these alterations and variations should be preserved. One group wants to impose its neat and ordered vision of the past on an unruly and incoherent present; the other wants to use the present, in all of its messiness and apparent incoherence, to understand the complex interplay of forces that compose a community's past.

So it is with trusteeship. Hardly any cities or towns in late-twentieth-century America are institutionally pristine. They contain different groups with different institutional orientations that intersect and overlap. In a pluralist society, boards of trustees are inevitably an arena for the playing out of different visions, expectations, and values. In a pluralist setting, can we assume that trusteeship can be prescribed without consulting those who share different conceptions of personal and collective responsibility and who have different values and goals?

Perhaps the time has come for those who would improve trusteeship to start listening and to initiate processes for the creation of shared meaning. Pluralism is a reality: nostalgia for the "good old days" of WASP hegemony leads nowhere; nor can we re-create new Americans as old WASPs. Whatever trusteeship looks like in the future—if it has a future—is bound to be very different from anything that we have had in the past. But there is nothing particularly threatening about this future. Trusteeship has always been in the process of evolution: the models that we hold forth as eternal verities are very proximate indeed.

5

Conflicting Managerial Cultures in Nonprofit Organizations

The increasingly managerial orientation of both staffs and trustees of nonprofit organizations appears to have led to conflict rather than cooperation. This chapter examines a case of an organizational crisis which illustrates how managerialism has obscured some of the unique constraints under which nonprofits operate and suggests ways of making these constraints more salient.

The professionalization of nonprofits management has been accompanied by efforts to encourage greater business participation in nonprofit governance. Nonprofits executives in particular hoped that alliances with business managers sharing similar approaches to problem solving would, in making their organizations more effective and efficient, also elicit higher levels of corporate support. Although these high hopes have largely been borne out, the marriage of professional managerial cultures has in some cases brought conflict severe enough to raise questions about the value of the new business voluntarism and the threat that it poses to the integrity of nonprofit enterprise.

Does conflict between managerial cultures in nonprofits rise from intrinsic organizational differences? Or does conflict stem from more proximate factors, such as the inexperience of many executive-level volunteers? The proliferation of nonprofits since the 1960s and their increasing dependence on corporate support over the past decade suggest the latter. Although efforts to train inexperienced executives for service on nonprofit boards have been initiated, this chapter suggests the need for other means of making salient the distinctive responsibilities of nonprofit directorship, specifically the creative use of charters and bylaws as frameworks to mediate relationships between directors and staffs.

Nonprofits, Business, and the Reagan Revolution

In the 1960s, nonprofits and businesses had more often been adversaries than partners. Although business could count on the friendship of donor nonprofits, such as United Way and grant-making foundations, its relationships to the donee side had steadily deteriorated. In the private universities, long the greatest beneficiaries of corporate largess, noisy constituencies clamored against business large and small. Museums and arts organizations, also traditionally favored by business donors, became less responsive to wealthy, often business-based trustees as their directors, and curators discovered the independence offered by funding from national arts and humanities endowments. On the community level, floods of Great Society money in the form of social-services grants and contracts empowered the underclass and led to the formation of thousands of grassroots nonprofits, most of them advocacy-oriented and hostile to private enterprise. A foundation officer's lament during this period might just as well have been expressed by a host of conscientious corporate contributions managers: "Why do they hate us? We didn't even give them a grant." Cynical nonprofiteers were wont to reply, "Corporate giving is to philanthropy as advertising is to literature."

Those were the bad old days, however. By the late 1970s, faced with crippling inflation, dwindling government spending, and stringent oversight, the more radical community-based nonprofits had either died off or matured into organizations more preoccupied with delivering services than with "mau-mauing the flak catchers."[1] Universities became quiescent, as students appraised their uncertain futures in the stagnant economy. Arts organizations and museums, burned by populist ventures such as the Metropolitan Museum of Art's controversial Harlem on My Mind exhibit, again turned their attention to art for art's sake. With the new president's clarion call for a new spirit of private-sector voluntary activism, there was every reason to believe that a new era of fruitful cooperation between nonprofits and business was at hand.[2]

The Reagan era brought a revolution in nonprofit management. This was no accident. The president fully expected that cutbacks in federal spending would force nonprofits to use their resources more efficiently and, in the search for new financial and human resources, to turn to the communities in which they operated for support. For this reason, the administration energetically promoted voluntarism, with a particular emphasis on the importance of business dollars and expertise to help nonprofits deal with diminished government funding.[3]

Both nonprofits and influential elements in the business community

initially greeted with skepticism the president's belief that private resources could fill the gaps left by federal retrenchment.[4] However, in
the long run their response was everything Reagan could have wished.
Nonprofits became more businesslike, seeking out professionally
trained managers and retooling veteran executives with expertise in
strategic planning, market research, cost-benefit analysis, sophisticated financial information systems, and entrepreneurial approaches to
raising revenue. Nonprofits energetically courted corporate donors,
proposed cooperative joint ventures, and invited business executives
onto boards and committees.[5]

Business had its own reasons for responding positively to Reagan's
courtship. Deeply disenchanted with big government, many were eager to back Reagan's alternative vision. Community-focused giving
programs, combined with enhanced business representation on donee
boards, promised to take control of the charitable agenda away from
the bureaucrats and return it to local leaders. Corporate liberals were
attracted by a concept of citizenship, expressed through voluntary
contributions and hands-on involvement, which promised business a
degree of public recognition and esteem which had been absent since
the days of Coolidge.

On the individual level, there were as many reasons for executives
and proprietors to welcome the president's call for new private-sector
initiatives as there were personal perspectives on the social role of
business. Some volunteers were idealists, schooled in the 1960s to believe in community involvement and to see corporations as powerful
forces for social change. Others, especially aspiring midlevel managers
faced with constricting opportunities for promotion into the top
ranks, saw voluntarism as a way of gaining a competitive edge over
their rivals, mindful not only of the visibility that volunteering could
bring but also of the usefulness of community contacts as sources of
new business. Ethnicity and religion were also factors. Before the
1980s, Catholics and Jews, seldom invited to join mainstream boards,
had generally restricted their involvement to organizations serving
their particular communities. But in the Reagan era, with the spiraling demand for capable executive volunteers, these distinctions
diminished.

As nonprofits eagerly sought business support and participation,
board membership, once the relatively restricted domain of senior executives with roots in the community, became invested with a certain
glamour. Although often lacking in board experience, rising young
executives sought out nonprofits in need of their help. They were
warmly welcomed by managerially oriented nonprofit chief executive
officers, who sometimes saw them as allies and kindred spirits.[6]

Cracks in the Façade

Now, a decade after the Reagan revolution, there is reason to believe that the business-nonprofits partnership, while yielding substantial benefits to both, has been far more troubled than generally suspected. Big-city newspapers seldom note such events, but in the press of small-to medium-sized cities, hardly a week passes without a feature on the resignation of a nonprofit executive director or a key staffer. These articles follow a curiously reliable format. They tell of the wonderful jobs by these managers—five-year plans drafted and implemented, growing membership, expanded services, and peak revenues. The articles speak of missions successfully accomplished and managers going on to new and more exciting challenges. Taken at face value, everything seems rosy.

The educated eye can discern unmistakable signs of conflict beneath the smooth phrases of these barely edited press releases. Departures of chief executive officers are often accompanied by unreported resignations of groups of trustees and major board reshufflings. Widely publicized programs suddenly vanish. Fund-raising initiatives are abruptly terminated. When initially questioned, staffers and trustees alike blandly assert that all is well—though a more complete story generally emerges with more careful questioning.[7]

The smallness of voluntary communities makes even big cities seem like small towns—and in small towns, no one wants to look bad. So it is with nonprofits: conflicts between boards and staffs may lead to resignations and purges, but both sides, out a common commitment to the organization's mission and out of a common desire to look good, do their best to assure the world that all is well.

Conflict is intrinsic to nonprofits, which, as fragile coalitions of diverse interests, must constantly struggle for the consensus that enables them to do their work. Although these conflicts have generally centered around interpretations of organizational missions, more concrete differences of values, background, and training have frequently underlain these substantive differences of viewpoint. For example, in museums one would expect conflict between wealthy lay trustees and ambitious career-minded directors. In hospitals, struggles between community-oriented governing boards and super-specialist physicians or between cost-conscious accountants and service-minded caregivers are common.[8]

What makes the hidden conflict within nonprofits so interesting is that there are so few obvious differences among contenders. The partnership of professional business managers on nonprofit boards and professional managers on nonprofit staffs seemed unlikely precisely because both seemed to have mastered the same body of managerial techniques and shared the same professional ideology. In most cases neither could boast of deep roots in the communities in which they worked. The value systems of nonprofits managers were frequently more complex than those of their business counterparts because the former often combined a managerial training with grounding in an academic discipline or learned profession. Nonetheless, there was every reason to believe that they could overcome the long-running conflict between altruism and self-interest through a common appreciation of organizational efficiency and the best means of achieving it. But, curiously, these similarities merely intensified the struggle.

A Case in Point

Like so many small new cultural enterprises, the Widget Museum had been started by a group of enthusiastic amateurs. The museum was a spinoff of the 1976 bicentennial celebrations of a mid-sized industrial city. The founders hoped to celebrate the community's historic contribution to widget-making and to preserve the site of one of the nation's pioneer widgeteers. After a period of intense but unproductive activity under the guidance of volunteers, the organization hired a professional director in 1982. Exhausted with conflict, the board sank comfortably into a ratifying mode.

It was an ideal situation for an entrepreneur-manager. Federal, state, and foundation funders were successfully tapped. Prize-winning exhibitions were mounted. Publications brought national awards. The museum's education programs became an integral part of local school curricula. Attendance increased. But as the activities of the museum took on more variety and excellence, its financial needs also increased. Although grants largely underwrote these programs, they made little contribution to the museum's overhead, which constituted more than 80 percent of its annual budget. Further, as the funding arena became more competitive and funders proved less willing to underwrite indirect costs, the executive director concluded that the time had come to seek local support, particularly from the business community.

From the start, the director acknowledged that corporate contributions would require an executive presence on the board. But, being himself a trained manager, the director welcomed this presence as an antidote to the board's longstanding passivity. Largely composed of absentee members, the board only met quarterly and had delegated most of its business to a small and easily mustered executive committee. The executive director hoped that business directors would not only gradually replace the museum's deadwood but also help to mobilize the trustees who remained.

Even in the favorable climate of the 1980s, finding business volunteers was not easy. Numerous prominent business people, individuals with demonstrated records of service on other community boards, were informally sounded out about becoming widget trustees. They declined, citing overcommitment to other, usually more prestigious boards. As outlines of the city's board hierarchy gradually became apparent, the executive director realized that, because the museum had a "stepping stone" board, it would have to set its sights considerably lower. Experienced board people were much sought after, and once they were captured by well-established high visibility institutions such as the city hospital, the community foundation, the symphony, and the historical society, they were unlikely to want to invest their limited time on the board of a small, new, and financially insecure museum.

By the time a young vice-president of a local corporation came to the director's attention, the museum's board had reached the depths of passivity. Its chairman had stepped down, and none of his fellow trustees was willing to take his place. The director met informally with the prospective trustee and candidly outlined the museum's difficult situation of the museum while also hoping to appeal to his entrepreneurial instincts by speaking enthusiastically of its unrealized promise. The candidate responded with appropriate enthusiasm, but set one condition to joining the board: that he be made chairman. Sensing a ally and a kindred spirit, the executive director readily agreed, and, with little discussion, the choice was speedily ratified at the museum's next annual meeting.

During the following year, much as the executive director had hoped, the chairman proved a magnet for increasing the business community's interest and participation in the museum. The executive presence on the board was increased with the addition of two colleagues of the new chairman. Although neither worked for the chairman's firm, both had substantial and profitable ties to it. With the three businessmen voting together on the five-member executive committee, the museum began to move out of the doldrums.

A joint promotional venture was mounted, cosponsored by the chairman's company, a local magazine, and the museum, to present an annual award to an outstanding widgeteer in the community. This presentation not only promised to bring the museum considerable attention and financial support from the region's business community, but also promoted the interests of the ward's business sponsors because, thanks to aggressive marketing, it gave both of these relatively new enterprises much-needed visibility. Moreover, the museum's executive director was delighted by the venture because the widgeteer award complimented the museum's programmatic focus on the historical importance of widget manufacturing. The winner was to be named by a jointly appointed committee. The three sponsors were to share expenses of the ceremony.

The widgeteer award was a spectacular success. By its second year, it had brought in nominations from throughout the state, the award-selection committee attracted prestigious business people and management faculty from the local university, and the award received lavish advance publicity. Nevertheless, there were subtle but unmistakable signs that the tail had begun to wag the dog. Press coverage featured participating businesses, but largely ignored the museum. The chairman's firm reneged on its commitment to bear its share of the costs of the award ceremony, promising instead to cover the shortfall with a generous contribution. More seriously, the chairman attempted to influence the awards process in favor of his firm's clients, undermining the award's credibility.

Open conflict began to develop between the business-based trustees and the executive director, which intensified as the executive committee shifted its attention from the promotional venture to the museum's purchasing and personnel policies. The museum's accounts were shifted into a bank to which their own firms were closely tied—although the museum's own bank offered the same services at the same cost—in order to encourage the new bank to make a large donation to the museum. When the museum was considering a substantial investment in office equipment, the chairman and his colleagues urged that it had to be obtained from a fellow trustee and client who operated an office-equipment firm. Having just sold an enormous equipment order to the chairman's firm, the vendor would be willing to make the sale to the museum at cost.

Under the chairman's leadership, the executive committee became involved in other domains previously delegated to the executive director. Frustrated by the slow pace of a complex negotiation with an adjoining property owner, the chairman took over as the museum's spokesman. His intervention brought short-term financial benefits, but, in endangering the historical integrity of museum-owned structures, threatened the museum's future eligibility for historic-preservation grant monies. At the same time, the executive committee overruled the director's decision to discharge a part-time employee, who, though outspokenly hostile to the museum's increasingly professionalized direction, commanded the loyalty of a large group of neighborhood volunteers.

The executive committee finally turned its attention to the museum's nationally recognized but unprofitable public programs. In the search for profit centers, temporary exhibitions were suspended in order to free up space for rental purposes. Programs serving schools were suspended and education grant funds were diverted to cover the shortfall resulting from the widgeteer award promotion. The museum's valuable collection of historic widgets, most of them received as gifts and bequests, was to be put on the block and resulting revenues were to be applied to its operating funds.

At this point, the executive director began to mobilize the non-business-based trustees to repudiate the actions of the executive committee. Arguing that the diversion of restricted funds and the series of self-dealing transactions violated the state's nonstock corporation law and that the suspension of public programs constituted a broad violation of public trust, the director indicated that the board would have to either repudiate the illegal actions of the executive committee or face serious problems of legal liability. The executive committee responded by formally requesting that the board "review the director's performance" and ratify its decisions to terminate the public programs of the museum, liquidate its collections, and allocate the proceeds to promotional expenses and budget-balancing.

A Conflict of Managerial Cultures

In a tale of this kind, it is easy to take sides. Trustees experienced in the ways of nonprofits will immediately discern the questionable areas of self-dealing and insensitivity to informal but commonly observed boundaries between board and staff prerogatives. But such experienced trustees in the Reagan era were the exception, especially in smaller stepping-stone nonprofits. There were no "bad guys" at the Widget Museum: the major actors were all well-intentioned but inexperienced managers laboring under consensual illusions. In their enthusiasm for managerial technology, they failed to understand the need to match their tools to the task—and that the duties, responsibilities, and ethical standards of boards in nonprofit settings differ significantly from those applicable to business ones. Further, because neither managers nor nonbusiness trustees had served on corporate boards, they failed to observe well-established norms that, in the corporate setting, constrain directors from "doing management's job."

The chairman and his allies did not believe that they were acting improperly. They had been invited into the museum to make it more businesslike—and they proceeded to do so. Their central concerns were appropriately fiscal. When they joined up, they found an enterprise whose financial-information system was a simple running check-book balance. The museum did not cost out its activities and was thus incapable of projecting future income and expenditures. Without this information, the museum could neither plan nor make effective presentations to potential business donors.

With the full approval of the executive director, the business group set up a financial management system that not only provided accurate month-by-month information on the cash position of the museum, but also enabled it to set a realistic budget and discipline the staff to live within it. Standard business accounting methods were used rather than the fund accounting system favored by many nonprofits, but no one objected to this, because the new system was such a dramatic improvement over the previous lack of information systems.[9]

The business-based trustees also pragmatically understood that "it takes money to make money." This rationale underlay the self-dealing transactions with the chairman's firm and those of his fellow business-based trustees. Tradeoffs would lead to contributions from their firms, which, when combined with the high visibility of the widgeteer award, would lay the groundwork for approaching other corporate donors. Although technically illegal under the state's nonstock corporation act, these self-dealing transactions would have been perfectly legal among business firms.[10] Citing a museum-ethics handbook that questioned the wisdom of such transactions, the executive director never suggested that they were illegal. Neither did the two attorneys on the board. Under the circumstances, the business-based trustees could hardly be blamed for their ignorance.

Having laid the basis for running the museum like a business—through its financial-information system and a series of mutually beneficial relationships with external constituencies—more extensive changes in the museum had to follow. There was little point in having accurate information about its finances unless it was used as a tool to make the museum more financially responsible by transforming its programs. Financial stability required zero-based budgeting: each budget line would have to be justified in terms of its potential to yield revenue either through user fees or grant income. Because revenue projections did not appear likely to cover even fixed costs—which absorbed over 80 percent of the museum's annual revenues—steps would have to be taken to remedy the situation. The most immediate solutions appeared to lie in cutting programs that yielded no revenue, seeking rental income, and converting collections and other idle assets into cash. The treatment of grant funds as unrestricted assets seemed perfectly natural because the accounting system did not reflect the restrictions attached to their use.[11]

Intervention in other aspects of the executive director's domain proceeded from a similar logic. Because the business trustees' concern was the museum's short-term cash position, eligibility for historic-preservation grants as a long-term proposition was not a salient issue when the chairman intervened in the negotiation with the adjoining property owner. The reinstatement of the part-time employee was motivated by an identical consideration. The employee not only managed the museum's main rental facility but also commanded the loyalty of a cadre of volunteers, whose donated labor to a major profit center made them a resource well worth conserving—in sharp contrast to the expensive professionally trained education staff, whose activities brought in little or no direct income.

Learning from Conflict

When the Widget Museum case was first presented to a group that included nonprofit staffers, trustees, and corporate contributions officers, most of them thought that the unidentified organization was one with which they had been connected in the recent past. This response suggests that conflicts of managerial cultures on nonprofit boards appear to be far more common than generally supposed. Some might be comforted by writing off such conflicts as artifacts of the 1980s. But to do so is to overlook the possibility that the Reagan revolution may have been only the political manifestation of a far more fundamental shift in our institutional arrangements. Whoever occupies the White House, the free-spending days of the 1980s are unlikely to return. For the foreseeable future, nonprofits will remain heavily dependent on business and other kinds of locally based participation and support.

Accordingly, there is no reason to believe that the conditions that have produced this conflict of managerial cultures are going to change in the foreseeable future. Business involvement is likely to increase rather than diminish. Despite instances of frustration and disappointment, business-based board members have found hands-on voluntarism to be both personally fulfilling and career enhancing.[12] More practically, as the scale of corporate contributions increases, firms will want to be able to more directly oversee their charitable investments.[13] At the same time, the managerial orientation of nonprofit executives is certain to increase because of intensifying competition for funding and audiences, a more stringent regulatory environment, and growing demands for services. In addition, as more management schools establish nonprofit courses and concentrations, degrees in management are likely to become the basic credentials for nonprofit employment.

What, if anything, can be done to reduce the likelihood of conflict between these two managerial cultures? Thus far, remedial efforts have focused on education. Business schools encourage students to take a course in nonprofit administration as part of their general management focus. Many communities have set up programs to acquaint business volunteers with the distinctive responsibilities of serving on nonprofit boards. The best of these programs supplement readings and lectures with role-playing exercises in which prospective board members and nonprofit executives act out conflict situations. These efforts appear to fall short of the mark. The major players in the Widget Museum case had been through such programs, which evidently had little impact on their subsequent behavior. These forms of "basic training" are intended to clarify the very real differences between nonprofit and for-profit governance and management responsibilities. But they overlook the particular difficulties that busy executives face in translating knowledge into practice when on the front lines of voluntary board service. A few evenings or afternoons of intensive learning are unlikely to overcome management perspectives that have developed over a lifetime and have formed the basis of successful executive careers. These perspectives, powerfully reinforced by the daily challenges and routines of work in the "real world," are unlikely to be shed when an executive sits down in the nonprofit boardroom.

In addition, the business perspective is ramified by the managerial culture of nonprofits. Because formalized managerial approaches are new to most nonprofits managers, they navely regard them as more powerful than they really are. Awed by the technicalities of financial-information systems and strategic analysis, most nonprofits managers forget that tools are only as good as the people using them—and that technique is no substitute for substance. This naïveté encourages executives on nonprofit boards to hold onto familiar business-management perspectives, regardless of lessons to the contrary. Finally, the ambiguities inherent in nonprofits, particularly the apparent fluidity of goals and lack of a clearly definable bottom line, tends to drive executives on charitable boards to cling to the most easily identifiable measures of performance, the financial ones with which they are most familiar.

The failure to attend to the important differences between the duties and responsibilities of nonprofit directors and for-profit ones is not restricted to business-based board members. As the Widget Museum case suggests, the lack of salience of these distinctions was universal. Even the two attorneys on the board were unaware of the stricter standard applied to self-dealing transactions by the state's nonstock corporation statute. Although the executive director knew that self-dealing was unwise, it was only after the conflict had reached its greatest intensity that he sought legal counsel and learned that the actions of the executive committee had violated the law.

A Basis for Resolution

Although the educational efforts of management schools and in midcareer board member training programs are important, it is clear that further steps are needed to make all nonprofit players, board and staff alike, familiar with their responsibilities. The most important of these steps may involve more imaginative use of charters and bylaws by nonprofit corporations. In regard to this, legal scholar Lizabeth Moody concluded that "it is prudent for each charitable corporation to develop its own internal law of director accountability and protection. Each charitable director should have concrete rules. It should be kept in mind that the director is more likely to read the organization's by-laws than the state's nonprofit corporation law. By-laws will thus be used as a blueprint for director conduct. They can contain provisions that make explicit matters ranging from conflicts of interest and disclosure requirements to attendance."[14]

There is a beautiful simplicity in Moody's approach to the problem of making distinctions between nonprofit organizations and for-profit ones salient. Acknowledging the diverse perspectives and interests that board members bring from their busy lives in the "real world" to the nonprofit boardroom, she understands that boundaries between them be made in the clearest and most accessible way. Just as fundamental differences between baseball and tennis are tangibly expressed by the physical arrangements of diamonds and courts, so the distinctive rules that govern the two sectors of private action can be made clear by using the charter and bylaws as a blueprint of board and staff conduct.

Anyone familiar with nonprofit charters and bylaws knows how far most of these documents fall short of Moody's desideratum. They tend to be lazily crafted assemblies of boilerplate, composed in a legalese that obscures rather than reveals their meanings. Usually drafted when an organization is set up, they are seldom referred to or updated. Often major changes in organizational structure and practice are seldom reflected in the bylaws, but are buried in equally incomprehensible and usually inaccessible minutes of board meetings. As a result, the rules governing behavior become personalized, informal, and folkloric; the signposts demarcating the boundaries between for-profit and nonprofit obligations become effaced; and the stage is set for organizational conflict. Because formal planning is now the vogue in the nonprofit sector, board members and staffs might begin this process by first turning to their charters and bylaws, regarding them as the ground rules and guidelines for the voluntary game, the specific terms of the contract between organizational participants and between the organization and the public it is meant to serve. These documents should not only be revised and updated but also placed in the hands of every trustee, committee member, and staffer as he or she joins the organization. Finally, like the old-time Congregationalists renewing the covenant, board members should annually review their contract with one another in order to remind themselves of the special responsibilities they have taken on as trustees of private corporations working in the public interest.[15]

Such an approach is no cure-all to what may be intrinsic conflicts between the goals and managerial cultures of eleemosynary and business enterprise. This approach will not be easy to implement, because it requires real willingness of nonprofit executives and their boards to cooperate—something difficult to come by in organizations under stress. Nevertheless, this common-sense approach to reducing the likelihood of unproductive conflict seems more promising than accusing business-based board members of greed and insensitivity or blaming nonprofit executive directors for being hopelessly impractical.

6

Paper Ephemera: Managers, Policymakers, Scholars, and the Future of American Philanthropy

Records management in foundations is generally treated as a support issue, akin to the paper-clip supply. It is seldom viewed as having any relationship to foundations' substantive grant-making activities, and it is not thought to have much bearing on either internal managerial and governance issues or external concerns of regulation and legitimacy. This chapter suggests that what records are kept and who has access to them have important bearing on what foundations do, how they do it, and by whom it is done—as well as on how those actions are viewed and interpreted by those outside the organization.

Ideally, it ought to be possible to address decisions about records management in terms of a relatively simple set of questions:

What records are needed to serve a foundation's own reference needs?
What records are foundations legally required to retain?
Who should have access to foundation records?
What formats will best serve these needs?
What will a records-management program cost?

The problem is that the answers even to these simple questions contain judgments about the purpose of a foundation, its mission and goals, its allocation of power between board and staff and within staff, and its accountability to external constituencies. How these questions are answered may not only reflect the character of the foundation as an organization but also, if made in an uninformed way, profoundly impact its purposes and processes in the future. The elusiveness and complexity of the answers to these kinds of questions are suggested by Peter Drucker's comments on the difficulties of assessing organizational effectiveness. How, he asks, should one measure whether a university is doing a good job?

By the jobs and salaries its students get twenty years after graduation? By that elusive myth, the "reputation" of this or that faculty, which all too often is nothing but self-praise and good academic propaganda? By the number of Ph.D.'s or scientific prizes alumni have earned? Or by the donations they make to their alma mater? Each such yardstick bespeaks a value judgment regarding the purpose of the university—and a very narrow one at that. Even if these were the right objectives, such yardsticks measure performance just as dubiously as the count of bed utilization measures performance in mental hospitals.[1]

There is always, as Drucker points out, a choice of yardsticks. And each one involves a different configuration of power within the organization, as well as a different posture in regard to external constituencies. Moreover, the value of each may depend on the age of an organization: performance measures suitable to a start-up organization, in which expectations are relatively unformed and consensus is relatively strong, may not be appropriate at later points. Their value of performance measures also obviously depends on the kinds of needs being served, which may change over time, either due to the success of the foundation's activities or for other reasons.

The capacity to make intelligent choices about yardsticks—about a foundation's mission and objectives—depends in large measure on whether it has the capacity, in terms of a coherent and accessible record of its own activities, to reflect on itself. Ultimately, effective management depends not only on the judgment, character, and technical competence of managers but also on the body of information available to help them understand their organizations and their roles in them, as well as the place of those organizations in the external environment.

Thus, to say that records-management policies must be weighed in terms of their "costs and benefits" begs the question. What is in the "best interest" of a foundation? Merely raising the issue suggests a range of uncertainties about who should determine such policies, what the foundation's purposes are, and the relative importance of various internal and external stakeholders in its activities.

Resolving these uncertainties is likely to be especially difficult for independent grant-making foundations, in which costs and benefits cannot be weighed in terms of profits, attracting capital, or customer satisfaction. For grant makers, the calculus of costs and benefits is framed by the charters of foundations, by the regulatory environment, by public opinion, and, ultimately, by assessments of whether their projects and programs are making any impact on the problems to which they are addressed.

Changing Foundations, Changing Information Needs

The extensive literature on foundations produced over the past thirty years tells us a great deal about what they are and what they do, but curiously little about how they actually operate. Despite all the rhetoric about philanthropic professionalization, as well as some promising proto-professional activities, including the formation of regional associations of grant makers, which permit informal exchanges of managerial intelligence, there really is no foundation-management literature comparable to the case studies, empirically based analyses, and theoretical reflections on organizational processes which illuminate the management of businesses and public agencies. This literature, which has focused increasingly on organizations as information systems and on the role of executives as information managers, has important bearing on records management and its place in the managerial process.

It is worth noting that analytical and empirical management literature is of relatively recent origin. It came into being over the past thirty years, largely in response to the breakdown of public and private managerial capacities in the face of rapidly changing economic and political conditions. Although rapidly changing conditions in the foundation world have increased foundation self-awareness and encouraged the hiring of full- or part-time staffs, a critical foundation-management literature has yet to be created.

Although foundation staffs increasingly consider themselves professionals, they seldom think of themselves as managers. They are generally recruited from the worlds of academia and social service, and few have received formal managerial training. And foundation trade publications (in contrast to trade publications in other nonprofits fields) have not partaken in any obvious way of the mainstream public- and private-management literature. As a result, grant makers have tended to remain relatively unsophisticated in their thinking about the role of information, current or retained, in the managerial process.

This situation may be coming to an end, however, due to changes in the foundation world which pose challenges as fundamental as those which have led to the development of a critical management literature for government, business, and nonprofits. Certainly the most important of these challenges involves the maturation of the foundation as an organizational form.

Although philanthropy itself boasts an ancient lineage, and a handful of grant-making entities may trace themselves back to the first decades of this century, the vast majority of foundations—some 77 percent—was created since 1950.[2] (An indicator of their relative novelty is the enormous confusion during congressional hearings of the 1950s on about the meaning of the term *foundation!*)[3]

The newness of foundations has important managerial implications, particularly with regard to the continuity of their missions and purposes.[4] This newness, in turn, has significant bearing on their capacity to formulate goals and objectives. Almost every foundation starts out being governed by individuals—donors, trustees, and staffs—who share a common sense of purpose. Although this is particularly true of foundations established by individual donors, who in many cases select family members or business associates as trustees, it is also true of community trusts and corporate foundations, which, though more formally institutionalized and broadly based, often reflect the collective values and vision of a particular group of community leaders or corporate directors and managers. These groups can have remarkable persistence: for example, one foundation in Pennsylvania, though established on the death of its donor in 1931, remained dominated by his long-lived personal associates until the early 1980s.[5] But those who shared in the founding vision eventually die off and are replaced by individuals with different viewpoints and values. When this happens, confusion and conflict over a foundation's mission and goals are bound to occur.

The changing nature of foundation management has accelerated this process. As professionalization has led to the development of a career orientation among foundation managers, staff turnover has dramatically increased. According to the *Foundation Management Report 1988,* half the chief executive officers of responding foundations had held their positions for less than five years—and 19 percent had held their positions for less than two. Although the report notes that 27 percent of these individuals had been promoted from within, the fact that nearly three-fourths of them were outsiders to their organizations offers compelling evidence of future problems in maintaining continuity. Unfortunately, the report offers no information on board turnover. Nonetheless, it seems inevitable that this also will increase.[6]

Information and Uncertainty

Demographic changes among foundation staffs and governing boards—whether involving temporal distance from the donor and his or her associates, increasing board and staff turnover, or growing staff professionalism—inevitably produce uncertainty and conflict over a foundation's mission and goals. Changes in the external environment—including changing public needs and expectations and more exacting regulatory oversight—introduce further uncertainties. One response to these changes has been increasing foundation interest in planning, evaluation, and self-assessment. Although no figures exist to show how many foundations have initiated such procedures, anecdotal evidence suggests that many have.[7]

Evaluation, self-assessment, and planning procedures originated in business and have more recently been adapted to nonprofits—both of which are dependent on external resources (capital/grants and contracts/donations, sales/user fees, customers/clients) for their survival.[8] Although these procedures were originally conceived of as methods for enabling organizations to adapt to changing external environments, critical examination of how they actually operate has led us to understand them as strategies affecting the flow and interpretation of information.[9] Rather than offering "objective" and "rational" criteria for assessing past performance or for projecting future activities, evaluation, assessment, and planning procedures are now understood to have an essentially political function, constituting "an interpretive framework that allows the organization to be understood by its internal and external stakeholders."[10] This understanding, in turn, forms a consensual or coalitional basis for the allocation of responsibility, resources, and accountability.

Conventional evaluation, assessment, and planning procedures were designed to serve the needs of resource-dependent organizations. Although the operational calculus of nonprofit organizations is informed to some extent by their charitable purposes, like for-profit enterprises they are still on the whole revenue maximizers that define their relation to their environments in terms of adjusting income to expenditures through efficient and effective use of resources.

Foundations are different. They are not resource-dependent. They do not have to seek out capital, contributions, or clients. Although they may *choose* to be concerned about using their resources effectively and efficiently, they do not have to be. Although government regulations and public scrutiny impose some constraints on foundations with regard the proportion of annual income used to defray administrative costs, they are immune to the market forces that lead businesses and nonprofits to initiate evaluation, assessment, and planning activities.

Foundations are unique in that they are *legitimacy*-maximizers rather than revenue-maximizers. The forces to which they are most subject do not involve sufficiency of financial resources. They involve internal agreement on mission, objectives, goals, and programs and seeking congruence between those internal agreements and the expectations of external constituencies—government agencies, legislators, the courts, the press, professional and trade associations, scholars, donees. When resource-dependent organizations do not operate efficiently or effectively, they are likely to either fail or reorganize. When foundations do not effectively or efficiently manage legitimacy, they are likely first to undergo internal conflict and, ultimately, to come to the attention of courts and regulatory agencies, which possess the power to compel reevaluation of their missions and goals.

Managing Legitimately, Managing Legitimacy

In such a setting, evaluation, assessment, and planning procedures obviously have to be implemented in a very different way. They may have in common the goal of generating shared understanding among internal and external stakeholders, but the information out of which such understandings are constructed may be significantly different. Particularly important for a foundation is the nature of its charter instrument. Businesses and nonprofits enjoy almost unrestricted freedom to alter their charters, but this is not the case for foundations. A foundation charter is more than a contract between living members of a corporation. It is a trust instrument that imposes enforceable obligations to fulfill the intentions of its founders. If these intentions cannot be fulfilled, trustees are not free to alter them at will. They are required to ask the courts for guidance in reinterpreting their purposes. Even in foundations whose purposes are open-ended injunctions to act "for the benefit of mankind," administrators and trustees have generally been attentive to the kinds of benefactions favored by donors during their lifetimes.

With the passage of time, as donors and their associates die off, as public needs change, and as management becomes increasingly professionalized, the interpretation of charter purposes is bound to become more problematic, involving greater uncertainty and greater potential for conflict among trustees, between board and staff, and between the foundation and external stakeholders. As this happens, foundations are likely to turn increasingly to formal evaluation, assessment, and planning procedures. But as they do so, they are bound to encounter the inability of these procedures to factor in divergent interpretations of charter purpose. How charter purpose is interpreted no small matter because of the legal force of founding documents and because of the standing of a variety of constituencies, internal and external, to compel judicial review of the actions of trustees and managers in carrying out their obligations under these instruments. As proceedings such as those involving the Buck Trust suggest, the courts may devote considerable attention to issues that seem essentially historical in nature.[11]

Businesses nonprofits can depend primarily on opinion research to define and prioritize stakeholder interests. But the interpretive framework within which internal and external stakeholders of a foundation shape their understanding of its mission and objectives is uniquely constrained by the past. As charitable trustees, they are legally bound by the documentary record that constitutes the record of their organization's activities, within which are embedded the motives and intentions of foundation donors and their successors and agents.

Conflict, Uncertainty, and the Politics of Information

As foundations mature organizationally, it seems inevitable that their trustees and managers will encounter greater uncertainty about their missions, goals, and objectives. The greater the uncertainty about these central concerns, the greater the likelihood of conflict between stakeholders and the greater the likelihood that they will look to objectively verifiable evidence to settle these disputes. In such conflicted settings, especially where their awareness of their organization's past is weak and where records are inaccessible or unavailable, control of retained information—the power to define the significant events in the past of the organization and to define its purposes—may assume considerable tactical importance.[12] Acknowledging the control of such records as instruments of power in organizations, two leading management scholars only half-humorously suggested that

> minutes should be written long enough after the event as to legitimize the reality of forgetfulness. They should be written in such a way as to lay the basis for subsequent independent action. In general, participants in the organization should be assisted in their desire to have unambiguous decisions actions taken today derived from the ambiguous decisions of yesterday with a minimum of pain to their images of organizational rationality and a minimum of claims on their time. The model of consistency is maintained by a creative resolution of uncertainty about the past.[13]

Quite clearly, each foundation constituency has its own stake in retained information, as well as its own capacity to enforce its claims to access organizational records.[14] The information needs of internal constituencies vary according to their function in the organization. Usually, staffs may only be concerned with convenience, in particular the extent to which records enable them to do their jobs more effectively and efficiently. But in a situation of conflict, they may also view records as means of documenting their contributions to the organization, which in turn may serve to legitimate their claims as stakeholders in its programs and policies. In addition, as staffs become more professionalized and career-minded, they develop an interest in the completeness and accessibility of records to the extent that they play a role in documenting their professional achievements and facilitating either promotion within the organization or movement into better positions elsewhere.

Another aspect of the status of retained records in regard to managerial professionalization involves the autonomy of management. Usually, the central task of managers is to control and interpret the flow of information between the organization and its external environment and among internal constituencies, including the board. This arrangement provides managers with the capacity not only to evaluate the performance of other employees and to assess programs, projects, and overall organizational performance, but also, in doing so, to set the policy options presented to the foundation's trustees. In a conflicted setting, what information is retained and who has access to it may have considerable bearing on the outcome of conflicts between managers and their boards.

The information needs of trustees are both the most comprehensive and the most limited of all. On the one hand, as the group bearing ultimate legal responsibility for a foundation's activities, they should have access to all information, retained or current. On the other hand, from a practical standpoint, exercising such a prerogative would fatally impair managerial effectiveness. By the same token, trustees generate information—particularly materials about personnel decisions and deliberations about recruiting fellow board members—that cannot, for practical reasons, be included among the official records of a foundation, but that nonetheless may have crucial bearing on interpreting its mission and goals. Usually, neither managers nor trustees have a compelling reason to transgress these domains of information—but in situations of conflict, they may seek to do so.

Certain external constituencies—regulatory agencies, legislatures, and the courts—have legal authority to enforce their information needs on foundations. Other constituencies, such as professional and trade associations, may have only moral authority to do so. The general public, the press, scholars, and grantees have neither legal nor moral authority to view foundation records. Nonetheless, because of the special legal status of foundations as tax-exempt charitable trusts, they cannot be excluded as parties interested in the retention and accessibility of foundation records.

Usually, the claims of external constituencies on retained foundation records are of little significance, consisting of little more than compliance with routine public reporting requirements. However, in situations of conflict the claims may be far-reaching. For example, when the Cox Committee investigated foundations in 1952, it required those with assets exceeding $10 million to respond to a ninety-item questionnaire, which, among other things, asked the respondents to list institutions, operating agencies, publications, specific projects, and individuals that had received grants from foundations, and the amounts, years, and nature of such grants since 1935. "For the larger foundations," as F. Emerson Andrews noted, "replies grew to book size (Henry Allen Moe's response for the John Simon Guggenheim Foundation ran to 329 pages)."[15]

These questions were relatively simple and, indeed, if asked today could be answered with little difficulty, because the kinds of issues the Cox Committee were concerned with ended up being embodied to a large extent in the regular annual reporting requirements imposed by the 1969 Tax Reform Act. But one can imagine more difficult kinds of questions being asked—questions unanswerable by the minimal records-retention requirements of current regulations. What if congressional committees became interested in decisionmaking processes within foundations, issues that could only be engaged through administrative memoranda, phone logs, appointment books, correspondence, and successive drafts of policy documents? That Congress would be interested in materials of this kind might seem incredible—but so, from the standpoint of foundation watchers before 1952, did the idea that the government might demand a full accounting of their grant-making activity.

Conclusion

Quite clearly, information is powerful. Control of and access to information are crucial in shaping the configuration of power within organizations, as well as profoundly influencing the outcome of internal conflicts. Because of the special character of foundation charter instruments and because of the peculiarities of foundations as legitimacy maximizers, retained records may be even more important than ever, not only in resolving internal conflicts but also in influencing the outcome of regulatory, investigative, and judicial interventions in foundation practices and policies.

If both internal and external constituencies have vital stakes in preserving and accessing foundation records and if control of such information constitutes a critical dimension of power in and over organizations, it follows that records-management policies need to be framed in the broadest terms—with a view not only to their immediate dollar costs but also in terms of managerial effectiveness, trustee responsibility, and organizational survival.

Implicit in this formulation is the likelihood that records-management policies will tend to be determined by the interests of whomever happens to be in control of the organization at any given time. As Elizabeth McCormack has noted with regard to foundation self-evaluation efforts, "self-evaluation is difficult; self-deception is easy."[16] Thus, it may be difficult for some grant makers to resist the urge to adopt selective and restrictive records-management policies, saving only the files that the law and executive convenience require and maximally limiting access to them (this is the practice followed by the vast majority of American foundations).[17] But, as Richard Nixon's missing eighteen minutes, Oliver North's deleted files, and the "lost" Atomic Energy Commission records of radiation-caused disabilities suggest, there may be limitations to this approach.[18] Pragmatically, it is nearly impossible to destroy information once it has been created and begins to move through an organization because for each person who has a stake in destroying or suppressing information there are always others who have a stake in its preservation. As the above examples suggest, destroying or unreasonably restricting access to information can be powerfully delegitimating for any organization. For foundations, which are legitimacy-maximizers, the consequences could be devastating.

This analysis points to the conclusion that records retention should be as inclusive as possible and that, in order to maintain the integrity of retained records and to place access policies under reasonably disinterested auspices, they should be placed in professionally operated archives centers rather than in-house repositories. This is admittedly a painfully expensive solution—costly both financially and politically. No organization wants to diminish its autonomy. Yet the fact that foundations are devoted to public purposes and have grown and flourished under a tax system that has accorded them and their donors certain valuable privileges may require sacrificing small degrees of independence in order to preserve more significant ones.

Moreover, these sacrifices may be well worth making, not only to enhance the overall legitimacy of private foundations in the public policy arena but also, more importantly and immediately, to enhance their effectiveness and to resolve the conflicts of mission and goals which seem likely to become more frequent and intense because of the death of donors and the professionalization of staffs.

There is a great deal that we do not know about foundations. Building a body of information about them which is sufficient to enhance their capacity to recognize their common political interests and, subsequently, to frame those interests in the language and concerns of contemporary public policy has come slowly, painfully, and—almost invariably—only after the occurrence of outbursts of regulatory enthusiasm.[19] Although surveys of foundation archival practices reveal a distressingly widespread indifference to the usefulness of such records, there are encouraging signs, especially among larger and better managed foundations, of a willingness to forearm themselves against internal and external crises, recognizing that their resolution will be profoundly shaped by the comprehensiveness and accessibility of their records.

7

Obstacles to Nonprofits Teaching and Research

The growth of nonprofits teaching and research over the past decade has been impressive but also selective. In many universities, the field has encountered substantial and deeply rooted resistance. This chapter points out some of the ways in which this resistance has been manifested, touches on some of its roots, and suggests some strategies for effectively institutionalizing the field.

Resistance

CASE 1

One major private university has received more than $5 million in nonprofits research funds over the past decade and is the site of the sector's "flagship" research enterprise. From the standpoint of the nonprofits field, the research center has been an outstanding success, attracting generous funders and distinguished visiting scholars, as well as publishing a large number of well-received scholarly books and articles.

Curiously, the research center has had little impact on the curriculum or faculty interests of the university with which it is affiliated. Faculty from other schools and departments seldom attend its seminars. No courses other than those taught by the handful of faculty members closely associated with the center have been initiated in the ten years of the center's existence. The management school, which has publicly committed itself to an interest in nonprofits administration, has restricted its commitment to a single survey course.

An anecdote suggests the situation of nonprofits studies in this university. A visiting scholar from the center recently raised with a senior faculty member the possibility of part-time teaching in one of the university's departments. He had prepared four course proposals, one of which focused on the history of nonprofit organizations. Although friendly to the work of the research center, the faculty member singled out the nonprofits course as the one least likely to interest the American studies faculty. He urged eliminating the course from the group of proposals because of the active hostility it was likely to arouse.

CASE 2

A year ago a school of public administration at a major private university in the Northeast decided to explore the possibility of a nonprofits management concentration. After extensive discussions with knowledgeable scholars throughout the country, the associate dean in charge of the enquiry endorsed the *idea,* but suggested that the university draw on its existing faculty resources rather than bringing in new members. When the faculty met on the matter, it decided that "its plate was already full" and that it would not commit its time or energy to another new program. The faculty urged the dean to seek the funding necessary for hiring new faculty to teach in the nonprofits area. At this point, the university's interest in the matter came to a halt.

REFLECTIONS ON THE CASES

Why have the oldest and most prestigious private universities resisted nonprofits studies, despite powerful administrative backing and substantial available funding? Why have such programs been more readily accepted in newer, less prestigious institutions? Should we be concerned about the hierarchical character of these preferences? It can be argued that nonelite institutions are more suitable settings for nonprofits studies, given the quintessentially democratic character of organized voluntarism. Even granting this, we still have to consider the possibility that resistance to nonprofits studies in elite universities may discourage talented scholars and teachers from entering the field.

These dilemmas require us to consider other efforts to institutionalize new fields. In particular, the nonprofits situation appears to parallel the development of education scholarship as depicted in Bernard Bailyn's *Education in the Forming of American Society.* For a whole generation of passionate crusaders for professionalism in education,

history was not simply the study of the past. It was an arcane science that revealed the intimate relationship between their hitherto despised profession and the destiny of man. . . . The development of this historical field took place, consequently, in an atmosphere of special professional purpose. It grew in almost total isolation from the major influences and shaping minds of twentieth-century historiography; and its isolation proved to be self-intensifying; the more parochial the subject became, the less capable it was of attracting the kinds of scholars who could give it broad relevance and bring it back to the public domain. It soon displayed the exaggeration of weakness and extravagance of emphasis that are the typical results of sustained inbreeding.[1]

In a similar fashion, nonprofits research has been to a large extent an effort to legitimate and justify charitable tax-exempt organizations, to set them apart as worthy of special treatment in public policy, and to promote managerial professionalization and the creation of the institutional infrastructure—academic programs, journals, conferences—rather than to dispassionately examine their role in society. Like education, nonprofits research and teaching finds itself ignored and resisted by the scholarly mainstream.

The Roots of Resistance

Resolving the dilemmas of institutionalization also requires that we consider the sources of resistance to the field. In doing so, it is useful to distinguish between resistance manifested institutionally, departmentally, and by academic professionals as individuals. The cases cited here suggest that there is little resistance of nonprofits studies on the institutional level. In both universities, nonprofits program proposals were initiated by top administrators and were promised or actually received generous outside funding. However, there is some evidence that the administrators may have been motivated more by financial considerations than by convictions about the intellectual value of the field. Generously funded institutes are profit centers for sponsoring universities, which earn substantial overhead from "soft" grant monies. The preeminence of the financial incentive is suggested by the failure of administrators to in any way match the nonprofit funders' commitments, by allocating discretionary funds to their support, or by encouraging departmental interest in nonprofits studies.[2] However, such opportunism can hardly be counted as a form of resistance.

Real resistance appears on the departmental and individual levels. Among these, resistance to courses and programs in the nonprofits area appears to involve three factors: scholarly ideology, academic structure, and the special characteristics of nonprofits studies.

IDEOLOGICAL RESISTANCE

Ideological resistance to nonprofit studies appears to stem from: (1) the overall political orientation of the academic profession; (2) the cultural factors involving the relationship of academics to the voluntary community; and (3) the sensitivity of scholars to lay influence on research and teaching.

One does not have to be a David Packard or a William F. Buckley, Jr., to discern the critical stance that many academics take toward private enterprise, whether in its self-interested or its altruistic garb. At best, academics are indifferent to private initiative; at worst, they are openly hostile to it.

Some years ago, Yale political scientist Robert Dahl studied the number of political-science dissertations and scholarly articles dealing with business issues since the establishment of his field sixty years earlier.[3] To his surprise, he found only a handful. This situation is mirrored in other disciplines: few outside the field of economics and management offer courses on private-sector issues, either for-profit or nonprofit. The average American college-level history text devotes no more than twenty of its thousand or so pages to business or philanthropy. Courses on business history, where they exist, are rare and are seldom part of the history or American studies curriculum.

Ironically, the very generosity and prestige of the sponsors of non-profits studies may intensify these underlying suspicions and work to harden resistance to the field. The inevitable association of philanthropy with names such as Ford, Rockefeller, Carnegie, Sloan, and other avatars of business civilization may inevitably handicap its efforts to gain academic acceptance. Further, the involvement of nonprofit intermediaries such as Independent Sector (IS) and the Council on Foundations—both commonly regarded as trade associations— may have also reinforced these suspicions because their leadership— Gardner, Filer, Lyman, and others—has been so closely identified with the foundations and corporations established by the very wealthy.

Academic attitudes toward nonprofits studies may also be shaped by the community-level relationship of professors to voluntary organizations. Academics are often nomadic, and few seek involvement in locally based voluntary organizations. Their participation is restricted to organizations with national and international concerns: few academics serve on local nonprofit boards or municipal commissions, but many are active in local chapters of organizations concerned with South Africa, Latin America, and disarmament.

It is difficult to say whether this lack of involvement is an artifact of their political outlook or their nomadic ways. Commitments with national and international foci can be more easily be transferred from community to community as scholars change jobs. However, these kinds of involvements may constitute another layer of resistance to nonprofits studies: the cosmopolitan orientation of academic life may lead professors to regard community-based nonprofit organizations as parochial enterprises smacking of Babbitry and boosterism.

STRUCTURAL OBSTACLES

Major obstacles to the growth of nonprofits studies also appear to be university authority structures and the bargaining process by which universities allocate financial and human resources. Although formally bureaucratic in structure, the administrative hierarchies of universities contain significant areas over which academic managers exercise only nominal power. The most important of these areas involve decisions about curriculum and personnel, over which administrators have little control and which are generally left to the discretion of departments. Authority within these units is exercised collegially by their tenured members.[4]

Tenure insulates departments from the influence of students, administrators, and the demands of society. To this extent, tenure prevents teaching and research from being market-driven. But tenure is a two-edged sword: while protecting the academic professions from outside interference, it also constitutes a significant obstacle to innovation. In the past tenure was less of an obstacle to innovation because university presidents felt more free to actively promote change by establishing new chairs and departments. For a variety of reasons, they are less willing to do this today. Curricular innovation is now usually left to the initiative of the tenured faculty—which has little incentive to promote change.

The budgetary process in universities reflects this shift in power from administrators to faculty, often taking the form of negotiations between established departmental interests. Curricular requirements become means of allocating students among departments in order to maintain current levels of staffing and budgeting. When resources are scarce, proposals for new programs and faculty appointments threaten resources available to existing ones and so are generally resisted. But even the availability of new resources may be perceived as threatening because of their potential influence on existing interdepartmental power arrangements. Under these structural constraints, innovation of any kind has little chance of success. Nonprofit studies labor under particular handicaps.

INTRINSIC OBSTACLES

Thus far, this chapter has dwelt on the demand side of resistance to nonprofits studies. Serious problems also exist on the supply side, particularly in the definition and organization of the field. These problems are not merely internal, but profoundly affect the way the broader academic environment perceives the field.

What do we mean by nonprofits studies? How should they be pursued? What forms of sponsorship and underwriting are most appropriate? These would be simple questions were it not for the inevitably close ties between nonprofits teaching and research, public policy, and organizational practice.

For two decades, scholars and policymakers have debated the existence of the nonprofit sector, the location of its boundaries, and the best strategies for studying it. Some scholars have emphasized the uniqueness of the sector and have urged that research focus on comparing and contrasting "independent institutions" with those of business and government. Others have suggested that more attention should be paid to the interpenetration and interaction of the sectors. Each viewpoint on nonprofits studies has important implications for both public policy and the place of the field in the curriculum.

Underlining the distinctiveness and independence of nonprofits has important consequences for the substance, disciplinary control, and institutional sponsorship of the field. Substantively, this approach emphasizes issues of organizational rationality and institutional effectiveness and efficiency. Within the curriculum, this approach promotes the power of disciplines predicated on concepts of rationality. In the realm of public policy, this approach promotes the reformist view of nonprofits which is favored by industry intermediaries. Moreover, this approach serves industry-sponsored efforts to professionalize nonprofits management.

That this approach to the field so closely ties scholarship to the legitimation of professional management may not be entirely healthy, as Bailyn's comments on education scholarship suggest. Although the field may yield short-term benefits in terms of grant support and other forms of industry sponsorship, it may, over the long term, stimulate the scholarly mainstream's resistance to nonprofits teaching and research and lead to the isolation and stagnation of the field.

Underlining interpenetration, interaction, and the commonalities between nonprofit, for-profit, and public organizations carries with it its own set of consequences. It advances the interests of disciplines attentive to the nonrational determinants of behavior. Substantively, it may question assumptions about the efficacy of reform, the efficiencies to be derived from rationalizing organizations, and the disinterestedness of professionals and volunteers. This approach may favor placing nonprofits studies within existing disciplinary foci rather than the establishment of new fields and programs. While not unfriendly to the professionalization of nonprofits management, the approach may favor training programs integrated into the general management curriculum rather than the establishment of nonprofits concentrations.

Because this perspective is essentially critical, it is necessarily less directly serviceable to nonprofits management professionalization and may be perceived as inimical to the political interests of the nonprofits industry. Although likely to be denied grant support and other forms industry sponsorship, the critical perspective may prove the most healthy line of development for the field over the long term. If the industry has a genuine interest in averting legislative and judicial interference, this perspective is essential to effective self-policing. Further, this approach is less likely to encounter resistance in the academic mainstream because it is more consistent with generally accepted standards of disinterested enquiry.

Strategic Dilemmas

The situation of nonprofits studies in the university setting presents serious dilemmas. How can the nonprofits research community best serve both the interests of scholarship and the real and pressing needs of the industry? Are the two hopelessly incompatible? More concretely, how can we create the boundaries necessary to free enquiry and retain the ties essential to the production of research useful to the industry while gaining academic acceptance for the field? These dilemmas are not insoluble, but solving them may require unusual candor and trust.

First, both the industry and the research community need to appreciate the extent to which academic resistance to the field stems from our failure to clearly distinguish nonprofits research from nonprofits advocacy. This lack of distinction is promoted by the current composition of the Independent Sector Research Committee, on which funders and industry representatives outnumber scholars by two to one. The committee is widely viewed, accurately or not, as having a key role in setting the research agenda, in brokering research funding, and in setting up the programs in which nonprofits scholars present their work. The dominance of the industry in the scholarly process is inimical to generally accepted standards of free enquiry.

Second, we must confront the role of grant-driven research in blurring the lines between research and advocacy. With the notable exception of the Lilly Endowment's recent blockbuster grant to Indiana University, most nonprofits funding has been piecemeal. Scholars and research centers tend to live hand to mouth, sponsoring only fundable research and eschewing less marketable projects. This situation also seems inimical to the spirit of free enquiry.

Establishing the conditions for free enquiry—and making nonprofits scholarship more acceptable in the scholarly mainstream— seems to require a selective disengagement of the industry and the research community. This disengagement requires that the industry be willing to trade off short-term utilities of control and the production of useful scholarship against the long-term benefits of a self-sustaining and reputable scholarly enterprise. Steps toward the latter end may include:

- The endowment of professorships in established departments and professional schools, with faculties selecting incumbents. These scholars, free to set their own research agendas, to teach regular courses, and to supervise graduate work, would be in a position to recruit a cadre of younger scholars with interests in the field. These positions would themselves constitute major incentives for talented teachers and researchers to make commitments to the area.
- Substantial no-strings grants and gifts to universities, management schools, and nonprofits research centers would, in permitting scholars to shape their own research agendas, enhance the field's acceptability to the scholarly mainstream.
- Increasing the representation of scholars on the IS Research Committee and the scholarly role in shaping the programs of IS's annual Research Forum and other "common meeting grounds" which bring together consumers and producers of nonprofits research. Enhancing the scholarly role strengthens the reputation of the field—while preserving the invaluable opportunities for scholars and industry representatives to meet and talk face to face.
- Promoting the usefulness of IS's annual Research Forum and similar events as common meeting grounds between scholars and the industry by placing conference registration costs more in line with the limited means of many scholars. IS might consider adopting membership and registration guidelines similar to those of the major professional societies, with annual dues and registration fees scaled to professional income. This would not only open the Research Forum for more scholars and practitioners, but also make it more financially self-sustaining.

- Requiring that nonprofits research centers follow the "principals and practices" currently required of IS and Council on Foundation member organizations. Encouraging fairness and openness in hiring, more open-ended conference programming, and a greater degree of participatory governance at research centers might bring the nonprofits research community more in line with accepted standards of free enquiry.

Strategic Alternatives

Some have argued that the best way of delineating the boundaries between the industry and the scholarly community is for the industry to establish a separate scholar-controlled organization and to use this as a basis for pursuing the institutionalization of the nonprofits field. The effectiveness of this exclusive strategy can be weighed historically against a more open mainstream approach to institutionalization. Business studies really began in the late 1940s, when a number of foundations underwrote a program of entrepreneurial studies at the Harvard Business School and numerous conferences. Out of this program came the journal *Business History Review* and the endowment of a handful of professorships, the most important at Harvard and Johns Hopkins.[5]

These auspicious beginnings did not lead to a burgeoning of interest in the field. A particular viewpoint quickly became dominant; the holders of that viewpoint became the gatekeepers to jobs, publication, and scholarly recognition; and the study of business, which might have profoundly influenced the core of historical discourse, became little more than a mutual-admiration society.[6] Today few universities teach courses on the history of business, and such courses are seldom offered by history departments.

The failure of business history was not due to insufficient resources or lack of institutional sponsorship. Conceptually, the field was, like nonprofits studies, intrinsically integrative, touching on almost every aspect of American culture, politics, and society and capable of drawing on all the social and humanistic disciplines. The failure of the field was a strategic one, stemming from its promoters' inability to recognize the relationship between integrative substance of the field and the need for the its structural and organizational features to reflect its integrative intent. Drawing too much on external sources of support, business history was perceived as a form of special pleading and was treated as such.[7]

American studies followed a very different—and conspicuously more successful—path. Like business history and more or less contemporary with it, American studies also took off in the late 1940s, fueled by major foundation grants. Although some proponents argued for an exclusive strategy, the dominant faction carefully avoided claiming that the movement was a distinct field, apparently understanding that genuinely integrative scholarly substance required an integrative organizational approach, which drew on—and at times supplemented—interests within established academic departments and programs.

The outcome of this strategy was dramatically different from that of business history. Students from Harvard, the University of Wisconsin, and the other academic centers of the American studies movement spread out through the country, taking jobs in departments of literature, history, music, art, and architecture. As faculty members, they promoted converging interests between disciplines in relatively unobtrusive and unthreatening forms, such as cross-listing courses, interdepartmental seminars, joint majors, and sponsored lectures and conferences.

These faculty members gradually gained influence over a provincial scholarly journal, the *Mississippi Valley Historical Review,* which, like the movement itself, gradually but effectively drew together highly diverse scholarly interests, eventually forming a broad coalition of literary scholars, art historians, and students of social, political, institutional, and intellectual life. By the 1960s, the movement was not only firmly and respectably established but also had transformed the definition of historical scholarship, which, only a few years earlier, had been restricted to the study of politics, government, and diplomacy. By the late 1970s, the movement had embraced studies in organizations, community development, ethnicity, gender, and the family and was building productive bridges to the social sciences.

Conclusion

Selective disengagement of scholarship and advocacy and implementation of an open institutionalization strategy will require a high degree of trust on the part of funders. They must be willing to underwrite and be tolerant of a degree of sometimes useless and sometimes critical research if they wish to gain a substantial, diverse, and respectable literature on nonprofits.

Freedom is risky and inefficient. But if the friends of the sector genuinely believe private voluntarism to be the foundation of a free society, they must be willing to foster freedom in their own ranks.

8

Dilemmas of Research on Philanthropy, Voluntarism, and Nonprofit Organizations

When a special-interest group seeks to promote academic research about itself, difficult dilemmas arise—for both the interest group and those who do research on it. On the one hand, such involvement is an essential component of the process through which groups—be they industries, political causes, or social movements—achieve public recognition and legitimacy. On the other hand, such involvement inevitably threatens the integrity and credibility of the research process itself.

Since the 1950s, research has become increasingly important in the efforts of charitable tax-exempt organizations to formulate guidelines for self-regulation, to build their case for tax consideration and other special forms of public consideration, and to protect themselves from outbursts of regulatory enthusiasm.

As it has grown more central to the activities of these organizations, research has come to reflect the tensions among the various stakeholders in its findings. These include charitable donors, grant-making and grant-receiving institutions, trustees and professional staffs of these institutions, constituencies served by these institutions, and regulatory agencies—as well as the scholars themselves.

As long as these tensions remained in the background of the research process, scholars were relatively unconcerned about them. Indeed, the diversity of stakes and stakeholders seemed to present "many doors to knock on," as one researcher said—a variety of sources of funding and alternative agendas. But over the past decade, charitable tax-exempt organizations, however diverse their activities, have succeeded recognizing their common interests. This growing unity of purpose has expressed itself institutionally in the form of increasingly well-defined expectations of the research process.

Some scholars have found these trends troubling. Reviewing the first major collection of research on nonprofit organizations in 1987, historian Barry Karl expressed deep disquiet about this confusion of research and advocacy. He argued that substituting the term *nonprofit* for *philanthropy* and *charity* served to enhance philanthropy's public character and obscure its ties to private interests by suggesting an organizational conception that was "presumably efficient, subject to cost-accounting standards of performance and principles of effective management." Similarly, he asserted, the use of the term *research* was "an umbrella that would cover the various aspects of advocacy without drawing critical attention to the process"—a process that used the rhetoric of open-ended scholarly enquiry, but was committed "to arguing the fundamental effectiveness of philanthropy."[1]

Examining the development of research on the nonprofit sector, as well as the origins of the term itself, permits us to view the tensions among the various stakeholders in the research process and to understand how they have encountered and attempted to creatively resolve the dilemmas inherent in research on special-interest groups.

Inventing the Nonprofit Sector

The term *nonprofit sector* as a category encompassing the complex domain of voluntary, philanthropic, and charitable organizations was coined barely two decades ago. As Karl has suggested, the term is more than descriptive. It involves powerful prescriptive assumptions about the management, funding, regulation, and responsibilities of these institutions. Disregarding vast differences of scope and scale, kinds of goods and services produced, sources of support and clientage, the term posits a single characteristic—tax-exempt status under the federal tax code—as the criterion for inclusion in the sector. This characteristic suggests a more than coincidental linkage between scholarship and public policy.

Scholars did not begin writing about the nonprofit sector simply "because it was there." Although there was a vast literature on particular kinds of nonprofits—charities, education, hospitals, museums, social welfare, and so on—no effort was made before the 1970s to treat these as part of a unified "sector" of activity. Indeed, the Commerce Department's National Income Accounts, which originated the concept of a sectored economy after World War II, had no "nonprofits" category until a decade ago. The terms *nonprofit sector, third sector,* and *independent sector* entered scholarly usage in the 1970s, and their appearance was specifically linked to the efforts of organized philanthropy to defend itself from government regulation and oversight.[2]

To understand how a unified conception of a nonprofit sector emerged, it is worth reviewing the background of the efforts of philanthropy to examine itself. Before the 1950s, foundations were indifferent or hostile to scholarly inquiries into their activities. Even the friendly efforts of the Russell Sage Foundation's F. Emerson Andrews to compile what became the *Foundation Directory* (which first appeared in 1960, though work on it had begun in 1957) were met with endless obstacles.[3] But in 1955 there was a major turnaround. Key funders suddenly became enthusiastic about generating information about themselves.

The chronology of congressional interest in organized philanthropy seems to suggest the motive for this sudden turnaround. The foundations had, almost miraculously, escaped congressional attention during the TNEC hearings in the late 1930s, though a number of officials, such as the Carnegie Corporation's Frederick W. Keppel, worried privately that the failure of foundation to "recognize their responsibility to the public enjoying exemption from taxation" by creating a public record of their activities would endanger "public confidence in the foundation as a social instrument."[4] Philanthropy's immunity from congressional enquiry ended with the advent of the Cold War. The 1948 investigation of Alger Hiss, president of the Carnegie Endowment for International Peace, was only the beginning of steadily broadening political and regulatory challenge to the autonomy of grant-making foundations. By 1955, foundations had been the subject of two major congressional investigations, each of which produced more stringent oversight through the federal tax code.

Not surprisingly, initiative for creating a public record of foundation activities came not from scholars, but from the foundations, which were finally heeding Keppel's warnings of a decade and a half before. In 1955, the Ford Foundation made its first grants to encourage the scholarly investigation of the role of philanthropy in American life, which produced pioneering volumes by University of Wisconsin historian Merle Curti and his associates.[5] In 1956, the Carnegie Corporation underwrote the establishment of "a new organization [that] would be a strategic gathering place for gathering and using knowledge about foundations"—the Foundation Center Library. Not content to merely gather information, the library also propagated it, first through the publication of the *Foundation Directory* and later through that of the *Foundation News*, which began publication in fall 1960.

Events of the tumultuous 1960s showed how much more needed to be done. On May 2, 1961, Congressman Wright Patman delivered the first of a protracted series of attacks on foundations. The efforts of Patman struck a chord among his colleagues, who were increasingly besieged by constituents unhappy with their mounting tax liabilities and unhappier still with the prospect that the wealthy were using charity to get a free ride. In response to this, the Treasury Department in 1965 issued its *Report on Private Foundations,* which, while far more moderate than Patman's recommendations, still pointed to the need for significant government intervention in what had heretofore been a virtually unregulated domain.

Although passed after lengthy, well-publicized, and sometimes acrimonious hearings, the 1969 Tax Reform Act was, despite the lamentations of many friends of foundations, far less draconian than it might have been. Still, its passage made it unmistakably clear not that foundations would never again enjoy immunity from public oversight and regulation, but that they existed on congressional sufferance. If foundations hoped to survive the next outburst of regulatory enthusiasm, they would have to justify themselves to a public that was increasingly skeptical about the capacity of private wealth to act in the public interest and increasingly inclined to look to government as the prime actor.

Even before the passage of the 1969 Tax Reform Act, there were major disagreements about how the charitable community should defend itself. One group, led by Andrews and Manning Pattillo of the Foundation Center, had called for a system of self-policing, complete with a formal system of accreditation. A second group, representing the largest national foundations and social-service agencies, was willing to "stonewall" Congress, using moralistic arguments about the essential Americanness of philanthropy and the necessity for it to be free of onerous regulation. A third group, convened by John D. Rockefeller 3rd and calling itself the Commission on Foundations and Private Philanthropy (better known as the Peterson Commission, after its chairman), advocated a more moderate course, which would recognize the public obligations of tax-exempt enterprises, while also seeking to preserve and enhance the tax incentives that Rockefeller and his associates viewed as essential to strengthening this aspect of the free-enterprise system.[6]

It was this awareness, combined with fears of further congressional action in the early 1970s, that led to the establishment of the Commission on Private Philanthropy and Public Needs (the Filer Commission). The commission was a unique hybrid: though nominally a public body operating under the authority of the Treasury Department, it was privately funded by over $2 million in donations from individuals, foundations, and corporations. Strategically, the Filer Commission represented a considerable risk for charitable tax-exempt organizations. Unlike previous task forces, it was, relatively speaking, a representative body with an ambitious and apparently open-ended research program. There was no way of predicting what its conclusions might be. Further, the Filer Commission was unique in that its scope of enquiry included not only foundations but also the whole realm of 501(c)(3) organizations—Community Chests, hospitals, museums, libraries, churches, neighborhood associations, and "associations of a thousand other kinds." For the first time all charitable tax-exempt agencies, from giant grant makers through grassroots activist organizations, were treated as part of a unified nonprofit sector. More than merely reporting on the current state of American philanthropy and voluntarism, the Filer Commission succeeded in creating a new language and a new conceptual framework, which would profoundly shape all subsequent research on voluntary, philanthropic, and charitable activity.[7]

Beyond the Filer Commission, 1975–1980

When the Filer Commission issued its report in fall 1975, many of its members and consultants realized that their work raised more questions than it answered. For that reason, the majority urged that the federal government establish a "permanent national commission on the nonprofit sector" to collect data on the sector's sources and resources, to explore and propose ways of strengthening private giving and nonprofit activity, to provide a forum for public discussion of issues affecting the nonprofit sector, to study its relationship to government, and to act as an ombudsman in protecting the sector's interests.[8] Commission members would be jointly appointed by Congress and the president, and funds for the commission's support would come half from government and half from private sources.[9]

This proposal also aroused sharply worded dissent from the commission's most conservative members: "The functions proposed . . . to be performed" by a "permanent national commission for the nonprofit sector" could be better executed by a recognized and supported private instrument. Indeed, the creation of this national commission by Congress is likely to lead to governmental intervention in the private nonprofit sector "that will weaken it rather than strengthen it."[10]

The more radical Donee Group, which generally favored greater federal regulation of tax-exempt organizations, gave the proposal only lukewarm endorsement, fearing that such an agency would quickly become the captive of larger and better organized interests.[11] But the final blow came from President Carter's new treasury secretary, Michael Blumenthal, who expressed skepticism about the ability of such a body to simultaneously represent the public interest and defend a private one.[12]

Had the Filer Commission's recommendation for a "Federal Bureau of Philanthropy" been followed, the development of the nonprofits research community would have followed a very different course—and the kinds of dilemmas facing nonprofit research would have been of a very different sort. By privatizing nonprofits research, the Carter administration insured that research would become the instrument of the various groups that were contending for leadership of the non-profit sector and, ultimately, of whichever emerged as the dominant one.

Even before the dismissal of the national commission early in 1977, an assortment of private groups, most of them led by former members of the Filer Commission, were scurrying to take its place. These groups included the Joint Committee on Research in Philanthropy, the Coalition of National Voluntary Organizations (CONVO), the Council on Foundations, the Foundation Center, the American Association of Fund Raising Counsel, the National Council on Philanthropy (NCOP), the National Committee for Responsive Philanthropy, and the Association of Voluntary Action Scholars (AVAS). All acknowledged the need for further research and some were prepared to do it themselves, though none had the financial resources to undertake a major research program and all seem to have understood that, as advocacy organizations, their research might lack credibility. Ultimately, the failure of these entities to inherit the research mantle of the Filer Commission was due to their close ties to one or another of the factions that had divided commission members.[13]

The Beginnings of Nonprofits Research

The plan to establish a nonprofits research center at Yale first surfaced in 1975, with a lengthy "Proposal for a Study of Independent Institutions," coauthored by university president Kingman Brewster, law school professor John G. Simon, and political scientist Charles E. Lindblom.[14] The original impetus for what would become the Program on Non-Profit Organizations (PONPO) came from Brewster, who, by the early 1970s, had grown increasingly alarmed about the impact of federal funding—and the strings attached to it—on the autonomy of private universities. Simon's interest stemmed not only from his role as the law school's specialist on charities but also from the fact that he was president of the innovative Taconic Foundation, trustee of the Council on Foundations and the Foundation Center, and former special consultant to the Filer Commission. Lindblom's involvement was based on his scholarly interest in promoting multidisciplinary and policy-relevant social-science research. By 1975, he had taken charge of Yale's Institution for Social and Policy Studies, which contained centers for the study of education, health care, and urban problems.

"It was a somewhat odd way to begin a research program," Simon said in 1980, two years after PONPO had finally begun its work:

> Most programs begin with a group of scholars who have ongoing work they want to finance. Or a program sometimes begins with a donor—a foundation or a government agency—that has money it wants to devote to meet some of its informational needs. Scholars or dollars launch most programs. Our program began without many scholars, without any dollars—with only an idea. Accordingly, it took some time to start up—to collect the financing and the personnel to get going.[15]

That the Yale program should have lacked scholars is hardly surprising. Although many of Yale's faculty had done work on activities supported by private philanthropy, the idea of a nonprofit sector that treated all of these as a unified and coherent entity was simply too new and strange. Indeed, even Lindblom, who was enthusiastic about creating the center, regarded its fundamental task as one of defining what was meant by the term *nonprofit sector*.[16]

It is surprising that the proposal also lacked dollars, given Yale's wealth and prestige and the evident post–Filer Commission interest in creating a research center. Despite its reputation, Yale, like so many other institutions during those inflationary years, was hemorrhaging financially. In addition, Brewster's controversial political stances had alienated many potential contributors to its fund drives.[17] Because the university could not give the program direct support, PONPO had to turn to the entities that the program was proposing to study.

There was no great rush to underwrite the Yale program, despite John D. Rockefeller 3rd's personal pledge of a quarter-million dollars. The primary reason for this lack of enthusiasm was summed up in the response of the Ford Foundation to its appeals for support. Ford officials believed that the program's research agenda placed "too much emphasis . . . on theory and not enough on quantitative measures" and that, as a result, "the research results would be of little relevance in the formulation of policy with regard to non-profit institutions."[18] As Simon said in 1980, "some third sector admirers . . . have to be prepared for research outcomes we might not find emotionally satisfying."[19] But at this stage of they game, they were not so prepared.

Finally, PONPO was only one of several research efforts seeking support.[20] These included the Committee for the Third Sector (which emerged in 1978 from the Aspen Institute and included John Gardner, Walter McNerney, Porter McKeever, and other Filer Commission

notables among its backers) and the National Center for Charitable
Statistics (established in 1979 by Filer Commission veterans Jack
Schwarz of the American Association of Fundraising Counsel and
Bayard Ewing of United Way). It was far from clear which research
effort would best serve the interests of the various and often conflicting
groups that composed the sector.

The situation began to change late in 1979, as various organized
factions began to overcome their differences. Efforts were underway to
merge CONVO, NCOP, and several lesser advocacy groups into Independent Sector (IS), a national organization that would represent the
interests of all charitable tax-exempt organizations. As this occurred,
leaders of the philanthropic community were able to agree on the kind
of research product they wanted and, as a result, were able to allocate
the task of examining "the philosophical basis and the long-term
societal aspects of the third sector" to the Yale program, while assign-
ing to IS the task of "focusing attention in, hopefully an objective way,
on near and medium-term issues in both a research and convening
role."[21] By the end of 1980, the Yale program had garnered over $1
million in commitments.

Despite the hope that the Yale program would be left free to pursue
a relatively unconstrained academic research effort, pressures to
pursue a more focused agenda—one that would yield "useful" results
and contribute to the sector's advocacy concerns—were unremitting.
It proved to be far easier to raise funds for special projects rather than
for general support, and this difficulty inevitably drew the academic
research effort away from unfundable basic research toward the "near-
and medium-term issues" that funders were more willing to underwrite.

Independent Sector and Nonprofits Research

From the beginning, IS had a stated commitment to fostering the
development of "a body of knowledge necessary to accurately define,
describe, chart, and otherwise understand the sector and the ways it
can be of greater service to society." IS pledged neither to do the
research itself nor to be a significant funder of it; it would seek to
"facilitate, encourage, and stimulate the work of others."[22] IS was as
good as its word. After 1980, funding became more abundant as the
audience for serious research on nonprofits grew. At the same time, IS's
commitment to an arm's-length relationship reassured many of those
who feared that industry sponsorship would impair the credibility of
their work.

The conception of the diverse and complex universe of charitable tax-exempt organizations as a unified and coherent sector grew easier to accept as these entities, working through IS, overcame their differences and suspicions of one another. As their policy interests converged, so also did their willingness to agree on their common stake in research.

In 1983, when IS's Research Committee was first convened, its members, which included scholars as well as representatives of donor and donee organizations, were willing to commit themselves to sustaining both applied and basic research, cautioning, however, of the necessity of establishing a balance between the two.[23]

By 1985, encouraged by the success of its early initiatives, the committee began to assume a far more proactive stance.[24] "Research agendas or priority research topics," the committee declared, have "become more necessary." Moreover, the committee urged that more attention be given to "supporting research institutions where the capacity can be built to accomplish and sustain such research."[25] Once again, these efforts were successful. By 1987, twelve research centers had been established in various universities; by 1988, twenty were in operation. In addition, by 1986 IS-affiliated groups such as the American Association of Fund Raising Counsel and the American Association of Colleges were underwriting courses and individual research projects in colleges and universities around the country.[26] IS was also able to attract major support to conduct its own interpretive studies of the sector.[27]

The Growth of Nonprofits Research and the Crisis of Credibility

The proliferation of research centers after 1985 fundamentally transformed the relationship between funders and researchers. More centers created increased demands for greater and more sustained support. This vastly complicated the decisionmaking process for grant makers, who now not only had to consider what kind of research was most worthwhile but also to decide which of twenty research institutions were most worthy of their benevolence. In addition to the university-based programs, mainstream industry groups such as IS, the Council on Foundations, and the Foundation Center, as well as other groups such as the National Committee for Responsive Philanthropy and the Center for Community Change, were requesting funds to underwrite their own in-house research.

As demands for funding increased, so also did funders' pressures for further rationalization of the research infrastructure: delineating agendas outlining the important topics; ranking researchers and research centers in terms of their reliability and quality; and informally dividing obligations among the major funders. Believing that it had the confidence of both he funders and the research community, IS began to formalize its brokerage role.

As IS and its Research Committee moved forward in their plans to further institutionalize the research effort, differences of opinion about its direction began to be heard. In a keynote address to the 1987 Spring Research Forum, David Mathews, Kettering Foundation president and Research Committee founding member, worried that the organizations of IS had failed to come to grips with its "larger political function" and that this "misreading of their history" threatened to "undermine the efforts of the Sector to develop a comprehensive strategy for responding to current political challenges." Concerned that nonprofits research had become narrowly preoccupied with short- and medium-range issues, Mathews proposed that the Research Committee "encourage studies to enrich the *concept* of the Sector":

> Ultimately . . . the purpose of a richer self concept in the Sector is not for tactical self defense. It is to inform what the Sector tries to do. Civic organizations have real political responsibilities that go beyond lobbying and providing services. They are basic, elemental political functions. . . . How people understand participation, how they come to join with one another, how they learn to talk with one another for public purposes, how public leadership is defined and developed—those are the overarching and common responsibilities of the Sector. There is a political environment that is just as real and just as important as the natural environment. And no group is more able to ensure its well-being than the organizations of the Independent Sector.[28]

Mathews' concern that IS's research focus had slipped into a trade-association mode, focusing on institutional interests rather than the public good, was echoed in early 1988 by Lance Buhl, a corporate contributions manager, who in reviewing the first phase of post–Filer Commission research complained that researchers had failed to look at the "large ideas—equity, justice, service, leadership—that relate to public purpose."[29]

The concerns of these funders paralleled those of certain veteran nonprofits researchers. In 1986, political scientist Lester Salamon, in a paper presented at the annual meeting of the Association of Voluntary Action Scholars, had argued that nonprofits research, in casting the charitable tax-exempt domain as an independent sector, had distorted its capacity to perceive the reality of its interdependence. Salamon believed that this overemphasis on the sector's independence was a product of the limitations of the conceptual lenses through which this reality was perceived. Moreover, both the theory of the welfare state and the theory of the voluntary sector leave much conceptual room for a flourishing government-nonprofit partnership. To the contrary, both suggest quite strongly that such cooperation could not, and should not, exist. It is no wonder that observers equipped with such theories have tended to overlook such cooperation when it appears.[30]

Although Salamon was circumspect in identifying the source of the "limitations of the conceptual lenses," others were not. Karl's 1987 review of the Yale handbook placed the blame squarely on those who had an interest in enhancing the public character of philanthropy and obscuring its ties to private interests by using "research" as "an umbrella that would cover the various aspects of advocacy without drawing critical attention to the process." Scholarship that represented itself as dispassionate and open-ended enquiry had become, thanks to its close ties to the industry it studied, committed "to arguing the fundamental effectiveness of philanthropy."[31]

Coming to Terms with Dilemmas of Nonprofits Research

Not surprisingly, IS's initial response to these criticisms was defensive. Some leaders worried that critical research would engender "outbursts of regulatory enthusiasm."[32] Nevertheless, events of 1988 and 1989 brought into the foreground of concern the dilemmas that faced both researchers and the industry that had a vital stake in research. Most importantly, it had become increasingly clear that the kinds of relationships appropriate to the first phase of developing nonprofits research would have to be reevaluated.

In the decade since the Filer Commission, the ability of scholars to do sustained work on nonprofits had depended on the willingness of funders to underwrite such work. Unlike other research funding arenas, in which the grant-making process was highly institutionalized and peer-review mechanisms gave the appearance of objective appraisal, the funding of nonprofits research had been highly personalized and dependent on powerful and well-connected sponsorship. Although IS's involvement in the research opened the process in important ways, particularly by enlarging opportunities for scholars interested in the field, the fact that IS represented the industry rather than scholars presented an additional set of problems.

The forums, workshops, committees, and retreats, as well as access to funding, made possible by IS's investment in knowledge development, succeeded in creating a community of scholars drawn from many fields. Unfortunately, the dependence of this community on IS had begun to isolate it from the academic mainstream, which tended to be suspicious of industry-sponsored research. Further, researchers themselves, troubled by this growing dependence, began to question their own motives: How self-serving had they been in offering opinions about the work of others? How far had they bent their thinking to suit the requirements of a funder or research center? Were they special pleaders who had traded away their commitment to objective scholarship? The industry, of course, faced a matching set of dilemmas. On the one hand, it had a vital stake in research: research of the right kind could enormously enhance both its effectiveness and its public image. Research of the wrong kind could have a devastating impact. Furthermore, funders believed that they were accountable for how research grants were used—how could they justify advancing funds to researchers without assurances that they would be used appropriately? On the other hand, subjecting the research process to oversight and control posed its own problems as far as the credibility of the research was concerned.

By September 1988, when the *Chronicle of Higher Education* featured a story on nonprofit research's "built-in conflict," it was no longer possible to avoid coming to terms with these dilemmas.[33] This article may have had an influence on IS's decision to restructure the Research Committee, placing a well-known scholar, Stanley Katz, in its chair and increasing the number of scholar members. This reshuffling coincided with the announcement of the creation of a "superfund" to centralize support for nonprofits research and to place it under the control of scholarly peer-review committees.[34] Discussions also were initiated with regard to creating a scholarly organization separate from IS, which would become the basis for constituting "philanthropy studies" as a field.[35] Accompanying these initiatives were efforts to create a formal scholarly apparatus through the establishment of journals and through the formation of a program committee to consider proposed sessions for future IS research meetings.[36]

These efforts were inevitably controversial. Some feared that IS had strayed far from its original intention not "to do the research or even be a significant funder of it" and worried that its involvement in the research process was diminishing "the very pluralism [that IS was] created to serve and enhance."[37] Others felt that IS had confronted the dilemmas and was struggling to find creative solutions to them.[38]

It may be that the dialectic of successive dissents, defenses, confrontations, and justifications is as characteristic of philanthropy as it is of the broader democratic political culture of which it is a part.[39] While there are pressures that confuse research and advocacy, there are also counterpressures. Counterpressures may prevent nonprofits scholarship from following the course of other fields that have developed "in a special atmosphere of professional purpose," isolated from the major influences and shaping minds of the academic mainstream, and its parochialism rendering it incapable of attracting the kinds of scholars "who could give it broad relevance and bring it back to the public domain."[40]

9

The "Me Generation" Grows Up: Thoughts on the Near Future of the Nonprofit Sector

When the National Health Council's director, Ed Van Ness, asked me to talk to the chief executives and board chairs of his organization in 1989, he "free associated" a series of questions which I might address:

Are Yuppies volunteering and giving?

Are volunteers coming forth and "sticking with it" in an era of two wage earners?

Is the American passion for advocacy (environment, civil rights, animal rights, diet and exercise) reducing the resources for mainline charities?

Are there really a "thousand points of light," or just flickering candles that could be extinguished by indifference, government regulation, or cynicism?

Are media critics informed enough, or are they the victims of their own deadlines, retreating to moralistic imperialism?

How many assaults on their public image (such as televangelists) can charities sustain before they lose the public's trust?

Is competition among charities causing inappropriate behavior?

What patterns are enduring between managers and board members? Who provides the leadership?

With a mandate such as this, I was reassured by his comment that I need not address them all—he was merely mentioning them to indicate the council's range of concerns.

I would have been tempted to believe Ed's disclaimer were it not for the fact that these questions—this range of concerns—have been mentioned to me so many times recently by so many people. The philanthropic community seems unusually anxious about its future. Independent Sector titled last year's Spring Research Forum "Looking

Ahead to the Year 2000"; the meeting's keynote speaker, outgoing
Rockefeller Foundation president Richard Lyman, expressed fear of a
future in which "some outburst of regulatory enthusiasm" would lead
to a nonprofit sector that was "overtaxed, over-regulated, and judged
more than anything else on its 'willingness to cooperate with governmental agencies and adjust to government plans.'" In a similar vein,
Elizabeth McCormack's keynote address to Independent Sector's annual meeting in September 1988 concluded with a peroration that mixed
optimism with anxiety. "Now, where do we go? What do we do?" she
asked:

> I submit that should the Independent Sector continue to limit its activities
> to its traditional causes and concerns, admirable and necessary as they are,
> it will have failed the nation. The sea changes I have referred to are not
> just new issues—they encompass and envelop all other issues. It is as
> though the machinery and amenities of a huge ship are under repair
> while the ship is sinking because of a hole in the bow. It is folly to rely
> on the first and second sectors in this situation. The stakes are too vast
> to be left in the hands of people concerned primarily with election and
> reelection, or to people riveted to the bottom line of the next quarterly
> report.[1]

Few would doubt that America is facing a crisis of enormous proportions—though as an historian I must suggest that it is of no greater
proportions than those of the 1930s, in which we confronted global
economic and political catastrophes and engaged them with remarkable élan. The difference between then and now is not the scale of the
challenge, but our confidence in our ability to meet it—in particular
the fear that the younger people now taking their places in the top
ranks of American institutions are inadequate to the great responsibilities of leadership.

Twenty-five years ago, *generation gap* was a popular term associated
with the baby boomers, who, as undergraduates, were becoming politically active. As the baby boomers graduated and began pursuing
careers and building families (or *not* building families), the pundits
fretted about the Me Generation. Eventually the term *Yuppie* was
coined to denote the former cultural and political revolutionaries who
were now busy building fast-track careers in government, philanthropy, and business.

Although the term *generation gap* is now a period piece, the sentiments behind it are far from obsolete. It is no coincidence that the
sharpest expressions of anxiety about the future of philanthropy and
voluntarism have been heard in the late 1980s—as the Me Generation
has finally begun to come into its own. The changing of the guard over
the past five years has been truly remarkable. In the foundation world

alone, the heads of the nation's second, fourth, seventh, and eighth largest foundations (Getty, MacArthur, Rockefeller, Pew, respectively) are individuals under the age of fifty.[2]

The changing of the guard is only one of many "sea changes" in the nonprofit sector. Not only are the faces on the established boards changing, but there are so many new boards and new faces! As of 1960, the *Foundation Directory* estimated that there were 12,000 foundations in existence. Today there are more than 24,000. In other words, over one-half the foundations currently in existence were created in the past thirty years. In the 1950s and 1960s, the IRS received seven thousand applications for tax-exempt status annually. By 1965, that number had more than doubled. By 1984 it had more than quadrupled, to 64,000 applications. Clearly, the nonprofit sector as we know it today is the creation of the past two decades. Indeed, the term *nonprofit sector,* which we now all use with such facility, is equally new, having only became current in the late 1970s with the publication of the Filer Commission's work.

But it is not merely that the nonprofit universe has grown in size and complexity over the past two decades. Its character has also fundamentally changed. Twenty-five years ago, corporate foundations were almost unknown: only 18 were considered large enough to be listed in the *Foundation Directory,* and their assets constituted a mere 2 percent of total held by all foundations. By 1988, 781 corporate foundations were listed, 69 percent created since 1975. Similarly, nearly one-half—111 of 240—the community foundations now operating came into being since 1960.[3] These numbers only dimly suggest the contemporary revolution in the charitable world, especially on the local level. Vastly increased corporate contributions and voluntary service by business managers, as well as joint ventures and partnerships among municipalities, charities, and businesses, have created a universe of philanthropy and voluntarism which is bewildering in its complexity. No wonder we had to invent a space-age term such as *nonprofit sector* to describe a range of activities and motives which could no longer be comfortably encompassed by old-fashioned terms such as *charity!*

The emergence of new patterns of organizational activity has been accompanied by transformations in traditional governance roles. My good friend and colleague Miriam Wood, who has been studying the boards of social-service agencies, invented a term to describe the new kind of board member—*MAPS,* or Middle-Aged Professionals.[4] The MAPs, as Wood describes them, are "typically in the age group 35 to 50"; "their approaches to problems and solutions tend to be expressed in bureaucratic terms and to rely on rationality implied by bureaucratic structure and process"; and they speak a rhetoric of "goals," "objectives," and "results" rather than of "mission." MAPs conceive

of their board service not only as "altruistic" and "civically valuable"
but also as a form of self-enhancement, an opportunity for "character
growth, character expression, maturation, and development." With
the MAPs have come "managerially-oriented executive directors," specialists credentialed not only in the fields in which they work, but
whose training, more often then not, has included management and
the acquisition of advanced management skills.

Small wonder that the senior leadership of nonprofitdom worries
about the future! How little the nonprofit sector, nationally or locally,
resembles the intimate world of the 1950s and 1960s!

What does all this have to do with the Me Generation, Yuppies, the
Generation Gap, and the evident uncertainty that the older generation
of nonprofit leaders has about passing the torch to those who have
become adults since the 1960s? Do these trends suggest that the genera-
tional issue is merely symbolic—and that the younger generation of
leaders is merely the lightning rod for its elders' discomfort with the
extraordinary institutional changes of the past quarter-century? If so,
it may not be inappropriate to take a closer look at the historical
experience of the younger generation of nonprofits leadership, to peel
away the symbols and slogans and emblems to see what they really
represent. This is no easy task because it means taking a dispassionate
look at myself and my contemporaries. Still, bear with me; I think you
will be as surprised as I was by what you shall find.

Recherche Du Temps Perdu

Right after I talked to Ed Van Ness, I wrote the foregoing portion
of my talk to the National Health Council. Having written the pro-
logue, I was, I must confess, stumped. Perhaps I had read too much.
When I thought of the late 1940s and the 1950s, the years in which I
was growing up, all that came to me were stereotypical newsreel and
textbook pictures of the period: images of Eisenhower and Joe
McCarthy and the fads of the era.

As luck would have it, while I was pondering all this my wife asked
me to help move some furniture—one piece of which was the desk that
I had used as a child. As I maneuvered the desk into my son's room,
a tiny square of paper fell to the ground. I picked it up. It was a stamp
depicting a little girl standing at the end of a hospital bed and reach-
ing out toward the viewer. Behind her was the enlarged face of a white-
haired woman. "Help . . . prevent polio crippling," read the legend
in red letters against a pale-blue background. And, along the bottom:
"Polio—Elizabeth Kenny Foundation."

That little square of paper was to my efforts to reconstruct the historical experience of my generation what Proust's madeleine was to his remembrance of things past. Its colors, images, and rhetoric set off a chain of association about growing up in the 1940s and 1950s which has led me to think about the near future of philanthropy and its leaders in a very different way then I had before. You will forgive my presumption in asserting that my experience was typical. But in the end, all history is biography—and if we really want to understand a generation we must tolerate efforts to generalize private experience.

The stamp, not unnaturally, got me to thinking about when and where I had received it—and, in turn, about the polio scare of the early 1950s. My school was one of the first in the country to get the Salk vaccine—we were one of the test groups to whom it was administered. And the stamps were given out to us as a little reward for having had to get shots. It is funny that, in a public-health program administered by a public elementary school, our attention should have been directed to a private foundation—but that is the way it was. Of course there was a lot more to it than getting polio shots. It seems evident, as I recollect it, that we were schooled in voluntary action. The March of Dimes had a virtually official status in my school, which was in a new long and low one-story building that stretched out for what seemed to me then a considerable distance. We made it our task one year to try to collect enough pennies to stretch along the center line of the central corridor of the school from one end to the other. Every day kids brought in more and more pennies, which were taped to paper strips and laid out along the corridor. Slowly but surely, we spanned the building! Then the money was all gathered up and sent off to the March of Dimes.

That was only one of the voluntary activities we learned in school. Back in the early 1950s people—at least where I came from—still looked to the United Nations as a real force for world peace. The Korean War was going on, after all, as a UN police action. And though the starving children of Asia had replaced those of Eastern Europe, their misfortunes were still held up before us as an example—and as an inducement not to waste food. For weeks before Halloween, in those days still safe enough to let children wander at will through the neighborhoods, we saved empty milk cartons, the little ones that came with lunch in the cafeteria. Then, a few days before the great night, we were set to the task of covering them in orange and black paper and decorating them with images and mottoes appropriate to UNICEF, the United Nations International Children's Fund—for which we all collected money while trick-or-treating, bringing the money in the next day to be sent where it would do the most good.

Such school-based activities were only the beginning of our education in voluntary action. Our lives out of school were even more framed by examples of giving and volunteering. Most of us, girls and boys, were Brownies or Cub Scouts; most of us, the boys anyway, belonged to the Y.M.C.A.; the [Rye] Free Reading Room, a wonderful public library whose major support came from private contributions, was a place of first resort on rainy days in that pretelevision era. Everybody, or so it seemed, went to church: my brother and our friends sang in a boys' choir, which rehearsed three days a week and paid us for our services.

Beyond the realm of our child concerns, most of the adults, especially the women, were involved in voluntary action. Our mothers took turns collecting for the Red Cross, the Community Chest, the United Hospital Fund, going from door to door in the evenings through our neighborhoods. From their ranks were recruited the leaders of the Cubs and Brownies. Women ran the Garden Club, which visibly beautified the town—and the Nearly New Shop, which benefited the United Hospital and from which all of us seemed to get our Best and Company church suits, trading them in as we grew.

Finally, we were keenly aware of the grand philanthropic gesture, the public-spirited generosity of the rich, of whom there were a few in the community. One prominent family had donated land at the center of town for civic uses, which included a beautiful park, a new (c. 1910) firehouse, and the Free Reading Room's magnificent Georgian building. Another had given its great mansion as a "center for building Christian principles into the everyday life of the world." While these places and structures constituted a setting for us, philanthropy of what we considered to be a grand scale touched even more directly on our young lives: a very wealthy man every year underwrote a trip to Playland, the local amusement park, for all the members of our church choir (giving each boy the then incredible amount of five dollars to spend on tickets!); I remember singing with the choir at his funeral and wondering whether some other benefactor would come along to fund our trips to Playland. Later I learned that he had left an endowment for this purpose—the first time that this term and concept entered my vocabulary.

The Me Generation and the Future of Philanthropy

The time has come to round off this remembrance of things past and to get back to the point on which I think it so centrally bears: the near future of philanthropy and, in particular, the kind of leadership that the nonprofit world can expect to have over the next decade. First and foremost, if my own experience is any guide, the foregoing suggests that the generation which was growing up in the 1940s and 1950s and graduating from college in the 1960s was a generation steeped in the values of philanthropy and voluntarism, perhaps more so than any other in our history. Whatever its objectionable aspects, the counter-culture of the 1960s in whatever form it took was distinctively communitarian, activist, and voluntaristic—and it was this very fact that framed its involvement with political reform and its ambivalent relationship to political reform and to government. To a generation raised as mine was, the idea of helping others, whether our friends and neighbors or people we did not know, seemed the most natural thing in the world because we had been schooled to it: the difference between gathering pennies for the March of Dimes and collecting for UNICEF while trick-or-treating and going to the South to work in voter-registration drives or to Africa to work in the Peace Corps was only a matter of degree. (In my own case, my political trajectory as an undergraduate was channeled by the very institutions that had framed out my childhood—I was a chorister as a child, and my attachment to religion led me to the Quakers as an adolescent; through the Friends, I ended up in an American Friends Service Committee work camp on an Indian reservation in Montana in 1963, where I got to experience firsthand some of the ironies and contradictions of helping.)

This orientation to voluntarism made our relationship to government complex and ambivalent: when programs of the Great Society emphasized voluntary action, we responded with outpourings of enthusiasm; when it emphasized coercion, as it did in the case of the Vietnam War, we opposed it—and did so through voluntary organizations of draft resisters, and so forth.

These same kinds of committed ambivalence remained strong after we graduated and went off into careers—a surprising number of us, by the way, choose careers in public service, especially in the world of voluntary action. We were the ones who spearheaded the proliferation of voluntary organizations so characteristic of the past twenty years. We were the ones who brought to the world of voluntary action the notion of professional management, whether serving as staffers or as board members. We were the ones who, once we made it onto boards, pushed for effectiveness, efficiency, and broader participation. We were the "self-actualizers" who, in Miriam Wood's view, saw voluntarism as an opportunity "for character growth, character expression, maturation, and development."

This brings us back to Ed Van Ness' series of questions:

Are Yuppies volunteering and giving? We most definitely are, though our motives and forms of volunteering may be rather different from those of our parents' generation. Our voluntarism tends to be far more closely tied to our personal needs, interests, and ambitions. For example, fathers may go into scouting because they have children of scouting age, not because they believe in the need for "character-building organizations"; businesspeople may get involved with organizations that directly or indirectly benefit their businesses.

Are volunteers coming forth and "sticking with it" in an era of two wage earners? Once again, we can answer this affirmatively. Because we have a personal and professional stake in our voluntarism, we are, if anything, more likely to stick with voluntarism: pulling an organization through a crisis becomes a point of pride; the success of the organizations we have helped enhances our professional reputations. Moreover—and this is especially true for volunteers involved with causes that benefit their own children—working with such organizations becomes a form of parenting, a way of being with and working with ones' children.

Is the American passion for advocacy reducing the resources for mainline charities? There is no easy answer to this one, because it bears as much on the nature of those charities as on the motives of volunteers. My impression is that the success of the mainline charities in commanding resources—time, loyalty, and contributions—depends very much on their ability to adapt their services, their image, and their organizational cultures to the interests of the postwar generation. Some have been more successful than others in doing this.

As to the impact of organizational proliferation on resources for nonprofits, I am inclined to look to my colleague the economist Gabe Rudney, who disputed the conventional assumption that charitable contributions were based only on what remained after basic consumption needs were satisfied.[5] He proposed instead that charitable-giving decisions could be as integral to the budgetary process of households as decisions about housing and food. This concept of "committed giving" is borne out in the recent finding that low-income Americans give a greater proportion of their income to charity than the more well to do. Rudney's finding has significant implications in assessing the impact of new nonprofits on resources available for the old: though not unlimited, the pool of dollars which might go to charity is clearly less finite than generally supposed. People will give, in other words, to what they believe in—and will sacrifice the necessities of life if the cause is important enough. From this perspective, then, new organizations *may not* cut into support for the mainline charities. The extent to which they do—or do not—will depend on whether those charities can demonstrate themselves *worthy* of support.

Let me skip down the list of questions to the last ones: How many assaults on their public image can charities sustain before the lose the public's trust? Is competition among charities causing inappropriate behavior? What patterns are enduring between managers and board members? Who provides the leadership? I would like to treat these as a single interrelated query with a single answer.

The public credibility of private charity and the appropriateness of charitable behavior depend, more than anything else, on the patterns enduring between managers and board members and the quality of organizational leadership on both the board and the staff level. Here is where we begin to run into problems as the postwar generation begins to take command.

First and foremost, there are the conflicts between boards and staffs which have become so evident and painful over the past decade. Why have these come about? They have a good deal to do with the professionalism of the postwar cohort: both board members and staffers are, these days, more likely to have received advanced professional training in their respective fields than at any time in the past. Although an overall professionalism gives them something in common—a commitment to the values of training and specialized knowledge—it also pulls them apart: the budgetary criteria (efficiency, cost-effectiveness, and whatnot) so important to M.B.A.'s serving on boards may not be as crucially important to a health professional, social-service worker, or curator, whose desiderata, though no less specialized and quantifiable, are likely to be more oriented to service. The problem is that their professional training gives them a tenacious attachment to what they know—they are less likely to want to "put on the corporate hat" or even to look to the interests of the community that they serve, setting aside their personal interests, than their predecessors might have been.

The proliferation of organizations is depleting an important but invariably overlooked resource—*experience.* When boards were few and communities were less fluid than they are today, it was easy to bring younger volunteers into board ranks with some assurance that, by the time they became trustees they knew what their responsibilities were and how to distinguish between their personal interests and their community obligations. In the good old days, board members of nonprofits tended to be senior businesspeople and professionals who had served on all kinds of boards, municipal, voluntary, and corporate. This kind of sustained training is simply no longer possible. Few live in communities long enough to go through such long apprenticeships—and even if they do, demand for their services far exceeds the supply of experienced people.

Inexperienced board members, however thoroughly committed—and do I think today's younger board members are extraordinarily so—are dangerous board members. By the same token, staffers well equipped with professional knowledge, but without significant attachments to the communities in which they will be working, are equally liable to destabilize the organizations with which they work.

One final aspect of the maturing of the Me Generation—and one that is almost invariably overlooked—involves the changing relationships between the helpers and the helped. Until recently, these roles, like those of staff and board, were fairly clear-cut. But now the beneficiaries of voluntarism and philanthropy are striving for inclusion on the governing boards and staffs of agencies established to help them. For some, this has been an easy transition. For others, as the "revolution" at Gallaudet College suggests, the movement has been stoutly—and disastrously—resisted. This inclusion of the helped in the helping process is an important sign of the fundamental transformation that the Me Generation is bringing to the nonprofit world: philanthropy and voluntarism, rather than just being a way for the able to assist the disabled, or the rich to help the poor, is becoming a means of empowerment. While empowerment has been part of the rhetoric of organized charity for the past century, it has seldom been more than that. For the new generation of philanthropic leadership, empowerment will become a far more important issue.

So where does this leave us as we contemplate the near future of philanthropy and voluntarism? It seems clear that there are no "easy outs." We live in interesting times, and the best that we can do is to brace ourselves to live through them. Internal conflict, intense interorganizational competition, inappropriate organizational behavior, and adverse public comment will be the inevitable consequences of the further maturing of the Me Generation. Along the way, some organizations will flourish; others will falter and die. Painful as this may be, I am not sure that this is necessarily a bad thing.

Facing the future requires that we become more tolerant of change and appreciative of the adaptability of philanthropy and voluntarism. No organization is indispensable—even the mainline charities, of which the oldest are of fairly recent creation. It may be necessary for some of them to decline, merge, or die. What is essential is that we not confuse the health of voluntarism with the fate of particular organizations. The important things are the continuing capacity of new organizations to emerge and the continuing willingness of people to pursue their ends through voluntary associations. Sociologist Carl Milofsky expressed this point succinctly:

> Movements exist in their moment. They are generated when members of a community share a sense of problem and their actions are fueled by enthusiasm and social commitment. Their shape is strongly determined by the cast of characters who create the organization and by the structure of opportunities and constraints those characters perceive. When the charter members no longer feel an urgency to participate, there tends to be an organizational crisis that leads to a shift in administrative form, a roll-over in central characters, or the death of the movement. [We] must recognize the vitality and energy inherent in transience and focus on the problems involved in building interest and in riding on a flood of collective enthusiasm.[6]

In light of these trends, I think we can be reassured about the near future of voluntarism and philanthropy and the capability of its new generation of leadership.

Notes

1. For an especially incisive discussion of the distinctions between charitable and noncharitable nonprofits, see Henry Hansmann, "Economic Theories of Nonprofit Organization," in W. W. Powell, ed., *The Nonprofit Sector: A Research Handbook* (New Haven: Yale University Press, 1987), 27-42.

2. For example, foundations are not voluntary organizations in the commonly accepted sense of the term. Nor are agencies involving high levels of professional expertise, such as hospitals. However, most service on municipal boards and commissions is voluntary and uncompensated. The broad issue of voluntary service as it applies across the sectors remains unexplored.

3. Basing their reasoning on the ideas put forth in Mancur Olson's *The Logic of Collective Action* (Cambridge: Harvard University Press, 1971), some economists, notably Henry Hansmann and Burton Weisbrod, have argued that a major reason for the existence of nonprofits is that they produce "public goods." Because the benefits of public goods (such as clean air, education, and public safety) cannot be fully captured by their purchasers, it is unremunerative for for-profit providers to produce them. Although government might be expected to provide these goods, the range of its activity is limited by the willingness of taxpayers to pay for them—by what James Douglas calls the "majoritarian constraint." The residual range of public goods not produced by government is, the argument runs, the domain of the private nonprofit sector. See Burton Weisbrod, "Toward a Theory of the Nonprofit Sector," in E. S. Phelps, ed., *Altruism, Morality, and Economic Theory* (New York: Russell Sage Foundation, 1975); and Burton Weisbrod, *The Nonprofit Economy* (Cambridge: Harvard University Press, 1988).

The public-goods argument ignores both history and common sense. Historically, any and every sort of public good has been produced by for-profit firms—and the shift toward nonprofit provision came about because elites made deliberate efforts to restructure markets in order to discourage proprietary firms from operating in fields of strategic importance to them. See James Wooten, "The Emergence of Nonprofit Legal Education in New York: A Case Study of the Economic Theory of Nonprofit Organizations," Working Paper no. 154 (New Haven: Program on Non-Profit Organizations, Yale University, 1990); and Paul J. DiMaggio, "Cultural Entrepreneurship in Nineteenth-Century Boston," in DiMaggio, ed., *Nonprofit Enterprise in the Arts: Studies in Mission and Constraint* (New York: Oxford University Press, 1986), 41-62. More to the point, there is no industry in which government, proprietary, and nonprofit firms do not compete—which is why the "unfair-competition" issue has loomed so large with regard to nonprofits over the past two decades.

4. On nonprofit revenues, see Lester Salamon, "Partners in Public Service: The Scope and Theory of Government-Nonprofit Relations," in Powell, ed., *The Nonprofit Sector,* 99–117.

5. Major efforts include Louis Galambos' seminal essays "The Emerging Organizational Synthesis in American History," in E. J. Perkins, ed., *Men and Organizations: The American Economy in the Twentieth Century* (New York: G. P. Putnam's Sons), and "Technology, Political Economy, and Professionalization," *Business History Review* 57 (1982): 471–93, as well as Louis Galambos and Joseph Pratt, *The Rise of the Corporate Commonwealth: United States Business and Public Policy in the Twentieth Century* (New York: Basic Books, 1988). No less important is Martin J. Sklar's *Corporate Reconstruction of American Capitalism: The Market, the Law, and Politics* (New York: Cambridge University Press, 1988). The earliest and most influential of these efforts is Robert Wiebe's widely read *The Search for Order, 1877–1920* (New York: Hill & Wang, 1967). Of course, it was Richard Hofstadter's *Age of Reform* (New York: Alfred A. Knopf, 1955) that really initiated this line of enquiry by pointing to the class characteristics shared by progressive leaders across the party spectrum.

6. The impact of Darwinism on American thought has yet to be fully assessed. Sadly, the definitive account of this remains Richard Hofstadter's revised Ph.D. dissertation, *Social Darwinism in American Life* (New York: Alfred A. Knopf, 1948).

7. The parallels in the use of Darwinist metaphors by Charles W. Eliot in his inaugural address as president of Harvard in "The New Education," *Atlantic Monthly* 23 (1869), and by Andrew Carnegie in his essays on labor and wealth in E. C. Kirkland, ed., *The Gospel of Wealth and Other Essays* (Cambridge: Harvard University Press, 1966), are striking.

8. See Guy Alchon, *The Invisible Hand of Planning: Capitalism, Social Science, and the State in the 1920s* (Princeton: Princeton University Press, 1985); and David F. Noble, *American By Design: Science, Technology, and the Rise of Corporate Capitalism* (New York: Oxford University Press, 1977). See also Barry D. Karl's valuable essays "Presidential Planning and Social Science Research: Mr. Hoover's Experts," *Perspectives in American History* 3 (1969): 347–409, and "Philanthropy, Policy Planning, and the Bureaucratization of the Democratic Ideal," *Daedalus* 4 (Fall 1976): 129–49.

9. On the growth of American historiography as a function of the consolidation of national economic and political leadership, see Carol F. Baird, "Albert Bushnell Hart and the Rise of the Professional Historian," in Paul Buck, ed., *The Social Sciences at Harvard* (Cambridge: Harvard University Press, 1965), 129–74. On the propagandistic function of American historiography, see Frances FitzGerald's superb *America Revised: History Schoolbooks in the Twentieth Century* (New York: Vintage Books, 1979). It is telling that no historian has yet undertaken a full-scale account of the development of American history as an academic discipline!

10. The best account remains Herbert Croly's description of the organization of the opposition to Bryan in the presidential campaign of 1896 in *Marcus Alonzo Hanna: His Life and Times* (New York: Macmillan Co., 1919), 209–27. Curiously, Peter Drucker is virtually alone in recognizing Hanna's importance. He describes the Ohio industrialist and statesman as "one of the true innovators in the history of politics" for having "invented a new political integration in which major economic interests are held together by their common interest in what we would now call economic development." See Drucker, *The New Realities in Government and Politics/in Economics and Business/in Society and World View* (New York: Harper & Row, 1989), 18–24.

11. Henry Adams, *The Education of Henry Adams* (Boston: Massachusetts Historical Society, 1918), 343.

12. One need only survey the papers presented at the annual research forums of Independent Sector to see how little interest there was in the ostensibly charitable mission of the sector during the 1980s. Elizabeth McCormack's keynote address at IS's 1988 annual meeting, "Looking Back to Look Forward," was devoted in large part to chiding the organization for its failure to look beyond its own self-interest and to address the real and compelling problems facing the nation and the world.

13. See Elizabeth Boris, *1988 Foundation Management Report* (Washington, D.C.: Council on Foundations, 1988); and Teresa Odendahl et al., *Working in Foundations: Career Patterns of Men and Women* (New York: Foundation Center, 1985).

14. Since the 1960s, federal application and reporting requirements for nonprofits have become increasingly complex and expensive. States have also greatly increased their regulatory expectations of nonprofits. Forming and operating a nonprofit now requires the ongoing assistance of lawyers and accountants. In addition, the 1969 Tax Reform Act restricted the activities of nonprofits in the area of political advocacy, making them far less attractive as vehicles for underclass empowerment. For a superb account of the recent history of nonprofits in this area, see J. Craig Jenkins, "Nonprofit Organizations and Policy Advocacy," in Powell, ed., *The Nonprofit Sector*, 296–320. See also Carl Milofsky, "Networks, Markets, Culture, and Contacts: Understanding Community Organizations," in Milofsky, ed., *Community Organizations: Studies in Resource Mobilization and Exchange* (New York: Oxford University Press, 1988).

15. See Charles Perrow and Mauro F. Guillen, *The AIDs Disaster: The Failure of Organizations in New York and the Nation* (New Haven: Yale University Press, 1990). Teresa Odendahl's *Charity Begins at Home: Generosity and Self-Interest among the Philanthropic Elite* (New York: Basic Books, 1990) also provides valuable insights into the preferences of contemporary donors for mutual-benefit activities (such as higher education and the arts) over charitable ones, such as human services.

16. Perhaps the darkest vision of the failure of reform through either public or private means is Willard Gaylin, Ira Glasser, Steven Marcus, and David Rothman's collection of essays, *Doing Good: The Limits of Benevolence* (New

York: Pantheon Books, 1979). An analog to this volume as a summary of the collapse of confidence in expertise is Thomas Haskell, ed., *The Authority of Experts: Studies in History and Theory* (Bloomington: Indiana University Press, 1984).

17. Drucker, *The New Realities*, 24–25.

18. Ibid., 94.

19. Ibid., 97. One would hesitate to place great faith in so frail a reed as Drucker's often shot-from-the-hip opinings were it not that some of the most compellingly interesting critical management literature of the past decade—especially that by Rosabeth Moss Kanter on organizational innovation, and Karl Weick, Jeffrey Pfeffer, and Gerald Salancik on the perception of organizational environments—emphasizes the significance of individual cognition in organizational processes. See especially Kanter, *Commitment and Community* (Cambridge: Harvard University Press, 1972); *Men and Women of the Corporation* (New York: Basic Books, 1977); and *The Change Masters* (New York: Simon & Schuster, 1983). See also K. E. Weick, *The Social Psychology of Organizing* (Reading, Mass.: Addison-Wesley, 1969); and Jeffrey Pfeffer and Gerald Salancik, *The External Control of Organizations: A Resource Dependence Perspective* (New York: Harper & Row, 1978).

20. Drucker, *The New Realities*, 195. Drucker's convictions about the importance of the nonprofit sector are further amplified in *Managing the Nonprofit Organization: Principles and Practices* (New York: Harper Collins, 1990).

21. Drucker, *The New Realities*, 205. On the importance of "knowledge workers" as a new constituency for nonprofits, see Miriam Wood's important essay "The Governing Board's Existential Quandary," Working Paper no. 151 (New Haven: Program on Non-Profit Organizations, Yale University, 1989), and Peter Dobkin Hall, "Conflicting Managerial Cultures in Nonprofit Organizations," *Nonprofit Management and Leadership* 1, no. 2 (Winter 1990): 153–65.

22. Obviously, as many critics of the Me Generation's involvement in non-profits have pointed out, knowledge workers can push organizations in either a narrow or a broad direction. See Frederick T. Miller, "Board Members from the 'Transitional Generation' Are the Key to Helping Organizations Move Ahead," *Chronicle of Philanthropy*, May 2, 1989, 36; and Peter Dobkin Hall, "Baby Boomers Have Demonstrated Commitment to the Non-Profit Sector: They Helped Create Most of It," *Chronicle of Philanthropy*, May 16, 1989, 29. Miriam Wood is also critical of the narrow perspectives of MAP (Middle-Aged Professional) board members in "The Governing Board's Existential Quandary." I am willing to argue, on the basis of personal experience as a board member and on the basis of extensive discussions of this point at the Lilly Endowment's December 1990 Leadership Education Conference, that in the long run knowledge workers will broaden the views of nonprofits of their missions—while making their managerial processes more rigorous. It is precisely this combination of outlooks which makes Drucker so optimistic about the possibilities of nonprofits.

23. Of course, such changes will not happen automatically. That is why the

ambitious "leadership-education" initiatives of midwestern foundations such as Lilly and Kellogg are so potentially important. They are predicated on the understanding that values and historical perspectives are as important in the armory of trustee skills as managerial acumen. See "Biographical Sketches and Project Descriptions," in *Leadership Education Conference, December 3–4, 1990* (Indianapolis: Lilly Endowment, 1990).

CHAPTER 1: INVENTING THE NONPROFIT SECTOR

1. Exact figures on the number of charitable tax-exempt organizations in existence before 1967, when the IRS began counting them, are elusive. In testifying to the Cox Committee in 1952, Norman Sugerman, assistant commissioner of the IRS, estimated the number of nonreligious charitable tax-exempt organizations as having been 12,500 in 1939, 27,500 in 1946, and 32,000 in 1950. See U.S. House of Representatives, 82nd Congress, 2nd Session, *Hearings before the Select Committee to Investigate Foundations and Comparable Organizations* (Washington, D.C.: Government Printing Office), 64. Figures for between 1967 and 1985 are from Burton Weisbrod's *The Nonprofit Economy* (Cambridge: Harvard University Press, 1988), 169–70. Figures for between 1985 and 1989 are from "The Nonprofit World: A Statistical Portrait," *Chronicle of Philanthropy* 2, no. 6 (January 9, 1990): 8.

2. Lester Salamon, "Partners in Public Service: The Scope and Theory of Government Nonprofit Relations," in W. W. Powell, ed., *The Nonprofit Sector: A Research Handbook* (New Haven: Yale University Press, 1987), 99–117.

3. Henry Hansmann, "Economic Theories of the Nonprofit Sector," in Powell, ed., *The Nonprofit Sector: A Research Handbook*, 27–42. Hansmann's ideas are grounded in the public-goods theory advanced by Mancur Olson in *The Logic of Collective Action* (Cambridge: Harvard University Press, 1971).

4. The best accounts of colonial efforts to create corporations are Joseph S. Davis, *Essays in the Earlier History of American Corporations*, 2 vols. (Cambridge: Harvard University Press, 1917); and Edwin M. Dodd, *American Business Corporations until 1860, with Special Reference to Massachusetts* (Cambridge: Harvard University Press, 1960). See also Peter Dobkin Hall, "Organizational Values and the Origins of the Corporation in Connecticut, 1760–1860," in Association for the Study of Connecticut History, *Three Hundred and Fifty Years—Legal and Constitutional Development in Connecticut, 1638-1988* (Willimantic: Connecticut Studies Center, 1989).

5. On the Puritans' rejection of English legal forms, see William E. Nelson, *The Americanization of the Common Law: The Impact of Legal Change on Massachusetts Society, 1760-1830* (Cambridge: Harvard University Press, 1975); and Morton J. Horowitz, *The Transformation of American Law, 1780-1860* (Cambridge: Harvard University Press, 1977). On the legal profession, see Gerald W. Gewalt, "Massachusetts Lawyers: A Historical Analysis of the Process of Professionalization, 1760-1840" (Ph.D. diss., Clark University, 1969); C. R. McKirdy, "Lawyers in Crisis: The Massachusetts Legal Profession, 1760-

1790" (Ph.D. diss., Northwestern University, 1969); and Maxwell Bloomfield, *American Lawyers in a Changing Society, 1776–1876* (Cambridge: Harvard University Press, 1976).

6. The best overall account of Harvard's complex corporate evolution remains S. E. Morison's *Three Centuries of Harvard* (Cambridge: Harvard University Press, 1936). Ronald Story's *The Forging of an Aristocracy: Harvard and Boston's Upper Class, 1800–1870* (Middletown, Conn.: Wesleyan University Press, 1980) provides a detailed account of the politics of privatization in the first half of the nineteenth century. On the importance of government support for Harvard, see M. S. Foster, *"Out of Smalle Beginnings . . .": An Economic History of Harvard College in the Puritan Period* (Cambridge: Harvard University Press, 1962); and Seymour Harris, *The Economics of Harvard* (New York: McGraw-Hill, 1970). Harris' discussion of the exaggeration of the importance of private contributions by the college's nineteenth-century chroniclers is especially noteworthy.

7. For an overview of the disintegration of traditional society, see James Henretta, *The Evolution of American Society, 1700–1815* (Lexington, Ky.: D. C. Heath, 1973); and Peter Dobkin Hall, *The Organization of American Culture, 1700–1900: Institutions, Elites, and the Origins of American Nationality* (New York: New York University Press, 1982).

8. For an excellent discussion of the reintegration of Americans into the "Atlantic culture," see James Deetz, *In Small Things Forgotten: The Archaeology of Early American Life* (Garden City, N.Y.: Doubleday, 1977).

9. The best discussion of the economic and political implications of the Great Awakening is Richard Bushman, *From Puritan to Yankee: Character and the Social Order in Connecticut, 1690–1765* (New York: W. W. Norton & Co., 1970).

10. Benjamin Franklin, *Autobiography and Other Writings* (New York: New American Library, 1961), 94.

11. Ibid., 106–7.

12. Ibid., 107.

13. Ola Elizabeth Winslow, *A Destroying Angel: The Conquest of Smallpox in Colonial Boston* (Boston: Houghton Mifflin Co., 1974). Ironically, Franklin opposed inoculation efforts at this time—primarily because of his political differences with Mather and other leading clerics. When his only legitimate son, Franky, died of smallpox, he had cause to regret his position—which he regarded as "one of the great errata of my life." Interestingly, religious opposition to public improvements remained strong in the mid-nineteenth century. New Haven's efforts to create a public water supply were blocked for more than two decades by religious opponents who viewed typhoid and cholera as "heavenly visitations." See Peter Dobkin Hall, *Waterworks* (Hamden, Conn.: Eli Whitney Museum, 1988).

14. Franklin, *Autobiography and Other Writings*, 73–74.

15. Ibid., 113.

16. Bushman, *From Puritan to Yankee.*

17. John Kewley, *Discourse Delivered at the Warren Lodge* (Hartford, 1811).

For an excellent general account of Freemasonry, see Dorothy Lipson, *Free-masonry in Federalist Connecticut* (Princeton: Princeton University Press, 1977).

18. On the turbulence of the revolutionary political mobs and their involvement with legislative leaders, see Willard Sterne Randall, *Benedict Arnold: Patriot and Traitor* (New York: William Morrow & Co., 1990), 476–83.

19. Timothy Dwight, "The Triumph of Infidelity," in V. L. Parrington, ed., *The Connecticut Wits* (New York: Thomas Y. Crowell Co., 1954), 272.

20. "An Act for the Support of Missionaries to Preach the Gospel in the Northern, and Western Parts of the United States, and among the Indian Tribes (October 1798)," *Public Records of the State of Connecticut, 1797-99* (Hartford: Connecticut State Library, 1953), 9: 266–67.

21. Ezra Stiles, *Literary Diary*, 3 vols. (New York: Henry Hoyt & Co., 1901), 3:457–58.

22. For a detailed discussion of the place of corporate charters in Connecticut's ecclesiastical politics, see Richard Purcell, *Connecticut in Transition, 1775-1818* (Middletown, Conn.: Wesleyan University Press, 1963).

23. *Connecticut Courant*, June 4, 1787.

24. James Sullivan, "Opinion of the Attorney General of Massachusetts on the Life of the Corporation," in Oscar Handlin and Mary Flug Handlin, *Commonwealth: A Study of the Role of Government in the American Economy—Massachusetts, 1774-1861* (Cambridge: Harvard University Press, 1969), 254–61.

25. Thomas Jefferson, "Notes on the State of Virginia, quoted in Adrienne Koch, ed., *The American Enlightenment* (New York: George Braziller, 1965), 389.

26. Ibid., 393.

27. On early Virginia corporations, see Samuel Shepard, *Statutes at Large of Virginia, from October Session 1792 to December Session 1806, Inclusive, in Three Volumes* (Richmond, 1835); and William Waller Henning, *The Statutes at Large: Being a Collection of All the Laws from the First Session of the Legislature, in the Year 1819*, 2 vols. (Richmond, 1821). On Jefferson's attitude toward common law, see "The Revisal of the Laws of Virginia," in Koch, ed., *The American Enlightenment*, 296–98. On trusts, see E. S. Hirschler, "A Survey of Charitable Trusts in Virginia," *Virginia Law Review* 25 (1939): 109–16.

28. Opinion of Henry St. George Tucker in "Gallego's Executor v. the Attorney General," *Leigh* 3 (1832): 462.

29. "An Act to Make Provision for the Support of Idiots, Lunatics, and Persons of Unsound Mind," in Henning, *The Statutes at Large* (1785), 2:167–69.

30. Thomas Jefferson, "Systematic Plan of General Education," in Koch, ed., *The American Enlightenment*, 298–99.

31. See Sadie Bell, *Church, State, and Education in Virginia* (Philadelphia: Science Press Publishers, 1930); George H. Callcott, *A History of the University of Maryland* (Baltimore: Maryland Historical Society, 1966); Eugene F. Cordell, *History of the University of Maryland School of Medicine* (Baltimore:

Press of I. Friedenwald, 1891); and Donald H. Hollis, *South Carolina College* (Columbia: University of South Carolina Press, 1951).

32. On the James River Company, see Henning, *The Statutes at Large*, 2:450–62; and Henry Sinclair Drago, *Canal Days in America* (New York: Crown Publishers, 1972), 75–86.

33. Quoted in Bray Hammond, *Banks and Politics in America* (Princeton: Princeton University Press, 1957), 606.

34. On New York State's hostility to private charity, see Austin Wakeman Scott, "Charitable Trusts in New York," *New York University Law Review* 26 (1951): 152–75; and James Barr Ames, "The Failure of the Tilden Trust," in *Essays in Legal History* (Cambridge: Harvard University Press, 1913). See also Stanley N. Katz, Barry Sullivan, and C. Paul Beach, "Legal Change and Legal Autonomy: Charitable Trusts in New York, 1777–1893," *Law and History Review* 3, no. 1 (Spring 1985): 51–89. On the regents, see John S. Whitehead, *The Separation of College and State: Columbia, Dartmouth, Harvard, and Yale, 1776–1876* (New Haven: Yale University Press, 1973.

Contrary to the argument of Katz et al. that New York's hostility to charities was an artifact of its legal system, the actions of the legislature up to the passage of the Tilden Act in 1893 remained unremittingly unfriendly to private eleemosynary institutions. In 1848, charitable, benevolent, literary, scientific, devotional, and missionary corporations were made subject to visitation of the state's Supreme Court (L. 1848, chap. 318, sec. 8, 1923). In 1871, the recently created State Board of Charities was empowered to investigate the affairs of charitable institutions (L. 1871, chap. 699, 2147). In 1882, the legislature reaffirmed the power of the regents over private colleges, forbidding their incorporation without that body's approval (L. 1882, chap. 367, 1929). No other state subjected its charities to such oversight and control.

35. W. H. Hitchler and S. R. Liverant, "A History of Equity in Pennsylvania," *Dickinson Law Review* 32, no. 2 (1933): 156–83.

36. The best account of Philadelphia's institutional ethos is E. Digby Baltzell's *Puritan Boston and Quaker Philadelphia: Two Protestant Ethics and the Spirit of Authority and Leadership* (New York: Free Press, 1979).

37. On the struggle to create corporations in the Northwest Territory, see Peter Dobkin Hall, "The Spirit of the Ordinance of 1787: Organizational Values, Voluntary Associations, and Higher Education in Ohio, 1803–1830," in Paul H. Mattingly and Edward W. Stevens, Jr., eds., ". . . *Schools and the Means of Education Shall Forever Be Encouraged* (Athens: Ohio University Libraries, 1987), 97–114.

38. On organizational taxonomy in Ohio, see James J. Burns, *Educational History of Ohio* (Columbus: Historical Publishing Co., 1905); and Edward A. Miller, *The History of Educational Legislation in Ohio from 1803 to 1850* (Columbus: F. J. Heer Printing Co., 1918). For a contemporary overview of institutional demography, see Colin B. Burke, *American Collegiate Populations: A Test of the Traditional View* (New York: New York University Press, 1982).

39. The best discussion of the controversy over the Bank of the United States is in Hammond, *Banks and Politics in America*.

40. Quoted in ibid., 606.

41. Ibid., 7.

42. The best account of the Society for Useful Manufacturers is in Davis, *Essays in the Earlier History of American Corporations,* 2:26off.

43. Quoted in ibid., 431–32 and 438.

44. A Virginia jurist of the period commented that acts of incorporation "ought never to be passed, but in consideration of the services rendered to the public." If the purpose of a corporation was "merely private or selfish," it had no "claim upon the legislature for privileges." Quoted in Hammond, *Banks and Politics in America,* 606.

45. On the organization of the opposition party, see Noble E. Cunningham, *The Jeffersonian Republicans in Power: Party Operations, 1801–1809* (Chapel Hill: University of North Carolina Press, 1963); and Paul Goodman, *The Democratic Republicans of Massachusetts* (Boston: Little, Brown & Co., 1964). Howard Rock's *Artisans of the New Republic: The Tradesmen of New York City in the Age of Jefferson* (New York: New York University Press, 1984) also sheds much valuable light on the role of voluntary organizations in the consolidation of Jeffersonianism.

46. Morison, *Three Centuries of Harvard,* 212–15; Story, *The Forging of an Aristocracy,* 135–60; and Whitehead, *The Separation of College and State,* 16–45.

47. James McBride, *Laws Passed by the Legislature Establishing the Miami University, and the Ordinances, Passed by the Trustees of Miami University—to Which Is Added, an Address to the Inhabitants of the Miami College Lands, Containing Brief Remarks and Observations* (Hamilton, Ohio: Privately Printed, 1814). In this remarkable pamphlet, a local legislator and trustee of Miami University anticipated the issues in the Dartmouth College case by five years. On the background to this controversy, see Walter Havinghurst, *The Miami Years, 1809–1969* (New York: G. P. Putnam's Sons, 1969).

48. On the Dartmouth College case, see Whitehead, *The Separation of College and State;* Howard S. Miller, *The Legal Foundations of American Philanthropy, 1776–1844* (Madison: Historical Society of Wisconsin, 1961); and Irvin G. Wyllie, "The Search for an American Law of Charity," *Mississippi Valley Historical Review* 40, no. 2 (1959): 203–21. See also Marilyn Tobias, *Old Dartmouth on Trial* (New York: New York University Press, 1982).

49. Quoted in Richard Hofstadter and Wilson Smith, eds., *American Higher Education: A Documentary History,* 2 vols. (Chicago: University of Chicago Press, 1961), 1:202–213.

50. "The Trustees of Dartmouth College v. Woodward," *Wheaton* 4 (1819): 625–54.

51. "Philadelphia Baptist Association v. Hart's Executors," *Wheaton* 4 (1819): 518.

52. *Proposed Revision of the Statute Laws of the State of New York* (Albany, 1828). These restrictions were repeatedly upheld by the courts in *Williams* v. *Williams,* 8 *New York Reports* 525 (1853), *Bascom* v. *Albertson,* 34 *New York Reports* 584 (1866), and *Cornell University* v. *Fiske,* 136 *U.S. Reports* 152 (1890).

53. *Vidal* v. *Girard's Executors,* 2 *How* 27 (1844). For an excellent account of the background of this case, see Robert A. Ferguson, "The Girard Will Case: Charity and Inheritance in the City of Brotherly Love," in Jack Salzman, ed., *Philanthropy and American Society: Selected Papers* (New York: Center for American Culture Studies, 1987), 1–16.

54. See Lawrence Friedman, *History of American Law* (New York: Simon & Schuster, 1985), 130–31; Hitchler and Liverant, "A History of Equity in Pennsylvania," *Dickinson Law Review* 37, no. 2 (1933): 156–83; and C. C. Binney, *The Life of Horace Binney* (Philadelphia, 1903).

55. Alexis de Tocqueville, *Democracy in America,* 2 vols. (New York: Alfred A. Knopf, 1945), 1:378.

56. Ibid., 1:187.

57. Ibid., 2:169.

58. See Charles I. Foster's *"An Errand of Mercy": The Evangelical United Front, 1790–1837* (Chapel Hill: University of North Carolina Press, 1960).

59. There is still no overview of the institution-building activities that emerged from the Second Great Awakening. Besides Foster's *An Errand of Mercy*, studies of particular components of the movement include David F. Allmendinger's examination of the American Education Society, *Paupers and Scholars: The Transformation of Student Life in Nineteenth-Century New England* (New York: St. Martin's Press, 1971); and Allen S. Horlick's *Country Boys and Merchant Princes: The Social Control of Young Men in New York* (Lewisburg, Pa.: Bucknell University Press, 1975). Mary P. Ryan's superb *Cradle of the Middle Class: The Family in Oneida County, New York, 1790–1865* (New York: Cambridge University Press, 1982) gives a detailed account of the interconnections between the evangelical impulse and institution-building in a particular locality. Burton J. Bledstein's *The Culture of Professionalism: The Middle Class and the Development of Higher Education in America* (New York: W. W. Norton & Co., 1976) provides an important account of the national dimensions of the movement.

60. See Donald M. Scott, *From Office to Profession: The New England Ministry, 1750–1850* (Philadelphia: University of Pennsylvania Press, 1978); and David Potts, "American Colleges in the Nineteenth Century: From Localism to Denominationalism," *History of Education Quarterly* 10 (1971): 72–86.

61. On the evangelical roots of the teaching profession, see Paul H. Mattingly, *The Classless Profession: American Schoolmen in the Nineteenth Century* (New York: New York University Press, 1975).

62. Paul E. Johnson's *Shopkeeper's Millennium: Society and Revivals in Rochester, New York, 1815–1837* (New York: Hill & Wang, 1978) suggests that the early credit agencies paid particular attention to the kinds of personal morality—often expressed in institutional participation—which the evangelical network fostered.

63. My "Family Structure and Class Consolidation among the Boston Brahmins" (Ph.D. diss., State University of New York at Stony Brook, 1973) provides the most detailed account of the Bostonians' responses to the challenges of postrevolutionary commerce. See also Story's *The Forging of an Aristocracy;*

and Robert F. Dalzell Jr.'s *Enterprising Elite: The Boston Associates and the World They Made* (Cambridge: Harvard University Press, 1987).

64. These claims for private actions were best articulated by Samuel Atkins Eliot in "Public and Private Charities of Boston," *North American Review* 61 (1845): 135–59, and "Charities of Boston," in *North American Review* 91 (1860): 154–61. See also his *Sketch of the History of Harvard College and Its Present State* (Boston: Ticknor & Fields, 1848), which is an ambitious attempt to re-write the history of the college as a private institution. See also Clifford S. Griffin, *Moral Stewardship in the United States, 1800–1865* (New Brunswick, N.J.: Rutgers University Press, 1960).

65. This claim of the patricians' special contribution to the Union's victory was explicitly proclaimed by Thomas Wentworth Higginson in his introduction to *The Harvard Memorial Biographies* (Cambridge: Sever & Francis, 1866) and later echoed by Charles W. Eliot in his inaugural speech as president of Harvard. George M. Frederickson's study of the U.S. Sanitary Commission, *The Inner Civil War: Northern Intellectuals and the Crisis of the Union* (New York: Harper & Row, 1965) provides the best account of the war's meaning to evangelical and metropolitan elites. See also Edmund Wilson's *Patriotic Gore* (New York: Farrar, Straus & Giroux, 1962).

66. Leonard D. White, *The Jacksonians: A Study in Administrative History* (New York: Macmillan Co., 1954), 550–51.

67. First-rate accounts of the organizational dimensions of the war are Stephen E. Ambrose's *Halleck: Lincoln's Chief of Staff* (Baton Rouge: Louisiana State University Press, 1962) and *Upton and the Army* (Baton Rouge: Louisiana State University Press, 1964). See also Emory Upton's *Military Policy of the United States* (Washington, D.C.: Government Printing Office, 1907).

68. See Hall, *The Organization of American Culture*, 220–39.

69. Charles W. Eliot, "Inaugural Address as President of Harvard," in *Educational Reform: Essays and Addresses* (New York: Macmillan Co., 1898), 1–38.

70. The fullest exposition of the thinking of Eliot and those who backed him can be found in "The New Education," *Atlantic Monthly* 23 (February 1869): 203–20, (March 1869): 358–67. For an excellent analysis of Eliot's ideas, see Hugh Hawkins, *Between Harvard and America: The Educational Leadership of Charles W. Eliot* (New York: Oxford University Press, 1972).

71. On the early history of the social sciences, see Thomas Haskell's *The Emergence of Professional Social Science: The American Social Science Association and the Nineteenth-Century Crisis of Authority* (Urbana: University of Illinois Press); and Paul Buck, ed., *The Social Sciences at Harvard* (Cambridge: Harvard University Press, 1965).

72. Jesse B. Sears, *Philanthropy in the History of American Higher Education* (Washington, D.C.: Bureau of Education, Department of the Interior, 1922), 23–24.

73. Thorstein Veblen, *The Higher Learning in America* (New York: B. W. Huebsch, 1918), 57.

74. Charles W. Eliot, "Views Respecting the Present Exemption from Tax-

ation of Property Used for Religious, Educational, and Charitable Purposes,"
in *Annual Report of the President and Treasurer of Harvard University* (Cambridge: Printed for the University, 1874), 369–94.

75. "An Act Concerning Associations for Religious, Charitable, Educational and Other Purposes," *Acts and Resolves Passed by the General Court of
Massachusetts in the Year 1874* (Boston: Wright & Potter, 1874), 412–14.

76. "Yale University v. Town of New Haven," *Connecticut Reports* 71 (1899):
316.

77. See "An Act in Relation to the Exemption of the Real Property of
Religious, Charitable, and Educational Corporations and Associations from
Taxation," *Laws of the State of New York Passed at the One Hundred and
Sixteenth Session of the Legislature* (Albany: James B. Lyon, Printer, 1893), 1,
chap. 498, 1077–87; and "An Act to Regulate Gifts for Charitable Purposes,"
in ibid., 2: chap. 701, 1748.

78. Richard Ely, "The Universities and the Churches," in *One Hundred
Seventh Report of the Regents, 1893* (Albany: University of the State of New
York, 1894), 361. I am grateful to James Wooten of the Yale Law School for
bringing this important speech to my attention. Wooten's essay "The Emergence of Nonprofit Legal Education in New York: A Case Study," Working
Paper no. 154 (New Haven: Program on Non-Profit Organizations, Yale University, 1990), is an invaluable study of the debate over privatization.

79. See T. J. Jackson Lears, *No Place of Grace: Antimodernism and the
Transformation of American Culture, 1880–1920* (New York: Pantheon Books,
1981).

80. Quoted in Hawkins, *Between Harvard and America*, 216.

81. Good overviews of the proliferation of philanthropic efforts during this
period include Robert M. Bremner's *From the Depths: The Discovery of Poverty
in the United States* (New York: New York University Press, 1956) and *The
Public Good: Philanthropy and Welfare in the Civil War Era* (New York: Alfred
A. Knopf, 1980), as well as Allen F. Davis' *Spearheads for Reform: The Social
Settlements and the Progressive Movement* (New York: Oxford University Press,
1967) and Nathan Huggins' *Protestants against Poverty: Boston's Charities,
1870–1900* (Westport, Conn.: Greenwood Press, 1971).

82. For a good panorama of these efforts, see Robert D. Cross, ed., *The
Church and the City* (Indianapolis: Bobbs-Merrill, 1967). Carol Smith-Rosen-
berg's *Religion and the Rise of the American City: The New York City Mission
Movement, 1812–1870* (Ithaca: Cornell University Press, 1971) is an excellent
case study. Ironically, given the quantitative significance of religious giving—
which amount to nearly two-thirds of current nonprofit revenues—the importance of religion both as a part of philanthropy and as a force behind it
remains largely unexamined.

83. On the elaboration of privatized elite cultural institutions during this
period, see Daniel M. Fox, *Engines of Culture: Philanthropy and Art Museums*
(Madison: State Historical Society of Wisconsin, 1963); Helen Lefkowitz
Horowitz, *Culture and the City: Cultural Philanthropy in Chicago, 1880–1917*
(Chicago: University of Chicago Press, 1976); and Thomas Bender, *New York*

Intellect: A History of Intellectual Life in New York City, from 1750 to the Beginnings of Our Own Times (New York: Alfred A. Knopf, 1987). The definitive account of this process will be offered by Paul DiMaggio's forthcoming volume on American culture. Portions of this study appeared as "Cultural Entrepreneurship in Nineteenth-Century Boston," in Paul DiMaggio, ed., *Nonprofit Enterprise in the Arts: Studies in Mission and Constraint* (New York: Oxford University Press, 1986); and "Class Authority and Cultural Entrepreneurship: The Problem of Chicago," Working Paper no. 155 (New Haven: Program on Non-Profit Organizations, Yale University, 1990).

84. An excellent primary account of the impulse behind these rationalization efforts is Amos G. Warner's *American Charities* (New York: Thomas Y. Crowell & Co., 1908). An excellent historical account of the movement is in Michael Katz, *In the Shadow of the Poorhouse: A Social History of Welfare in America* (New York: Basic Books, 1986).

85. See, for example, such early "social novels" as Thomas Bailey Aldrich's *The Stillwater Tragedy* (Boston: Houghton Mifflin Co., 1880) and John Hay's *The Breadwinners: A Social Study* (New York: Harper & Brothers, 1883).

86. Henry George, *Progress and Poverty* (1879; reprint, New York: Henry George School of Social Science, 1940).

87. Ibid., 1.

88. The handful of works on the social ideas and reform activities of businessmen in this period include Arthur H. Cole's *Business Enterprise in Its Social Setting* (Cambridge: Harvard University Press, 1959); Alfred D. Chandler's "Henry Varnum Poor: Philosopher of Management," in William Miller, ed., *Men in Business: Essays on the Historical Role of the Entrepreneur* (New York: Harper & Row, 1962); Edward Chase Kirkland's *Dream and Thought in the Business Community, 1860–1900* (Ithaca: Cornell University Press, 1956); and Robert Weibe's *Businessmen and Reform* (Cambridge: Harvard University Press, 1962). Certainly the best, though least-known, study in this area is Morell Heald's *The Social Responsibilities of Business: Company and Community, 1900–1960* (Cleveland: Press of Case Western Reserve University, 1970).

89. See Charles M. Shelton's 1897 novel *In His Steps* (Springdale, Pa.: Whitaker House, n.d.), which describes the efforts of an upper-middle-class congregation to practice Christian social ethics amidst the poverty and dislocation of the 1890s. This immensely popular novel, which has sold more than thirty million copies since its publication, remains in print.

90. See Daniel Aaron, *Men of Good Hope* (New York: Oxford University Press, 1951); Sylvia E. Bowman, *The Year 2000: A Critical Biography of Edward Bellamy* (New York: Bookman Associates, 1958); Arthur Mann, *Yankee Reformers in the Gilded Age: Social Reform in Boston, 1880–1900* (Cambridge: Harvard University Press, 1954); and John G. Sproat, *"The Best Men": Liberal Reformers in the Gilded Age* (New York: Oxford University Press, 1968).

91. Henry Adams, *The Education of Henry Adams* (Boston: Massachusetts Historical Society, 1918), 344.

92. Upton, *Military Policy of the United States,* and Ambrose, *Upton and the Army.*

93. Eliot, "Views Respecting the Present Exemption from Taxation of Property Used for Religious, Educational, and Charitable Purposes," 369.

94. Quoted in Bliss Perry, *Life and Letters of Henry Lee Higginson* (Boston: Houghton Mifflin Co., 1921), 64.

95. Gabriel Kolko, *The Triumph of Conservatism: A Reinterpretation of Progressivism* (Chicago: Quadrangle Books, 1963).

96. Richard Hofstadter, *Age of Reform* (New York: Alfred A. Knopf, 1955).

97. Robert Wiebe's *The Search for Order* (New York: Hill & Wang, 1967) initiated this comprehensive reinterpretation of Progressivism, by describing the reformers as members of a "new middle class," which cut across traditional political, occupational, and geographical divisions and which was characterized by not only its educational base but also its distinctive bureaucratic and professionalized orientation. Bledstein's *The Culture of Professionalism* traced the nineteenth-century origins of this group. Most recently, Martin Sklar's *Corporate Reconstruction of American Capitalism, 1890–1916* (New York: Cambridge University Press, 1988) provided both a comprehensive overview of the emergence of this group and explored its impact on law and politics. Of particular importance in the emergence of the reinterpretation of this key period in American history are Louis Galambos' provocative essays "The Emerging Organizational Synthesis in Modern American History," in Edwin J. Perkins, ed., *Men and Organizations: The American Economy in the Twentieth Century* (New York: G. P. Putnam's Sons, 1977), and "Technology, Political Economy, and Professionalization: Central Themes of the Organizational Synthesis," *Business History Review* 57 (1983): 471–93 .

98. See Louis Galambos, *Competition and Cooperation: The Emergence of a National Trade Association* (Baltimore: Johns Hopkins University Press, 1966); and Robert D. Cuff, *The War Industries Board: Business-Government Relations during World War I* (Baltimore: Johns Hopkins University Press, 1973).

99. The best account of the evolution of Carnegie's career and ideas is Joseph Frazier Wall's *Andrew Carnegie* (New York: Oxford University Press, 1970).

100. Andrew Carnegie, "An Employer's View of the Labor Question," *Forum* 1 (August 1886): 114–25.

101. Andrew Carnegie, "Wealth," *North American Review* 148 (June 1889): 653–64; 149 (December 1889): 682–98.

102. Ibid.

103. Quoted in John Ensor Harr and Peter J. Johnson, *The Rockefeller Century* (New York: Charles Scribner's Sons, 1988), 51–52. Gates, trained as a minister, but ultimately building a career as one of John D. Rockefeller's closest associates, represents an especially interesting example of the convergence of the organizational culture of evangelical religion and that of big business. His autobiography, *Chapters in My Life* (New York: Free Press, 1977), is a key to understanding both the shift from "retail" to "wholesale"

philanthropy and the interrelation of business and philanthropy. The best study of Rockefeller remains Alan Nevins' *John D. Rockefeller: A Study in Power* (New York: Charles Scribner's Sons, 1953).

104. Harr and Johnson, *The Rockefeller Century*, 59.

105. A useful and insightful discussion of the general problem of the legitimacy of the foundation as a charitable instrument was offered by Barry D. Karl and Stanley N. Katz in "The Legitimation of the Philanthropic Foundation in the United States, 1890–1930" (Paper delivered at the Shelby Collum Davis Center, Princeton University, January 30, 1981).

106. See "Schouler, Petitioner," *Massachusetts Reports* 134 (1883): 426 and "Minot v. Baker," *Massachusetts Reports* 147 (1888): 348.

107. The Peabody and Slater funds, pioneer foundations, have attracted curiously little scholarly interest. On them, see Robert Bremner, *American Philanthropy* (Chicago: University of Chicago Press, 1988) and *The Public Good: Philanthropy and Welfare in the Civil War Era* (New York: Alfred A. Knopf, 1980). See also Franklin Parker, "George Peabody, 1795–1869" (Ph.D. diss., University of Texas, 1957).

108. "Tilden v. Green," 130 *New York* 29, 44 (1891).

109. David Graham Phillips, "The Treason of the Senate," in Arthur Weinberg and Lila Weinberg, eds., *The Muckrakers* (1906; reprint, New York: Capricorn Books, 1964), 71–83.

110. John M. Glenn, Lilian Brandt, and F. Emerson Andrews, *The Russell Sage Foundation, 1907-1947* (New York: Russell Sage Foundation, 1947), remains the definitive account of this pioneer foundation. See also David C. Maddox and David Hammack, ed., *The Russell Sage Foundation: Social Research and Social Action in America, 1907-1947* (Frederick, Md.: Congressional Information Service, 1988).

111. Most accounts of the Russell Sage Foundation have minimized Mrs. Sage's role in its establishment, giving most of the credit to her legal adviser, Robert De Forest. The papers of Mrs. Sage, now deposited at the Rockefeller Archive Center, suggest that she played a far more active role. See James A. Smith and Melissa A. Smith, "Margaret Olivia Sage: A Life" (forthcoming).

112. Two superlative studies of Carnegie's foundations are Ellen Condliffe Lagemann's *Private Power for the Public Good: A History of the Carnegie Foundation for the Advancement of Teaching* (Middletown, Conn.: Wesleyan University Press, 1983) and *The Politics of Knowledge: The Carnegie Corporation, Philanthropy, and Public Policy* (Middletown, Conn.: Wesleyan University Press, 1989).

113. On the Rockefeller Institute (later Rockefeller University), see George W. Corner, *A History of the Rockefeller Institute, 1901-1953: Origins and Growth* (New York: Rockefeller Institute Press, 1964). The extensive critical studies of the Rockefellers' patronage of science and medicine include Gerald Jonas' *The Circuit Riders: Rockefeller Money and the Rise of Modern Science* (New York: W. W. Norton & Co., 1989); Stephen C. Wheatley's *The Politics of Philanthropy: Abraham Flexner and Medical Education* (Madison: University of Wisconsin Press, 1988); John Ettling, *The Germ of Laziness: Rockefeller*

Philanthropy and Public Health in the New South (Cambridge: Harvard University Press, 1981); and E. Richard Brown, *Rockefeller Medicine Men: Medicine and Capitalism in America* (Berkeley: University of California Press, 1979).

114. On the General Education board, see Raymond B. Fosdick, *An Adventure in Giving: The Story of the General Education Board* (New York: Harper & Row).

115. On the Rockefeller Foundation, see Raymond B. Fosdick, *The Story of the Rockefeller Foundation* (New York: Harper & Row, 1952). Harr and Johnson, *The Rockefeller Century*, shed interesting new insights on the foundations' origins.

116. One of the best accounts of this controversy can be found in Peter Collier and David Horowitz's *The Rockefellers: An American Dynasty* (New York: New American Library, 1976). See also U.S. Senate, 62nd Congress, 3rd Session, *The Rockefeller Foundation* (Washington, D.C.: Government Printing Office, 1913); U.S. Senate, 61st Congress, 2nd Session, Rep. 405, *Incorporation of the Rockefeller Foundation* (Washington, D.C.: Government Printing Office, 1910); and *Industrial Relations: Final Report and Testimony Submitted to Congress by the Committee on Industrial Relations* (Washington, D.C.: Government Printing Office, 1916).

117. Quoted in Collier and Horowitz, *The Rockefellers*, 63–64.

118. See Lagemann, *Private Power for the Public Good;* Barry D. Karl and Stanley N. Katz, "The American Private Foundation and the Public Sphere, 1890–1930," *Minerva* 19 (1981): 236–70; and Barry D. Karl and Stanley N. Katz, "Foundations and Ruling Class Elites," *Daedalus* 116, no. 1 (1987): 1–40. See also Thomas James' valuable essay "The Private Nonprofit Sector, Public Policy, and Urban Schooling in the United States, 1900–1929," in *Conference Papers, Conference on Private Action and Public Policy: The Impact of Federations and Associations in the American Metropolis, 1900–1929* (Cleveland: Case Western Reserve University, Social Policy History Program, 1989).

The influence of foundations on public policy remains a controversial but poorly examined topic. For interesting samples of the scholarly debate on the topic, see Donald Fisher, "The Role of Philanthropic Foundations in the Reproduction and Production of Hegemony," *Sociology* 17 (1983): 204–33; Martin Bulmer and Donald Fisher, "Debate," *Sociology* 18 (1984): 573–87; and Joan Roelofs, "Foundations and the Supreme Court," *Telos* 62 (Winter 1984–85): 59–87. See also Edward H. Berman, *The Influence of the Carnegie, Ford, and Rockefeller Foundations on American Foreign Policy: The Ideology of Philanthropy* (Albany: State University of New York Press, 1983).

119. *Industrial Relations: Final Report and Testimony.* See also Graham Adams, Jr. *Age of Industrial Violence* (New York: Columbia University Press, 1966).

120. On the influence of these pioneer think tanks, see James A. Smith, *The Idea Brokers: Think Tanks and the Rise of the New Policy Elite* (New York: Free Press, 1991).

121. For a contemporary critique of this, see Harold J. Laski, "Foundations,

Universities, and Research," in *The Dangers of Obedience and Other Essays* (New York: Harper & Brothers, 1930), 150–77. Lucid and insightful analyses of this debate include Barry D. Karl, "Presidential Planning and Social Science Research: Mr. Hoover's Experts," *Perspectives in American History* 3 (1969): 347–409; Barry D. Karl, "Philanthropy, Policy Planning, and the Bureaucratization of the Democratic Ideal," *Daedalus* 105, no. 4 (Fall 1976): 129–49, and Guy Alchon, *The Invisible Hand of Planning: Capitalism, Social Science, and the State in the 1920s* (Princeton: Princeton University Press, 1985). See also Stanley N. Katz, "Grantmaking and Research in the US, 1933–1983," *Proceedings of the American Philosophical Society* 129, no. 1 (1985): 1–19.

122. See Sanford M. Jacoby, *Employing Bureaucracy: Managers, Unions, and the Transformation of Work in American Industry, 1900–1945* (New York: Columbia University Press, 1985); Stuart Brandes, *American Welfare Capitalism* (Chicago: University of Chicago Press, 1976); and Daniel Nelson, *Workers and Managers: Origins of the New Factory System in the United States, 1880–1920* (Madison: University of Wisconsin Press, 1975). See also David Brody's valuable essays "The American Worker in the Progressive Era" and "The Rise and Decline of Welfare Capitalism," in *Workers in Industrial America: Essays on the Twentieth Century Struggle* (New York: Oxford University Press, 1980).

123. See Robert F. Dalzell, "The Rise of the Waltham–Lowell System and Some Thoughts on the Political Economy of Modernization in Ante-Bellum Massachusetts," *Perspectives in American History* 9 (1975): 229–68. An interesting case study of some of the later variants of model industrial villages is Stanley Buder's *Pullman: An Experiment in Industrial Order and Community Planning, 1880–1930* (New York: Oxford University Press, 1967). The factory village was an analog to the use of asylums and penitentiaries as models for the reorganization of society and the resocialization of its members, a point on which David Rothman has written brilliantly in *The Discovery of the Asylum: Social Order and Disorder in the New Republic* (Boston: Little Brown & Co., 1971).

124. The extent to which the scientific-management movement shared broad social reform concerns is evident in Frederick W. Taylor's own work, including "A Piece Rate System, Being a Step Toward the Partial Solution of the Labor Problem," in *Transactions of the American Society of Mechanical Engineers* 16 (1895): 850–903, and *Principles of Scientific Management* (1911; reprint, New York: W. W. Norton & Co., 1967). The latter begins with a set of quotations from Theodore Roosevelt. This was not mere opportunism on Taylor's part, but represented deeply held and widely shared convictions in the early managerial community—as in Henry Towne's "The Engineer as Economist," *Transactions of the American Society of Mechanical Engineers* 7 (1886): 120–28, and "Gain Sharing," *Transactions of the American Society of Mechanical Engineers* 10 (1889): 600–640.

125. On corporate investment in the Y.M.C.A., see F. Emerson Andrews, *Corporation Giving* (New York: Russell Sage Foundation, 1950); Brandes, *American Welfare Capitalism;* Heald, *The Social Responsibilities of Business,* 10–14; and Pierce Williams and Frederick E. Croxton, *Corporate Contributions*

to Organized Community Welfare Services (New York: National Bureau of Economic Research, 1930).

126. Buder, *Pullman.*

127. On community-wide welfare capitalism in mid-sized industrial cities with diversified economies, see Peter Dobkin Hall and K. L. Hall, "Allentown, 1870–1900" and "Allentown, 1929–1939," in Mahlon Hellerich, ed., *Allentown, 1762–1987*, 2 vols. (Allentown, Pa.: Lehigh County Historical Society, 1988), 1:81–147, and 2:150–95. See also Peter Dobkin Hall, "'Unmitigated Materialism with a Degree of Something Resembling Civilization': Civil Society in Cleveland, 1870–1930," in *Conference Papers, Conference on Private Action and Social Policy: The Impact of Federations and Associations in the American Metropolis, 1900–1929* (Cleveland: Case Western Reserve University, Social Policy History Program, 1989).

128. There is, lamentably, no thorough scholarly study of the board-of-trade and chamber-of-commerce movements. Suggestive primary sources on the subject include Alexander Orr, "Commercial Organizations," in Chauncey M. DePew, ed., *One Hundred Years of American Commerce* (New York: D. O. Haynes & Co., 1895), 50–54; Kenneth A. Sturges, *American Chambers of Commerce*, Williams College, David A. Wells Prize Essays, no. 4 (New York: Henry Holt & Co., 1915); and Kenneth A. Sturges, *Trade Associations: Their Economic Significance and Legal Status* (New York: National Industrial Conference Board, 1925).

129. On Hanna's involvement in the National Civic Federation, see Herbert Croly, *Marcus Alonzo Hanna: His Life and Work* (New York: Macmillan Co., 1919). It is a measure of the importance of Hanna that his biography was written by the chief ideologue of the Progressive movement and the founder of the *New Republic,* the leading progressive periodical. Although much maligned by generations of liberal historians, Hanna's reputation is being rediscovered. Management guru Peter Drucker describes Hanna as "one of the true innovators in the history of politics" and credits him with having "deflected American politics away from ideology" by integrating organized economic interests into political life (Drucker, *The New Realities* [New York: Harper & Row, 1989], 19–26). The National Civic Federation and its local affiliates were crucial mechanisms in this process.

130. On the origins of federated giving, see Scott Cutlip, *Fund Raising in the United States: Its Role in American Philanthropy* (New Brunswick, N.J.: Rutgers University Press, 1965), 29–109; and John R. Seeley et al., *Community Chest: A Case Study in Philanthropy* (Toronto: University of Toronto Press, 1957). See also Peter Dobkin Hall, "The Community Foundation in the United States," in Richard Magat, ed., *Philanthropic Giving* (New York: Oxford University Press, 1989).

131. On the early origins of the Community Chest, see Charles Whiting Williams, "Cleveland's Federated Givers," *Review of Reviews* 48 (1913): 472–75; and E. M. Williams, "Essentials of the Cleveland Experiment in Cooperative Benevolence," *Proceedings of the Conference on Charities and Corrections* (New York: Conference on Charities & Corrections, 1913), 111–15.

132. See Hall, "The Community Foundation in the United States"; and David C. Hammack, "Community Foundations: The Delicate Question of Purpose," in Richard Magat, ed., *An Agile Servant: Community Leadership by Community Foundations* (New York: Foundation Center, 1989), 23–50.

133. On the founding rationale for early community foundations, see Walter Greenough, "Private Wealth for Public Needs," *Scribner's* 74 (December 1923): 697–705.

134. Herbert Clark Hoover, *American Individualism* (New York: Doubleday, Doran & Co., 1922). Hoover, like Hanna, has been scorned by liberal historians who have characterized him, quite inaccurately, as an advocate of laissez-faire capitalism. More recent interpretations of the life and work of Hoover underscore his role as the most articulate spokesman for—and implementer of—an important variant of the progressive polity. See Ellis W. Hawley, ed., *Herbert Hoover as Secretary of Commerce: Studies in New Era Thought and Practice* (Iowa City: University of Iowa Press, 1974); and E. W. Hawley, "Herbert Hoover, the Commerce Secretariat, and the Vision of an 'Associative State,'" in Edwin J. Perkins, ed., *Men and Organizations* (New York: G. P. Putnam's Sons, 1977), 131–48. For an interesting discussion of Hoover's place in the evolution of the liberal state, see Paul Johnson, *Modern Times* (New York: Harper & Row, 1983), 203–60.

135. Hoover, *American Individualism*, 39.

136. Ibid., 38.

137. Ibid., 41–43.

138. Ibid., 24.

139. Ibid., 25.

140. Ibid., 4–5.

141. Hawley, "Herbert Hoover, the Commerce Secretariat, and the Vision of an 'Associative State,'" 132–33.

142. Ibid., 143.

143. Herbert Clark Hoover, "Consequences of the Proposed New Deal," in *Addresses upon the American Road, 1933–38* (New York: Charles Scribner's Sons, 1938), 7.

144. Although harshly critical, David F. Noble's *America by Design: Science, Technology, and the Rise of Corporate Capitalism* (New York: Oxford University Press, 1977) gives the best overview of the thought and action of top industrial managers in the 1920s. See Alchon's *The Invisible Hand of Planning* and Karl's "Presidential Planning and Social Science Research."

145. On Swope, see David Loth, *Swope of GE* (New York: Simon & Schuster, 1958).

146. Loth, *Swope of GE*, 70–71.

147. See Tillmann Buddensieg, *Industiekultur: Peter Behrens and the AEG* (Cambridge: MIT Press, 1979).

148. Quoted in Loth, *Swope of GE*, 162.

149. To date, no biography of Gifford has appeared. Material on his life and thought can be found in a variety of places, including the reports of the Harvard class of 1905 and in W. S. Gifford, *Addresses, Papers, and Interviews,*

4 vols. (New York: American Telephone & Telegraph Co., 1929-49). For a critical account of Gifford's stewardship of the company, see N. R. Danielian, *AT&T: The Story of Industrial Conquest* (New York: Vanguard Press, 1939.

150. The activities of Page—and those of other corporate leaders of the period—are documented in his papers at the Wisconsin Historical Society. For a good account of Page and his group, see Merle Curti, *Philanthropy in the Shaping of American Higher Education* (New Brunswick, N.J.: Rutgers University Press, 1965).

151. See Hall and Hall, "Allentown, 1870-1900" and "Allentown, 1929-1939"; and Peter Dobkin Hall, "Philanthropy as Investment," *History of Education Quarterly* 22, no. 2 (1982): 185-91. See also William H. Wilson, *The City Beautiful Movement in Kansas City* (Columbia: University of Missouri Press, 1964).

152. Lance E. Davis and Daniel J. Kevles, "The National Research Fund: A Case Study in the Industrial Support of Academic Science," *Minerva* 12 (1974): 206-20. See also Committee on Recent Social Trends, *Recent Social Trends in the United States*, 2 vols. (New York: McGraw-Hill, 1933). These volumes are monuments to the close relationship among government, business, universities, and philanthropy during the 1920s.

153. See Heald, *The Social Responsibilities of Business*, 150; and Loth, *Swope of GE*, 216-40.

154. Williams, "Cleveland's Federated Givers," 472.

155. Yale University, *Yale Roll Call, Final Edition* (New Haven: Yale University, 1928), vi.

156. These patterns were reconstructed from donor lists in Harvard University, *Report of the President and Treasurer* (Cambridge: Printed for the University, 1927), 119-55, and from the relevant classbooks.

157. Williams and Croxton, *Corporate Contributions to Organized Community Welfare Services*, 93.

158. Ibid., 221-22.

159. Danielian, *AT&T*, 200-42.

160. Loth, *Swope of GE*, 216-40; and Brody, "The Rise and Decline of Welfare Capitalism," 66-78.

161. See Ernest V. Fricke's excellent "The Impact of the Depression on Allentown, Pennsylvania, 1929-1940" (Ph.D. diss., New York University, 1974).

162. 295 US 495; 55S Ct. 837; 79L. Ed. 1570 (1935).

163. Heald, *The Social Responsibilities of Business* 148-73.

164. John Price Jones, *Yearbook of Philanthropy 1940, Presenting Information and Statistics Covering American Philanthropy since the Year 1920* (New York: Inter-River Press, 1940), 10.

165. Ibid., 8-10.

166. Andrews, *Corporation Giving*, 158.

167. Ibid., 209.

168. The best study of foundation formation is Teresa Odendahl et al.,

America's Wealthy and the Future of Foundations (New York: Foundation Center, 1987).

169. James F. Harris and Anne Klepper, "Corporate Public Service Activities," and Thomas Vasquez, "Corporation Giving Measures," in *Research Papers Sponsored by the Commission on Private Philanthropy and Public Needs*, 6 vols. (Washington, D.C.: Department of the Treasury, 1977). Hayden W. Smith has provided the most thoughtful and careful evaluation of corporate giving trends in *A Profile of Corporate Contributions* (New York: Council for Aid to Education, 1983) and *Corporate Contributions Research since the Filer Commission* (New York: Council for Aid to Education, 1984).

170. Andrews, *Corporation Giving*, 29.

171. Curti, *Philanthropy*, 238–58.

172. *A. P. Smith Manufacturing Company* v. *Barlow*, 13 N.J. Sup. Ct. 147 (1954). For background on this case, see Heald, *The Social Responsibilities of Business*, 207–42.

173. Robert H. Hays and William J. Abernathy, "Managing Our Way to Economic Decline," *Harvard Business Review* 58, no. 4 (1980): 67–77.

174. Alan J. Matusow, *The Unraveling of America: A History of American Liberalism in the 1960s* (New York: Harper & Row, 1984), 32.

175. See Joseph Galaskiewicz, *The Social Organization of an Urban Grants Economy: A Study of Business Philanthropy and Nonprofit Organizations* (Orlando, Fla.: Academic Press, 1985), and Michael Useem, *The Inner Circle: Large Corporations and the Rise of Business Political Activity in the U.S. and U.K.* (New York: Oxford University Press, 1987). An excellent primary document is Arthur White and John Bartolomeo's *Corporate Giving: The Views of Chief Executive Officers of Major American Corporations* (Washington, D.C.: Council on Foundations, 1982).

176. See note 1 above.

177. Weisbrod, *The Nonprofit Economy*, 169.

178. See Carolyn Webber and Aaron Wildavsky, *A History of Taxation and Expenditure in the Western World* (New York: Simon & Schuster, 1986), 494–506.

179. Lester Salamon, "Of Market Failure, Voluntary Failure, and Third Party Government: Toward a Theory of Government–Nonprofit Relations in the Modern Welfare State," in Susan A. Ostrander et al., eds., *Shifting the Debate: Public/Private Sector Relations in the Modern Welfare State* (New Brunswick, N.J.: Transaction Books, 1987), 29–49.

180. See Wood, Struthers and Company, *The Trusteeship of Charitable Endowments* (New York: Macmillan Co., 1932), 6; F. Emerson Andrews, *Philanthropic Giving* (New York: Russell Sage Foundation, 1950), 70; John Copeland, "Financial Data from Form 990 Returns for Exempt Charitable, Religious, and Educational Organizations and Private Foundations," in *Research Papers Sponsored by the Commission on Private Philanthropy and Public Needs*, 143–55. The most up-to-date survey of long-term foundation formation trends is Odendahl et al., *America's Wealthy and the Future of Foundations*.

181. See Teresa Odendahl, *Charity Begins at Home: Generosity and Self-Interest among the Philanthropic Elite* (New York: Basic Books, 1990).

182. On the origins of the Ford Foundation, see Dwight MacDonald, *The Ford Foundation: The Men and the Millions* (New York: Reynal & Co., 1955). For an excellent historical overview of the creation of major foundations in this period, see Waldemar Neilsen, *The Big Foundations* (New York: Columbia University Press, 1972).

183. The obvious tax-avoiding purposes of the Ford Foundation was only one of many abuses of the tax system in the name of philanthropy during the postwar years. This aura of self–servingness, combined with the aggressively liberal mandate of some foundations, helped to focus public and congressional attention on tax-exempt organizations in the early 1950s. Of course, not all foundations were liberal. Donal L. Bartlett and James B. Steele's *Empire: The Life, Legend, and Madness of Howard Hughes* (New York: W. W. Norton & Co., 1979) provides fascinating insights into the abuse of nonprofit entities by a leading right-winger.

184. Because of the sensitivity of the topic, there has been no thorough or disinterested study of the use of foundations and other tax-exempt organizations as instruments of public policy during this period. The Reece Committee's report, despite its anti-Communist fervor, contains much useful information on this; see U.S. House of Representatives, 83rd Congress, 2nd Session, *Hearings before the Special (Reece) Committee to Investigate Tax Exempt Foundations and Comparable Organizations* (Washington, D.C.: Government Printing Office, 1954). Mark L. Chadwin's *The Warhawks: American Interventionists before Pearl Harbor* (New York: W. W. Norton & Co., 1965) contains much suggestive material on this point, as does Walter Isaacson and Evan Thomas' important *The Wise Men: Six Friends and the World They Made* (New York: Simon & Schuster, 1986).

185. The studies of this power elite by C. Wright Mills and G. William Domhoff are well known. Less so are those by Philip Burch, published as a three-volume study, *Elites in American Society* (New York: Holmes & Meier, Publishers, 1981). For Burch's appraisal of the establishment, see 69–167.

186. Numerous first-rate studies of the impact of postwar federal policies on the health-care industry have recently appeared. These include Rosemary Stevens's *In Sickness and in Wealth: American Hospitals in the Twentieth Century* (New York: Basic Books, 1989); Daniel M. Fox's *Health Policies, Health Politics: The British and American Experience* (Princeton: Princeton University Press, 1986); and Paul Starr's *The Social Transformation of American Medicine* (New York: Basic Books, 1982). A superb case study of the impact of changing federal policies on a particular institution is Lawrence J. Friedman's *Menninger: The Family and the Clinic* (New York: Alfred A. Knopf, 1990).

187. These critical volumes include Harold Laski, *The Dangers of Obedience and Other Essays* (New York: Harper & Brothers, 1930); Eduard Lindemann, *Wealth and Culture: A Study of One Hundred Foundations and Community Trusts and Their Operations during the Decade 1921–1930* (New York: Harcourt Brace & Co., 1936); Ferdinand Lundberg, *America's Sixty Families* (New York:

Vanguard Press, 1937); Horace Coon, *Money to Burn: What the Great American Foundations Do with Their Money* (New York: Longmans, Green & Co., 1938); and William H. Allen, *Rockefeller: Giant, Dwarf, Symbol* (New York: Institute for Public Service, 1930). Allen is one of the least-known and most interesting critics of foundation philanthropy. His *Modern Philanthropy: A Study of Efficient Appealing and Giving* (New York: Dodd, Mead & Co., 1912) is a pioneering analysis of philanthropic practices. On Allen, see Peter Dobkin Hall and George A. Marcus, "The Empty Tomb: The Social Construction of Dynastic Identity," in Hall and Marcus, *The Empty Tomb and Other Essays on American Dynasties* (Boulder, Colo.: Westview Press, forthcoming).

188. Quoted in Coon, *Money to Burn*, 334–35. See also Frederick Keppel's *The Foundation: Its Place in American Life* (New York: Macmillan Co., 1930).

189. Stephen Becker, *Marshall Field III: A Biography* (New York: Simon & Schuster, 1964), 241–48.

190. On the general background of McCarthyites and their ties to isolationism and populism, see Michael Paul Rogin, *The Intellectuals and McCarthy: The Radical Specter* (Cambridge: MIT Press, 1969). For a detailed account of the motives of the Cox Committee and its members, see Helen Hill Miller, "Investigating the Foundations," *Reporter* 9 (November 24, 1953): 37–40.

191. H. Res. 561, 82nd Congress, 2nd Session, "Resolution," in *Hearings before the Select Committee to Investigate Tax-Exempt Foundations and Comparable Organizations*, 1.

192. F. Emerson Andrews, *Foundation Watcher* (Lancaster, Pa.: Franklin & Marshall College, 1973), 133–37. This little-known volume, which the Foundation Center has blessedly kept in print, is essential reading for anyone seriously interested in the evolution of philanthropy's self-awareness between 1940 and 1969.

193. *Hearings before the Select Committee*, 259, 262.

194. Select Committee to Investigate Foundations, 82nd Congress, 2nd Session, House Report No. 2514, *Final Report* (Washington, D.C.: Government Printing Office, 1953).

195. This is a summary of the "Introductory Material" in Special Committee to Investigate Foundations and Comparable Organizations (Reece Committee), 83rd Congress, 2nd Session, House Report No. 2681, *Tax-Exempt Foundations—Report* (Washington, D.C.: Government Printing Office, 1954), 1–14.

196. Andrews gives a detailed account of these responses in *Foundation Watcher*. They included the convening of the Princeton Conference in December 1955. This two-day meeting, underwritten by the Ford Foundation, brought together a group of leading scholars, led by historian Merle Curti, to define a strategy for studying—and thereby creating a place for—philanthropy in the historical and social-science literature. This meeting not only marked the beginning of nonprofits scholarship but also set the paradigm of grants-driven research which has characterized the field ever since. Working with Ford money, Curti and a number of his colleagues and students (including Irvin Wyllie, Daniel M. Fox, Howard Miller, David Allmendinger, and Paul

Mattingly) produced valuable and important studies. But typically, when the money ran out, interest waned. On this important meeting, see *Report of the Princeton Conference on the History of Philanthropy* (New York: Russell Sage Foundation, 1956).

197. Andrews, *Foundation Watcher*, 175-94. See also Foundation Library Center, *Annual Reports*, 1956-, and *Foundation News—Bulletin of the Foundation Library Center* 1, no. 1 (September 1960): 1-3.

198. U.S. Senate, "Limitation on Deduction in Case of Contributions by Individuals for Benefit of Churches, Educational Organizations, and Hospitals—Report Together with Minority and Supplemental Views," 87th Congress, 1st Session, Report No. 585 (July 20, 1961), 7-8.

The Rockefeller Archives contain important material on philanthropy lobbying efforts in connection with this bill: see memorandum from F. Roberts Blair to Laurence S. Rockefeller, "Recent Proposed Federal Legislation on Unlimited Deduction for Charitable Contributions," October 1, 1959, Rockefeller Archives Center (Family, RG3, JDR3rd, Box 24, "Taxes—Unlimited Deduction"); F. Roberts Blair to John D. Rockefeller 3rd, "Federal Income Tax—Qualification for Unlimited Deduction for Charitable Contributions," October 8, 1959, in ibid.; Weston Vernon to John D. Rockefeller 3rd, "Re: Unlimited Charitable Deduction," February 24, 1961, in ibid.; F. Roberts Blair to John D. Rockefeller 3rd and Laurence S. Rockefeller,, "Unlimited Deduction Averaging Proposal," April 21, 1961, in ibid.; Weston Vernon to John D. Rockefeller 3rd, June 5, 1961, in ibid.; F. Roberts Blair to John D. Rockefeller 3rd, "Charitable Contributions H.R. 2244," in ibid. In the latter, Blair described the minority report as "interesting reading" and called attention to "the hostility that exists in the Committee to tax-exempt foundations and to measures which encourage contributions to charities."

Responses to H.R. 2244 are interesting for two reasons. First, because they mark the beginning of John D. Rockefeller 3rd's active efforts to shape public policy regarding philanthropy—they, in effect, planted the seed of the Filer Commission. Second, because the usually acute F. Emerson Andrews completely missed the significance of the bill and the minority report. Because Andrews has been relied on as the sole interpreter of events of this period, subsequent commentators have pointed to Patman as the chief instigator of the attack on the foundations and have used this as a pretext for avoiding the real issues of foundation abuses.

199. On Patman, see Robert Sherill, " 'The Last of the Great Populists' Takes on the Foundations, the Banks, the Federal Reserve, the Treasury," *New York Times Magazine*, March 16, 1969.

200. *Congressional Record—House*, 87th Congress, 1st Session, 107:73 (May 2, 1961), 6560.

201. "The Power and Influence of Large Foundations," in ibid. (May 3, 1961), 6780-81; and "Foundations Fail to Give Adequate Financial Reports," in ibid. (May 8, 1961), 7053-63. See also "IRS Needs Sharper Tools," in ibid. (August 7, 1961): 13751-56. For initial responses to these charges by the philanthropic community, see Andrews, *Foundation Watcher*, and *Patman and the*

Foundations: Review and Assessment (New York: Foundation Center, 1968). See also *Foundation News* 2, no. 4 (July 1961): 1–4; 2, no. 6 (November 1961): 3–4; and 3, no. 6 (November 1962): 3–5.

202. *Congressional Record,* August 7, 1961, 13751–56.

203. Patman's reports included *Tax-Exempt Foundations and Charitable Trusts: Their Impact on Our Economy,* Chairman's Report to the Select Committee on Small Business, House of Representatives, 87th Congress, December 31, 1962 (Washington, D.C.: Government Printing Office, 1962); *Tax-Exempt Foundations and Charitable Trusts: Their Impact on Our Economy,* Second Installment, Subcommittee Chairman's Report to Subcommittee No. 1, Select Committee on Small Business, House of Representatives, 88th Congress, October 16, 1963 (Washington, D.C.: Government Printing Office, 1963); ibid., Third Installment, March 20, 1964; *Tax-Exempt Foundations: Their Impact on Small Business,* Hearings Before Subcommittee No. 1 on Foundations, Select Committee on Small Business, 88th Congress, 2nd Session (Washington, D.C.: Government Printing Office, 1964); *Tax-Exempt Foundations and Charitable Trusts: Their Impact on Our Economy,* Fourth Installment, December 21, 1966; *Tax-Exempt Foundations and Charitable Trusts: Their Impact on Our Economy,* Fifth Installment, April 28, 1967; *Tax-Exempt Foundations: Their Impact on Small Business,* Hearings Before Subcommittee No. 1 of the Select Committee on Small Business, House of Representatives, 90th Congress, 1st Session (1967); *Tax-Exempt Foundations and Charitable Trusts: Their Impact on Our Economy,* Sixth Installment, March 26, 1968.

204. Ferdinand Lundberg, *The Rich and the Super-Rich: A Study in the Power of Money Today* (New York: Lyle Stuart, 1968). In this volume, Lundberg devoted over seventy pages to discussing Patman's findings. For an interesting precis of other books and articles produced in response to Patman's efforts, see "Spotlight on Foundations," *Foundation News* 6, no. 2 (March 1965): 25.

205. Chief among these officials was Stanley Surrey, lawyer, tax expert, and Harvard professor, who served as assistant secretary of treasury for tax policy from 1961 to 1969.

206. *Treasury Department Report on Private Foundations,* Printed for Use of the House Committee on Ways and Means, February 2, 1965. See also *Written Statements by Interested Individuals and Organizations on Treasury Department Report on Private Foundations Issued on February 2, 1965,* Submitted to Committee on Ways and Means, 89th Congress, 1st Session (Washington, D.C.: Government Printing Office), vols. 1 and 2, 493–771. For organized philanthropy's response, see "Treasury Report," *Foundation News* 6, no. 2 (March 1965): 29; and John Holt Myers, "Foundations and Tax Legislation," *Foundation News* 6, no. 3 (May 1965): 51–54.

Once again, the Rockefeller Archives contain invaluably detailed material on philanthropy's responses to Treasury Department proposals. See John E. Lockwood and Dana Creel to Laurence S. Rockefeller, "Treasury Department Proposals Relative to Taxation of Foundations," June 30, 1965 (Family, RG3, JDR3, Box 367, "Philanthropy: T–Z"); G. Raymond Empson to John D.

Rockefeller 3rd, "Briefing for Meetings with Russell Billiu Long and Wilbur Daigh Mills on June 17, 1965" (Family, RG3, JDR3, Box 370, "Philanthropy—JDR3rd"). The latter document is especially important because it traces the history of pending legislation affecting charitable giving and provides the stances that Long, Mills, and other key congressional figures took on similar proposals.

The Empson memorandum also alludes to the little-known fact that in 1963 President Kennedy had proposed the abolition of the unlimited charitable deduction—but had been prevented from doing so by Congress. This initiative suggests that the 1965 Treasury Department report was more than a reluctant response to Patman—Andrews describes the department was being "under the Patman lash." It was, rather a presidential initiative, as suggested by the appointment of Stanley Surrey, an avid advocate of tax reform, as the man in charge of tax policy in the Treasury Department. All this sheds interesting light on Kennedy's ambivalent relationship to the Establishment!

207. Quoted in Andrews, *Foundation Watcher*, 253.

208. Raymond A. LaMontagne to John D. Rockefeller 3rd, "A Possible National Association of Foundations," September 21, 1964 (Family, RG3, JDR3, Box 370, "Philanthropy—JDR3rd"). See also Donna McKinnon (Ford Foundation) to Donald McLean, untitled memorandum regarding John D. Rockefeller 3rd's proposal for "a closer association of foundations," October 23rd, 1964 (Family, RG3, JDR3, Box 368, "Association of Foundations"); Chauncey Belknap (family legal adviser) to John D. Rockefeller 3rd, November 2, 1964, legal opinion concerning the pros and cons of an association of foundations; Raymond A. LaMontagne to John W. Gardner (Carnegie Corporation), November 20, 1964, summarizing views "on the subject of 'a trade association of the foundation industry' "; Paul Ylvisaker (Ford Foundation) to Donald McLean (Rockefeller family associate), December 2, 1964, on the usefulness of the association in influencing the actions of new foundations, especially in the Southwest; Leonard Silverstein (Washington, D.C., lawyer specializing in charities and tax law) to Joseph D. Hughes (Mellon family office), December 14, 1964, on the advantages of an association, to which is appended a legal opinion entitled "the legality of an association of tax-exempt foundations with a purpose among others of opposing legislation detrimental to the interest of foundations."

209. Raymond A. LaMontagne, one of John D. Rockefeller 3rd's associates, had been asked, to sketch out ideas on philanthropy which would address both Rockefeller's growing concerns about congressional attacks on philanthropy and the failure of philanthropy to acknowledge its place in a changing political and economic system. Rockefeller had been asked to write an article for *Harper's* and to give a speech to the Cleveland Welfare Federation—both of which presented unusual opportunities to voice his ideas. The phrases in the text are from LaMontagne's September 21 memorandum, 8. On the *Harper's* article, see memoranda and drafts in Family, RG3, JDR3, Box 367, "Philanthropy: G–H". Especially notable in this body of material is a memoranda from associate John W. McNulty to John D. Rockefeller 3rd (September 10,

1965), in which he McNulty advises Rockefeller not to write the article because the Patman Committee had been inactive lately.

210. Andrews, *Foundation Watcher.*

211. Quoted in "Ways and Means Hearings on Foundations," *Foundation News* 10, no. 3 (May 1969): 1. See also Andrews, *Foundation Watcher,* 252–55.

212. The testimony of foundation leaders and other friendly witnesses are in *Foundations and the Tax Bill: Testimony on Title I of the Tax Reform Act of 1969 Submitted by Witnesses Appearing before the United States Senate Finance Committee, October 1969* (New York: Foundation Center, 1969); and House of Representatives, 91st Congress, Part 1, *Hearings before the Committee on Ways and Means* (February 18, 19, 20, 1969) (Washington, D.C.: Government Printing Office, 1969). The published testimony of the hearings, because its is edited and seldom reveals the jockeying behind the various positions taken by witnesses, only provides a partial documentation of the tension and turmoil in the world of philanthropy during this period.

Three sources are especially useful in reconstructing the events of 1969 and interpreting their meaning. First, *Foundation News,* which had come under the control of the Council on Foundations, presented a number of important pieces on the 1969 Tax Reform Act hearings and the foundations' strategizing. These include "Ways and Means Hearings on the Foundations," 10, no. 3 (May–June 1969): 93–96; "House Ways and Means Report," 10, no. 4 (July–August 1969): 139; "A Program of Self-Regulation by Philanthropic Foundations," 10, no. 6 (November–December 1969): 213–15; "National Leaders Support Foundations," 10, no. 6 (November–December 1969): 217–21; and Robert D. Calkins, "The Role of the Philanthropic Foundation," 11, no. 1 (January–February 1970): 1–13.

Second, *Nonprofit Report* (now the *Philanthropy Monthly*), an independent newsletter focusing on public-policy issues affecting philanthropy, provided insightful, if opinionated, coverage of the hearings. Especially useful articles include: "Foundation Associations and Tax Reform," "Treasury Testimony on Tax Reform," and "Report—Interview: Background on the Treasury Proposals," 2, no. 5 (May 1969); "Foundations Urged to be United in Own Defense," "The Private Sector Is in Trouble—Dana Creel," and "Mills Announces Proposed Tax Reforms," 2, no. 6 (June 1969); "Pifer Finds Mills Proposals 'Shocking,' " 2, no. 7 (July 1969); "House Responds to 'Taxpayers Revolt,' " and "The Tax Reform Act of 1969," 2, no. 8 (August 1969); "Senate Hearings on Tax Reform," "Kennedy and Cohen Testify for Nixon Administration," "Javits Critical of Foundation-Related Reforms," and "Open Letter to Senator Russell B. Long," 2, no. 9 (September 1969); "Senate Finance Committee and Tax Reform" and "Mr. Bundy Isn't Overly Concerned," 2, no. 11 (November 1969); "The Christmas Tree Act of 1969" and "Senator Kennedy Lists the 'Secret Provisions' of the Tax Reform Bill," 2, no. 12 (December 1969).

Finally, the files of John D. Rockefeller 3rd and his associates and the working files of the Council on Foundations, both of which are in the Rockefeller Archive Center, not only abundantly document the internal debate within the world of philanthropy about how to best respond to Congress, but also contain unedited stenographic transcriptions of much of the congressional testimony. In addition, both collections contain extensive clipping files of coverage of the hearings by national and local newspapers and periodicals.

213. Clarification of the meaning of the 1969 Tax Reform Act was carried out through an intricate and protracted set of negotiations between congressional staffers, led by Lawrence Woodworth, Treasury Department officials, representatives from the Council on Foundations, and tax lawyers in private practice—such as former IRS Assistant Commissioner Norman Sugerman and Washington, D.C., lawyer and lobbyist Leonard Silverstein—who operated in the Treasury Department–foundation industry network. See memoranda and correspondence in the Council on Foundations files at the Rockefeller Archives Center, Filer, Box 4. Also useful are the 1970 and 1971 articles in *Foundation News* and *Non-Profit Report* which seek to interpret the act's technical provisions.

214. Efforts to gauge the impact of the 1969 Tax Reform Act became a minor industry in the 1970s. A definitive study, the Project on Foundation Formation and Termination, was conducted in the mid-1980s by Yale's Program on Non-Profit Organizations, under the direction of Teresa Odendahl. Its findings appeared as Odendahl et al., *America's Wealthy and the Future of Foundations*. By the late 1980s, most philanthropic leaders conceded that the 1969 Tax Reform Act had done more good than harm.

Although is was ultimately possible to concede that the 1969 Tax Reform Act did not mark the beginning of the end for private philanthropy, the congressional hearings of 1969 left a deep scar on the consciousness of a whole generation of nonprofits executives. Most seriously, the trauma of the hearing impaired their capacity to tolerate either candid self-evaluation or criticism. This fearfulness had a major impact on the development of industry-funded research on nonprofits. See Barry D. Karl, "Nonprofit Institutions," *Science* 234 (May 22, 1987): 984-85; and Anne Lowry Bailey, "Philanthropy Research's Built-In Conflict," *Chronicle of Higher Education* 35 (September 21, 1988): A36. For a typical example of the way those traumatized by the events of 1969 respond to critical research, see Richard Lyman, "Looking Forward to the Year 2000: Public Policy and Philanthropy" (Keynote address delivered at the Independent Sector Spring Research Forum, San Francisco, March 1988). In the original text of this speech, Lyman, president of the Rockefeller Foundation, warned scholars against doing work that might "stimulate outbursts of regulatory enthusiasm" and singled out two researchers—Teresa Odendahl and Robert Bothwell—for censure. The text of this speech, along with extensive correspondence with Lyman about the appropriateness of his remarks, is in the author's collection.

215. On John D. Rockefeller 3rd's controversial testimony at the 1969 Tax Reform Act hearings, see "Mr. R3 re Statement, Tax Reform Bill," unrevised stenographic minutes of testimony to the House Ways and Means Committee, February 27, 1969 (Family, RG3, JDR3, Box 37, "Tax Reform Bill/State-

ments"). See also Box 371, "Tax Reform Bill—Clippings," for responses to John D. Rockefeller 3rd's remarks.

216. John D. Rockefeller 3rd had been thinking along these lines as early as the mid-1960s—see "Thoughts on Philanthropy" (Family, RG3, JDR3, Box 370, "Philanthropy—JDR3rd/Book"). His ideas along these lines were much stimulated by Alan Pifer's May 1968 speech "The Foundation in the Year 2000," in ibid. Pifer helped Rockefeller understand the fluidity of circumstances and the necessity for philanthropy to be able to respond to extraordinary change with flexibility—a view very much in contrast to the rigidity and defensiveness of most "philanthropoids" and wealthy donors in this period. John D. Rockefeller 3rd acknowledged his intellectual debt to Pifer by appointing him to the Filer Commission. He was the only foundation executive so honored.

217. See Henry C. Suhrke, "Foundation Replies: "Dear Mr. Patman," *Non-Profit Report* 5, no. 9 (September 1972).

218. "Peril in Treasury's Tax Proposals," *Non-Profit Report* 6, no. 5 (May 1973).

219. Henry C. Suhrke, "Foundations on the Senate Griddle," *Non-Profit Report* 6, no. 10 (October 1973): 1, 4–7.

220. Ibid., 7.

221. The Peterson Commission's final report appeared in published as Commission on Foundations and Private Philanthropy, *Foundations, Private Giving, and Public Policy* (Chicago: University of Chicago Press, 1970). On the commission's activities, see "The Role of Foundations in Society: Two Studies," *Non-Profit Report* 2, no. 5 (May 1969): 8–9; and "The Peterson Study: The Role of Foundations in the U.S.," *Non-Profit Report* 2, no. 8 (August 1969): 13. See also Andrews, *Foundation Watcher*, 255–56. The papers of John D. Rockefeller 3rd and his associate Datus Smith contain extensive material on the establishment and activities of the commission.

222. John D. Rockefeller 3rd to Wilbur Mills, November 1, 1972 (Family, RG3, JDR3rd, Box 369, "Committee on Tax Incentives"); Wilbur Mills to John D. Rockefeller 3rd, November 8, 1972, in ibid., and Datus C. Smith to Mills, November 13, 1972, in ibid.

223. Memorandum from Datus C. Smith, Jr., to John D. Rockefeller 3rd, "Committee on Tax Incentives," December 7, 1972, in ibid. This memorandum summarizes the group's thinking about the committee's purposes, composition, program, and budget. Evidently, the effort was originally conceived as a modest effort—budgeted at only $80,000. By the time it completed its work in 1978, the committee—better known as the Filer Commission—raised and spent over $2 million! The original list of members was compiled by John D. Rockefeller 3rd's staff and congressional staffer Lawrence Woodward. On Woodward's involvement, see Datus Smith to Laurence N. Woodward, chief of staff, Joint Committee on Internal Revenue Taxation, November 13, 1972 (Family, RG3, JDR3rd, Box 369, "Commission on Philanthropy"). Interestingly, of the twenty-five proposed members, not one was a foundation executive.

224. Henry C. Suhrke, "Watergate Foundation Testimony," *Non-Profit Report* 6, no. 10 (October 1973): 34. In this issue, which also included coverage of the Hartke hearings, Suhrke speculated that Hartke, who was otherwise densely ignorant about philanthropy, was simply trying to cash in on public interest in Watergate.

225. I am grateful to Hayden W. Smith for his account of the origins of the 501(c)(3) Group, of which he was a member from the early 1970s until its disbanding in 1987. According to Smith, the founders included Charles Sampson of the United Way, Jack Schwartz of the American Association of Fundraising Counsel, John Leslie of the American College Public Relations Association, and tax lawyers Connie Tytell and Stan Whitehorn. Hayden Smith was interviewed by the author on December 13, 1989.

226. This literature included William D. Andrews, "Personal Deductions in an Ideal Income Tax," *Harvard Law Review* 86, no. 2 (1972): 309–85; Boris I. Bittker, "The Propriety and Vitality of a Federal Income Tax Deduction for Private Philanthropy," in *Tax Impacts on Philanthropy* (Princeton: Tax Institute of America, 1972); R. Goode, *The Individual Income Tax* (Washington, D.C.: Brookings Institution, 1964); Harry C. Kahn, *Personal Deductions in the Federal Income Tax* (Princeton: Princeton University Press, 1960); Paul R. McDaniel, "An Alternative to the Federal Income Tax Deduction in Support of Private Philanthropy," in *Tax Impacts on Philanthropy*, 171–209; Paul R. McDaniel, "Federal Matching Grants for Charitable Contributions: A Substitute for the Income Tax Deduction," *Tax Law Review* 27, no. 3 (Spring 1972): 377–413; Joseph A. Pechman, *Federal Tax Policy* (New York: W. W. Norton & Co., 1971); David Rabin, "Charitable Trusts and Charitable Deductions," *New York University Law Review* 41 (1966): 912–25; Henry C. Simons, *Personal Income Taxation* (Chicago: University of Chicago Press, 1938); Stanley S. Surrey et al., *Federal Income Taxation* (Mineola, N.Y.: Foundation Press, 1972); William S. Vickrey, "Private Philanthropy and Public Finance," unpublished paper, 1973; William S. Vickrey, "One Economist's View of Philanthropy," in Frank Dickinson, ed., *Philanthropy and Public Policy* (New York: National Bureau of Economic Research, 1962), 31–56; Murray Weidenbaum, "A Modest Proposal for Tax Reform," *Wall Street Journal*, April 4, 1973, 18; Melvin White, "Proper Income Tax Treatment of Deductions for Personal Expense," in *Tax Revision Compendium*, Compendium of Papers on Broadening the Tax Base submitted to the Committee on Ways and Means, House of Representatives, U.S. Congress (Washington, D.C.: Government Printing Office, 1959), 1:370–71; and Department of the Treasury, *Tax Reform Studies and Proposals*, U.S. Congress, House Ways and Means Committee and Senate Finance Committee, 91st Congress, 1st Session, 1969.

A number of these authors had a standing in both the academic and public-policy domains, most notably Stanley S. Surrey, who was both a professor at Harvard Law School and, between 1961 and 1969, assistant secretary of treasury for Tax Policy.

227. Hayden W. Smith, interview with author, 13 March 1990.

228. Feldstein formally presented his proposal to Hayden W. Smith, chair

of the 501(c)(3) Group, in a letter of January 22, 1973 (Family, RG3, JDR3rd, Box 371, "Tax Reform Act of 1969").

229. On the group's ambivalence, see Lindsley F. Kimball's letter of March 9, 1973, to John E. Lockwood of the Rockefeller Family Office, in ibid. Kimball notes that Feldstein "has developed an argument with his sponsors. He very naturally as a scholar want to produce his own book, subject to no restrictions. The congeries of social agencies want him to agree to suppress his book if they don't like it. For my money this would destroy both its objectivity and its persuasive credibility. I am trying to work out a reasonable compromise without getting my fingers burnt through over-involvement."

230. See Lindsley F. Kimball's memorandum of February 14, 1973, to J. R. Dilworth (head of the Rockefeller Office) and memoranda of April 22, 1974, to Dilworth, John E. Lockwood (Rockefeller legal adviser), Dana Creel and Robert Scrivner, and Donal O'Brien. These describe and recap the circumstances under which the study was sponsored and detail the Rockefeller's "invisible support" of Feldstein's work. Kimball's letter of March 13, 1973, to James A. Norton of the Cleveland Foundation provides further details on financing arrangements and the anticipated impact of the study. Correspondence between David Freeman of the Council on Foundations and Lindsley F. Kimball (December 13, 1973), between Richard Salamon of the Rockefeller family office and David Freeman (December 27, 1973 and January 24, 1974), David Freeman and Laurence S. Rockefeller (January 15, 1974).

Of this body of material, the most important is Lindsley F. Kimball's February 7, 1973, memorandum to Rockefeller legal adviser Donal O'Brien, which describes the search for a suitable economist and plans for secretly funding an econometric study. As Kimball noted in discussing the 501(c)(3) Group, "they have fire in the boilers, but not much leadership. . . . If we were to put up the balance anonymously [of the $25,000 needed for the study] we would have a good handle in directing the course of the enterprise." Looking ahead to what would become the Filer Commission, he noted that "we could perfectly well use the Harvard study as background material for setting up a conference which would be pushed by all of the charitable receivers, and I think might be very influential indeed."

231. "Outstanding Service Awards," *Philanthropy Monthly* 7, no. 12 (December 1974): 4.

232. Memorandum from William Howard Beasley III to Mr. [William] Simon, "Advisory Group on Private Philanthropy," May 11, 1973 (Family, RG3, JDR3rd Confidential Files, Box 14, "Commission on Philanthropy").

233. Memorandum from Porter McKeever to Howard Bolton and Leonard Silverstein, "Subject: John Filer," July 16, 1973 (Family, RG3, JDR3rd Confidential Files, Box 14, "Commission on Philanthropy"); and memorandum from Leonard Silverstein to Commission on Private Philanthropy Advisory Committee, untitled (to apprise the Advisory Committee of developments since its August 13 meeting), August 1973, in ibid. This important summary of the Filer Commission's preliminary discussions specifically details the range of its informational needs and policy concerns. Porter McKeever, author

of the first memorandum, had replaced Datus Smith as John D. Rockefeller 3rd's point man on the philanthropy front. McKeever would be a key background figure in activities of the Filer Commission and in institutionalizing its legacy with the formation of Independent Sector.

The papers of the Filer Commission, donated by executive director Leonard Silverstein to Independent Sector, are not available to researchers. However, the papers of John D. Rockefeller 3rd and his associates and the working files of the Council on Foundations—all of which are at the Rockefeller Archive Center—cover the ground fairly well.

234. "Citizens Committee on Private Philanthropy to Begin Study," press release, November 5, 1973 (Family, RG3, JDR3rd, Confidential Files, Box 14, "Commission on Philanthropy").

235. Memorandum from Robert Goheen to Eugene Struckhoff, untitled, in Council on Foundations files, Box 3, "Agency File, 8/73–4/74." Because it had been left out of the planning process, the council's publication, *Foundation News*, virtually ignored the commission's existence, mentioning it only twice in 1974. By contrast, see its treatment in *Non-Profit Report*, beginning in November 1973.

236. See interview with William C. Archie in *Non-Profit Report* 4, no. 2 (February 1971): 1–2; and "Gardner Report," *Non-Profit Report* 3, no. 6 (June 1970). These pieces refer to a Temporary Committee on Foundation Standards, originally organized by individuals who hoped to devise a scheme of foundation self-regulation along the lines proposed by F. Emerson Andrews and his successor, Manning Pattillo. The committee was reorganized by Gardner, who disposed of its most critical members and scrapped the self-policing plan. Instead, its revised report proposed "increased research, analysis, and publication about foundations," the initiation of special efforts "to develop greater public understanding of Foundations on the part of the general public and key leaders of opinion," development of voluntary standards of good practice, the provision of "a central clearinghouse and forum to facilitate an exchange of information, cooperation, and counseling on mutual problems," and the establishment of continuing arrangements for governmental relations. It was, in short, to be a broadly based lobbying–public relations effort organized along trade-association lines— and it would, the committee hoped—be carried out by a " 'broad membership organization,' to be called the American Council of Foundations," which would be created by a merger of the Foundation Center and the Council on Foundations.

237. Sources on the elements of this faction are scattered. *Non-Profit Report* for 1969–71 contains a number of important references to its activities, especially on Manning Pattillo—who the Gardner group would displace from the Foundation Center in 1971—and on Merrimon Cuninggim, then head of the Danforth Foundation.

The papers of John D. Rockefeller 3rd and his associates abundantly document their dislike for many top foundation leaders and, especially, their distrust of Gardner, with whom they maintained superficially cordial relations. A key document on the interrelationship of the anti-Gardner group is

Datus Smith's letter to Peter G. Peterson, August 2, 1972 (Family, RG3, JDR3rd, Box 369, "Commission on Philanthropy"), in which he comments on Cunningim's book *Private Money and Public Service* and its discussion of the Peterson Commission's responsibility for the pay-out provision in the 1969 Tax Reform Act. ("How True!" wrote Smith, "and 'Bully for Peterson!' ") See also Datus Smith to Peter G. Peterson, November 18, 1971, in which he discusses the involvement of David Freeman and Al Neal—both members of the 501(c)(3) Group—and the American Association of Fundraising Counsel (whose president, Jack Schwartz was a charter member of the group) in preliminary efforts to organize the Filer Commission.

There is no single collection of 501(c)(3) Group papers, though many appear in the John D. Rockefeller 3rd, Datus Smith, and Porter McKeever files at the Rockefeller Archive Center. I am especially grateful to Hayden W. Smith, a member of the group and former research director of the Council for Aid to Education, for sharing his recollections and his files on its activities.

The best expression of the views of this group are Waldemar A. Nielsen's *The Big Foundations* (New York: Columbia University Press, 1972); and Cunningim's *Private Money and Public Service: The Role of Foundations in American Society* (New York: McGraw-Hill Book Co., 1972). Many regard Nielsen as an irresponsible critic, and it is generally unknown that his study was undertaken with the full encouragement and support of John D. Rockefeller 3rd. See Waldemar A. Nielsen to Earl Newsom, September 16, 1963, and Earl Newsom to John D. Rockefeller 3rd, September 20, 1963, regarding Neilsen's plans for an ambitious and wide-ranging study of foundations (Family, RG3, JDR3rd, Box 370, "Philanthropy—JDR3rd"). Neilsen would remain associated with John D. Rockefeller 3rd as a consultant until the latter's death in 1978 and would be part of the group—including McKeever, Elizabeth McCormack, and Walter McNerney (president of Blue Cross)—that conducted the negotiations that led to the establishment of Independent Sector.

238. For unusually candid and revealing discussions of these political jockeyings, see "Foundation Leadership in the Seventies—A Conversation with David Freeman," *Non-Profit Report* 4, no. 9 (September 1971): 13-16; and Richard Fitzgerald, "Foundation Standards and Accrediting," *Non-Profit Report* 5, no. 1 (January 1972): 1-14. Freeman was a top official in the Council on Foundations and a member of the 501(c)(3) Group. He was also virtually a secret operative of the "antiphilanthropoids" in the Rockefeller family office. His description of the unsuccessful efforts of the Gardner group to force a merger of the Council on Foundations and the Foundation Center in the wake of the 1969 Tax Reform Act is priceless.

239. The first volume was Report of the Commission on Private Philanthropy and Public Needs, *Giving in America: Toward a Stronger Voluntary Sector* (Washington, D.C.: Commission on Private Philanthropy & Public Needs, 1975). The six volumes of research papers were published as *Research Papers Sponsored by the Commission on Private Philanthropy and Public Needs* (Washington, D.C., Department of the Treasury, 1977).

240. Department of the Treasury, "Treasury Secretary Blumenthal Cuts Ad-

visory Committees," press release, March 15, 1977; Advisory Committee on Private Philanthropy and Public Needs, "Minutes—April 7, 1977 Meeting"; John D. Rockefeller 3rd to Michael Blumenthal, April 7, 1977; Leonard Silverstein to Porter McKeever, April 18, 1977; memorandum from Leonard Silverstein to Commission Members [this untitled memorandum summarizes the status of the Treasury Committee on Private Philanthropy and Public Needs], April 18, 1977; Michael Blumenthal to Leonard Silverstein, April 27, 1977; memorandum from John D. Rockefeller 3rd to Porter McKeever, "Re: Conversation with Walter McNerney," June 22, 1977—all in Porter McKeever Papers, RG 17, McKeever, Box 1, "Filer Commission." See also "PM Newsletter," *Philanthropy Monthly* 10, no. 3 (March 1977): 4.

241. See "Comments and Dissents," in Report of the Commission on Private Philanthropy and Public Needs, *Giving in America*, 197-222; and "Private Philanthropy: Vital and Innovative or Passive and Irrelevant—The Donee Group Report and Recommendations," in Commission on Private Philanthropy and Public Needs, *Research Papers Sponsored by the Commission on Private Philanthropy and Public Needs*, 49-88. I am grateful to Pablo Eisenberg, Gabriel Rudney, and David Horton Smith for sharing their recollections of debate within the commission over its recommendations.

242. For an excellent overview of these groups, see "Organizing Charity," *Philanthropy Monthly* 9, no. 11 (November 1976): 7-11. Documentation of their efforts includes W. Homer Turner, "Resolving the Permanent National Commission Proposal of the Filer Commission" (Paper prepared for the members of the National Council on Philanthropy, February 27, 1976); letter from Pablo Eisenberg to Porter McKeever, April 2, 1976, regarding the Committee for Responsive Philanthropy (an outgrowth of the Filer Commission's dissenting Donee Group); memorandum from Porter McKeever to John D. Rockefeller 3rd, "Meeting with Messrs. Haley of Monsanto and Aramony of United Way," June 20, 1977, in which McKeever warns about the dangers of becoming too involved with United Way; letter from Porter McKeever to Landrum Bolling, January 12, 1978, regarding the John D. Rockefeller 3rd Fund's disappointment with the Council on Foundations; letter from Porter McKeever to Leslie Luttgens, May 18, 1978, in which he describes the council as "a narrowly focused trade association infused with eastern elitism"; memorandum from Porter McKeever to John D. Rockefeller 3rd, "Re: Meetings with John Gardner and Walter McNerney in Washington, D.C., May 12 and 16, 1978," regarding the efforts of Walter McNerney, who had taken charge of the Filer Commission's legacy, to negotiate with the various contenders for Third Sector leadership—all in Porter McKeever Papers, RG 17, Box 1. Also important are a letter from Porter McKeever to Frederick J. Davis, June 20, 1978, on McNerney and his role as mediator, and a letter from Porter McKeever to Wayne Thompson, February 16, 1979, on the impending success of the merger between CONVO and NCOP (Family, RG 3, JDR 3rd, Confidential Files, Box 19, "Daily Chron.").

243. Coalition of National Voluntary Organizations and National Council

on Philanthropy, *To Preserve an Independent Sector-Organizing Committee Report* (Washington, D.C., 1979), vi.

244. Ibid., 23.

245. Independent Sector, *Program Plan (as Amended and Approved by the Membership, October 24, 1980)* (Washington, D.C.: Independent Sector, 1980), 37.

246. Ibid., 38. On political tensions within IS during this period, see Henry C. Suhrke, "Independent Sector, Inc.—The 'How' and 'Why' of a Proposed Organization," *Philanthropy Monthly* 12, no. 10 (October 1979): 5–9; and Henry C. Suhrke, "Who Speaks for Philanthropy?" *Philanthropy Monthly* 17, no. 10 (October 1984): 13–17.

247. On the President's Task Force on Private Sector Initiatives (Verity Commission), see *Building Partnerships* (Washington, D.C.: Government Printing Office, 1982); *Corporate Community Involvement* (New York: Citizen's Forum on Self-Government/National Municipal League, 1982); and *Investing in America: Initiatives for Community and Economic Development* (Washington, D.C.: Government Printing Office, 1982). For a conservative critique of the task force, see Marvin Olasky, "Reagan's Second Thoughts on Corporate Giving," *Fortune*, September 20, 1983.

248. Conservatives charged that the Verity Commission was sabotaged by the liberal Knauft; see Marvin Olasky, "Reagan's Second Thoughts on Corporate Giving," *Fortune*, September 20, 1983. I am grateful to Burt Knauft for sharing his recollections of the commission with me.

249. Lester Salamon and Alan Abramson, "The Federal Government and the Nonprofit Sector: Implications of the Reagan Budget Proposals" (Washington, D.C.: Urban Institute, 1981). This research was funded by the 501(c)(3) Group. After Feldstein's 1973 study, it ranks as one of the most important single pieces of research ever done on the nonprofit sector.

250. According to "The Non-Profit World: A Statistical Portrait," *Chronicle of Philanthropy* 2, no. 6 (January 9, 1990): 8, the number of nonreligious nonprofits continued to grow through the 1980s: these 501(c)(3) and (4) organizations numbered 406,000 in 1977, 454,000 in 1982, 483,000 in 1984, and 561,000 in 1987—an increase of nearly 40 percent.

251. The best critical appraisal of these changes is Jon Van Til's *Mapping the Third Sector: Voluntarism in a Changing Social Economy* (New York: Foundation Center, 1988). Also valuable is Virginia A. Hodgkinson et al., eds., *The Future of the Nonprofit Sector* (San Francisco: Jossey-Bass Publishers, 1989).

While encouraged by circumstances, the professionalization of nonprofits management has been strongly encouraged by major nonprofit groups, including the United Way and Independent Sector. The chief spokesman for professional training of nonprofits managers is Dennis R. Young, who heads the Mandel Center for Nonprofit Organizations at Case Western Reserve University. Young's work in this area includes "Executive Leadership in Nonprofit Organizations," in Powell, ed., *The Nonprofit Sector*, 167–79; "Entrepreneurship and the Behavior of Nonprofit Organizations: Elements of a

Theory," in Susan Rose-Ackerman, ed., *The Economics of Nonprofit Institutions: Studies in Structure and Policy* (New York: Oxford University Press, 1986), 161; (with Lilly Cohen), *Careers for Dreamers and Doers: A Guide to Management Careers in the Nonprofit Sector* (New York: Foundation Center, 1989); and (with Michael O'Neill), *Educating Managers of Nonprofit Organizations* (New York: Praeger, 1988). For a valuable, if not somewhat outdated, critical overview of existing literature in this area, see Melissa Middleton, "Nonprofit Management: A Report on Current Research and Areas for Development," Working Paper no. 108 (New Haven: Program on Nonprofit Organizations, Yale University, 1986).

Although management schools and schools of public administration have generally resisted the effort to create degree programs—and even special courses—for nonprofit managers, the movement received significant encouragement recently from management guru Peter Drucker, who has decided that nonprofits represent a new managerial frontier. See Drucker, *The New Realities* (New York: Harper & Row, 1989), and *Managing the Nonprofit Organization: Principles and Practices* (New York: Harper Collins, 1990).

Despite Drucker's endorsement, the question of whether nonprofits administration is sufficiently distinctive to warrant a special place in management curricula remains controversial, especially in view of the rapid disappearance of clear distinctions between nonprofits and for-profits. See James M. Ferris and Elizabeth Graddy, "Fading Distinctions among the Nonprofit, Government, and For-Profit Sectors," in Hodgkinson et al., eds., *The Future of the Nonprofit Sector*, 123–39.

252. On these trends, see Miriam Wood's important "The Governing Board's Existential Quandary," Working Paper no. 150 (New Haven: Program on Non-Profit Organizations, Yale University, 1990); and Peter Dobkin Hall, "Conflicting Managerial Cultures on Nonprofit Boards," *Nonprofit Management and Leadership* 1, no. 2 (Winter 1990): 153–65.

253. On these changing patterns, see Anne Lowry Bailey, "Big Gains in Giving to Charity," *Chronicle of Philanthropy* 3, no. 1 (October 16, 1990), which reports on the publication of Virginia Hodgkinson and Murray Weitzman, *Giving and Volunteering in the United States, 1990* (Washington, D.C.: Independent Sector, 1990). The results of this survey point to major changes in patterns of giving and volunteering in the late 1980s. Especially notable is the downward shift in the age cohorts of givers.

254. United Way originally supported sets of organizations deemed by local leaders to best represent the interests of their communities. On this, see Seeley et al., *Community Chest*. A recently published reprint of this classic study includes an introduction by sociologist Carl Milofsky, which sheds valuable light on the relation between the traditional Community Chest and the modern United Way (New Brunswick, N.J.: Transaction, 1989), vii–xxi.

As communities became more pluralistic—and as previously unempowered constituencies, especially blacks and women, became more insistent in their demands for community services—United Way found it increasingly difficult to serve their needs. Moreover, it found itself facing competition from rival federated charities designed to serve minority interests. In the course of the 1980s, donor designations, which permitted contributors to target particular recipient organizations either positively or negatively, and program support supplanted earlier forms of institutional subvention. See Deborah Kaplan Polivy, "The United Way: Understanding How It Works Is the First Step to Effecting Change," in Carl Milofsky, ed., *Community Organizations: Studies in Resource Mobilization and Exchange* (New York: Oxford University Press, 1988), 157–69. See also Deborah Kaplan Polivy, "A Study of Admissions Policies and Practices of Eight Local United Way Organizations," Working Paper no. 49 (New Haven: Program on Non-Profit Organizations, Yale University, 1982); and Bruce Millar, "United Ways and the Charities They Support Will Face Fast-Paced, Dramatic Changes in the 1990s, Report Says," *Chronicle of Philanthropy* 2, no. 4 (November 28, 1989). I am grateful to Harold Brown, treasurer of United Way of Connecticut, for sharing his insights into the challenge that pluralism is posing for the organization's traditional conception of its role in the community.

255. See Peter Dobkin Hall, "Understanding Nonprofits Trusteeship," *Philanthropy Monthly* 23, no. 3 (March 1990): 10–15; and the proceedings of the "Lilly Endowment Education Conference, December 3–4, 1990," which contains historical background on this midwestern foundation's developing interest in these issues and summaries of more than thirty different leadership/ education projects currently funded by the endowment. Similar efforts are being underwritten by another important midwestern philanthropy, the Kellogg Foundation.

256. See Sidney Blumenthal, *The Rise of the Counter-Establishment: From Conservative Ideology to Political Power* (New York: Harper & Row, 1988). See also Smith, *The Idea Brokers.*

257. The opening shot of this battle was Irving Kristol's 1980 essay "Foundations and the Sin of Pride: The Myth of the 'Third Sector,' " which questioned the idea of the foundations that they could in any way represent the public interest. The battled heated up in 1982, with the appointment of outspoken liberal James Joseph, as president and chief executive officer of the Council on Foundations; see *Foundation News* 23 (January–February 1982): 53. In the same year, Joseph articulated his ideas at Yale Law School in his speech "Justice for All: The New Public Philosophy and the Role of Private Philanthropy," in which he offended conservatives by boldly asserting that private philanthropy had public obligations, particularly in the areas of affirmative action (a copy of the text of this speech is in the author's collection).

In 1980, the Council on Foundations' directors had adopted a statement of "Recommended Principles and Practices for Effective Grantmaking," which urged grant makers to follow a designated set of standards of open decisionmaking, public reporting, and pluralistic leadership. In April 1983, the directors decided that all members of the council should pledge themselves to abide by the statement of principles and practices. This "loyalty oath" set off a storm of protest among conservative foundations, which culminated in a bitter private debate at the council's annual meeting in August 1986. By the fall of that year, a full-scale—but ultimately unsuccessful—effort was underway to establish a conservative alternative to the council. This was organized under the aegis of Kristol's Institute for Educational Affairs.

For a good overview of these events, see "Principles and Practices Prescribed for Foundations," *Philanthropy Monthly* 19, no. 8 (September 1986): 5–14. I am grateful to Philip N. Marcus, then president of the Institute for Educational Affairs, and Leslie Lenkowsky, one of the organization's moving spirits, for sharing with me their thoughts on these events.

258. The best overview of the Buck Trust controversy is *University of San Francisco Law Review* 21, no. 4 (Summer 1987), the entire issue of which is devoted to various aspects of the case.

259. See Estelle James, ed., *The Nonprofit Sector in International Perspective: Studies in Comparative Culture and Policy* (New York: Oxford University Press, 1989); Virginia Hodgkinson, ed., *The Nonprofit Sector (NGO's) in the United States and Abroad: Cross-Cultural Perspectives–1990 Spring Research Forum Working Papers* (Washington, D.C.: Independent Sector, 1990); and James Joseph, *The Charitable Impulse: Wealth and Social Conscience in Communities and Cultures outside the United States* (New York: Foundation Center, 1989). For background on this sudden interest in international dimensions, see Anne Lowry Bailey, "Leaders of Philanthropy Call on Foundations to Join Forces, Seek Solutions to Global Ills," *Chronicle of Philanthropy* 2, no. 3 (November 1989); and Stephen G. Greene, "For U.S. Philanthropy, Opportunity in the Turmoil of Eastern Europe," *Chronicle of Philanthropy* 2, no. 4 (November 28, 1989).

Chapter Two: Reflections on the Nonprofit Sector in the Postliberal Era

1. Alexis de Tocqueville, *Democracy in America*, 2 vols. (1835, 1849; reprint, New York: Alfred A. Knopf, 1945), 115.

2. Ibid., 2:115.

3. Ibid., 1:202.

4. Ibid., 1:203.

5. Kingman Brewster, Charles E. Lindblom, John G. Simon, "Proposal for a Study of Independent Institutions," unpublished grant proposal, 1976.

6. Ibid., 2.

7. *Research Papers Sponsored by the Commission on Private Philanthropy and Public Needs*, 6 vols. (Washington, D.C.: Department of the Treasury, 1977), 9.

8. Quoted in Henry Adams, *History of the United States during the Administrations of Jefferson and Madison* (Englewood Cliffs, N.J.: Prentice-Hall, 1963), 38.

9. Mary Flug Handlin and Oscar Handlin, *Commonwealth: A Study of the Role of Government in the American Economy* (New York: Alfred A. Knopf, 1947); and Peter Dobkin Hall, *The Organization of American Culture, 1700–*

1900: Institutions, Elites, and the Origins of American Nationality (New York: New York University Press, 1982).

10. Lester Salamon and Alan Abramson, *The Federal Budget and the Nonprofit Sector* (Washington, D.C.: Urban Institute, 1981). See also Lester Salamon, "Partners in Public Service: Government and the Nonprofit Sector in Theory and Practice," in W. W. Powell, ed., *The Nonprofit Sector: A Research Handbook* (New Haven: Yale University Press, 1987), 99–117; and Lester Salamon, "Of Market Failure, Voluntary Failure and Third-Party Government: Toward a Theory of Government-Nonprofit Relations in the Modern Welfare State," in Susan Ostrander et al., eds., *Shifting the Debate: Public-Private Sector Relations in the Modern Welfare State* (New Brunswick, N.J.: Transaction Books, 1987), 29–49.

11. Salamon, "Partners in Public Service," 3.

12. Austin Wakeman Scott, *The Law of Trusts,* 4 vols. (Boston: Little Brown & Co., 1967), 3:2767.

13. Samuel Atkins Eliot, "The Charities of Boston," *North American Review* 61 (1845): 135–59.

14. Ibid., 150.

15. Andrew Carnegie, "Wealth," *North American Review* 148 (1889): 653–64; 149 (1889): 682–98.

16. Eduard Lindeman, *Wealth and Culture* (New York: Harcourt, Brace & Co., 1936), 58.

17. Waldemar A. Nielsen, *The Big Foundations* (New York: Columbia University Press, 1972), 273–74.

18. Teresa Odendahl et al., *Working in Foundations: Career Patterns of Men and Women* (New York: Foundation Center, 1985), 43.

19. Lindeman, *Wealth and Culture,* 58.

20. See Robert H. Hayes and William J. Abernathy, "Managing Our Way to Economic Decline," *Harvard Business Review* 58 (1980): 66–77; and James Fallows, "The Case against Credentialism," *Atlantic Monthly* 256 (December 1985): 49–67.

21. Institute for Educational Affairs, *Independent Philanthropy* (New York: Institute for Educational Affairs, 1983), 4.

22. James A. Joseph, "Justice for All: The New Public Philosophy and the Role of Private Philanthropy" (Speech delivered at John Filer Symposium, Yale Law School, March 1982).

23. Henry Ford II, quoted in William E. Simon, "Reaping the Whirlwind," *Philanthropy Monthly* 13 (1980): 5–8.

24. Ibid., 8.

25. Milton J. Bloch, "Growing Pains: The Maturation of Museums," *Museum News,* June 1984, 8–14.

26. In surveying *Museum News* over the past two decades, it is interesting to observe the shifting viewpoint on the relation between staff and board. In 1965, the journal published a symposium on museum-organization and -personnel policies. The participants, while acknowledging the importance of the staff's professional prerogatives, emphasized the preeminence of the board and

viewed the most important attribute of the staff professional as his ability to
be "sympathetic with its [the board's] policies and purposes." Walter Muir
Whitehill, "Professional-Staff Relationship," 1965, 25. By the late 1970s, the
director's role had been dramatically recast and enhanced in importance. As
a 1978 article on the duties of museum personnel noted, "the director provides
conceptual leadership through specialized knowledge of the discipline of the
museum, and is responsible for policymaking and funding [with the governing board], planning, organizing, staffing, directing, and supervising/coordi-
nating activities through the staff." "Museum Positions." 1978, 25:

The article went on to list thirteen other possible professional staff positions
whose responsibilities required specialized training of a sort generally beyond
the capabilities of the enthusiastic amateurs on whom small museums have
traditionally depended.

By the 1980s, articles such as Milton J. Bloch's "Growing Pains" were
focusing on the problems of young professionals "at the early stages of [their]
administrative careers, eager and obviously frustrated" (8). Bloch's article reverses Whitehill's 1965 formulation and views the good board as one that
"never asks a director to compromise his position by pressing for favors or
lobbying for a viewpoint at either the staff or board level" (12). The shifting
position of *Museum News* on the professional role is indicative of the extension of professionalism from large organizations to "small or possibly new
museum with limited resources" (8), organizations that had traditionally depended on amateurs rather than professional staffs.

27. The dependence of nonprofits on large donors is remarkably constant
over the past century and a half. Ronald Story's discussion of Harvard's financial history in *The Forging of an Aristocracy: Harvard and Boston's Upper Class,
1800-1870* (Middletown, Conn.: Wesleyan University Press, 1980), 26–27,
shows that in the subscription drives from 1805 to 1826, over one-half the
funds subscribed came from between 10 percent and 20 percent of the subscribers. Four percent (24) of the 597 subscribers to Yale's first endowment fund
drive in 1832 contributed 40.3 percent of the total raised by the college. A
century later, .03 percent (63) of 22,123 contributors to Yale's 1926–28 capital
fund drive gave 53 percent of the $21 million total. Even small regional in-
stitutions such as Reed College in Poland remain dependent on large donors.
The results of its ongoing (1985–86) capital fund drive show that .03 percent
(17) of 6,536 donors gave 67.1 percent of the $21.6 million raised. The level of
participation in fund drives has unquestionably increased since the early nineteenth century: in Yale's 1832 drive, less than 20 percent of living alumni
contributed; over 60 percent supported the 1926–28 effort; Seymour Harris's
study of Harvard's finances shows a steady growth in alumni participation in
twentieth-century annual appeals, from 12.9 percent of living graduates in
1926 to 39.8 percent in 1967 (Seymour Harris, *The Economics of Harvard* [New
York: McGraw-Hill, 1970], 302). Despite these increases in the overall number
of participants over 150 years, the proportion given by small numbers of large
givers has remained remarkably constant.

28. Paul J. DiMaggio, "Can Culture Survive the Marketplace?" *Arts Management Review* 13 (1983): 34–25.

29. Horace Coon, *Money to Burn: What the Great American Foundations Do with Their Money* (London: Longmans, Green & Co., 1939); Ferdinand Lundberg, *America's Sixty Families* (New York: Vanguard Press, 1937) and *The Rich and the Super-Rich* (New York: Lyle Stuart, 1968); and Waldemar A. Nielsen, *The Big Foundations* and *The Golden Donors: A New Anatomy of the Great Foundations* (New York: E. P. Dutton, 1985). Unlike the other critics, Nielsen is a supporter of private philanthropy—though he laments its many failings.

30. Alexis de Tocqueville, *The Old Regime and the French Revolution* (1856; reprint, New York: Alfred A. Knopf, 1955), 110.

31. Bernard Bailyn, *Education in the Forming of American Society* (Chapel Hill: University of North Carolina Press, 1960), 3–4.

32. Ibid., 9.

33. John S. Whitehead, *The Separation of College and State* (New Haven: Yale University Press, 1973).

34. Colin Burke, *American Collegiate Populations: A Test of the Traditional View* (New York: New York University Press, 1982).

35. On the neglect of the economic history of universities, see Peter Dobkin Hall, "Veritas et Pecunia: The Historical Economy of Education," *History of Education Quarterly* 17, no. 4 (Winter 1974): 177–25.

36. Salamon and Abramson, *The Federal Government and the Nonprofit Sector.*

37. Ibid., 46.

38. Salamon, "Partners in Public Service," 99.

39. Ibid., 100.

40. See Walter Isaacson and Evan Thomas, *The Wise Men: Six Friends and the World They Made* (New York: Simon & Schuster, 1986); David Halberstam, *The Best and the Brightest* (New York: Random House, 1972); Philip Burch, *Elites in American Society* (New York: Holmes & Meier, Publishers, 1981). See also C. Wright Mills, *The Power Elite* (New York: Oxford University Press, 1956), and the work of G. William Domhoff—*Who Rules America?* (Englewood Cliffs, N.J.: Prentice-Hall, 1967), *The Higher Circles: The Governing Class in America* (New York: Vintage Books, 1970), and *The Powers That Be* (New York: Vintage Books, 1979). Unfortunately, very little of this literature—of which those works listed are but a small sample—study career patterns. Most focus on interlocking relationships.

41. John S. Stanfield, *Philanthropy and Jim Crow in American Social Science* (Westport, Conn.: Greenwood Press, 1984), 187. More recent studies of such networks include E. Richard Brown, *Rockefeller Medicine Men: Medicine and Capitalism in America* (Berkeley: University of California Press, 1979); Stephen C. Wheatley, *The Politics of Philanthropy: Abraham Flexner and Medical Education* (Madison: University of Wisconsin Press, 1988); Gerald Jonas, *The Circuit Riders: Rockefeller Money and the Rise of Modern Science* (New York: W. W. Norton & Co., 1989); and Ellen Condliffe Lagemann, *The Politics of*

Knowledge: The Carnegie Corporation, Philanthropy, and Public Policy (Middletown, Conn.: Wesleyan University Press, 1989).

42. Stanfield, *Philanthropy and Jim Crow in American Social Science,* 127.

43. Teresa Odendahl, Elizabeth Boris, and Arlene Daniels, *Working in Foundations: The Career Patterns of Men and Women* (New York: Foundation Center, 1985).

44. See Barry D. Karl and Stanley N. Katz, "The American Private Philanthropic Foundation and the Public Sphere, 1890–1930," *Minerva* 19 (1981): 236–70; and James A. Smith, *The Idea Brokers: Think Tanks and the Rise of the New Policy Elite* (New York: Free Press, 1991).

45. See Mark L. Chadwin, *The Warhawks: American Interventionists before Pearl Harbor* (New York: W. W. Norton & Co., 1968). By the 1930s, internationalists were old hands at using private nonprofit entities to shape public policy, having used similar organizations and techniques in the "preparedness movement" preceding American entry into World War I.

46. Paul J. DiMaggio and Walter W. Powell, "The Iron Cage Revisited: Conformity and Diversity in Organizational Fields," Working Paper no. 52 (New Haven: Program on Non-Profit Organizations, Yale University, 1982), 4. This important paper later appeared as "The Iron Cage Revisited: Institutional Isomorphism and Collective Rationality in Organizational Fields," *American Sociological Review* 48 (1983): 147–60.

47. DiMaggio and Powell, "The Iron Cage Revisited: Conformity and Diversity in Organizational Fields," 10.

48. This body of critical work is best summarized in chapter 1 of David McClelland, *The Achieving Society* (New York: D. Van Nostrand, 1961). See also Thomas Cochran's important essay "The Role of the Entrepreneur in Capital Formation," in *Capital Accumulation and Economic Growth* (New York: National Bureau of Economic Research, 1955).

49. See Alvin Gouldner, *The Coming Crisis in Western Sociology* (New York: Basic Books, 1970); Paul Johnson, *Modern Times: The World from the Twenties to the Eighties* (New York: Harper & Row, 1983); and Alan Matusow, *The Unraveling of America: A History of Liberalism in the 1960s* (New York: Harper & Row, 1984).

50. See Louis Galambos, "The Emerging Organizational Synthesis in Modern American History," in E. J. Perkins, *Men and Organizations: The American Economy in the Twentieth Century* (New York: G. P. Putnam's Sons, 1970); Louis Galambos, "Technology, Political Economy and Professionalization," *Business History Review* 57 (1982): 471–93; Robert Weibe, *The Search for Order, 1877–1920* (New York: Hill & Wang, 1967); Burton J. Bledstein, *The Culture of Professionalism* (New York: W. W. Norton & Co., 1976); and Peter Dobkin Hall, "Social Perception and Social Policy: Some Thoughts on the Task of Cultural History," *Intellectual History Group Newsletter* 5 (1983): 15–22. See also Martin J. Sklar, *The Corporate Reconstruction of American Capitalism, 1890–1916: The Market, Law, and Politics* (New York: Cambridge University Press, 1988), and, for an especially sophisticated effort, W. E. Bijker, Thomas P. Hughes, and Trevor Pinch, *The Social Construction of*

Technological Systems: New Directions in the Sociology and History of Technology (Cambridge: MIT Press, 1987).

51. For example, Arthur Stinchcombe, "Social Structure and Organizations," in James March, ed., *The Handbook of Organizations* (Chicago: Rand McNally, 1965), 142–93; John W. Meyer and Brian Rowan, "Institutionalized Organizations: Formal Structure as Myth and Ceremony," *American Journal of Sociology* 83 (1977): 340–63; Alfred D. Chandler, William Ouchi, and Charles Perrow, "Markets, Hierarchies, and Hegemony," in A. H. Van de Ven, ed., *Perspectives on Organizational Design and Behavior* (New York: J. W. Wiley & Sons, 1981), 347–406; Lewis Coser, Charles Kadushin, and Walter W. Powell, *The Culture and Commerce of Book Publishing* (New York: Basic Books, 1982); and Paul J. DiMaggio, "Cultural Entrepreneurship in Nineteenth Century Boston," in DiMaggio, ed., *Nonprofit Enterprise in the Arts: Studies in Mission and Constraint* (New York: Oxford University Press, 1986).

52. See *Foundations and the Tax Bill: Testimony on Title I of the Tax Reform Act of 1969 Submitted by Witnesses Appearing before the United States Senate Finance Committee, October 1969* (New York: Foundation Center, 1969); and *Hearings before the Committee on Ways and Means*, House of Representatives, 91st Congress, Part 1 (February 18–20, 1969) (Washington, D.C.: Government Printing Office, 1969). See also F. Emerson Andrews, "Introduction," in Marianna Lewis, ed., *Foundation Directory*, 10th ed. (New York: Foundation Center, 1985), xv; and F. Emerson Andrews, *Patman and the Foundations: An Assessment* (New York: Foundation Center, 1968).

53. Andrews, "Introduction," in Lewis, ed., *Foundation Directory*, xv.

54. Alan Pifer, *Philanthropy in an Age of Transition* (New York: Foundation Center, 1984), 102.

55. Andrews, "Introduction," in Lewis, ed., *Foundation Directory*, 7–51.

56. See Hayden Smith, *Corporate Contributions Research since the Filer Commission* (New York: Council for Aid to Education, 1984).

57. Arthur White and John Bartolomeo, *Corporate Giving: The Views of Chief Executive Officers of Major American Corporations* (Washington, D.C.: Council on Foundations, 1982). The most thorough study of the motives of corporate donors are Joseph Galskiewicz's *The Social Organization of an Urban Grants Economy: A Study of Business Philanthropy and Nonprofit Organizations* (Orlando, Fla.: Academic Press, 1985) and "Corporate Contributions to Charity: Nothing More Than a Marketing Strategy?" in Richard Magat, ed., *Philanthropic Giving: Studies in Varieties and Goals* (New York: Oxford University Press, 1989), 246–60.

58. See Daniel M. Fox, "The Consequences of Consensus: American Health Policy in the Twentieth Century," *Milbank Memorial Fund Quarterly* 64 (1986): 76–99. See also Rosemary Stevens, *In Sickness and in Wealth: American Hospitals in the Twentieth Century* (New York: Basic Books, 1989).

59. Michael B. Katz, *Class, Bureaucracy and the Schools: The Illusion of Educational Change in America* (New York: Praeger Publishers, 1975) and *In the Shadow of the Poor House: A Social History of Welfare in America* (New

York: Basic Books, 1986); and David J. Rothman et al., *Doing Good: The Limits of Benevolence* (New York: Pantheon Books, 1978).

60. David F. Allmendinger, *Paupers and Scholars: The Transformation of Student Life in Nineteenth-Century New England* (New York: St. Martin's Press, 1973); Thomas Haskell, *The Emergence of Professional Social Science: The American Social Science Association and the Nineteenth-Century Crisis of Authority* (Urbana: University of Illinois Press, 1977); and David F. Noble, *American by Design: Science, Technology, and the Rise of Corporate Capitalism* (New York: Oxford University Press, 1977).

61. Galambos, "Technology, Political Economy and Professionalization," 471–93.

62. Bledstein, *The Culture of Professionalism*.

63. Michael Paul Rogin, *The Intellectuals and McCarthy: The Radical Specter* (Cambridge: MIT Press, 1967).

64. Thomas Bender, *Community and Social Change in America* (New Brunswick, N.J.: Rutgers University Press, 1978).

65. In addition to works already cited by Allmendinger, Bledstein, Galambos, Haskell, Hall, Hawley, and Story, see Alan Dawley, *Class and Community: The Industrial Revolution in Lynn* (Cambridge: Harvard University Press, 1976); Paul E. Johnson, *A Shopkeeper's Millennium: Society and Revivals in Rochester, New York, 1815–1837* (New York: Hill & Wang, 1981); and Mary P. Ryan, *Cradle of the Middle Class: The Family in Oneida County, New York, 1790–1865* (New York: Cambridge University Press, 1981).

66. William Miller, ed., *Men in Business: Essays on the History of Entrepreneurship* (Cambridge: Harvard University Press, 1952); and Alfred D. Chandler, *The Visible Hand: The Managerial Revolution in American Business* (Cambridge: Harvard University Press, 1977).

CHAPTER 3: "A BRIDGE FOUNDED UPON JUSTICE AND BUILT OF HUMAN HEARTS": REFLECTIONS ON RELIGION AND PHILANTHROPY

1. Virginia Hodgkinson, ed., *Research in Progress, 1986–87: A National Compendium of Research Projects on Philanthropy, Voluntary Action, and Not-for-Profit Activity* (Washington, D.C.: Independent Sector, 1988); Program on Nonprofit Organizations, *Research Reports* 9 (Winter 1988); and Daphne Niobe Layton, *Philanthropy and Voluntarism: An Annotated Bibliography* (New York: Foundation Center, 1987).

2. Gabriel Rudney, "The Scope and Dimensions of Nonprofit Activity," in W. W. Powell, ed., *The Nonprofit Sector: A Research Handbook* (New Haven: Yale University Press, 1987).

3. Loren Renz and Stan Olson, eds., *The Foundation Directory*, 11th ed. (New York: Foundation Center, 1987), xxxvi.

4. Independent Sector, *Annual Report, 1986* (Washington, D.C.: Independent Sector, 1987), 2–12.

5. Figures on the relative sizes of religious denominations are from *The World Almanac and Book of Facts* (New York: Pharos Books, 1986), 339–40.

6. Andrew Carnegie, "Wealth," in E. C. Kirkland, ed., *The Gospel of Wealth and Other Timely Essays* (Cambridge: Harvard University Press, 1962), 26.

7. Ibid., 27.

8. Andrew Carnegie's analysis of the industrial transformation of society and the resulting interdependencies are best presented in his essays "An Employer's View of the Labor Question," *Forum* 1 (April 1886): 114–25, and "Results of the Labor Struggle," *Forum* (August 1886): 538–51.

9. Alfred D. Chandler, *The Visible Hand: The Managerial Revolution in American Business* (Cambridge: Harvard University Press, 1977), 266–69.

10. Amos G. Warner, *American Charities* (New York: Thomas Y. Crowell & Co., 1908), 445. Warner's book was not an odd tract. First published in 1894, it became a standard source book on American charity and went through numerous revised editions, the last of which appeared in 1930.

11. "An Act for the Support of Missionaries to Preach the Gospel in the Northern, and Western Parts of the United States, and among the Indian Tribes" (October Session, 1798), in *The Public Records of the State of Connecticut* (Hartford: Published by the State, 1953), 9:266. As both the title and the substance of the act make clear, the Missionary Society's primary targets were not Indians, but freethinkers and other "infidels." On the role of the Second Great Awakening as the major nursery of American voluntarism, see Charles I. Foster, *"An Errand of Mercy": The Evangelical United Front, 1790–1837* (Chapel Hill: University of North Carolina Press, 1961).

12. Mary P. Ryan provides a paradigmatic account of the secularization of the associational impulse in *The Cradle of the Middle Class: The Family in Oneida County, New York, 1790–1865* (New York: Cambridge University Press, 1983), 60–144.

13. Complaints about the multiplicity of charitable efforts appear as early as 1845; see Samuel Atkins Eliot, "Public and Private Charities in Boston," *North American Review* 61 (July 1845): 149–50.

14. On the Sanitary Commission and its religious roots, see George M. Frederickson, *The Inner Civil War: Northern Intellectuals and the Crisis of the Union* (New York: Harper & Row, 1965), 7–22.

15. Ibid., 104.

16. Ibid., 105.

17. Ibid., 106.

18. Ibid., 212.

19. Warner, *American Charities*, 3–32, provides an interesting summary of the evolving accommodation between political economy and philanthropy.

20. Ibid., 25.

21. On the origins of political economy as an empirical rather than a philosophical enquiry, see Edward S. Mason, "The Harvard Department of Economics from the Beginning to World War II," *Quarterly Journal of Economics* 97, no. 3 (August 1982): 386–433. On the business community's objections to

the laissez-faire stance of traditional political economy, see Samuel Eliot Morison, "Francis Bowen, an Early Test of Academic Freedom," *Massachusetts Historical Society Proceedings* 65 (January 1936): 507–11. See also Paul Buck, ed., *The Social Sciences at Harvard* (Cambridge: Harvard University Press, 1965).

22. Charles W. Eliot, the most important institutional reformer of the late nineteenth century, opened his famous essay "The New Education" with this phrase—*Atlantic Monthly* 23 (January 1869): 203. On the American Social Science Association, see Thomas Haskell, *The Emergence of Professional Social Science and the Nineteenth-Century Crisis of Authority* (Urbana: University of Illinois Press, 1977).

23. Martin J. Sklar, "Periodization and Historiography: The Corporate Reconstruction of American Society, 1896–1914" (Paper delivered at the Annual Meeting of the Organization of American Historians, Los Angeles, March 1984). See also Martin J. Sklar, *The Corporate Reconstruction of American Capitalism, 1890–1916: The Market, the Law, and Politics* (New York: Cambridge University Press, 1988).

24. Warner, *American Charities*, 23–24.

25. Ibid., 25.

26. Ibid., 31.

27. Timothy L. Smith, *Revivalism and Social Reform: American Protestantism on the Eve of the Civil War* (New York: Harper & Row, 1957), 166.

28. Robert D. Cross, ed., *The Church and the City* (Indianapolis: Bobbs-Merrill Co., 1967), ix.

29. Walter Rauschenbusch, *Christianity and the Social Crisis* (New York: Harper & Row, 1964), 238.

30. Charles M. Shelton, *In His Steps* (1897; reprint, Springdale, Pa.: Whitaker House, n.d.).

31. Ibid., 16–19.

32. On the transformation of Kansas politics, see *Historical Statistics of the United States* (Washington, D.C.: Bureau of the Census, 1961), 679.

33. Jane Addams, *Twenty Years at Hull House* (New York: New American Library, 1961), 95–97. "The Subjective Necessity for Social Settlements," which Addams included in her autobiography, was originally written and presented in 1892.

34. Ibid., 122–23.

35. Ibid., 123.

36. Henry Steele Commager, "Forward," in ibid., xiv.

37. Michael B. Katz, *In the Shadow of the Poorhouse: A Social History of Social Welfare in America* (New York: Basic Books, 1986), 160–62.

38. Sydnor H. Walker, "Privately Supported Social Welfare Work," in *Recent Social Trends in the United States* (New York: McGraw-Hill Book Co., 1933), 1169.

39. Katz, *In the Shadow of the Poorhouse*, 170–71.

40. Among the best studies of the failure or rationalization efforts are Janet A. Weiss, "Substance versus Symbol in Administrative Reform: The Case of

Human Services Coordination," *Policy Analysis* 7, no. 2 (1981): 21–45; Marc Friedman, "The Elusive Problem of Management Cooperation in the Performing Arts," in Paul DiMaggio, ed., *Nonprofit Enterprise and the Arts: Studies in Mission and Constraint* (New York: Oxford University Press, 1986), 199–213; and Susan Hunter, "Failure Factors in Multi-Institutional Systems," *Health Care Management Review* 8, no. 2 (1984): 37–50.

41. Walt Harrington, *The Hospital Memoirs* (Allentown, Pa.: Call-Chronicle Newspapers, 1979), 9. This is one of the most interesting and detailed studies of the failure of a rationalization effort.

42. Chester Barnard, *The Functions of the Executive* (Cambridge: Harvard University Press, 1966).

43. Carl Milofsky, "Neighborhood-based Organizations: A Market Analogy" in Powell, ed., *The Nonprofit Sector*, 280. See also Carl Milofsky, ed., *Community Organizations: Studies in Resource Mobilization and Exchange* (New York: Oxford University Press, 1988).

44. Milofsky, "Neighborhood-based Organizations," 291.

45. Ibid., 291.

46. Jacob Riis, *How the Other Half Lives* (New York: Sagamore Press, 1957), 226.

CHAPTER 4: CULTURES OF TRUSTEESHIP IN THE UNITED STATES

1. Successive editions of Austin Wakeman Scott's *Law of Trusts*, 4 vols. (Boston: Little, Brown & Co., various dates), devote considerable attention to the differences between the case and statute law bearing on trusts in various states.

2. See Lizbeth Moody, "State Statutes Governing Directors of Charitable Boards," *University of San Francisco Law Review* 18, no. 3 (Summer 1984): 749–61.

3. "Harvard College and Massachusetts General Hospital v. Francis Amory, Trustee," *Massachusetts Reports* 9 (1830): 446. In this case, Harvard and the hospital brought suit against Amory, who was trustee of an estate in which the institutions held a residuary interest, claiming that his investments in industrial securities were imprudent. As major investors in and promoters of industrial ventures, the directors of the hospital and the college had no objections to such investments. This was a test case that the directors hoped would eliminate legal obstacles to their investing institutional endowments in such securities.

4. One of the major concerns of the 1969 Tax Reform Act was the use of foundations as vehicles for maintaining donor control of family firms. By requiring foundations to diversify their portfolios, the tax law eliminated any incentives their trustees might have for investment policies that promised anything other than maximum return over the short term. The transformation of the Prudent Man Rule in regard to testamentary trustee practice has not, as far as I know, been systematically studied. Among the notable cases sug-

gesting that such a transformation took place is that involving the Bingham family of Louisville, in which a suit by a disgruntled family member forced the trustees to accept "an offer that couldn't be refused" for stock in its communications empire. On this, see David Leon Chandler, *The Binghams of Louisville* (New York: Crown Publishers, 1987). The recent struggle within the Dorrance family in regard to family trust holdings in the Campbell Company shows similar features, with tensions between trustees trying to sustain what they regard as the family's long-term interests by holding on to Campbell stock and dissident family members urging the sale of that stock to takeover specialists.

5. In testimony before the Select Committee to Investigate Tax-Exempt Foundations and Comparable Organizations (Cox Committee) in 1952, Norman Sugarman, then an assistant commissioner of the IRS, estimated the number of charitable tax-exempt organizations as having been 12,500 in 1939, 27,500 in 1946, and 32,000 in 1950. U.S. House of Representatives, 82nd Congress, 2nd Session on H. Res. 561, *Tax Exempt Foundations, Hearings before the Select Committee to Investigate Tax-Exempt Foundations and Comparable Organizations* (Washington, D.C.: Government Printing Office, 1953), 64.

6. The best current figures on the number of charitable tax-exempt organizations chartered by year are in Burton Weisbrod's *The Nonprofit Economy* (Cambridge: Harvard University Press, 1988).

7. Lester Salamon, "Partners in Public Service," in W. W. Powell, ed., *The Nonprofit Sector: A Research Handbook* (New Haven: Yale University Press, 1987), 99–117.

8. The basic task of the Commission of Private Philanthropy and Public Needs (Filer Commission), as acknowledged in the preliminary meetings held and memoranda exchanged among those who organized it, was to reconcile public policy, especially tax regulations, to the increasingly complex institutional realities of charitable tax-exempt entities as they had developed by the 1970s. These materials can be found in the papers of John D. Rockefeller 3rd and his associates Datus Smith and Porter McKeever, as well as in the files of the Council on Foundations—all of which are at the Rockefeller Archive Center.

9. See Joseph Galaskiewicz's comments on changing corporate culture in the Twin Cities in *The Social Organization of an Urban Grants Economy* (New York: Academic Press, 1986).

10. The best general treatment of these organizations is Carl Milofsky, ed., *Community Organizations: Studies in Resource Mobilization and Exchange* (New Haven: Yale University Press, 1988).

11. Mary P. Ryan's account of the origins of voluntary associations in *Cradle of the Middle Class: The Family in Oneida County, New York, 1790–1865* (New York: Cambridge University Press, 1982) is must reading for anyone interested in American institutional cultures. Also useful, though less broad-ranging, is Paul Johnson's *Shopkeeper's Millennium: Society and Revivals in Rochester, New York, 1815–1837* (New York: Hill & Wang, 1978).

12. David Rosner, "From First Person to Third Party: Financing Health

Services in the Great American Metropolis" (Paper delivered at the Conference on Private Action and Social Policy at Case Western Reserve University, September 15, 1989), includes a detailed account of the variety of voluntary organizations created by immigrants in American cities in the late-nineteenth and early-twentieth centuries.

13. This material is drawn from an extensive unpublished study of institutional culture in Allentown, Pennsylvania. Portions of the study have appeared in K. L. Hall and Peter Dobkin Hall, *The Lehigh Valley* (Woodland Hills, Calif.: Windsor Publications, 1982), and in K. L. Hall and Peter Dobkin Hall, "Allentown, 1869–1900" and "Allentown, 1929–1940," in Mahlon Hellerich, ed., *Allentown, 1762–1987* (Allentown, Pa.: Lehigh County Historical Society, 1988).

14. The relative acceptance of the German Jewish elite in New York is described in Stephen Birmingham, *Our Crowd: The Great Jewish Families of New York* (New York: Dell Publishing Co., 1967); and Cleveland Amory, *Who Killed Society?* (New York: Harper & Brothers, Publishers, 1960).

15. The Judaic roots of organized philanthropy are brilliantly detailed in Paul Johnson's *History of the Jews* (New York: Harper & Row, Publishers, 1987).

16. *Worcester Directory for the Year Commencing January 15, 1878* (Worcester, Mass.: Drew, Allis & Co., Publishers, 1878). Similar lists of "Societies, Libraries, &c." are contained in virtually every nineteenth-century city directory. They constitute an important, but virtually unutilized, basic source on the institutional life of American communities.

17. The "official" historiography of hospitals has tended to minimize the roles of exclusion and discrimination in the emergence of Catholic institutions. However, a number of recent sources have highlighted the importance of these issues. See Mark J. Mininberg, *Saving New Haven* (New Haven: Fine Arts Publications, 1988).

18. Walt Harrington's *The Hospital Memoirs* (Allentown, Pa.: Call-Chronicle Newspapers, 1979) provides a detailed and intimate examination of the interactions within and between ethnic and mainstream boards of trustees in Allentown. Harrington's work is an especially valuable case study of the impact of conflicting understandings of trusteeship on efforts to rationalize the health-care delivery system in Lehigh Valley during the 1970s.

19. In "Conflicting Managerial Cultures on Nonprofit Boards," *Nonprofit Management and Leadership* 1, no. 2 (Winter 1990): 153–65, I examine the efforts of a largely ethnic clique on the board of a Connecticut museum to impose "objective" management criteria on fellow trustees and staff. The group I examined is of particular interest, because it not only was multiethnic—including Jewish, Italian, and Polish Americans—but also was part of a larger network of newly successful ethnic businesspeople and professionals who aggressively, and with considerable success, sought entry to mainstream boards in the city under study. The overall impact of this group on board culture remains to be thoroughly assessed.

20. The inclusiveness of midwestern civic cultures and the rapid develop-

ment of an ethnic trusteeship tradition are suggested by the institutional histories in David Van Tassel and John Grabowski, eds., *Cleveland Encyclopedia* (Cleveland: Western Reserve Historical Society, 1988). My study of Allentown, Pennsylvania, confirms the significance of this phenomenon, with ethnics well represented on "mainstream" for-profit and nonprofit boards by the turn of the century. The question of ethnocentric counterforces to assimilation remains largely unexamined. The Jewish community center movement of the 1950s and the "ethnic pride" and "ethnic heritage" activities of the 1970s and 1980s suggest that these phenomena are worthy of further study, particularly as they relate to trusteeship issues.

21. Alexis de Tocqueville, *Democracy in America,* 2 vols. (New York: Alfred A. Knopf, 1945), 2:114.

22. Richard T. Ely, "The Universities and the Churches," in *One Hundred Seventh Annual Report of the Regents, 1893* (Albany: University of the State of New York, 1894), 361. I am grateful to Jim Wooten of Yale Law School for bringing this speech to my attention.

23. Ibid., 357.

24. Ibid., 362.

25. For an overview of this struggle, see Peter Dobkin Hall, "The Spirit of the Ordinance of 1787: Organizational Values, Voluntary Associations, and Higher Education in Ohio, 1803–1830," in Paul Mattingly and Carl Kaestle, eds., *"Education and Means of Education Shall Forever Be Encouraged": Education in the Old Northwest, 1787–1887* (Athens: Ohio University Library, 1987).

26. James Sullivan, "Opinion of the Attorney General of Massachusetts on the Life of Corporations, 1802," quoted in Oscar and Mary Flug Handlin, *Commonwealth: A Study of the Role of Government in the American Economy, 1774–1861* (Cambridge: Harvard University Press, 1969), 260.

27. James McBride, *Laws Passed by the Legislature Establishing the Miami University, and the Ordinances, Passed by the Trustees of Miami University— to Which Is Added, an Address to the Inhabitants of the Miami College Lands, Containing Brief Remarks and Observations* (Hamilton, Ohio, 1814). McBride's analysis of Miami University's legal situation anticipated by five years the argument that Daniel Webster would advance in the Dartmouth College Case regarding the corporation as a constitutionally protected contract.

28. Robert Hamilton Bishop, "Inaugural Address," in *Oxford Addresses* (Hanover, Ind., 1835), 20–21.

29. "The Yale Report of 1828," quoted in Richard Hofstadter and Wilson Smith, eds., *American Higher Education—A Documentary History,* 2 vols. (New York: Alfred A. Knopf, 1965), 1:278.

30. Colin B. Burke, *American Collegiate Populations: A Test of the Traditional View* (New York: New York University Press, 1982), 6–7.

31. James J. Burns, *Educational History of Ohio* (Columbus, Ohio: Historical Publishing Co., 1905), 323.

32. Ibid., 324.

33. Ibid., 326–27.

34. Ibid., 328–30. On Miami University, see also Walter Havinghurst, *The Miami Years, 1809–1969* (New York: G. P. Putnam's Sons, 1969).

35. J. Burns, *Educational History of Ohio*, 358–65. On Ohio University, see also T. N. Hoover, *History of Ohio University* (Athens: Ohio University Press, 1937).

36. Edward Alanson Miller, *The History of Educational Legislation in Ohio from 1803 to 1850* (Columbus, Ohio: F. J. Heer Printing Co., 1918), 107–19. Miller's views of Ohio's institutional taxonomy, like Burns's, represent interesting efforts to make sense of the region's unusual organizational culture in terms of the northeastern models of civil privatism which were becoming dominant in the early twentieth century.

37. I encountered, as part of my broader study of cultures of trusteeship, an unusually high rate of institutional participation among Yale graduates, which was more than double that of Harvard alumni at the turn of the century. In this population of college men twenty-five years after graduation, certain cities—among them Cleveland—appear to have been especially notable in enlisting the energies of individuals for civic purposes.

Yale was quite clearly the institution of choice for educating members of Cleveland's economic elite—though those who attended Yale were by no means solely recruited from the elite. The *Directory of the Living Graduates of Yale University* for 1910 lists 208 residents of Cleveland—one of the largest concentrations of alumni outside the Northeast. Unlike most Yale graduates, who seldom returned to where they were born, Clevelanders did so in unusually large numbers. Of the 43 graduates of Yale College living in Cleveland at the time of their deaths, 28—nearly two-thirds—spent their whole lives in the city; an additional 6 migrated to the city after graduation; only 9 (20 percent) went elsewhere (see *Yale Obituary Record*, 1914–39). This pattern suggests an unusually vital and intact culture. Moreover, Clevelanders were outstandingly generous to Yale.

The Yale Roll Call—Final Edition, which summarizes contributions to the university's 1925–28 fund drive, rates Cleveland the third most generous in its survey of "the results of the campaign in large centers"—of the city's 463 alumni (the eighth largest concentration in the country), 85 percent gave to the drive—a total contribution of $460,172, averaging $1,165 per donor.

38. On the paradoxical anti-institutionalism of Whigs in the Western Reserve, see Stephen E. Maizlish, *The Triumph of Sectionalism: The Transformation of Ohio Politics, 1844–1856* (Kent, Ohio: Kent State University Press, 1982), 19.

39. The Western Reserve was populated largely by migrants from Connecticut, but this does not imply that most were Congregationalists. Of the six colleges founded in the area before 1850, two were Congregationalist, two were Baptist, one was Methodist, and the affiliation of one are unknown. There is considerable evidence that dissenters from Connecticut's Standing Order were especially attracted to the Western Reserve.

40. On the founding of Case Institute and Western Reserve University, see Burns, *Educational History of Ohio*, 339–40, and D. D. Van Tassel and J. J.

Grabowski, The Encyclopedia of Cleveland (Bloomington: Indiana University Press, 1987), 156–58.

41. Of the 181 Clevelanders listed in the 1910 *Directory of Living Graduates* as having received undergraduate degrees from Yale, only 65 attended the Sheffield Scientific School.

42. Van Tassell and Grabowski, eds., *Cleveland Encyclopedia*, 157. I have inferred Case's intentions regarding the Case block from similar circumstances in other cities with strong associational traditions. When William R. Nelson, owner of the *Kansas City Star*, died in 1910, his will, in leaving his entire estate to the Nelson Trust, specified that it should be invested in real estate in a certain part of the city. Jesse Nichol, who developed the University District of Kansas City, used the holdings of the Nelson Trust to create a model of planned urban land use comparable in many ways to Cleveland's University Circle. See *William Rockhill Nelson* (Cambridge: Riverside Press, 1915); I. F. Johnson, *William Rockhill Nelson and the Kansas City Star* (Kansas City, Mo.: Burton Publishing Co., 1935); and William H. Wilson, *The City Beautiful Movement in Kansas City* (Columbia: University of Missouri Press, 1964). In a similar way, the real-estate holdings of the H. C. Trexler estate in Allentown, Pennsylvania, were used to develop the Hamilton Parkway district and the area surrounding Muhlenburg College. See Peter Dobkin Hall and K. L. Hall, "Allentown, 1929–1940," in Mahlon Hellerich, ed., *Allentown, 1762–1987* (Allentown, Pa.: Lehigh County Historical Society, 1987).

43. On the history of Western Reserve University, see Burns, *Educational History of Ohio*, 330–32; and Van Tassel and Grabowski, eds., *Cleveland Encyclopedia*, 157–59, 366, 502–3.

44. The parsimony of Clevelanders toward Western Reserve University is in marked contrast to their generosity to Yale. As Van Tassel and Grabowski note, Clevelanders "by 1986 had not yet provided [the university] with quite enough support to allow it to realize its full potential" (767). On this curious phenomenon, see Peter Dobkin Hall, "Philanthropy as Investment," *History of Education Quarterly* 22, no. 3 (Summer 1982): 185–203, which compares the generosity of Allentown, Pennsylvania, toward Muhlenburg College, which became the crucible of its civic sensibilities, with the failure of Scranton, Wilkes-Barre, and other Lackwanna Valley cities to make comparable institutional investments—with, as it turned out, devastating consequences for their future growth.

45. Van Tassel and Grabowski, eds., *Cleveland Encyclopedia*, 159.

46. There is, lamentably, no thorough scholarly study of the board-of-trade and chamber-of-commerce movements in the United States. My insights are drawn primarily from my study of the activities of Allentown, Pennsylvania's Board of Trade, which are summarized in Peter Dobkin Hall and K. L. Hall, *The Lehigh Valley* (Woodland Hills, Calif.: Windsor Publications, 1982), and "Allentown, 1870–1900" and "Allentown, 1929–1940," in Hellerich, ed., *Allentown, 1762–1987*. Also useful for general background is Alexander Orr, "Commercial Organizations," in Chauncey M. DePew, ed., *One Hundred Years of American Commerce* (New York: D. O. Haynes & Co., 1895), 50–54.

47. The central role of Cleveland's Chamber of Commerce is repeatedly referred to in articles on the city published from 1900 to 1930. See also Van Tassell and Grabowski, eds., *Cleveland Encyclopedia*, 469. The role of the board or chamber as the central mediator of public and private resources in cultures in which associational modes were dominant is a phenomenon especially worthy of further study. Also worthy of study are service clubs such as Rotary, Kiwanis, and Lions—all of which, according to Charles F. Marden's 1923 study, originated in midwestern cities with strong associational cultures. Charles F. Marden, *Rotary and Its Brothers: An Analysis and Interpretation of the Men's Service Club* (Princeton: Princeton University Press, 1935).

48. William R. Thayer, *The Life of John Hay*, 2 vols. (Boston: Houghton Mifflin & Co., 1916).

49. Ibid., 2:1–2.

50. Anonymous (John Hay), *The Breadwinners—A Social Study* (1883; reprint, New York: Harper & Brothers Publishers, 1900), 55–56.

51. Thayer, *The Life of John Hay*, 7–8.

52. These essays include "An Employer's View of the Labor Question" and "Results of the Labor Struggle," which appeared in the *Forum* in April and August 1886, respectively. Both are reprinted in E. C. Kirkland, ed., *The Gospel of Wealth and Other Essays* (Cambridge: Harvard University Press, 1956). All references are to the Kirkland edition. These essays present Carnegie's analysis of the industrial revolution, without which his later essay on wealth is incomprehensible.

53. Carnegie, "An Employer's View of the Labor Question," 98–99.

54. Carnegie, "Results of the Labor Struggle," 106–7, 115. Carnegie's characterization of the intellectuals' ignorance of business still holds true today.

55. Ibid., 110–11.

56. Carnegie, "Wealth," 28. This essay first appeared in the *North American Review* in June 1889. It is probably the single most important essay written on philanthropy. As I suggest, Carnegie's statements have been read in a variety of ways. Those with a national outlook tended to emphasize the essay's concern with the causes of poverty, whereas those rooted in regional cultures were most sensitive to its statements about the role of philanthropy in the process of economic self-renewal.

57. Ibid., 31.

58. Ibid., 19–21. Carnegie's views parallel those of certain other social Darwinist social commentators. See especially the attack on spendthrift trusts by Boston legal scholar John C. Gray in *Restraints on the Alienation of Property* (Boston: Boston Book Co., 1895).

59. Carnegie, "Wealth," 37.

60. Ibid., 47.

61. Ibid., 48.

62. Carnegie's antipathy to Wall Street before his final sellout to Morgan in 1901 is abundantly documented in Joseph Frazier Wall's superb biography *Andrew Carnegie* (Pittsburgh: University of Pittsburgh Press, 1989). Although Carnegie moved to New York City in 1867, most of his time was spent shuttl-

ing between Pittsburgh and England. In any event, he seems to have maintained the viewpoint of a midwestern manufacturer for many years after taking up residence in New York—which may account for why Clevelanders took
him seriously. His labor essays are notable in that many of the managerial and
labor relations reforms to which he refers were initiated by midwestern employers. Not coincidentally, the first stirrings of the scientific-management
movement, which combined a technological focus with an interest in the
social relations of production—as well as the whole relation of society—first
emerged at the Annual Meeting of the American Society of Mechanical Engineers in Chicago in 1886.

63. The only biography of Hanna, *Marcus Alonzo Hanna: His Life and Work*
(New York: Macmillan Co., 1919), was written by Herbert Croly, founder of
the *New Republic* and chief ideologist of the Progressive movement. Although
Croly's own biographer, David Levy, in *Herbert Croly of the New Republic*
(Princeton: Princeton University Press, 1985), dismisses the Hanna biography
as a piece of hack work, my own reading of the text, combined with an
appreciation of the background of Croly in the real-estate trade press, suggests
that he took Hanna's transformation into a reformer quite seriously. Hanna
seems to be the model "political specialist" described by Croly in *The Promise
of American Life* (New York: Macmillan Co., 1909). Because Hanna was the
most important political organizer of the early-twentieth century, his career
really deserves a modern scholarly examination.

64. Croly, *Hanna*, 84–95.

65. Ibid., 386–410.

66. Ibid., 409–10.

67. Ibid., 409.

68. Ibid., 410.

69. Croly's view of the role of business in the process of reform is outlined
in *The Promise of American Life*, 105–17. More a comprehensive view of progressivism and the professionalization of business management is Morrell
Heald's outstanding *The Social Responsibilities of American Business* (Cleveland: Case Western Reserve University Press, 1960). See also Peter Dobkin
Hall, "Business Giving and Social Investment," in Richard Magat, ed., *Philanthropic Giving: Studies in Varieties and Goals* (New York: Oxford University
Press, 1989), 221–45.

70. Although some admirers of the legacy of Johnson may quarrel with my
suggestion that he had anything in common with Marc Hanna, it is a matter
of record that, when Hanna proposed that the two of them form a partnership
to operate their traction and steel interests, Johnson begged off on the grounds
that "they were too much alike, that they 'would make good opponents, but
not good partners.' " See Hoyt L. Warner, *Progressivism in Ohio* (Columbus:
Ohio Historical Society, 1964), 57. That so many businessmen—in Cleveland
and elsewhere—became followers of Henry George is yet another subject
worthy of more serious exploration.

71. On the origins of federated giving, see Scott M. Cutlip, *Fund Raising in
the United States: Its Role in American Philanthropy* (New Brunswick, N.J.:

Rutgers University Press, 1965), 29–109. On its Cleveland origins, see Charles Whiting Williams, "Cleveland's Federated Givers," *Review of Reviews* 48 (1913): 472–76; C. W. Williams, "Cleveland's Group Plan," *Survey* 29 (1913): 603–6; and E. M. Williams, "Essentials of the Cleveland Experiment in Cooperative Benevolence," in *Conference on Charities and Corrections* (New York: Henry Holt & Co., 1913), 111–15.

72. Williams, "Cleveland's Federated Givers," 472.

73. Ibid., 473.

74. Pierce Williams and William R. Croxton, *Corporate Contributions to Organized Community Welfare Services* (New York: National Bureau of Economic Research, 1930), contains the most complete list of Community Chests established before 1930—see 91–138 and 247–53. See also Cutlip, *Fundraising in the United States*, 73–81. The community-chest idea was spread through an aggressive education campaign under the leadership of the U.S. Chamber of Commerce.

75. R. L. Duffus, "Cleveland: Paternalism in Excelsis," *New Republic*, April 4, 1928. I am grateful to David Hammack for calling this important article to my attention.

76. On the background of the establishment of the Cleveland Foundation, see "Cleveland Foundation Not Self-Perpetuating," *Survey* 31 (January 31, 1914): 511; I. M. Tarbell, "He Helps Capitalists to Die Poor," *American Mercury* 78 (September 1914): 56–57; "Survey of Cleveland by New Foundation," *Survey* 31 (March 21, 1914): 763; "Private Wealth for Public Needs," *Independent* 70 (January 12, 1914): 50; and "Trust Company and the Community," *Outlook* 106 (January 17, 1914): 108–9. The best early overview of the community-trust movement is Walter Greenough, "The Dead Hand Harnessed: The Significance of Community Trusts," *Scribner's* 74 (December 1923): 697–705. The impression given by these primary sources that the foundation was an immediate success is corrected by Richard Pogue's *The Cleveland Foundation at Seventy-Five* (New York: Newcomen Society of the United States, 1989), which points out that the endowment of the Cleveland Foundation grew very slowly. At the time of Goff's death in 1923, the endowment was yielding less than $25,000 annually—so little that its famous surveys were primarily underwritten by Goff personally and by a subsidy from the Cleveland Trust. The endowment did not reach the $10 million mark until 1946! The best general study of community foundations is David Hammack's "Community Foundations: The Delicate Question of Purpose" (Cleveland: Mandel Center Discussion Paper Series, 1989).

Primary sources on the spread of community trusts include "Four New Community Trusts Established," *Survey* 34 (June 12, 1915): 239–40; "Charity Federation and Its Fruits," *Survey* 36 (May 13, 1916): 187–88; W. J. Norton, "Progress of Financial Federation," *National Conference on Social Work* (1917): 503–7; F. M. Hollingshead, "Community Foundations," *Survey* 45 (January 29, 1921): 639–40; F. J. Parsons, "New York Community Trust," *American City* 23 (August 1920): 138–39; T. Devine, "Uniform Trust for Public Uses," *Survey* 45 (February 12, 1921): 694; T. Devine, "Community Trusts in

Chicago," *Survey* 45 (March 26, 1921): 918-19; F. D. Loomis, "Community Trusts," *Survey* 46 (April 13, 1922): 219; R. M. Yerkes, "Science and Community Trusts," *Science* 53 (June 10, 1921): 527-29; J. Cowan, "Community Trust," *Canadian Magazine* 63 (July 1924): 169-74; Raymond Moley, "Community Trust," *National Conference on Social Work* (1921): 427-32; Ralph Hayes, "To Help the Dead Hand by a Living Mind," *American City* 29 (December 1923): 600-602; Pierce Williams, "Could Community Trusts Work?" *Survey* 58 (May 15, 1927): 223-24; Ralph Hayes, "Dead Hands and Frozen Funds," *North American Review* 227 (May 1929): 607-14; H. Wickenden, "What the Community Trust Is Doing for American Cities," *American City* 40 (January 6, 1929): 124-26; and "Community Trust Funds in the United States," *Survey* 66 (April 15, 1931): 100. Eduard Lindeman's *Wealth and Culture: A Study of One Hundred Foundations and Community Trusts and Their Operations during the Decade 1921-1930* (New York: Harcourt Brace & Co., 1936) lists twenty community trusts with their establishment dates.

77. Among the most notable of these quasi-public entities in Cleveland were the City Plan Commission, which oversaw the development of the Group Plan for the Mall, and the Metropolitan Park District Commission. According to Pogue, the designation of public officials with power to appoint members of the Cleveland Foundation's distribution committee was suggested by Livy S. Richard, an editorial writer at the *Cleveland Press*. This was a not uncommon feature of community-oriented endowment trusts in cities with strong associational cultures. The trustees of Kansas City's Nelson Trust (see note 19 above) were appointed by the curators of the University of Missouri. (Richard may well have gotten this idea from Nelson, who had died the year before the Cleveland Foundation was formed.) Similarly, the trustees of Allentown, Pennsylvania's H. C. Trexler Foundation, formed in 1933, were appointed by the chief judge of the Lehigh County Orphan's Court (Pennsylvania's probate court). Interestingly, there appears to be a connection between these forms of public appointment and the concern about the "dead hand" of the past controlling the charity of the present which so preoccupied Goff and many of his contemporaries. Allentown's Trexler originally considered limiting the life of his foundation to twenty-five years, following the example of Julius Rosenwald, but ultimately settled on public appointment. For the thoughts of Rosenwald on this question, see his "Principles of Public Giving," *Atlantic Monthly*, May 1929, 599-606.

78. Greenough, "The Dead Hand Harnessed," 698.

79. George F. Baer to William F. Clark, July 17, 1903, in William Cahn, *A Pictorial History of American Labor* (New York: Crown Publishers, 1972), 189.

80. The class histories published from the mid-nineteenth century on provide detailed accounts, usually in the words of the graduates, of their personal, professional, and civic activities. Beginning with the year of graduation, class histories generally appeared at five-year intervals until the fiftieth—and sometimes the sixtieth—"year out." The classbooks are most useful, not only for investigating the collective experiences of particular cohorts of educated young men as they mature, but also for studying civic and corporate cultures.

My observations on civic participation are drawn from *Harvard Class of 1905—Twenty-Fifth Anniversary Report* (Cambridge: Privately Printed for the Class by the Plimpton Press, 1930); and *History of the Class of 1905—Yale College* (New Haven: Published under the Direction of the Class Secretaries Bureau, 1930).

81. Oliver Wendell Holmes, *Autocrat of the Breakfast Table* (New York: Sagamore Press, 1957), 119-20.

82. An interesting description of the Hapgood family's activities is included in Kurt Vonnegut's novel *Jailbird* (New York: Dell Publishing Co., 1979), 18-19. The protagonist of this book is, like the Hapgoods, a Harvard-educated Hoosier. Although Vonnegut is generally disliked by the philanthropic community and is something of a source of embarrassment to his native place, his work contains valuable observations on the civic and institutional culture of Indianapolis, which resembled that of Cleveland in many respects.

83. Norman Hapgood, "Modern Charity," *Harper's Weekly* 51 (March 20, 1915): 268.

84. Like so many pioneers of alternatives to the dominant private model of philanthropy, Rosenwald has been overlooked by scholars and biographers. The best available study of the community setting in which he operated—and one that, happily, gives serious attention to his importance—is Kathleen McCarthy's *Noblesse Oblige: Charity and Philanthropy in Chicago, 1849-1929* (Chicago: University of Chicago Press, 1982).

85. Julius Rosenwald, "Charity," *Harper's Weekly* 51 (March 27, 1915): 522.

86. An indication of the quasi-monopoly status of private universities in higher education in the Northeast is suggested by the fact that Massachusetts, Connecticut, and New York did not develop comprehensive state-financed universities until the 1960s. Charles W. Eliot's correspondence in the 1880s and 1890s is full of fervid arguments against establishing a national university under federal auspices.

87. Lester Salamon, "Partners in Public Service: The Scope and Theory of Government-Nonprofit Relations," in Powell, ed., *The Nonprofit Sector*, 101.

88. Duffus, "Cleveland."

89. Donald Holbrook, *The Boston Trustee* (Boston: Marshall Jones Co., 1937).

90. The origins of the leading Brahmin families are recounted in Mary Caroline Crawford, *Famous Families of Massachusetts* (Boston: Little, Brown & Co., 1930).

91. On the status of corporations in colonial Massachusetts, see E. M. Dodd, *American Business Corporations until 1860, with Special Reference to Massachusetts* (Cambridge: Harvard University Press, 1960); and J. S. Davis, *Essays in the Earlier History of American Corporations* (Cambridge: Harvard University Press, 1917).

92. On the question of the status of Harvard as a private institution, see John S. Whitehead, *The Separation of College and State* (New Haven: Yale University Press, 1976); and Ronald Story, *Forging of an Aristocracy* (Middletown, Conn.: Wesleyan University Press, 1980). The best general account of

the debate over the public/private status of corporations is in Oscar and Mary Flug Handlin, *Commonwealth: A Study of the Role of Government in the American Economy, 1774–1861* (Cambridge: Harvard University Press, 1969), 93. See also "Prescott v. Tarbell," *Massachusetts Reports* 1 (1804): 204.

94. "Parsons et ux. v. Winslow," *Massachusetts Reports* 6 (1810): 169.

95. The interrelations between the law of testamentary and charitable trusts are recounted in Peter Dobkin Hall, "Family Structure *and Class Consolidation among the Boston Brahmins*" (Ph.D. diss., State University of New York at Stony Brook, 1973).

96. "Harvard College and Massachusetts General Hospital v. Francis Amory, Trustee," *Massachusetts Reports* 26 (1830): 446.

97. On the rise of democratic politics in Massachusetts, see Richard Buel, *Securing the Revolution: Ideology and Politics, 1789–1815* (Ithaca: Cornell University Press, 1972); Noble E. Cunningham, *The Jeffersonian Republicans in Power: Party Operations, 1801–1809* (Chapel Hill: University of North Carolina Press, 1963); and Paul Goodman, *The Democratic Republicans of Massachusetts* (Boston: Little, Brown & Co., 1964).

98. For a detailed account of this search, see Peter Dobkin Hall, "Institutional Values and the Origins of the Corporation in Connecticut," *Connecticut Studies* 29 (November 1988): 63–90.

99. The strategic importance of the colleges is attested to by the sobriquet "seminaries of sedition" applied to them by the British during the Revolution. Later, a Federalist clergyman was quoted as stating that "when all the colleges are under our control it will establish our sentiments and influence, so that we can manage the civil government as we please." See Dr. Burton, *To the Public: Priestcraft Exposed and Primitive Christianity Defined: A Religious Work* (Lockport, N.Y., 1828). For a detailed discussion of the political impact conservatives expected colleges and other private institutions to have, see Charles Foster, *An Errand of Mercy* (Chapel Hill: University of North Carolina Press, 1963).

100. Story, *Forging of an Aristocracy*, 135–59, provides an excellent account of the political dimensions of alterations in Harvard's charter.

101. Samuel Eliot Morison, *Three Centuries of Harvard* (Cambridge: Harvard University Press, 1936), 212.

102. "Dartmouth College v. Woodward," 4 *Wheaton* 518; 4 L. Ed. 629 (1819).

103. Asahel Stearns and Lemuel Shaw, *The General Laws of Massachusetts* (Boston, 1823), chap, 190, sect. 37. For an incisive discussion of the distinction between equity and common law, see Scott, *Law of Trusts* (1939), 1:8.

104. Hall, "Family Structure and Class Consolidation among the Boston Brahmins," 195–322.

105. Oliver Wendell Holmes, *Elsie Venner* (New York: New American Library, 1961), 19.

106. See Peter Dobkin Hall, *The Organization of American Culture* (New York: New York University Press, 1982), 55–75.

107. See Hall, "Family Structure and Class Consolidation among the Boston Brahmins," 323–469.

108. On changes in the organization partnerships, see Peter Dobkin Hall, "Family Structure and Economic Organization," in Tamara Hareven, ed., *Family and Kin in Urban Communities* (New York: New Viewpoints, 1976).

109. Holmes, *Autocrat of the Breakfast Table*, 212.

110. Samuel Atkins Eliot, "Public and Private Charities of Boston," *North American Review* 61 (July 1845): 135–59, and "Charities of Boston," *North American Review* 76 (July 1860): 149–65.

111. See Hall, "The Model of Boston Charity," *Science and Society* 38, no. 4 (1974): 464–77.

112. See Gerald T. White, *The Massachusetts Hospital Life Insurance Company* (Cambridge: Harvard University Press, 1957).

113. Story, *Forging of an Aristocracy*.

114. Henry Adams, *The Education of Henry Adams* (New York: Modern Library, 1931), 54–55.

115. Ibid., 55.

116. Alfred D. Chandler, *The Visible Hand: The Managerial Revolution in American Business* (Cambridge: Harvard University Press, 1977), 345–76.

117. Ibid., 608–9.

118. James Jackson Putnam, *A Memoir of Dr. James Jackson* (Cambridge: Privately Printed, 1905), 81.

119. The best scholarly study of the Jacksons and related families is K. W. Porter's *The Jacksons and the Lees* (Cambridge: Harvard University Press, 1937).

120. Hall, "Family Structure and Class Consolidation among the Boston Brahmins," 226–30.

121. Barrett Wendell to Charles W. Eliot, April 20, 1890. C. W. Eliot Papers, Harvard University Archives.

122. Charles W. Eliot, "The New Education," *Atlantic Monthly* 23 (February 1869): 218.

123. Ibid., 212.

124. Charles W. Eliot, "Inaugural Address as President of Harvard," in Hofstadter and Smith, eds., *American Higher Education*, 609.

125. Ibid.

126. Eliot, "The New Education," 212.

127. Ibid., 216.

128. Ibid., 203.

129. Croly, *The Promise of American Life*, 438–39. On Croly himself as a product of the New Education, see David W. Levy, *Herbert Croly of the New Republic* (Princeton: Princeton University Press, 1985).

130. Charles W. Eliot, "Views Respecting the Tax Exemption," in Harvard University, *Report of the President and Treasurer* (Cambridge: Printed for the University, 1874), 369–94.

131. Eliot, "Inaugural Address as President of Harvard," 619.

132. Ibid., 620.

133. Ibid., 617.

134. Ibid., 618.

135. Eliot, "Public and Private Charities of Boston," 164.

136. Ibid.

137. See works such as Robert Wiebe, *The Search for Order, 1877-1920* (New York: Hill & Wang, 1965); Burton Bledstein, *The Culture of Professionalism* (New York: W. W. Norton & Co., 1976); and Martin J. Sklar, *The Corporate Reconstruction of American Capitalism* (New York: Cambridge University Press, 1988).

138. Hall, *The Organization of American Culture*, 95-124.

139. For example, A. W. Scott, "Charitable Trusts in New York," *New York University Law Review* 26, no. 2 (April 1951): 251ff.

140. These include "Williams v. Williams" *New York Reports* 8 (1853): 525; "Bascom v. Albertson" *New York Reports* 34 (1866): 584; and "Cornell University v. Fiske," *One Hundred Thirty-Sixth U.S. Reports* 152 (1890). According to Scott, had the Tilden bequest been made in New York, Michigan, Minnesota, Maryland, Virginia, or West Virginia, it would have been held invalid. He is probably understating the case, because he failed to recognize the extent to which the bequest was open-ended in its charitable purposes, focusing instead on the technical issue of naming as trustee corporations not yet in existence.

141. "Tilden v. Green," in *Reports of Cases Decided in the Court of Appeals of the State of New York* (Albany: James B. Lyon, 1892), 29-87.

142. James Barr Ames, "The Failure of the Tilden Trust," in *Lectures in Legal History* (Cambridge: Harvard University Press, 1913).

143. James Wooten, "The Emergence of Nonprofit Legal Education in New York: A Case Study," Working Paper no. 154 (New Haven: Program on Non-Profit Organizations, Yale University, 1990).

144. On the heterogeneity of New York's elite, see Moses Yale Beach, *Wealth and Biography of the Wealthy Citizens of New York* (New York, 1845).

145. On the emergence of New York's elite legal culture, see Wooten, "The Emergence of Nonprofit Legal Education in New York"; and Jerold S. Auerbach, *Unequal Justice: Lawyers and Social Change in Modern America* (New York: Oxford University Press, 1976).

146. See Thomas Bender, *New York Intellect: A History of Intellectual Life in New York City, from 1750 to the Beginnings of Our Own Time* (New York: Alfred A. Knopf, 1987).

147. On the peculiarities of New York's charitable culture, see Lindsley F. Kimball, "Oral History," in the Rockefeller Archive Center. Pierce Williams and Frederick E. Croxton's *Corporation Contributions to Organized Community Welfare Services* (New York: National Bureau of Economic Research, 1930) provides a comparative context for assessing the relative weakness of New Yorkers' charitable efforts. A more recent appraisal is Julian Wolpert's *Philanthropy in the New York Region* (New York: New York Regional Association of Grantmakers, 1989).

148. Clarence Day, *Life with Father* (New York: E. P. Dutton, 1936); Sinclair Lewis, *Babbitt* (New York: Charles Scribner's Sons, 1960); and John P. Marquand, *The Late George Apley* (Boston: Little Brown & Co., 1936). Lewis

presents an especially interesting example of the interaction of the federationist and civil-privatist orientations in the chapter dealing with the involvement of Babbitt with his church's Sunday school. Such accommodations of these two civic styles must have been fairly common during the 1920s.

149. Ellis Hawley, "Herbert Hoover, the Commerce Secretariat, and the Vision of an 'Associative State,' " in E. J. Perkins, ed., *Men and Organizations* (New York: G. P. Putnam's Sons, 1977).

150. See especially A. T. Vanderbilt, *Fortune's Children: The Fall of the House of Vanderbilt* (New York: William Morrow & Co., 1989).

151. Grace Goulder, *John D. Rockefeller: The Cleveland Years* (Cleveland: Western Reserve Historical Society, 1972).

152. Chandler, *The Visible Hand*, 419–26.

153. Raymond Fosdick and Henry Pringle, *An Adventure in Giving: The Story of the General Education Board* (New York: Harper & Row, Publishers, 1962).

154. Raymond Fosdick, *The Story of the Rockefeller Foundation* (New York: Harper & Brothers, 1952), 17.

155. Ibid., 20.

156. Ibid., 21.

157. See appendices in Fosdick and Pringle, *An Adventure in Giving;* and Fosdick, *The Story of the Rockefeller Foundation.*

158. John Harr and Peter Johnson, *Rockefeller Century* (New York: Charles Scribner's Sons, 1988), 305.

159. Raymond Fosdick to John D. Rockefeller 3rd, undated, RG-2/JDR3rd/Box 1/Folder 2.

160. John D. Rockefeller 3rd to Raymond Fosdick, 6/24/1932.

161. John D. Rockefeller 3rd to Roger Greene, 6/23/1932.

162. John D. Rockefeller 3rd to Roger Greene, 6/23/1932.

163. Raymond Fosdick to John D. Rockefeller 3rd, 6/26/1932.

164. Harr and Johnson, *Rockefeller Century,* 306.

165. Henry Fairfield Osborn to John D. Rockefeller, Jr, 7/17/1933, RG-3/JDR3/Confidential Files/Box 3/Folder: Mr. JDR, 1930–35.

166. John D. Rockefeller 3rd to John D. Rockefeller, Jr., 12/28/1934, RG-2/JDR3/Box 1/ Folder 2.

167. Stuart Crocker to John D. Rockefeller 3rd, 11/14/1936.

168. Arthur Packard to John D. Rockefeller 3rd, 11/18/1936.

169. John D. Rockefeller 3rd to Thomas Debevoise, 12/29/1934, RG-2/JDR3/Box 1/Folder: correspondence with former employees.

170. "Boards and Committees—Mr. J.D.R., 3rd as of May 15, 1941," RG-2/JDR3rd/Box 2/Folder 1.

171. Memorandum from Robert Goheen to Eugene Struckoff, Council on Foundations Papers, Box 5, RAC. This undated note, obviously written within minutes of the council's learning of the formation of the commission, expresses the philanthropic mainstream's disapproval in no uncertain terms. Goheen doubted that this group of "lawyers and highly institutionalized establishment types" had anything to teach "philanthropy's traditional practi-

tioners." In line with this, the council's bimonthly publication, *Foundation News*, ignored the existence of the commission until the issuance of its report in 1975.

172. Leon Harris, *Only to God* (New York: Athenaeum, 1967).

173. John D. Rockefeller, Jr., to John D. Rockefeller 3rd, 12/18/1934, RG3/ JDR3/Confidential Files/Box 3/ Mr. JDRJr., 1930–35.

174. Detailed information on the activities of John D. Rockefeller 3rd as a trustee of such organizations as Lincoln Center, the Population Council, Japan House, the Rockefeller Foundation, the Rockefeller Brothers Fund, and the Corporation for Public Broadcasting are included in his papers. One interesting dimension of the family office's use of associates was as members of boards in which the family had an interest but, for one reason or another, did not wish to serve personally. As the Lindsley F. Kimball interview suggests, this practice dated back to John D. Rockefeller, Jr.'s time, when Kimball served as his patron's point man at the New York Community Fund and United Service Organizations.

175. George Marcus, "The Making of Pious Persons within Contemporary Notable Families," *Sociological Perspectives* 32, no. 2 (1989): 253–68.

176. Ibid.

177. George Marcus, "The Problem of the Unseen World of Wealth for the Rich: Toward an Ethnography of Complex Connections," *Ethos* 17 (1989): 11–19.

178. Kenneth Rose's "The State of Foundation Archives" (Paper delivered at the Annual Meeting of the Society of American Archivists, Saint Louis, October 18, 1989) indicates that only a handful of foundations even have records-management policies, much less archives. Those such as Ford and the Carnegie Corporation, which have in-house archives, are very restrictive in making accessible potentially sensitive materials.

179. Teresa Odendahl's *Charity Begins at Home: Generosity and Self-Interest among the Philanthropic Elite* (New York: Basic Books, 1990) sheds considerable light on these issues.

180. Federationist charitable vehicles, the Community Chest and the community foundation, were energetically promoted by their founders—see notes 71 and 76 above.

181. For example, in New Haven such services are offered through Business Volunteers for the Arts, which is a program of the New Haven Arts Council, the Volunteer Action Center, and Development and Technical Assistance. The New Haven Foundation has not only generously funded these organizations but also directly underwritten the efforts of organizations to upgrade their boards.

182. These community-based leadership-education and board-intervention activities are connected to national ones in a variety of ways, both through the New Haven Foundation, which is a member of Independent Sector (which is turn operates the National Center for Nonprofit Boards) and through the United Way. Local chapters of national federations, such the Girl Scouts, have

also been active in promoting trustee education and in producing materials for locally based programs.

183. Notable examples of such theoretically informed but clinically applicable literature are books and articles by Rosabeth Moss Kanter, Clayton Alderfer, and Thomas Gilmore.

184. Although many academic centers now focusing on philanthropy, voluntarism, and nonprofit organizations offer "short courses" for trustees, their primary curricula are, almost without exception, devoted to training managers. Nonprofits research shows a similar bias toward the study of managers over trustees: for example, of the 145 Working Papers published by Yale's Program on Non-Profit Organizations since 1978, only three have specifically focused on boards of trustees.

185. Frederick T. Miller, "Board Members from the 'Transitional Generation' Are the Key to Helping Organizations Move Ahead," *Chronicle of Philanthropy* 1, no. 14 (May 2, 1989): 36.

186. Judith Huggins Balfe, "The Baby-boom Generation: Lost Patrons, Lost Audience?" in Margaret Jane Wyszomirski and Pat Clubb, eds., *The Cost of Culture: Patterns of Private Arts Patronage* (New York: ACA Books, 1989), 14.

187. Ibid., 15.

188. Our knowledge of the process through which individuals become trustees—how they are recruited, at what age, into what kind of institution—is negligible. The best of the studies, such as those done by Dan Fenn on executives as volunteers, and by Meyer Zald, date only from the late 1960s and early 1970s. Although the data exist to reconstruct these patterns back to the early-nineteenth century, no scholar has yet taken on the task. Clearly any reliable conclusions about the changing nature of trusteeship require that such a study be undertaken!

189. Myron Magnet, "Changing Business Ethics," *Fortune,* December 8, 1986.

190. For an example of this, see my "Conflicting Managerial Cultures in Nonprofit Organizations," 153–65.

191. Among the best studies on the process of reconciling these competing assumptions are Rosabeth Moss Kanter and David Sommers, "Doing Well While Doing Good," in Powell, ed., *The Nonprofit Sector;* and Melissa Middleton, "Governing Boards and the Planning Process: Exploring the Relationship" (Ph.D. diss., Yale University, 1990).

192. See Robert B. Winans, "The Folk, the Stage, and the Five-String Banjo in the Nineteenth Century," in Glenn Lomey, ed., *Papers and Proceedings of the Conference on the Musical Theater in America* (Westport, Conn.: Greenwood press, 1984), 71–97); and Hans Nathan, *Dan Emmett and the Rise of Early Negro Minstrelsy* (Norman: University of Oklahoma Press, 1962).

193. On multiple levels of meanings of artifacts, see James Deetz, *In Small Things Forgotten* (New York: Anchor Books, 1977). On reading the multiple meanings of organizations as artifacts, see Peter Dobkin Hall, "Organiza-

tion as Artifact," in Joan Scott, ed., "Essays in Honor of William R. Taylor" (New York: Wadsworth Publishing Co., forthcoming).

CHAPTER 5: CONFLICTING MANAGERIAL CULTURES IN NONPROFIT ORGANIZATIONS

1. Tom Wolfe, *Radical Chic and Mau-Mauing the Flak Catchers* (New York: Farrar, Straus & Giroux, 1970).

2. Israel Unterman and Richard Hart Davis, "The Strategy Gap in Not-for-Profits." *Harvard Business Review* 60, no. 3 (May–June 1982): 30–40.

3. President's Task Force on Private Sector Initiatives, *The Task Force* (Washington, D.C.: President's Task Force on Private Sector Initiatives, 1982).

4. Lester M. Salamon and Alan J. Abramson, *The Federal Government and the Nonprofit Sector* (Washington, D.C.: Urban Institute, 1981).

5. Despite the enormous investment in "leadership-training" programs designed to educate trustees, there has been hardly any empirical research on the changing composition of boards and the backgrounds of trustees. Miriam M. Wood's paper "The Governing Board's Existential Quandary: An Empirical Analysis of Board Behavior in the Charitable Sector," Working Paper no. 143 (New Haven: Program on Non-Profit Organizations, Yale University, 1990) is especially notable for the attention that it gives to this issue. See also Judith Huggins Balfe, "The Baby-Boom Generation: Lost Matrons, Lost Audience," in Margaret-Jane Wyszomirski and Pat Clubb, eds., *The Cost of Culture: Patterns and Prospects of Private Arts Patronage* (New York: ACA Books, 1989); Dan H. Fenn, Jr., "Executives as Community Volunteers," *Harvard Business Review* 49, no. 2 (March–April 1971): 4–16; Peter Dobkin Hall, "Baby-Boomers Have Demonstrated Commitment to the Non-Profit Sector: They Helped Create Most of It," *Chronicle of Philanthropy* 1, no. 15 (May 16, 1989): 29; Peter Dobkin Hall, "Cultures of Trusteeship in the United States," Working Paper no. 153 (New Haven: Program on Non-Profit Organizations, Yale University, 1990); Melissa Middleton, "Nonprofit Boards of Directors: Beyond the Governance Function," in W. W. Powell, ed., *The Nonprofit Sector: A Research Handbook* (New Haven: Yale University Press, 1987), 141–53; and Frederick T. Miller, "Board Members from the 'Transitional Generation' Are the Key to Helping Organizations Move Ahead," *Chronicle of Philanthropy* 1, no. 14 (May 2, 1989): 36.

6. Wood, "The Governing Board's Existential Quandary."

7. Peter Dobkin Hall, "To Make Non-Profit Organizations More Effective, and the 'Secret Wars' between Boards and Staffs," *Chronicle of Philanthropy* 1, no. 3 (November 22, 1988): 32.

8. See Charles Perrow, "Goals and Powerstructures: A Historical Case Study," in Eliot Friedson, ed., *The Hospital in Modern Society* (New York: Free Press, 1963).

9. Regina E. Herzlinger and H. David Sherman, "Advantages of Fund Ac-

counting in 'Nonprofits,' " *Harvard Business Review* 58, no. 3 (May–June 1980): 94–105.

10. Lizabeth Moody, "State Statutes Governing Directors of Charitable Corporations," *University of San Francisco Law Review* 18, no. 3 (Summer 1984): 749–61.

11. Herzlinger and Sherman, "Advantages of Fund Accounting in 'Nonprofits,' " 97–98.

12. In November 1986, "Business Involvement in School Reform," a conference jointly sponsored by the American Enterprise Institute and the U.S. Education Department, reported on business voluntarism in a half-dozen states. One of the most surprising findings of the conference was the uniform expression of the personal satisfactions of voluntarism reported by participating business executives.

13. Adam Stern and Mark Vermillion, "Corporate Social Investment," *Foundation News* 27, no. 2 (November–December 1986): 8–66.

14. Moody, "State Statutes Governing Directors of Charitable Corporations," 779.

15. Clayton P. Alderfer, "The Invisible Director on Corporate Boards," *Harvard Business Review* 64, no. 6 (November–December 1986): 38–52.

CHAPTER 6: PAPER EPHEMERA: MANAGERS, POLICYMAKERS, SCHOLARS, AND THE FUTURE OF AMERICAN PHILANTHROPY

1. Peter Drucker quoted in Rosabeth Moss Kanter and David Sommers, "Doing Well while Doing Good: Dilemmas of Performance Measurement in Nonprofit Organizations," in W. W. Powell, ed., *The Nonprofit Sector: A Research Handbook* (New Haven: Yale University Press, 1987), 156.

2. Tables in the eleventh edition of the *Foundation Directory* show that of the 5,148 directory foundations established before 1986, 3,959 were established after 1950 (New York: Foundation Center, 1987), viii.

3. F. Emerson Andrews, *Foundation Watcher* (Lancaster, Pa.: Franklin & Marshall College, 1973), 136. As Andrews pointed out in discussion the 1952 Cox Committee investigation, the issue of how foundations were defined had a dramatic impact on the question of how many there were. By the government's definition, there were 35,000; by Andrews' "tighter definition," there were only 1,007. Because the rapid proliferation of foundations was one of the major factors leading Congress to investigate tax-exempt organizations, the definitional question was crucially important.

4. On the strains that maturation puts on the ability of organizations to define their missions and goals, see Dennis N. T. Perkins et al., *Managing Creation: The Challenge of Building a New Organization* (New York: John Wiley & Sons), 1984); Walter W. Powell and Rebecca Friedkin, "Organizational Change in Nonprofit Organizations," in Powell, ed., *The Nonprofit Sector,* 180–94; and Miriam M. Wood, "The Governing Board's Existential Quandary:

An Empirical Analysis of Board Behavior in the Charitable Sector," Working Paper no. 143 (Program on Non-Profit Organizations, Yale University, 1989).

5. See Peter Dobkin Hall, "The Community Foundation and the Foundations of Community," Working Paper no. 34 (Program on Non-Profit Organizations, Yale University, 1980). See also Fran Henry, "Suffering from Founder's Syndrome?" *Foundation News* 30, no. 4 (July–August 1989): 56–58.

6. Elizabeth T. Boris and Deborah Brody, *Foundation Management Report 1988* (Washington, D.C.: Council on Foundations, 1988), 74. See also Teresa Jean Odendahl, Elizabeth Trocolli Boris, and Arlene Daniels, *Working in Foundations* (New York: Foundation Center, 1985).

7. No foundation has reflected more conscientiously on the problem of self-evaluation than the Lilly Endowment. See Lilly Endowment, Inc., *Evaluation Notebook* (Indianapolis: Lilly Endowment, 1989). I am grateful to D. Susan Wisely for sharing this important document with me, as well as two important background memoranda relating to the endowment's own self-evaluation process, "Invitation to Reflection" and "An Introduction to Foundation Evaluation."

Lilly's unique approach to this problem owes a great deal to the business tradition of self-assessment, which is grounded in the critical management literature. Robert Greenleaf, who, as a consultant, played a key role in shaping Lilly's policies, had been head of personnel management at AT&T. AT&T's executive cadre in the days when Greenleaf was active there included Chester Barnard, whose *Functions of the Executive* (Cambridge: Harvard University Press, 1938) is generally regarded as the basis of modern organization and management theory.

8. See Kanter and Sommers, "Doing Well while Doing Good," 154–66.

9. On the analysis of organizations as information systems, see Richard L. Daft and Karl E. Weick, "Toward a Model of Organizations as Interpretation Systems," *Academy of Management Review* 9, no. 2 (1984): 284–95; and Jeffrey Pfeffer and Gerald Salancik, *The External Control of Organizations* (New York: Harper & Row, 1978), particularly their chapter "The Organizational Environment and How It Is Known," 62–91.

10. On planning as an interpretive and essentially political process, see Jane Covey and L. David Brown, "Beyond Strategic Planning: Strategic Decisions in Nonprofit Organizations," Working Paper no. 5 (Institute for Development Research, Boston, 1985); and Melissa Middleton, "Planning as Strategy: The Logic, Symbol, and Politics of Planning in Nonprofit Organizations" (Ph.D. diss., Yale University, 1989). See also John W. Meyer and W. Richard Scott, *Organizational Environments: Ritual and Rationality* (Beverly Hills: Sage Publications, 1983).

11. On the role that historical issues played in the Buck Trust case, see *University of San Francisco Law Review* 21, no. 4 (Summer 1987): 585–762.

12. On the significance of records and record-keeping formats on the internal politics of organizations, see David J. Cooper, David Hayes, and Frank Wolfe, "Accounting in Organized Anarchies: Understanding and Designing Accounting Systems in Ambiguous Situations," *Accounting, Organizations,*

and Society 6, no. 3 (1981): 175–91; Regina Herzlinger, "Why Data Systems in Nonprofit Organizations Fail," *Harvard Business Review,* January–February 1977, 47–52; Regina Herzlinger and and H. David Sherman, "Advantages of Fund Accounting in 'Nonprofits,' " *Harvard Business Review* 58, no. 3 (May–June 1980): 94–105; and M. Lynne Markus and Jeffrey Pfeffer, "Power and the Design and Implementation of Accounting and Control Systems," *Accounting, Organizations, and Society* 8, nos. 2–3 (1983): 205–18.

13. Michael D. Cohen and James G. March, *Leadership and Ambiguity: The American College President* (New York: McGraw-Hill Book Co., 1974), 214–15.

14. On the politics of information and its role in shaping the politics of governing boards, see Clayton Alderfer, "The Invisible Director on Corporate Boards," *Harvard Business Review* 64, no. 6 (November–December 1986): 38–52; and Peter Dobkin Hall, "Conflicting Managerial Cultures in Nonprofit Organizations," *Nonprofit Management and Leadership* 1, no. 2 (Winter 1990): 153–65.

15. Andrews, *Foundation Watcher,* 134.

16. Elizabeth McCormack, "Looking Back to Look Forward" (Keynote address delivered at the Annual Meeting of Independent Sector, Houston, October 23, 1988). I am grateful to Dr. McCormack for providing me with her text.

17. Kenneth Rose, "The State of Foundation Archives: Results from the Rockefeller Archive Center's Survey of the Thousand Largest American Foundations" (Paper delivered at the Annual Meeting of the Society of American Archivists, Saint Louis, October 18, 1989). See also Paul Ylvisaker, "Today's Administrative Memo Is Tomorrow's Historical Document," *Foundation News,* March–April 1978, 32; and Charles T. Morrissey, "Ideas and Creative Philanthropy: Does Grant Making Have a Life of the Mind?" *Foundation News* 19 (March–April 1979): 21–22.

18. See Clifford T. Honicker, "The Hidden Files," *New York Times Magazine,* November 19, 1989.

19. Recent congressional inquiries into the procedures of scientific research, as well as recent court decisions on the confidentiality of university tenure decisions, suggest that governmental interest in organizational processes is likely to increase in the future.

CHAPTER 7: OBSTACLES TO NONPROFITS TEACHING AND RESEARCH

1. Bernard Bailyn, *Education in the Forming of American Society* (Chapel Hill: University of North Carolina Press, 1960).

2. As of 1988, of nineteen academic centers, only five received more than one-third of their funding from their host institutions. Independent Sector, *Academic Centers and Research Institutes Focusing on the Study of Philanthropy, Voluntarism, and Not-for-Profit Activity—A Progress Report* (Washington, D.C.: Independent Sector, 1988), 35.

3. Robert Dahl, "Business and Politics: A Critical Appraisal of Political

Science," *American Political Science Review* 53, no. 1 (March 1959): 1–34.

4. See Michael D. Cohen and James G. March, *Leadership and Ambiguity: The American College President* (New York: McGraw-Hill Book Co., 1974).

5. I am grateful to economic historian William N. Parker for his insights into the problematic relationship between American studies and economic scholarship.

6. The ambitiously broad outlook of the first wave of business history was summed up in William Miller, ed., *Men in Business: Essays on the Historical Role of the Entrepreneur* (Cambridge: Harvard University Press, 1952). This promise failed to be realized. Until recently, business history has been dominated by the protégés of Harvard's Alfred D. Chandler, who have tended to share a highly rationalistic, technologically deterministic view of American economic development. The hegemony of this viewpoint has recently been challenged by a younger generation of scholars based in sociology and the history of science and technology. For a good example of this new work, see Wiebe E. Bijker, Thomas P. Hughes, and Trevor Pinch, *The Social Construction of Technological Systems* (Cambridge: MIT Press, 1989).

7. The Arthur W. Page Papers at the Wisconsin State Historical Society contain valuable material on foundation underwriting of American studies and business history. Page, a former vice-president of AT&T in charge of public relations and trustee of a number of leading foundations, was one of a group of top corporate people who, in the years following World War II, sought, through strategic grant-making, to promote opinions favorable to the free-enterprise system and to the United States' distinctive values.

CHAPTER 8: DILEMMAS OF RESEARCH ON PHILANTHROPY, VOLUNTARISM, AND NONPROFIT ORGANIZATIONS

1. Barry D. Karl, "Nonprofit Institutions," *Science* 236 (22 May 1987): 984–85.

2. The best introduction to the conceptual framework of sectoring is in Carolyn Webber and Aaron Wildavsky's *A History of Taxation and Expenditure in the Western World* (New York: Simon & Schuster, 1986), 476–559. On the implementation of these concepts, see National Income Division, U.S. Department of Commerce, *National Income, 1954 Edition* (Washington, D.C.: Government Printing Office, 1954). On the reformulation of the national income accounts to include a nonprofit sector, see Richard and Nancy D. Ruggles, "Integrated Economic Accounts of the United States," Working Paper no. 841 (Institution for Social and Policy Studies, Yale University, New Haven, 1980), 4–30.

3. F. Emerson Andrews' account of the difficulties encountered in assembling the first *Foundation Directory* are to be found in his autobiography, *The Foundation Watcher* (Lancaster, Pa.: Franklin & Marshall College, 1973), 156–58, 201–2, 217–19.

4. Quoted in Horace Coon, *Money to Burn: What the Great American Phi-*

lanthropic Foundations Do with Their Money (London & New York: Longmans, Green & Co., 1938), 334–35.

5. These volumes, most of them now out of print, include Merle Curti, *American Philanthropy Abroad* (New Brunswick, N.J.: Rutgers University Press, 1963); Merle Curti and Roderick Nash, *Philanthropy in the Shaping of American Higher Education* (New Brunswick, N.J.: Rutgers University Press, 1965); Scott M. Cutlip, *Fundraising in the United States: Its Role in American Philanthropy* (New Brunswick, N.J.: Rutgers University Press, 1965); Howard S. Miller, *The Legal Foundations of American Philanthropy* (Madison: State Historical Society of Wisconsin, 1961); and Daniel M. Fox, *Engines of Culture: Philanthropy and Art Museums* (Madison: Department of History, University of Wisconsin, 1963).

6. The most easily available, though necessarily partisan, overview of strategizing in the era of the 1969 Tax Reform Act is Andrews, *Foundation Watcher*. Detailed, critical, and gossipy reporting by Richard Fitzgerald on the congressional hearings in *Non-Profit Report* (now *Philanthropy Monthly*) is invaluable. The most comprehensive files of unpublished materials on lobbying on the 1969 Tax Reform Act are in the Rockefeller Archive Center's collections in the papers of John D. Rockefeller 3rd and his associate Datus Smith and in the recently donated files of the Council on Foundations.

7. To date, there is no written history of the Filer Commission. The best published sources on its composition, methods, and impact are in *Non-Profit Report/Philanthropy Monthly* 6, no. 11 (November 1973); 7, no. 7 (July 1974); 7, no. 8 (August 1974); 8, no. 6 (June 1975); 8, no. 12 (December 1975); 9, no. 11 (November 1976); and 10, no. 1 (January 1977). The John D. Rockefeller 3rd, Datus Smith, Porter McKeever, and Council on Foundations Papers at the Rockefeller Archive Center provide detailed information on every aspect of the commission's activities. The commission's own files, donated by Leonard Silverstein, its executive director, to IS, are not available to researchers.

8. Commission on Private Philanthropy and Public Needs, *Giving in America: Toward a Stronger Voluntary Sector* (Washington, D.C.: Commission on Philanthropy and Public Needs), 26.

9. "A National Commission on Philanthropy—an Excerpt of Donald R. Spuehler's Report to the Filer Commission," *Philanthropy Monthly* 9, no. 6 (June 1975): 10–16.

10. Needs, *Giving in America*, 221–22.

11. "Private Philanthropy: Vital and Innovative or Passive and Irrelevant—The Donee Group Report and Recommendations," in *Research Papers Sponsored by the Commission on Private Philanthropy and Public Needs*, 6 vols. (Washington, D.C.: Department of the Treasury, 1977), 84.

12. Following the issuance of its report, the Filer Commission's members were able to persuade Treasury Department Secretary William Simon to establish an advisory committee on philanthropy in the Treasury Department. It was hoped that this would become the nucleus of the "permanent national commission" (Pablo Eisenberg, telephone interview, March 21, 1989; "PM Newsletter," *Philanthropy Monthly* 10 [March 1977]: 4). On the fate of this

plan once the Carter administration took office, see Leonard Silverstein, "Memorandum to Commission Members," April 18, 1977, and the clipping "Treasury Secretary Blumenthal Cuts Advisory Committees," *Treasury News,* March 15, 1977 (Rockefeller Archive Center, RG-17, Porter McKeever Papers, Filer Commission folder).

13. "Organizing Charity," *Philanthropy Monthly* 9, no. 11 (November 1976): 7–11, gives an excellent overview of the groups vying for the national commission's mantle. See also *Journal of Voluntary Action Research* 1, no. 1 (Winter 1972). I am grateful to Jon Van Til, David Horton Smith, and Pablo Eisenberg, who shared their recollections of this period in telephone interviews on March 21, 1989. Once again, the papers of John D. Rockefeller 3rd and Porter McKeever contain invaluable information both on the groups themselves and on the concerns of funders with regard to the research problem.

14. Kingman Brewster, John G. Simon, and Charles E. Lindblom, "Proposal for a Study of Independent Institutions" (unpublished grant proposal dated October 1975), author's collection. On how this proposal was regarded, see "Organizing Charity," *Philanthropy Monthly* 9, no. 11 (November 1976): 9–10.

15. John G. Simon, "Research on Philanthropy" (Speech given at the twenty-fifth anniversary conference of the National Council on Philanthropy, Denver, November 8, 1979). The text of this speech was published as an Independent Sector Research Report in July 1980.

16. Lindblom's ideas about the purposes of the program are scattered through the minutes of the 1978–79 workshop on nonprofit organizations. Minutes of these meeting, taken by John Simon's student Bob Boisture, are in the author's collection.

17. On the precarious position of Brewster at Yale by 1976–77, see his obituary in the *New York Times,* November 9, 1988.

18. Comments of Richard Sharpe, Ford Foundation program officer to the Yale nonprofits workshop, Seminar Minutes, January 16, 1979.

19. Simon, "Research on Philanthropy," 13.

20. "PM Newsletter," *Philanthropy Monthly* 11, no. 10 (October 1978): 3; "PM Newsletter," *Philanthropy Monthly* 12, no. 6 (June 1979): 3; and John J. Schwartz, "New Center for Charitable Statistics," *Philanthropy Monthly* 14, no. 3 (March 1981): 18–19.

21. Memorandum of Porter McKeever to John D. Rockefeller 3rd, "Re: Meetings with John Gardner and Walter McNerney in Washington, May 12" (May 16, 1978), and Porter McKeever's letter to Wayne Thompson, February 16, 1979 (Rockefeller Archive Center, RG-17S, Box 1). For background on political tensions within IS during this formative stage, see Henry C. Suhrke, "Independent Sector, Inc.—the 'How' and 'Why' of a Proposed Organization," *Philanthropy Monthly* 12, no. 10 (October 1979): 5–9, and "Who Speaks for Philanthropy," *Philanthropy Monthly* 15, no. 10 (October 1984): 13–17.

22. Independent Sector, *Program Plan* (as amended and approved by the membership, October 24, 1980), 37.

23. Independent Research Committee Minutes, September 13, 1983. See also

"*IS* Research Plan: A Program for the Development of Knowledge in the Independent Sector," September 1984, 1.

24. "Research Program Plan, 1985–86—First Working Draft," September 1985.

25. "Seminars, Colloquia, Workshops—A Plan to Stimulate the Development of Knowledge on the Independent Sector," September 1984, 2.

26. Independent Sector, *Academic Centers and Research Institutes Focusing on the Study of Philanthropy, Voluntarism, and Not-for-Profit Activity—A Progress Report* (Washington, D.C.: Independent Sector, 1988); and Virginia L. Hodgkinson, "Research on the Independent Sector: A Progress Report," August 1987. On the industry's understanding of the significance of IS's work in knowledge development, see David Johnston, "Nonprofit Pied Piper," *Foundation News* 30, no. 2 (March–April 1989): 67–69.

27. IS's expenditures for research went from $354,664 in 1985 to $658,270 in 1986, increasing to $825,554 by the end of 1987. Part of this increase can be accounted for by the merger of IS and the National Center for Charitable Statistics, but an increasing proportion was being devoted to in-house interpretive work. The first product of this in-house research effort was *From Belief to Commitment: The Activities and Finances of Religious Congregations in the United States—Findings from a National Survey* (Washington, D.C.: Independent Sector, 1988).

28. David Mathews, "The Independent Sector and the Political Responsibilities of the Public" (Keynote address delivered at the IS Spring Research Forum, New York City, March 6, 1987). In delivering the speech, Mathews referred to those pushing for an enlarged view of the sector as "an embattled minority" on the Research Committee, suggesting that there was some unhappiness within IS about the tendency of research to focus on "near- and medium-term issues."

29. Lance Buhl, "As We're Seen by Social Scientists," *Foundation News* 29, no. 1 (January–February 1988): 71–72 (review of W. W. Powell, ed., *The Nonprofit Sector: A Research Handbook*).

30. Salamon's paper "Of Market Failure, Voluntary Failure, and Third-Party Government: Toward a Theory of Government-Nonprofit Relations in the Modern Welfare State," was originally delivered at the Association of Voluntary Action Scholars (AVAS) Annual Meeting in 1986. It was later published in *Journal of Voluntary Action Research* 16, nos. 1–2 (January–June 1987): 29–49, and in Susan A. Ostrander, Stuart Langton, and Jon Van Til, eds., *Shifting the Debate: Public/Private Sector Relations in the Modern Welfare State* (New Brunswick, N.J.: Transaction Books, 1987), 29–49.

31. Barry D. Karl, "Nonprofit Institutions," 984–87.

32. See Richard Lyman's keynote address delivered at the 1988 IS Spring Research Forum, San Francisco, March 17, 1988, "Looking Forward to the Year 2000: Public Policy and Philanthropy," particularly his comments on the work of Bob Bothwell and Terry Odendahl (16). In a speech presented at the same meeting, John G. Simon responded forcefully to Barry D. Karl's review in *Science* (a tape recording of this speech in the author's possession).

33. Anne Lowry Bailey, "Philanthropy Research's Built-in Conflict," *Chronicle of Higher Education* 34 (September 21, 1988): A36.

34. David Arnold, "Concept Paper—National Fund for Research on Philanthropy and the Nonprofit Sector" (1988). Arnold was kind enough to provide me with a copy of this paper.

35. On efforts to establish a field of "philanthropy studies," see Robert L. Payton to author, April 3, 1988, and Payton, "The Emergence of a Field," unpublished essay submitted to the *Chronicle of Higher Education,* April 1988.

36. Jon Van Til has been kind enough to share memoranda from December 1987 to March 1989 regarding the AVAS/IS relationship. These and my correspondence with Jossey-Bass editor Alan Schrader have provided an understanding of the ties among AVAS, IS, and Jossey-Bass, which publishes *Nonprofit and Voluntary Sector Quarterly* (formerly the *Journal of Voluntary Action Research*), *Nonprofit Management Review,* and anthologies compiled from papers presented at IS meetings. Jon Van Til and Dennis Young have provided me with information about IS use of a program-committee apparatus for its research meetings.

37. Peter Dobkin Hall, "Obstacles to Nonprofit Teaching and Research" (Paper delivered at the IS Academic Retreat, Indianapolis, June 7–8, 1988), and the six-part series "Dilemmas of Nonprofits Research," *Philanthropy Monthly,* January–June 1989.

38. Responses to the series, particularly letters from Stanley N. Katz, Harvey Dale, Robert L. Payton, Richard Magat, and Brian O'Connell, have effectively presented the view of these dilemmas by IS and its efforts to deal with them. The best and most extensive public discussion of these issues occurred at the IS Academic Retreat and Professional Forum in Durham, North Carolina, July 6, 1989. Portions of statements from this meeting are in Peter Dobkin Hall, "Who Speaks for the Research Community?" *Philanthropy Monthly* 22, no. 6 (June 1989): 9–13.

39. These ideas were voiced in an unpublished letter written by Barry D. Karl to the editor of the *Chronicle of Higher Education* in response to Bailey's "Philanthropy Research's Built-in Conflict."

40. Bernard Bailyn, *Education in the Forming of American Society* (New York: Vintage Books, 1960), 8–9. Bailyn's analysis of the relation among scholarship, the institutional interests of education, and the professionalization of educators presents a paradigm of the dilemmas of special-interest research.

Chapter 9: The "Me Generation" Grows Up: Thoughts on the Near Future of the Nonprofit Sector

1. Elizabeth McCormack, "Looking Back to Look Forward" (Keynote address delivered at the Independent Sector 1989 Annual Meeting, Houston, October 23, 1988).

2. On new philanthropic leadership, see "Most Big Foundations Select New Presidents from Outside the Field," *Chronicle of Philanthropy* 1, no. 10 (March

7, 1989). See also "Rockefeller's Goldmark: 'Every Major Foundation Should Have an International Dimension," *Chronicle of Philanthropy* 2, no. 3 (November 14, 1989): 6–7; "Special Report: Women and Foundations," *Chronicle of Philanthropy* 1, no. 2 (November 8, 1988): 13–14; and "A New Generation of Foundation Leaders," *Chronicle of Philanthropy* 2, no. 22 (September 4, 1990).

3. Foundation Center, *Foundation Directory*, 12th ed. (New York: Foundation Center, 1988).

4. Miriam M. Wood, "The Governing Board's Existential Quandary: An Empirical Analysis of Board Behavior in the Charitable Sector," Working Paper no. 143 (New Haven: Program on Non-Profit Organizations, Yale University, 1990).

5. Barry Dennis, Gabriel Rudney, and Roy Wyscarver, "Charitable Contributions: The Discretionary Income Hypothesis," Working Paper no. 63 (New Haven: Program on Non-Profit Organizations, Yale University, 1983).

6. Carl Milofsky, "Neighborhood-Based Organizations: A Market Analogy," in W. W. Powell, ed., *The Nonprofit Sector: A Research Handbook* (New Haven: Yale University Press, 1987), 291–92.

Index

Designed by Laury A. Egan

Set in Baskerville text and Univers display by Blue Heron, Inc.

Printed on 50-lb. Glatfelter Offset, B-16, and

bound in Joanna Arrestox cloth by Thomson-Shore, Inc.